Taxation

Taxation
Policy and Practice

9th edition 2002/2003

Andy Lymer
Dora Hancock

THOMSON
™

Australia • Canada • Mexico • Singapore • Spain • United Kingdom • United States

Taxation: policy and practice – 9th Edition 2002/2003

Copyright © 2003
Andrew Lymer and Dora Hancock

The Thomson logo is a registered trademark used herein under licence.

For more information, contact Thomson, High Holborn House 50/51 Bedford Row, London, WC1R 4LR or visit us on the World Wide Web at: http://www.thomsonlearning.co.uk

British Library Cataloguing-in-Publication Data
A catalogue record for this book is available from the British Library

ISBN 1–86152–592–3

First edition 1993
Second edition 1994
Third edition 1995
Fourth edition 1996
Fifth edition 1997
Sixth edition 1999
Seventh edition 2001
Eighth edition 2002
Ninth edition 2003

Cover design by Hot Chilli

Printed in Great Britain by TJ International, Padstow, Cornwall

Contents

Note: each chapter is numbered individually

Preface to 9th Edition

This is the third edition I have been responsible for having taken over editorial control of the book from Dora Hancock with the 7th Edition. Dora Hancock started producing this book at a time when there was an important gap in the market for tax textbooks. Excellent material already existed which covered a legal approach to tax, an economic/public sector approach and very detailed technical materials. What was missing, however, was an introductory level text that took a combined, interdisciplinary view on the subject, written in a readable style. Over the six editions of the text until I was involved in this project, Dora had been very successful in creating a book to achieve this important goal. Many of us, as users of her efforts, have been able to construct different kinds of tax courses around this book because of the different perspective on the subject it gives to students.

In attempting to continue to provide a complete, but readable, university student tax textbook I have also tried to provide as wide a coverage as possible of professional level introductory UK tax courses. This book is therefore suitable as a supplement to most of the UK accounting and business professional examinations particularly in providing greater depth to the courses you may be undertaking towards professional exams to help enhance your understanding of this topic.

A number of key changes were made in this edition including

1   Updating the book fully for the 2002 Budget and Finance Bill 2002.
2   Splitting the previous Chapter 5 into two parts. The new Chapter 6 contains all the details on capital allowances and trading losses for business taxation that previously formed the second part of Chapter 5.
3   The UK Tax Budget summaries have been moved to a new Appendix B from their previous position as part of Chapter 1.

How to use this text

This textbook is not written as a reference text, although the detailed indices and glossary it contains will help direct you to specific areas of material when you need this help. It is written to be read. To gain the most from this text I would advise you to read chapters in their entirety, preferably starting at the beginning of the chapter!

I have included regular activities in the text to illustrate the important points you will need to understand and to give you a chance to practice what you are learning as you go through the book. Although there may be a significant 'urge' to jump straight from the activity to the feedback provided, you will miss much of the benefit of the activities if you do not first attempt them yourself.

You will also find a number of exam level questions at the end of each chapter that cover the material explained in the chapter. Some of these have answers provided in the back of the book, some on the website. For others you will have to obtain the answers from your lecturer or teacher, as they will only be provided to them via their section of the website.

As you read the text you will regularly meet new tax terms. You will find all the terms you will need to be familiar with in the glossary at the back of the book. Use this resource as you come across the terms so you can gradually build up your tax vocabulary as you learn new tax ideas and techniques.

Website

Last year we created a website (http://www.taxstudent.com/uk) to support this text. It contains a range of materials and resources that will help you gain the most from your studying of the UK's taxation system. This includes answers to questions not available at the back of the book, a series of case studies provided by KPMG's Tax Business School®, a regularly updated news service targeted at introductory level students, multiple choice based self-test questions for each chapter, a range of links and other resources to help with your wider reading for this subject and any assignments/dissertations you may need to undertake associated with a course you may be taking. The website is frequently updated throughout the year so check it from time to time for updates.

Acknowledgements

As in previous years I acknowledge the effort put into the production of this text by other people. These include the Thomson Learning 'team' – Publishers (Jennifer Pegg/Patrick Bond), Production (Fiona Freel), Website (Melody Woolard) and Marketing (Sarah Mouncey) and my typesetter Joanne Smith.

I am also grateful for the specialist tax help provided to me by my reviewer, Lynne Oats, who has helped reduce the errors in this book to an absolute minimum. It should be noted, however, that any errors still remaining in the text belong to Dora and I.

Please note, whilst every attempt has been made in writing this text to be accurate and true to the current UK tax system it should not be solely relied upon as a definitive source of information on current tax rules. Readers are advised to seek specific professional advice in their tax planning affairs. The authors and publishers accept no legal responsibility for loss related to actions taken based on material contained in this book.

Any suggestions for future development of this book, or the associated website, would be appreciated. The authors can be contacted for this purpose at a.lymer@taxstudent.com (although, please do not use this address for general queries as we are unable to answer other email queries).

Andrew Lymer
May 2002

Taxation: Policy and Practice – website

http://www.taxstudent.com/uk

Accountingeducation.com, in conjunction with Thomson Learning and the authors of this text, have created a website to be used in conjunction with their text book.

Visit the above address to find:

1. Constantly updated UK tax news (including free email update service you can subscribe to)
2. Answers to questions at the end of each chapter (note – some are reserved for lecturer use only as a teaching aid)
3. Additional chapter on Inheritance Tax
4. KPMG Tax Business School® Cases in Personal Tax, Business Tax, Corporate Tax and Capital Gains Tax
5. Multiple choice questions – self test questions for each chapter
6. Links – large list of tax related links for further reading, dissertation etc.
7. Easy to print rates and allowance pages.

Other material to be released during the year includes:

a) Introduction to International Taxation
b) Guide to the UK Stamp Duty system

1 The framework of UK taxation

Introduction

Ever since people started to gather together in groups and provide resources for the community, taxes had to be raised to pay for services to be used by the whole community such as defense. In the latter part of the 20th century taxes are used to achieve a number of government objectives as well as raise revenue to fund Parliament's spending. In 21st-century Britain we largely accept taxation as a necessary part of our society. However, this has not always been the case.

At the end of this chapter you will be able to:

- discuss the historical background of taxation, particularly in the UK
- describe the main features of the UK tax system today, including the systems for collecting taxes, the legal framework of taxation and the administration of taxation
- discuss the impact of taxation on the behaviour of individuals and organisations
- define fiscal neutrality
- identify progressive and regressive taxes and discuss their characteristics
- compare and contrast tax evasion, tax avoidance and tax mitigation

A brief history of taxation

Before we study the history of tax we must understand what a 'tax' is. All taxes have some features in common. They are a compulsory levy, imposed by government or other tax raising body, on either income, expenditure or capital assets, for which the taxpayer receives nothing specific in return. The primary purpose of imposing a tax is to raise money for public spending purposes. However, they are also used as a tool to influence the behaviour of the taxpayer. The collection of all the taxes in operation in an economy and the rules related to these taxes is called a 'tax system'.

Throughout history tax has been a sensitive issue between rulers and governments and their subjects or citizens. Significant civil unrest, even wars, have resulted from tax disputes. This section reviews some of these events in ancient history, and more recently in British history, illustrating the dynamic nature of tax systems. Note how the complexity of the tax system develops overtime but that many features of taxation have in fact remained fairly constant.

Taxation in Roman times

In the time of Julius Caesar Roman citizens did not pay tax. All the revenue required by the empire, including the cost of the military operations, was requisitioned from the people who lived in territories which had been occupied by the Romans. Only indirect taxes* were raised in Rome itself because direct taxes were seen to be humiliating and undignified.

Indirect taxes, such as customs duties, are paid by an individual through purchasing goods and services, and are not directly related to the personal circumstances of the taxpayer. On the other hand, direct taxes, such as income tax, can directly reduce the taxpayer's income and can be directly related to the taxpayer's personal circumstances. Romans resisted direct taxes, not so much because of an unwillingness to pay them, but because of the loss of privacy which such taxes necessitated.

Requisitioning required every citizen to assist the Roman state with his labour and property. The system had a number of serious disadvantages, principally its lack of certainty. This led to tax demands being levied in an unpredictable and arbitrary way.

The Romans introduced a system of collective responsibility so that members of the taxpayer's family, neighbours and community could be called upon to pay any taxes which the taxpayer defaulted on. Tax collection was undertaken by publican companies under contract to the Emperor and there was a considerable amount of corruption by both the Emperors and the publican companies.

Occasionally it was necessary to raise a direct tax, called a *tributum*, on the citizens of Rome, leading to the necessity of a census. Often the *tributum* was repaid by the state after the need for it passed. In addition some indirect taxes were raised by charging import and export duties.

Augustus realised that a fairer system of tax would have to be introduced and created a civil service to administer the tax. He introduced a 5% inheritance tax, which was payable on the death of a taxpayer from his estate, a 1% sales tax on public auctions and a 4% tax on the sale of slaves.

Tiberius, when encouraged to increase the direct taxation from the provinces, refused saying 'A good shepherd should shear his flock, not skin it.' Indeed this offered wisdom is hung prominently inside No. 11 Downing Street. Chancellors today seem to agree with Tiberius, operating now with a top rate of tax of 40%, but in the 1970s some taxpayers paid tax at rates as high as 98% on their investment income. Most people would consider this to be skinning not shearing.

The Romans also introduced a rudimentary system of social security by paying a form of family allowance nearly 2,000 years ago.

Between the 2nd and 3rd centuries AD inflation was extremely high and the taxes described above were allowed to lapse. Instead taxes were raised in the form of goods rather than money.

At the beginning of the 4th century AD Diocletian introduced *capitatio*, a poll tax, and *jugatio*, a tax on landed property. The land was divided into four classes: vines, olive trees, arable land and pasture land, each class with further sub-classes. Land of a higher quality fell into a higher class leading to greater taxes than land of a lower quality, regardless of the way in which the land was actually used. This is the

---

*   where you meet a term like this for the first time you may want to check its meaning in the glossary at the back

first example of the capacity to generate wealth being taxed, rather than taxing the wealth generated.

An individual paid poll tax for himself and all his employees. The tax on women was a fraction of the tax for a man. The fraction varied across the empire. A man was taken as being a unit of tax with all other taxes, including land taxes, expressed as a fraction of a man.

The Empire decided how much tax should be raised in total and allocated this to regions, which then calculated the tax which must be levied on a man. From this all tax liabilities were calculated and collected from the citizens. Taxes were still based on payment in kind rather than cash and the majority of the taxes were collected at source. Hence landowners with tenants were required to pay taxes for themselves and their tenants. Individuals who were not wealthy landowners or tenants paid their taxes directly to the local municipal council. In practice the tax tied citizens to their land, limiting prospects for advancement, and was extremely progressive.

Under a progressive tax system a taxpayer who is better off pays a higher proportion of his income in tax than a less well off individual. In contrast, in a regressive tax system the burden of tax falls heavily on the poorest. The direct tax system in operation the UK now is progressive because taxpayers on relatively low incomes pay a relatively low proportion of their income in income tax while better off taxpayers pay a higher proportion. For a tax system to be progressive it is not enough for better off taxpayers to pay more tax than the less well off: the better off must pay proportionately more in tax than the less well off.

In fact, the system in Diocletian's time in Rome was so progressive that the higher a taxpayer's income before tax the lower his income after tax, i.e. the tax paid on an extra unit of income was greater than 100%. This tax system was blamed for the decline in both economic prosperity and personal freedom and ultimately contributed significantly to the downfall of the Roman Empire.

The introduction of taxation in the UK

Medieval taxation

In medieval times kings had access to revenue from three sources. They received income from Crown property and also from feudal rights, which were considered to provide the kings with sufficient revenue to meet their normal expenditure. In addition kings could raise customs duties and grants in times of emergency, provided that Parliament approved. In practice Parliament usually did not grant the king the right to raise all the revenue he asked for. The role of Parliament was to act as a brake on public expenditure. Ironically today, it is more likely to be Parliament which is restrained by the Treasury than the other way round.

The customs duties were levied on both imports and exports. Initially the funds raised were used for naval purposes and consequentially offered some protection to merchants against piracy. Merchants consequently saw the tax as something of an insurance premium. However, in much the same way as with the road fund licence today, the revenue raised was soon diverted to other uses. Most of the goods which were imported were luxury goods and so the tax was ultimately paid by wealthy people, who probably gained most benefit from the money raised. The peasants would have been largely unaffected by the taxes.

The feudal services and the right to a payment in lieu of such services are examples of direct taxes, while customs duties are indirect taxes. The indirect taxes proved to be both easy and economical to collect while the direct taxes were difficult and expensive to collect. Citizens were able to challenge an assessment to tax in the courts and case law is still an important source of law today. There were, and are, a number of advantages of customs taxes. Firstly, during this time there was a large volume of overseas trade, primarily with Europe, so that a relatively large amount of tax could be raised from a relatively low rate of tax. Secondly, the tax was relatively cheap and easy to collect although tax evasion, through smuggling, was widespread.

As you have already seen, kings could raise money from a variety of feudal services, or payments in lieu of services, and from their income-generating assets, which were primarily land. However, income from both these sources was expensive to collect and evasion and avoidance was widespread. Tax evasion, unlike tax avoidance, is illegal. For instance, if a trader conceals some of his revenue from the authorities in order to reduce his burden of taxation he is evading tax, but if he legally arranges his affairs so as to reduce the amount of tax payable this is tax avoidance and is permissible. For example, a man may transfer investments to his non-working wife in order for the income from them to escape tax. However, as we shall see, the courts are taking an increasingly tough line on tax avoidance and artificial schemes which have no business purpose other than to reduce a tax liability are open to challenge by the Inland Revenue.

Taxation in the Middle Ages

In times of war the king was unable to raise enough revenue to fund the military effort. The king had no absolute right to raise additional funds and so had to negotiate with his wealthier subjects. These subjects usually insisted that the king follow the formal procedures which meant that Parliament had to be convened for the king to request either increases in customs duties or to raise a lay subsidy, called the system of the fifteenths and tenths, which was a tax on all movable property and income. Some personal goods such as clothes and armour were exempt from the tax. The members of Parliament were the country's wealthiest citizens, who were also the people most likely to be affected by an increase in the king's tax raising power. However, these members were also the people with the most to lose if the king was unsuccessful in the war, and so Parliament usually granted the king his request. In fact increases in these taxes had the effect of redistributing wealth from the king's wealthier subjects to the peasants who became soldiers. However, there was a great power struggle between the monarchy and Parliament, which of course was eventually won by Parliament.

In 1377 Parliament gave the king permission to levy a poll tax of four old pence on all his adult male subjects. Two years later the king was granted permission to raise a graduated poll tax. Peasants still paid four old pence but subjects with positions were taxed at higher rates depending on their status: up to £4 for barons, earls and mayors. In real terms the poll tax represented about 2% of the King's income. The amount which was levied varied according to the income of the individual, but there were no mechanisms for determining fluctuating incomes and so only fixed incomes were taxed.

On both occasions the general populace rebelled and evasion was widespread. Two years later Parliament once again, and with reluctance, granted the king the right to levy a poll tax, this time at one shilling (12 old pennies) a head. Because the tax was not graduated by reference to the taxpayer's wealth it was regressive, that is the burden of tax fell most heavily on the poorest members of society, and was once again widely evaded. In fact the peasants revolted and nearly brought about the downfall of the king. (Perhaps if Margaret Thatcher had read her history she might have survived the challenge to her leadership in 1990 which was due, in part, to the unpopular 'poll' tax (or community charge) she had instigated in the UK in the late 1980s) Interestingly the evidence suggests that the revolt was not so much due to an inability to pay as to an unwillingness to pay this new tax which was set at a relatively high level.

In 1435 and 1450 a graduated income tax was introduced as a temporary measure. The tax was levied at a rate of 2.5% on small incomes and 10% on large incomes. Once again only fixed incomes were taxed.

By Henry VIII's reign a mixture of the two systems was operating. Individuals whose income could easily be ascertained, such as the clergy, wage-earners and landowners, were subject to income tax while individuals whose income fluctuated, such as merchants, professional men and tenant farmers, were subject to tax on their movable property. During the reign of Elizabeth the income tax rate was 20% while movables were taxed at a rate of two-fifteenths. Movables included coins, plate, merchandise, household goods and debts owing less debts owed to the taxpayer. Even the poor were subject to these taxes as exemption limits were set very low. As before both these taxes were only raised during times of financial urgency. However, by the middle of the 16th century the exemption limits had been raised and only the upper and middle classes paid taxes.

Taxation became a contentious issue between the King and Parliament during the reign of the Stuarts primarily because, as is now generally agreed, the Stuarts had insufficient revenue to fulfill their royal functions. This led to King James applying to Parliament for financing the ordinary expenses of government which caused bitter quarrels. King Charles I, James's son, also suffered from this problem and Parliament refused to grant him the right to raise revenue through customs duties for life, as had been done in the past, but granted the duties for 12 months. Eventually Charles levied the duties without the consent of Parliament. The differences between the monarch and Parliament became insurmountable and finally there was a civil war and Charles was executed. From that day until the present, Parliament has ruled in the UK, although a limited monarchy as we have it today was restored with Charles II. One interesting result of this struggle is that the Board of the Inland Revenue receive their commission to act from the Crown rather than from Parliament. Thus the Board is deemed to have inherited some of the qualities of the Crown, in particular justice, equity and mercy. We will not have the opportunity to evaluate the performance of the Inland Revenue against these criteria in this book, but you might like to consider the matter during your working life.

Excise duties on food, drink and other essentials were introduced in 1643. They were unpopular because the burden of the tax fell on everyone including the poor but had the advantage of being easy to collect. Like the poll taxes before them, excise duties on the necessities of life are regressive, that is, the poor pay a larger proportion of their income in duty than the better off.

Parliament attempted to reform the personal tax system after Charles's execution but was largely unsuccessful. The country was divided into regions which were required to raise a set amount of revenue, with little guidance about the way in which the tax should be levied and little supervision. The tax soon became a tax on land rather than on income or other assets.

In 1662 a hearth tax was introduced which was readily avoided by the simple practice of blocking up hearths.

In 1688 a graduated poll tax and the General Aid system was introduced. Individuals paid poll tax according to their rank. Under the General Aid system three types of tax were levied. Individuals with property in goods, merchandise, money and debts were required to pay 5% on their annual profits which were deemed to equal 6% of their net capital. Employees paid 5% of their salary in tax. Finally a tax of 5% was levied on the true yearly value of all lands, tenements, tithes and mines. By 1692 the rate had increased to 20%. Initially the General Aid tax was successful but the revenue raised fell over the years and in 1698 the poll tax was abandoned and a fixed quota system for each region was reintroduced, although this time the basis for assessment to tax was clearly laid down together with the rates at which tax should be paid. Salaries were taxed at 15% and the balance of the quota was to be raised from the Land Tax which was a rate on land, tenements, tithes and mines in the district. Over time the tax on income proved to be largely uncollectible and the Land Tax became the sole source of direct tax for Parliament. The Land Tax was finally repealed in 1949. One of the reasons for the longevity of the Land Tax is the ease of collecting the tax and the virtual impossibility of tax evasion. These advantages outweighed the many disadvantages of the Land Tax. The Council Tax introduced in April 1993 is a form of land tax, with reliefs for low income groups and single occupancy accommodation. Despite its many disadvantages has proved to be much easier to collect than its predecessor, the Community Charge, was.

In 1747 a window tax was introduced in an attempt to make taxes less regressive. It was argued that the rich had larger houses and therefore more windows and so would pay more tax than poorer citizens. Like the hearth tax before, it was possible to avoid the tax by bricking up a window and lying about the number of windows in the house was widespread. In 1851 the window tax was abolished on the grounds of public health.

The modern era of taxation

Modern-day income tax has its roots in the tax introduced by William Pitt (The Younger) in 1799. When the Napoleonic Wars started William Pitt borrowed money against future excise revenue, in order to finance the war. However, it became apparent that the war was going to last too long to enable this method of financing to be sustained. Pitt needed to find a new way to raise taxes. He introduced an income tax at a rate of 10% which was targeted on the rich middle and upper classes, the people with the most to lose if the war was lost. There was massive evasion of the tax and only £6m was raised in the first year rather than the £10m anticipated.

Although the poorest people were not subject to income tax it is estimated that by 1810 a labourer earning £22 a year paid £11 in indirect tax, a truly colossal proportion of his income. It did not seem possible to fund the war by increasing indirect taxes. Taxpayers earning over £60 per annum were required to make a return listing all their sources of income and calculating the amount of tax which was due on that income.

The law did not allow for any control over the correctness of the return. In an attempt to reduce evasion, which was widespread, withholding taxes were introduced by the Bank of England. For example, the Bank paid dividends net of tax. Pitt resigned in 1801 and his income tax was repealed in 1802 by Addington because it was seen as a wartime tax only. In 1803 Addington introduced a new income tax which introduced the five Schedules, A to E, which have largely survived, (apart from Schedule B which was abolished in 1988 and Schedule C, abolished in 1996), until today. Addington was also responsible for 'taxation at the source' and rent, salaries, pensions and interest were all paid net of basic rate tax. Because of these innovations to what had been done before it is probably fair to say that Addington is the true father of income tax, rather than Pitt who has generally been awarded the honour. Addington's income tax was progressive and ranged from 1% on an income of £60 to 10% on an income of over £200. Income tax was repealed once again in 1816.

In 1842 Peel reintroduced income tax as a temporary measure, at a very low level, to deal with an inherited budget deficit of £5 million. Peel drew on Addington's Act of 1803 for his legislation, making only minor amendments. Peel rejected proposals to impose high rates of tax on the wealthy, arguing that it would lead to them closing their businesses or even leaving the country. A second major criticism of income tax was the need to undertake an annual investigation, or as Peel put it: 'A certain degree of inquisitorial scrutiny is, therefore, inseparable from an income tax.' It was this rather than the actual rate of the tax which was generally opposed. It seems that income tax was as unwelcome in the 19th century as it was in Roman times.

Income below £150 was exempted and income above this figure was taxed at 3% regardless of the amount of the income. At the same time indirect taxes were reduced in order to help the country's manufacturing, trading and commercial sectors.

The income tax was supported, despite its drawbacks, because it was seen to be temporary and set at a low level and industrialists believed that if the government were to raise all its revenue by means of indirect taxation it would cut consumer spending and increase inflation. Ironically these measures received more approval from the opposition than from Peel's own party. Not all income was taxed in full: for example, farmers were taxed on the rental value of their land rather than their farming profits. Farmers were not taxed on their income until 1941.

Peel also created a system of Special Commissioners, who were experts in taxation, with whom businessmen could deal rather than the General Commissioners, who were local businessmen, from whom the taxpayer might want privacy. In addition, if the taxpayer disputed the amount of tax which was deemed to be payable he could choose to appeal to either the Special Commissioners or the General Commissioners. This system remains in force today.

Peel also introduced a fixed penalty of £50 for any taxpayer who was found to be 'neglectful in connection with his return of income'. The penalty was abolished in 1923 but today the Inland Revenue can impose interest charges as well as penalties on taxpayers who fail to pay the full amount of tax due.

William Gladstone introduced 13 budgets during the last half of the 19th century. At the time of his first budget in 1853 public expenditure was over £50 million a year and nearly £30 million of the total was used to pay interest on the National Debt. Gladstone claimed that the cause of the deficit was the prevailing level of income tax. Less tax was raised in 1853 from income tax than was collected in each of the years from 1806 to 1815. Gladstone was aware of the limitations of the system of income tax, especially self-assessment which led to widespread fraud. To start to redress the balance Gladstone extended legacy duty so that land and businesses were subject to tax on the death of their owner. He reduced the rates of indirect taxation, believing that this would stimulate consumption and thus not actually reduce the net receipts to the government. This, together with the reforms introduced by Peel, helped to free the restrictions on trade by encouraging imports and enabling exports to be sold as cheaply as possible. However, Gladstone has been criticised for failing to reduce the National Debt or spend money on social issues such as public health and housing.

Gladstone intended to phase income tax out by 1860, but for a number of reasons this did not prove to be possible and the rate of income tax had to rise. Public expenditure was already growing rapidly, much to Gladstone's regret, and this made it impossible ever again to consider abolishing income tax.

Harcourt introduced Estate Duty, referred to as Death Duties, in 1894. The Estate Duty removed many of the injustices of the old legacy duties which had evolved over many centuries and so suffered from inconsistencies. The origin of the present-day inheritance tax can be traced to 1694 and probate duties. This new tax fell most heavily on the landowners. Harcourt justified this bias by claiming that property values had been greatly increased since the railways were built. The duty was at the rate of 1% on estates worth between £100 and £500, with estates worth more than £1 million taxed at 8%. The money raised was largely used to fund the expansion of the Navy. The new tax was highly unpopular with the families who were affected by it. They argued that an individual who chose to spend his money could avoid paying the tax which would be levied on the estate of the careful man who accumulated assets to pass on to the next generation. Others argued that future Chancellors would be unable to resist the temptation to increase both the rate of the tax and its scope. The question of tax avoidance was also raised, commentators arguing that by simply giving the estate away during the lifetime of the testator the tax could be completely avoided. Harcourt defended his tax, arguing that estate duty was the only opportunity to tax non-income-generating assets such as the taxpayer's main residence.

Harcourt next turned his attention to income tax, considering the possibility of making it progressive. Harcourt was strongly in favour of the system of deduction of tax at source, which applied to about three-quarters of all income tax collected, arguing that it meant that there was no 'inquisitorial prying' into the affairs of individuals. The Revenue argued that were it not for the system of deduction at source the investigations that they would have to make and the penalties which they would have to impose for mis-declarations would 'render the collection of the Income Tax so odious as to imperil its existence and in all probability make it impossible to maintain the tax.' He concluded that the system of deduction at source, which he approved of, made a progressive income tax system impossible.

Taxation in the 20th century

Until the 20th century tax was paid on earned income by less than a million people. Hence tax was still paid only by the better off. However, during the 20th century public expenditure increased phenomenally. In 1907 Asquith introduced personal allowances, which exempted a proportion of earned income from income tax. In 1908 old-age pensions were introduced. This, together with a need to increase spending on the Navy, necessitated an increase in taxation. In 1909 Lloyd George introduced the first progressive tax on income in the so-called 'People's Budget'. The budget was not generally accepted and was rejected by the House of Lords in November 1909 but eventually became law in 1910. The power of the House of Lords to veto budgets was

ended on Lady Day, which was 25th March, the first quarter day in the calendar year (and the date of the start of the church year as the Feast of the Annunciation of the Virgin Mary – exactly nine months before Christmas Day). In 1752 the government adopted the Gregorian calendar which necessitated the loss of 11 days between the 2nd and 14th of September to bring the calendar year back into line with the solar year. However, the government was unwilling to have an accounting period which did not run for 365 days and so moved their year end forward by 11 days to 5th April. Hence today a fiscal year runs from 6th April to the following 5th April: the fiscal year 2002/03 runs from 6th April 2002 to 5th April 2003. At the beginning of each fiscal year the Inland Revenue sends out a 'Tax Return' to many taxpayers. If a taxpayer receives a return it must be completed and returned to the inspector by:

- The later of
    - 31st January following the end of the fiscal year and
    - 3 months after the date of issue of the return
  if the tax payer has calculated their own tax liability and
- The later of
    - 30th September following the end of the fiscal year and
    - 2 months after the date of issue of the return
  if the taxpayer wishes the Inland Revenue to calculate their tax liability (TMA 1970 s8).

The taxpayer must include details about his or her income for the previous fiscal year as well as claiming allowances and reliefs for the same year. If the taxpayer runs a business he or she may also be required to submit accounts to the revenue unless the business turnover (or rental income) is less than £15,000, in which case a statement simply consisting of three figures (turnover, total expenses and profit) is sufficient, although the Inland Revenue still may request the full accounts.

The Inland Revenue has the right to impose penalties if the tax return is late. Not every taxpayer receives a tax return each year but if a taxpayer becomes chargeable to either income tax or capital gains tax he or she must notify the Inland Revenue within six months of the end of the year of assessment for which he or she is chargeable (TMA 1970 s7(1)).

In 1996/97 a system of self-assessment was introduced which was intended to make taxpayers complete their own tax returns and calculate their own tax liability (hence being called self-assessment). In 2000/1 8,795,949 tax returns were made (an increase from 8,506,741 made the previous year). More recently still taxpayers can now submit their tax returns to the Inland Revenue electronically if they want to.

Estimated number of taxpayers (Source: Inland Revenue website – Tax receipts and Taxpayers section, Numbers: thousands)*

	Income Tax Number of individuals	Corporation Tax	Capital Gains Tax[3]
2001/2	27,400[1]	–	120
2000/1	27,800[2]	–	190[1]
1999/0	26,900	515	220[1]
1998/9	26,900	470	160[3]
.	.	–	.
1988/9	25,200	355	150
.	.	–	.
1983/4	24,000	230	115
.	.	–	.
1978/9	25,900	185	225
.	.	–	.
1973/4	23,100	175	285

[1] Projected in November 2001 Pre-Budget Report

[2] Provisional Figures

[3] After 1990/91 married couples count as two if both have CGT liabilities as a result of independent taxation. Prior to this they only counted as one.

For more details of the administration of UK tax see the Inland Revenue website (http://www.inlandrevenue.gov.uk).

The UK budget

The most critical event of the annual taxation calendar in the UK (most years) is the annual Budget Statement made by the Chancellor of the Exchequer. This is usually made during March each year, although the 2002 Budget was not until 17th April 2002. This statement outlines the Government's budget plans for the year, which correspondingly have to be balanced with how they will raise the money to finance these plans. It is in this statement each year that most tax changes for the year are therefore to be found.

The Treasury is in fact legally bound to provide two economic forecasts each year. Between 1993 and 1997 this was done in the Budget in November and the Summer Economic Forecast (given late June or early July).

Under the Labour Government elected in May 1997, however, the system changed back to a Spring Budget with the addition of a Pre-Budget report in the autumn before (usually in November). This Pre-Budget statement gives an update on the state of the economy, Government expenditure and outlines ideas and plans for the forthcoming Budget. This new pattern allows for much wider debate on the proposals for tax changes than previously had been the case and also results in less surprises on Budget day. (Details of this year's Budget, and summaries of those of the last few years, can be found in the appendices.)

The operation of a national budget is not a new thing. In fact, it goes back to the

Norman period in the UK. The Normans established the two government departments still operating in the UK today to deal with national finances. These are the Treasury, who received and paid out money on behalf of the King, and the Exchequer, which received money in connection with the Treasury, and regulated the King's accounts.

Income taxed at source

A key feature of the UK's tax system is the extent to which income is taxed at source. For example, if an individual taxpayer receives interest from a bank account tax will have already been deducted by the payer of the interest. An individual who is not liable to income tax can usually reclaim this tax deducted at its source from the Inland Revenue. The amount of tax deducted at source is independent of the taxpayer's personal circumstances.

Taxpayers who are employed pay tax under the PAYE scheme. Although this tax is deducted at source it is somewhat different to the other examples because the amount of tax deducted is dependent on the taxpayer's personal circumstances. Income collected via the self assessment system is an example of direct assessment which is the usual alternative to tax at source.

The income tax schedules and corporation tax

Until 1965 individuals and companies were taxed under the same rules. In 1965 corporation tax was introduced for companies but there are still many similarities between the taxation of the two groups.

Income is taxed with reference to a number of Schedules and Cases. For example, income from employment, including pensions, is taxed under Schedule E. Income from a trade or profession is taxed under Schedule D Case I. Each source of income received by a taxpayer is assessed under a Schedule. Schedule D Case VI is used to tax annual profits or gains not falling under any other Case of Schedule D and not charged by virtue of Schedules A or E (ICTA 1988 s18(3)). Each Schedule has its own rules which determine how much income should be assessed, what deductions are allowed and when the tax should be paid. We will study these rules in detail in later chapters.

Corporate income is taxed under the same Schedules and Cases as personal income tax. The principal difference is that for a company tax is due to be paid either nine months after the end of the accounting period or, if a large business, on a quarterly basis whereas individuals will make interim payments on 31st January in the tax year and 31st July following the tax year and a final payment on 31st January following the tax year.

Direct and indirect taxation

Direct tax is tax which is suffered directly by the taxpayer. Income tax is an example of a direct tax. Indirect tax is a tax which is paid to the tax collector by someone other than the person who is pays the tax. VAT is an example of an indirect tax as it is collected by the retailer but paid for by the purchaser of whatever product or service the retailer is selling.

The current tax legislation

There are a number of sources of tax law today. Income tax and corporation tax is legislated for in the Income and Corporation Taxes Act 1988 (ICTA 1988). Capital allowances are regulated by the Capital Allowances Act 2001 (CAA 2001). Capital gains tax is legislated for in the Taxation of Chargeable Gains Act 1992 (TCGA 1992). Value Added Tax is dealt with in the Value Added Tax Act 1994 (VATA 1994). In each of the above cases the rules may be changed by the annual Finance Acts. The latest of these Acts is the Finance Act 2001 (although the 2002 Finance Act will prpobably become law during the summer 2002). In addition the Taxes Management Act 1970 (TMA 1970) deals with the administration of taxes.

Whilst we look at the current law as we examine each tax issue, this text does not include a detailed consideration of the administration of taxation. In addition to UK tax law, the UK's tax system is determined by a number of other laws, cases and guidance statements.

Because the UK is a member of the European Union, EU Law must be adhered to in the UK and EU law takes priority over UK law where they disagree. The UK's tax system is what is termed case law system. This means specific laws created by Parliament, in our case tax laws, are interpreted by judges in courts to explain how the laws are to be applied. Throughout this book you will meet cases that are used in this way to determine how the law should be applied to specific circumstances.

The UK's tax authorities, such as the Inland Revenue, also periodically issue guidance of various types for taxpayers and their advisors. Whilst this is not legally binding on taxpayers and can be challenged, it does provide useful advice on the tax authority's view on how specific tax issues should be handled. Taking a look at the Inland Revenue's website for example, you will find guidance in the form of Statements of Practice (their interpretation of the law), Extra-statutory Concessions (specific relaxations to the law allowed by the Inland Revenue), Press Releases (various statements on tax issues) Internal Manuals (publicly published internal manuals to illustrate how tax issues are to be handled) and leaflets (general advice usually that provides overviews for taxpayers). The boundaries between these guidance forms are disappearing with the growth of the Internet where technologies, such as search engines, make it easier for taxpayers to discover information they need in a timely fashion.

Key issues in taxation

The first part of this chapter was intended both to set taxation today in its historical context and to explore the history of tax to see if it is possible to learn lessons that can be applied today. We also briefly considered the administration of taxation today. In this section we will discuss some other framework ideas and concepts which are relevant to taxation today.

Hypothecated taxes

Taxes which are raised to provide specific benefits are termed hypothecated taxes. They are generally unpopular with the Treasury who see these taxes as undermining its control of public expenditure.

The Treasury argues that the revenue raised by hypothecated taxes oscillates in line with the economic cycle. That is, when the economy is strong a relatively large amount of revenue is raised but relatively little revenue is raised when the economy is weak.

However, there are a number of examples of hypothecated taxes that have been raised in the UK: vehicle excise duties were originally intended to fund highway construction and maintenance and the television licence fee was intended to fund the BBC. In practice the vehicle excise duties are used for general expenditure but the television licence fee is still used exclusively to finance the BBC.

The British Medical Association considered a proposal for the National Health Service (NHS) to be funded by way of a hypothecated tax because it believed that taxpayers would be willing to pay more taxes if a clear link between the tax and health care could be established. A new hypothecated tax was proposed by the then Chancellor, Kenneth Clarke, in his November 1993 budget. The 2002 Budget announced a rise from April 2003 in National Insurance Contributions to pay for a growth in the NHS. This is an indication that we may see more hypothecation of this type in the future (if it is successful politically at least). As soon as it is technically possible electronic road pricing will be introduced to raise revenue from the use of motorways to finance motorways.

Equitable taxes

Some taxes raise very little money but are seen as necessary to make a tax system equitable (fair). The main example of this is capital gains tax, which is often subject to rumour about its abolition because so little revenue is raised directly from the tax but remains in place because it is seen to be necessary for a 'fair' tax system. Capital Gains Tax allows for taxing of capital growth whilst income tax taxes income gains. In combination they make it harder for people to switch between capital growth and income for wealth gains (eg both increases in share values and wages are taxed in the UK systems). Not every country has a capital growth tax of this kind.

Fiscal neutrality

Like the window tax of the 18th century many taxes affect the behaviour of individuals and companies. Some argue that the introduction of road-pricing for motorways will encourage drivers to use other roads, particularly A roads. This potential transfer of traffic is generally seen as an unwelcome consequence of charging for motorway use. The accident rate per mile driven is higher on roads which are not motorways, leading to fears of an increase in road traffic accidents after the scheme is introduced. It also seems likely that congestion will increase on roads which do not carry a charge. This might increase journey times and fuel consumption for all road users and the accident rate might rise still further. To minimise these effects the Chancellor will have to set the cost per mile travelled at such a level that relatively few road users are deterred from using motorways.

This 'knock-on' effect caused by the presence of taxes is common. Tax systems which do not distort the decisions made by individuals and companies are termed fiscally neutral.

During the 1980s there was a move towards the reformation of tax throughout the world. There were moves to limit the level of public expenditure. Then the assessment of taxation was reformed. Tax rates were reduced throughout the world but the tax base was broadened. That is, more of a taxpayer's income is taxed but the tax rate applied per pound is lower. In 1979 the highest rate of tax in the UK was 98% (on some types of income from investments). This was rightly seen as undesirable, if only because the incentives to avoid (legal, but currently 'frowned upon') or even evade (illegal) tax were so large. Today the highest rate of income tax in the UK is 40%, and in the USA it is only 28%. The lower the rate of tax the more the taxpayer keeps of their income and so the less incentive there is to avoid or evade tax.

Since 1979, although the rates of tax have fallen, the tax 'base' has been broadened by decreasing the range of allowances which taxpayers could use to reduce their taxable income and adding taxes to more things that previously were not taxed. The removal of the tax deduction (called a 'relief') available for interest paid on mortgages and the benefit of the married couple's allowances are recent examples of this broadening of the tax base.

In addition, the 100% first-year allowances (deductions from business taxation due) on capital expenditure on plant and machinery which at one time were available to all businesses were phased out for large businesses, leaving only a 25% writing down allowance to be claimed. At the same time the rate of corporation tax was reduced from 52% to 35%. This has subsequently been reduced to 30%.

This is not to say that the government is committed to fiscal neutrality to the extent of never introducing policies which are intended to distort the economic decisions made by individuals and businesses. Tax advantageous treatment has been bestowed on new forms of investments, particularly pensions, but also ISAs (Individual Savings Accounts) and on items of expenditure like recently he reduction in the vehicle licence fee for the cleanest and smallest cars.

We will return to the subject of fiscal neutrality in Chapter 2.

The tax implications of the single European market

Now a new challenge faces UK Chancellors. As Europe draws ever closer as a trading market, and companies become more sophisticated, the harmonisation of tax rates in Europe becomes more important. Efforts were initially concentrated on VAT, customs and excise duties. After a number of years of work it has proved possible to reach some agreement about the ranges at which VAT will be charged in member states (currently set at no lower than 15%), although problems such as the UK's zero rate for food and children's clothing are still to be resolved. Attention is now being turned to the harmonisation of direct taxes, particularly corporation tax. This process of harmonisation also raises questions about sovereignty. The UK government, among others, believes that the right to raise taxes is one of the fundamental rights of a government and is reluctant to cede power to the EU, at least at the present time.

Progressivity

When examining a tax system, or an individual tax, the burden placed on a tax payer will either be

- proportional – the amount of tax to be paid increases directly in line with rising income (or which ever tax base is being used)
- progressive – increases faster than the rising income/other tax base
- regressive – increases slower than the rise in income/other tax base.

In most tax systems, including the UK's, there is a generally accepted principle that income tax should be progressive, that is that better off taxpayers should pay a higher proportion of their income in tax than less well off taxpayers. In fact a detailed analysis of tax paid and benefits received shows that the net tax paid as a proportion of income is not always progressive in the UK tax system.

A tax can still be progressive if it only has two rates of tax. Consider two taxpayers, one earning £10,000 per annum and the other earning twice that, £20,000 per annum. Assume both taxpayers have personal allowances of £5,000. This means that the first £5,000 of income is not subject to income tax. The rest of the income is taxed at 25%. The taxpayer earning £10,000 per annum will pay £1,250 ((£10,000 – 5,000) × 25%) tax, 12.5% of their income, while the higher earning taxpayer will pay £3,750 ((£20,000 – 5,000) × 25%) tax, 18.75% of their income.

This example is simplified from reality of course to illustrate the point about how progressivity works. When other tax factors are taken into account, for example tax relief on contributions paid into a pension fund, or when combined with the effects of other taxes, the analysis may not give the same results.

VAT, on the other hand, is not a progressive tax. Wealthy individuals spend proportionally less of their income than poorer taxpayers on VAT who consequently suffer a higher proportion of their income being paid in VAT. This problem is ameliorated to some extent by policies to reduce VAT on some essential goods, such as the zero rate of indirect tax on most food and some other basic goods. Less well off people generally spend higher proportions of their income on food and basic goods and so benefit most from this strategy. However, this zero rate taxing does not apply to all basic items. Less well off people also spend proportionately more on fuel than the better off, which led to a political outcry when VAT was introduced on domestic fuel.

Personal allowances and progressivity

Every individual who lives in the UK is entitled to at least a single personal allowance. This allowance entitles everyone to earn a certain amount of income before they become liable for any tax. Chapter 4 contains a complete list of personal allowances and the conditions which must be satisfied to claim them. Earnings have consistently increased by more than the rate of inflation and allowances do not always increase at the same rate. This leads to more individuals being liable to pay income tax and increases the proportion of income which is paid in tax for all taxpayers. Any increase in personal allowances benefits individuals with lower income proportionately more than better-off individuals. Hence increases in personal allowances help to increase the progressivity of an income tax system. The next activity illustrates this point.

Average earnings increase by 20% during a period in which personal allowances increase by only 10%. The personal allowance was worth one quarter of average earnings at the beginning of the period and the basic rate of tax is 22%. Find the increase in the tax paid by the following taxpayers expressed as a percentage of total earnings:

- Ben who has an income equal to half average earnings
- Laura who has an income equal to average earnings
- Ashley who has an income equal to twice average earnings

Feedback

Let A = average earnings at the beginning of the period.
First calculate the proportion of income paid in tax at the beginning of the period.

	Ben	Laura	Ashley
Income	0.5A	A	2A
Less personal allowances	0.25A	0.25A	0.25A
Taxable income	0.25A	0.75A	1.75A
Tax paid	0.055A	0.165A	0.385A
Proportion of income paid in tax	11%	16.5%	19.25%

Next calculate the proportion of income paid in tax at the end of the period.

	Ben	Laura	Ashley
Income	0.6A	1.2A	2.4A
Less personal allowances	0.275A	0.275A	0.275A
Taxable income	0.325A	0.925A	2.125A
Tax paid	0.0715A	0.2035A	0.4675A
Proportion of income paid in tax	11.92%	16.96%	19.48%

This result may surprise you. However, a little thought may help to explain your results. Because incomes have risen faster than personal allowances, each of the taxpayers has paid tax on a higher proportion of their income at the end of the period than they did at the beginning. Hence you should expect the proportion of tax paid to increase for all the taxpayers.

You might have expected the proportion of tax paid to increase by more for the lower income taxpayer than the other taxpayers, because the personal allowance forms a greater proportion of his income and hence the impact of its falling value as a proportion of his income is relatively greater relative than for the other taxpayers. Of course the tax system is still progressive but it is less progressive than it was.

Anti-avoidance legislation and the relationship between statute and case law and in the UK today

As we have already seen, people throughout the ages have found ways of circumventing a liability to tax. Some evade tax, for instance by smuggling. Tax evasion is illegal and is punishable by fines and/or imprisonment. Tax avoidance on the other hand is legal. Some avoidance is simple and completely acceptable. For instance, saving money in an ISA rather than an ordinary Building Society account has the result that income from the account is paid without deduction of tax. This therefore is a (legal) scheme which enables taxpayers to avoid paying tax on investment interest received. Individuals may also attempt to avoid paying tax by using schemes devised by tax planning experts who try to exploit loopholes in the tax legislation. Many of the schemes were incredibly complicated and completely artificial, that is they served no real purpose, other than to avoid or postpone paying tax.

In the past the Inland Revenue took a very reactive role to anti-avoidance activity. They simply plugged any loopholes which the tax experts exposed. There were three main problems with this approach. Firstly, tax legislation is not usually retrospective. Hence the Inland Revenue can stop the scheme being used again but legislation cannot be used to foil a scheme which has already been executed. Secondly, the anti-avoidance legislation which was needed created increasingly complex Finance Acts, (the 2000 Finance Bill was approximately 600 pages long, for example). During the 1980s and 1990s accountants lobbied the Chancellor of the Exchequer not to give more and more tax reliefs, but to simplify the legislation. The more complex legislation is the more likely there are to be anomalies which were not detected when the legislation was drafted but which cause endless difficulties for the people who have to deal with the consequences of the legislation. The third disadvantage of anti-avoidance legislation is that it often creates new loopholes which can be exploited by the increasingly sophisticated tax avoidance industry.

The other avenue of attack open to the Revenue is to challenge the legitimacy of any scheme in the courts. Certainly the Inland Revenue have the resources to do this but until recently the courts were unwilling to be seen to be creating new tax law. That is they chose merely to interpret the law as it stood and so would only consider the legal nature of the scheme, as in the case of *IRC v Duke of Westminster* (1936). In this case servants were not paid wages but received an income from a deed of covenant. A deed of covenant is valid only if no valuable consideration is provided by the recipient in return. However, the Duke of Westminster and his servants had an understanding that so long as the deed of covenant operated the servants would not claim the wages due to them. The scheme enabled the Duke to claim tax relief for the amounts paid to his servants whereas payment of wages to servants would not be an allowable deduction from income tax. Today such a scheme could not be used because payments made under deeds of covenant are no longer tax effective when paid to individuals. The House of Lords found for the Duke, declaring that they would only consider the legal nature of the transaction. Until the mid-1980s this case remained a precedent and the Inland Revenue were rarely successful in challenging tax avoidance schemes in the courts.

(Before you read about the details of these schemes it would be useful if you knew a little about capital gains tax. As you might have expected, transactions of a capital nature rather than a revenue nature are subject to capital gains tax. A capital gains tax liability only arises when an asset is disposed of. Hence a taxpayer may defer a capital gains tax liability simply by refraining from selling an asset.)

In *WT Ramsey Ltd v IRC* (1981) the House of Lords took a completely different view of an anti-avoidance scheme.

The case involved an 'artificial scheme' which was used to create a large capital loss. The company had realised a capital gain and intended to set the artificial loss against a chargeable gain to avoid paying tax on the gain. The scheme was artificial because it was made up of a series of preordained steps which were to be carried out in rapid succession. The scheme required that all steps be completed once the first one had been made. At the end of the series of steps the taxpayers would be in the same position as they had been at the beginning and any loss created would not be a real loss. In fact the only losses which had been suffered were the professional fees which were paid for the scheme's operation. The House of Lords decided that although each step in the scheme was a separate legal transaction it was possible to view the scheme, not as a series of separate legal transactions, but as a whole, by comparing the position of the taxpayer in real terms at the start and finish of the scheme. When this was done no real loss was incurred and the scheme was self-cancelling.

Lord Wilberforce explained the decision thus:

> While obliging the court to accept documents or transactions, found to be genuine, as such, it does not compel the court to look at a document or a transaction in blinkers, isolated from any context to which it properly belongs. If it can be seen that a document or transaction was intended to have effect as part of a nexus or series of transactions, or as an ingredient of a wider transaction intended as a whole, there is nothing in the doctrine to prevent it being so regarded; to do so is not to prefer form to substance, or substance to form. It is the task of the court to ascertain the legal nature of any transaction to which it is sought to attach a tax, or a tax consequence, and if that emerges from a series, or combination of transactions, intended to operate as such, it is that series or combination which may be regarded.

The *Ramsay* principle was extended in *Furniss v Dawson* (1984). This time the objective was to defer capital gains tax by using an intermediary company based in the Isle of Man. The scheme was not circular or self-cancelling. The House of Lords decided that the scheme should still be set aside for tax purposes because once again the scheme required a series of steps to be carried out in quick succession.

The case of *Craven v White* (1989) was used by the House of Lords to limit the application of the *Ramsay* principle. Once again an intermediary company in the Isle of Man was used to defer a capital gains tax liability. The key difference between *Craven v White* and *Furniss v Dawson* was that when the shares were transferred to the Isle of Man company the final disposal of the shares had not been agreed. Hence no preordained series of steps existed at the time that the first transaction was undertaken. Consequently the House of Lords refused to view the series of transactions as a whole and the scheme was successful. This case has great significance for anti-avoidance schemes generally. It makes planning well in advance critical. If transactions are undertaken before the final step is known with certainty there is a greater likelihood of the scheme being successful.

In the early part of 1993 it became public knowledge that John Birt, the then new Director General of the BBC, was not on the payroll as an employee of the BBC but was employed, through his own company, as a consultant to the organisation. In this capacity John Birt was able to arrange his affairs so that his tax liability was much less than it would have been had he been an employee. The details of his financial arrangements were published in virtually all the national newspapers and widely discussed on television and radio. Although there was no suggestion that such an arrangement was illegal – indeed it was claimed that for some groups of staff within the BBC it was normal – there was widespread condemnation of the situation. It was soon announced that John Birt would become an employee of the BBC and pay tax under the PAYE system.

More recently, the introduction of restrictions on the general use of 'personal service companies' has been imposed as the Inland Revenue argues these companies are used as tax avoidance vehicles for people who may often be treated as employees under other circumstances. Being an employee has tax implications for both parties. It can often be the case however, that the tax paid to the Revenue will be a lower amount, or paid at a different time at least, if an intermediary company entity is used. These rules are referred to as the IR 35 rules.

It seems to be clear that tax avoidance schemes which are substantially artificial in nature have become less acceptable as well as being less useful because of the case law described above.

Money raised and spent by the UK Government

The table opposite shows the current taxes in operation in the UK for 2002/03. It shows how much each tax contributes to the total revenue raised by the Government each year. You will see that the most important UK taxes in terms of the revenue they raise for the Government are income tax (predicted to raise the UK's tax revenue in 2002/03 before credits), VAT, corporation tax and social security contributions.

How does the UK spend its money?

The following table shows how the Government is planning to spend the revenue it raises in 2002/03. To give you a comparison we have also given you the figures for 2000/01 and 2001/2 expenditure and the projections for 2003/04 and 2004/5. We have not shown all the expenditure here, but all the big costs are given. Note that the largest costs are in social security benefits, health and local government/regional policy.

From Table C7: Public Sector Current Receipts – Budget: April 2002 – Financial Statement and Budget Report. Crown copyright is produced with the permission of the Controller of Her Majesty's Stationery Office (for full notes to this table please see the full report available on the HM Treasury website).

£ billion	Outturns		Projections
	2000–01	2001–02	2002–03
Inland Revenue			
Income tax (gross of tax credits)	106.0	110.2	117.5
Corporation tax	32.4	32.4	33.2
Tax credits	−1.2	−2.6	−3.9
Petroleum revenue tax	1.5	1.3	1.4
Capital gains tax	3.2	2.9	1.8
Inheritance tax	2.2	2.3	2.5
Stamp duties	8.2	7.1	8.2
Social security contributions	60.6	63.2	65.0
Total Inland Revenue taxes (net of tax credits)	**212.9**	**216.9**	**225.6**
Customs and Excise			
Value added tax	58.5	61.1	63.9
Fuel duties	22.6	21.9	23.1
Tobacco duties	7.6	7.8	7.7
Spirits duties	1.8	1.9	2.0
Wine duties	1.8	2.0	2.2
Beer and cider duties	3.0	3.1	3.1
Betting and gaming duties	1.5	1.4	1.3
Air passenger duty	1.0	0.8	0.8
Insurance premium tax	1.7	1.9	1.9
Landfill tax	0.5	0.5	0.5
Climate change levy	0	0.6	0.9
Aggregates Levy	0	0	0.2
Customs duties and levies	2.1	2.0	2.1
Total Customs and Excise	**102.2**	**104.9**	**109.7**
Vehicle excise duties	4.3	4.4	4.5
Oil royalties	0.6	0.6	0.5
Business rates	17.2	18.2	18.5
Council Tax	14.2	14.9	16.1
Other taxes and royalties	9.0	10.6	10.7
Net taxes and social security contributions	**360.4**	**370.3**	**385.6**
Accrual adjustments on taxes	2.8	0.9	0.8
less own resources contribution to EU budget	−6.3	−6.1	−5.4
less PC corporation tax payments	−0.1	−0.1	−0.2
Tax credits	1.2	1.2	1.6
Interest and dividends	4.8	4.2	4.2
Other receipts	19.4	20.4	20.6
Current receipts	**383.0**	**390.8**	**407.2**
Memo:			
North sea revenues	*4.3*	*5.2*	*5.3*

Selected from Table C14 – Departmental Expenditure Limits (resource budgets – selected). Financial Statement and Budget Report April 2002. Crown copyright is reproduced with the permission of the Controller of Her Majesty's Stationery Office (for the full table and associated notes to this table please see the full report).

| | £ Billion | | | |
	2000/01 (Outturn)	2001/02 (Estimate)	2002/03 (Projections)	2003/04 (Projections)
Education and employment	14.3	17.0	20.2	21.4
Health (NHS)	43.6 (42.7)	48.8 (47.7)	53.4 (51.2)	58.5 (56.1)
Transport and the regions	3.7	4.2	5.2	5.2
Local Government	35.3	36.9	37.4	40.1
Home Office	8.4	9.6	9.4	9.6
Defense	19.2	18.9	18.9	18.9
Foreign and Commonwealth Office	1.2	1.3	1.3	1.2
International Development	2.4	2.8	2.9	3.2
Trade and Industry	3.0	3.9	3.7	3.3
Scotland	2.6	14.2	15.3	16.3
Wales	6.8	7.7	8.2	8.8
Northern Ireland (Executive and office)	5.3	6.3	6.3	6.5
Work and pensions (admin)	5.9	6.3	6.9	7.5

(Note: Social Security benefits/expenditure for same periods £99.1, £105.1, £109 and £113.9 billions. Source: Table C11 Total Managed Expenditure (FSBR - April 2002)

To give some idea of who pays income taxation this table gives details of the number of UK income tax payers over the last twenty years.

Number of income taxpayers (in thousands)

Year	Number of individuals paying tax	Number of lower-rate taxpayers	Number of basic rate taxpayers	Number of higher rate taxpayers
1979–80	25,900	–	25,226[b]	674
1984–85	23,800	–	22,870[b]	930
1989–90	25,600	–	24,040[b]	1,560
1994–95	25,300	5,180	18,170	2,000
1998–99	26,900	7,300	17,200	2,200
1999–00[a]	26,900	3,700[c]	20,800	2,300

(Notes: [a] provisional statistics, [b] includes both lower-rate and basic rate taxpayers, [c] includes savings rate taxpayers ie those whose only income is from either savings or dividends)

Sources: Inland Revenue Statistics (http://www.inlandrevenue.gov.uk/stats/index.htm)

Progressivity revisited

Throughout this chapter we have considered the progressive nature of many taxes. You have seen how successive budgets in the 1980s and 1990s have reduced the progressive nature of the UK tax system with the move to indirect taxation and the reduction in the marginal rates of taxation for high-income taxpayers. As you have seen, although tax systems were progressive in the past they were also proportional to the expenses incurred by the kings on behalf of the taxpayer and to the benefits received by the taxpayer. That is, only relatively wealthy individuals paid tax and these were also the people with most to lose if the kings were unsuccessful in their defence of the realm.

In the 19th and 20th centuries the principle of progressivity became entrenched in the fiscal system. Socialists espoused the concept as part of their belief in the redistribution of wealth. Economists developed the law of diminishing marginal utility which states that the amount of satisfaction which is derived from the consumption of successive units of the same good or service will decline. It was argued that for there to be equality of sacrifice the better off would have to pay proportionately more of their income in tax. However, many economists challenged the validity of this law. Seligman in *Progressive Taxation in Theory and Practice* concluded that

> The imposition of equal sacrifices on all taxpayers must always remain an ideal impossible of actual realisation. Sacrifice denotes something psychical, something psychological. A tax takes away commodities, which are something material, something tangible. To ascertain the exact relations between something psychical and something material is impossible. No calculus of pains and pleasures can suffice.

It is argued by many today that it is the better off who accumulate capital and invest in resources to generate wealth in the future. A progressive system of tax interferes with these activities and may impair a nation's ability to invest in its future.

You have been presented with the arguments for and against progressivity and must make up your own mind. However, when the electorate was invited to vote for a top rate of tax of 50%, against the 40% in force, in 1992 there was a convincing rejection of the proposal. Since the general election in 1992 in the UK the electorates in the USA and Australia have also rejected proposals to increase taxation. The Labour government elected in the UK in May 1997 has repeatedly committed itself to not increasing the rates of tax paid by individuals and companies – although the extent to which this has been achieved in practice in perhaps more of a political issue and best debated elsewhere.

Summary

In this chapter we have laid the foundations which you will need to study taxation. We have drawn on the lessons of history to try to understand how taxation affects all of us today. You are now able to trace the history of taxation over more than 2,000 years. The difficulties facing Parliament today have been faced by leaders throughout the centuries. Governments must raise revenues in ways which are seen by the electorate as being fair and equitable.

A modern Chancellor is likely to have many conflicting objectives when setting out his tax proposals in the annual budget. He must decide how much tax he wishes to raise and then determine exactly how that tax should be raised. To do this a Chancellor must be aware of the potential consequences of his legislation on individuals and businesses. For example, a large increase in taxation may lead to a reduction in the economic activity in the private sector which is not compensated for by an increase in the economic activity in the public sector. A Chancellor is also likely to have an opinion about where the burden of tax should fall. In recent years the UK tax system has become less progressive, suggesting that Chancellors do not consider the redistribution of wealth to be an objective of our tax system.

In this chapter we have been able to explore the complex relationship between legislation and case law and understand the limitations of each.

Finally, we have thought a little about the nature of taxation and we are now in a position to define a successful tax. For a tax to be successful it should be difficult to avoid or evade in order to increase the equitable nature of tax and to maximise the revenue raised. In Chapters 2 and 3 we will consider in more detail the nature of a 'good' tax, if indeed any tax can be considered to be good.

In the remaining chapters of the book we will study current taxation in some detail.

Project areas

There are a number of areas covered in this chapter which would provide good material for projects. These include the following:

- a comparison of the progressive nature of the tax systems of a number of countries
- surveys of taxpayers to determine current attitudes to taxation, for example a study of the effect of phasing out MIRAS on the attitude to home ownership or removal of the married couples allowances or other tax reducers
- an evaluation of the impact of the changes in capital gains tax for individuals
- a comparison of ISAs with TESSAs and PEPs
- an investigation into the behaviour of small and medium-sized businesses as a result of the extension of first year allowances
- history of UK taxation
- implications of tax harmonisation in Europe.

Discussion questions

Question 1. Road fund licenses were originally introduced to pay for road building and maintenance. This is a tax based not on an ability to pay but according to use. In practice much of the road fund licence fee is used for other purposes. Is this a good way to raise taxes?

Question 2. Do you think that the decision in *W T Ramsay* v *IRC* was the right one?

Question 3. Do you think that people will be more likely to work if they receive support through the tax system rather than the benefits system?

Question 4. Design a fair method of identifying which individuals should receive child benefit net of higher rate tax.

Question 5. Will a General Anti-avoidance Rule (GAAR) ever be enacted in the UK?

Further Reading

History and Administration

- Inland Revenue website on the history of income tax and current administration procedures; http://www.inlandrevenue.gov.uk
- Dowell, S. (1965 - 3rd Edition, first published in 1884) A History of Taxation in England (4 volumes), Frank Cass & Co. Ltd.
- Sabine, B.E.V. (1966) A History of Income Tax, George Allen & Unwin.

Progressivity – James, S. and Nobes, C. (1999) *The Economics of Taxation: 1999/ 2000 Edition*, Chapter 2, Prentice-Hall: Hemel Hempstead.

Dates in UK Tax System – 'A year beginning on 6 April' – by J. Jeffrey-Cook, Taxation, 5 April 2001, p8.

2 The impact of the UK tax system

Introduction

As we have already seen in Chapter 1, tax can affect the economic decisions made by taxpayers. When a tax on windows was introduced in 1747 homeowners blocked up their windows, leading to health problems. Today the government uses taxpayers' eagerness to avoid tax to influence their behaviour. For example, in the Finance Act 1991 the Chancellor introduced tax relief for the payer of private health insurance premiums on individuals aged 60 and over. Until its recent scrapping this concession did much to encourage older people, who are generally more expensive than younger people to provide medical facilities for, to provide some of the cost of their health care needs directly for themselves. When making this relief available the Chancellor must have undertaken some sort of cost/benefit analysis. For example, if the only people who took advantage of the scheme were those who were already subscribers to private medical insurance the Chancellor would have lost some revenue he would otherwise have collected without encouraging anyone to reduce the costs of the National Health Service by investing in health insurance. (Note– that this relief was abolished in the Finance Act (No 2) 1997 but it is a useful illustration of the point.) In this chapter we will look at a number of other ways in which the tax system in the UK affects the decisions made by taxable persons. Having laid this foundation, we can then examine the detailed rules of the current UK tax system in subsequent chapters.

At the end of this chapter you will be able to discuss the:

- distorting effects of UK taxation on the decisions made by individuals, businesses and companies
- impact of tax on the personal investment decision
- impact of tax on the business investment decision
- problems of moving towards fiscal neutrality.

Fiscal neutrality

A tax system can be said to be fiscally neutral if it does not discriminate between economic choices. That is, the introduction of the tax system does not change the economic choices made by taxpayers. Hence a fiscally neutral system seeks to raise revenue in ways which avoid distortionary effects.

A tax has a distortionary effect if it changes the relative cost of goods and services. Consider, for example the tax (VAT) that is levied when you purchase a product. VAT is added to the purchase of chocolate biscuits like Hobnobs because they are a luxury good, but not on Jaffa Cakes which are deemed to be cakes and therefore an item of food. The law of supply and demand tells us that an increase in the price of Hobnobs without a corresponding increase in the price of Jaffa Cakes will lead to a decline in the number of boxes of Hobnobs sold compared to the number of boxes of Jaffa Cakes sold. This will normally cause a reduction in demand for Hobnobs because of the increase in price. Indeed, some individuals may purchase Jaffa Cakes rather than Hobnobs because of the charged price differential. This switch from one product to another, because of taxation, is called a distortionary substitution effect. (Of course some people just prefer Hobnobs and will continue to buy them – but there are always exceptions to the rule!)

Until the autumn of 1993 there was a similar distortion between freshly squeezed fruit juice, which was not subject to VAT, and long-life fruit juice which was taxed at 17.5% as a luxury good. This tax treatment had the effect of making freshly squeezed juice relatively more attractive than long-life juice. In the autumn of 1993 the government announced that freshly squeezed juice would also be taxed at 17.5%, thus removing the substitution distortion between the two products. Other such anomalies can be found throughout the UK tax system, as you will discover.

VAT would be fiscally neutral if all goods and services were taxed at the same rate. If this was so the marginal rate of substitution of one product for another will be the same including and excluding VAT.

If a tax system is not fiscally neutral the economic loss to the community may be greater than the revenue raised by the tax. The difference between the economic loss and the revenue raised is termed the economic, or excess, burden of taxation. While you are reading this chapter, and the next one, try to decide if there is an excess burden of taxation in each case.

Since VAT is charged only when money is spent, VAT makes saving relatively more attractive than spending money. This is another example of the inefficiencies introduced into our economy by our tax system and explains why turnover taxes can be recessionary – because they encourage saving at the expense of consumption.

What about the taxing of investment? If investments are to be taxed neutrally the amount of tax paid will need to be related to the returns earned and will be independent of the particular investment vehicle used.

This all implies that in a fiscally neutral environment all forms of income and all types of savings would be subject to the same taxation.

You may feel that tax systems should be fiscally neutral. In practice this is almost certainly impossible even if desirable and most governments and businesses therefore do not demand fiscal neutrality from their tax systems. As we will examine throughout this chapter, and chapter 3, the fact the presence of tax may affect economic decisions is an important feature of the tax system which can then be used to achieve political, social and economic goals.

Decisions about work and leisure activities

Whilst not always the case, in most jobs there is a direct relationship between how hard you work and how well you are paid. Many individuals therefore have the opportunity to choose whether to earn more money or not by working harder. Some people may be able to work overtime, others may choose to do jobs which have longer basic working hours in order to earn more money and still others may work many extra hours in the hope of gaining promotion. Of course, many people also make decisions which reduce their income, for instance taking early retirement, working part time or taking unpaid holidays.

In this section we will consider the factors which influence an individual when making a decision about how hard to work and then briefly consider the effect of their decisions on wealth creation and the revenues collected by governments.

Marginal rates of taxation

When considering the role that tax plays in the decision to work harder or not it is the marginal rate of tax (MRT) which is important, rather than the average rate of tax (ART). The marginal rate of tax is the rate of tax which is due if the taxpayer earns £1 more than their current income (the average rate of tax is the amount of tax paid as a proportion of their total income).

$$\text{MRT (on income)} = \frac{\text{amount of tax paid on next £1 of income}}{1}$$

$$\text{ART (on income)} = \frac{\text{total tax due on income}}{\text{total income}}$$

One of the reasons given for the reduction in the top rate of tax is that lower marginal rates of tax can encourage individuals to work harder. Another supposed benefit is that people will be less reluctant to pay tax if the tax rate is low, thus reducing the attractiveness of tax evasion and avoidance.

Full details of national insurance contributions and income tax rates are contained in Chapter 4. However, in order to understand this section you need to know a few basic facts about the current UK tax system, namely that:

- individuals are entitled to a personal allowance (they get the first £4,615 of their income free of income tax)
- employees' national insurance contributions (primary) are a percentage of earnings between £89 and £585 per week. Income over this limit does not incur a further liability to national insurance contributions for employees
- income tax is levied at up to five marginal rates, depending on the nature of the income, which increase at certain points as the taxpayer's income increases.

We will start by determining the marginal rates of tax which are in force in the UK at the current time. The effective rate of tax on earned income can be considered to be the combined rate of income tax and national insurance contributions, since they are both compulsory. However, national insurance contributions are technically not a tax, but a contribution 'insurance' paid to earn the rights to certain benefits – however, as they are a compulsory levy on an employee's income the are effectively a tax in all but name.

It is not possible to list the marginal rates absolutely because they depend, in part, on the personal circumstances of the taxpayer. Let us consider a single man, without investment income (i.e. any dividends or savings), who does not contribute to a pension scheme. His marginal rates of tax are:

Annual income	Income tax rate %	NIC rate %	Effective MRT rate %
0–4,615	0	0	0
4,616–4,628	10	0	10
4,629–6,535	10	10	20
6,536–30,420	22	10	32
30,421–34,515	22	0	22
34,516 +	40	0	40

This table may surprise you. You should note the UK currently has an income tax system which, when combined with national insurance contributions, levies a marginal rate of tax of 32% on an individual with income of £9,000 per annum, 22% on an individual with income of £32,000 and 40% on an individual with income of £36,000. Note that individuals who earn more than £4,628 must pay national insurance contributions of 10% on earnings over this amount (£89 × 52) up to the annual limit of £30,420 (£585 × 52). The section on national insurance contributions in Chapter 4 explains how this system has evolved to become what it is today and why these calculations apply as they do.

Our income tax system is progressive because the marginal rate of tax exceeds the average rate of tax at all times once you start to pay tax (try the numbers yourself if you are not sure). However, you may like to reflect on the 'fairness' of a system which incorporates a drop in the marginal rate of tax as income increases between particular levels and where national insurance contributions by employees stop for earnings greater than £585 per week. The UK electorate were offered the opportunity to change this situation in the general election in 1992 when the Labour Party manifesto included a commitment to remove the upper limit on national insurance contributions. As the Labour Party failed to win this election, this policy was never enacted and was not explicitly offered again once they finally were in the position to form the Government from 1997. The 2002 Budget has hinted at possible changes to the upper limit restriction on employee's national insurance contribution. An increase to these payments from April 2003 of 1% will be due on all income above the lower limit. This extra payment will not cease at the upper limit as other contributions will do. Whilst this represents only a small payment to those on high incomes, it does mark the breaking of the barrier and may result in further increases in the future.

To work or play?

As already suggested, many taxpayers are able to decide whether or not to increase their income by increasing their work effort. Let us take a simple example where an employee is offered the opportunity to work for an extra hour one evening. When making the decision an individual is likely to weigh the benefit of any extra money they might earn against the cost of working an extra hour.

Some individuals will be offered pay at a higher hourly rate to encourage them to undertake overtime. Of course, employers offer their employees the opportunity to work overtime because they believe that the marginal cost to them is less than the marginal benefit to be gained from the work which the employee will do.

In addition to the extra money being earned, an employee should also consider the tax consequences of the decision. An employee who undertakes overtime will, of course, pay tax at his or her marginal rate on their overtime income.

To examine these tax consequences for any individual overtime decision we must assess the relative benefits that will be gained against any costs that will be incurred. On the benefit side, of course there is their overtime pay. There may also be some cost savings associated with working these longer hours; for example, the employee might have socialised with friends if he or she had not worked overtime and will therefore save the cost of the drinks etc. they would have bought.

There may also be some benefits from working overtime which are difficult to express in monetary terms. For example, if some kind of emergency has brought about the need for overtime, there may be an enjoyable sense of camaraderie among the individuals who undertook extra work.

Now let us consider the costs of working overtime. These may be zero but other employees may incur significant costs if they work for an extra hour including any of the following:

- extra child care costs
- transport costs
- additional eating out, and so on.

In addition, there may be many other costs which cannot easily be assigned a monetary value, for example, missing spending time with their family.

Now that we have identified some of the costs and benefits of making the decision to work overtime we can consider the marginal utility of an extra £1 to a taxpayer. For example, individuals may be willing to work more overtime in the month before they go on holiday than at other times. Try and think of some more circumstances in which either an employee would rather work more hours at one time than another or one employee might choose to work overtime and another might decline the offer.

We have now identified one reason for the employer to offer extra work: the marginal benefit is greater than the marginal cost. For the employee the decision will be based on the same criteria, that is the collective marginal benefit is greater than the collective marginal cost. In practice, of course, identifying the marginal benefits and the marginal costs is likely to be difficult sometimes but, as employees, most people are able to make this rational decision even if we cannot fully justify why in monetary terms.

Now let us extend our argument to consider the effect of taxation on the decision to work overtime. Once again we will only consider marginal rates of taxation rather than the total tax paid or the average rates of tax. Suppose an employee habitually works overtime. If their marginal rate of tax is increased they may choose to work more hours to maintain their net income. Alternatively they may decline to work overtime because their net income per hour is such that the marginal costs exceed the marginal benefits. We can illustrate this with two examples. The first is an individual with a large mortgage who has to earn a given amount in overtime each month to sustain his lifestyle. The second is an individual with children who has to pay a childminder an hourly rate to look after the children. The first taxpayer may choose to increase his hours of overtime to maintain his level of income because his marginal rate of tax has increased. The second taxpayer may conclude that the net benefit of working overtime, that is the extra gross income less the tax and the costs of childcare, is too low to be worthwhile.

Similarly a drop in the marginal rate of tax may provide an incentive to work extra hours to some taxpayers while others may limit the hours they work so as to maintain their previous net income. However, if we return to our original hypothesis, that the work would be undertaken so long as the marginal costs are less than the marginal benefits, then the lower the marginal rate of tax the higher the marginal benefits and the more likely it is that individuals will undertake the extra work.

So far we have only considered individuals who are already working and are deciding whether or not to accept overtime. We could also consider the situation of those who do not currently work but may be able to obtain work if they chose to. This category may include single-parent families, who may have to rely on the state benefit system instead of any earned income they would otherwise be able to receive. If these individuals move into work often their benefits are reduced once they earn over a relatively low limit. Once single parents start to work their effective marginal rate of tax can be extremely high. Not only do they pay tax and national insurance contributions but they lose state benefits and may incur other direct costs such as extra travelling and child care costs. This can mean the overall cost impact to them is prohibitive – much more than others on similar incomes may be bearing.

The Chancellor went some way towards addressing these problems recently when he provided single parents with some relief for the cost of child care and substantial additional help for low income families in the March 1998 budget. This was helped further by the introduction in 2001/02 of the Children's Tax Credit Scheme and will be further developed by the provision of the Child Tax Credit from April 2003.

There are many other important issues in judging the decision to work or play which are beyond the scope of this text, but we can generally conclude that the lower the marginal rate of tax the more likely it is that individuals will choose to work harder.

Do-it-yourself or subcontract?

So far we have considered the marginal costs and benefits without looking in detail at the impact on this decision caused by the varying alternatives to working overtime. This section looks at some of these alternatives and how they may affect this decision.

Activity

Suppose that a taxpayer can choose to work overtime regularly on Saturday morning. If the overtime is worked the taxpayer will employ a sole trader to maintain his garden. Let us assume that the taxpayer does not enjoy gardening any more than he enjoys work and that he works less efficiently in the garden than in his normal job. We will also assume that the gardener, who has special skills and equipment, works more efficiently in the garden than our taxpayer. List the tax implications of the two situations. You may assume that all the transactions are recorded and tax is not evaded.

Feedback

If the taxpayer chooses to reject the opportunity of overtime and maintains his own garden there are the following direct tax consequences:

- his direct income taxation is unchanged
- his employer does not benefit from his extra work and so his profits are not increased and the corporation tax payable is unchanged
- the taxpayer is likely to be working less efficiently than an experienced gardener and the economic value of the work he produces is likely to be less valuable than

the economic value of the work which he would have undertaken during the period of overtime he has declined.

If the taxpayer chooses to work the overtime and employ a gardener there are the following tax consequences:

- his direct income taxation increases as his earnings increase
- his employer's profits (should) increase and so the corporation tax payable increases
- the gardener receives an income
- the amount of direct income tax paid by the gardener increases
- the gardener may also charge VAT on his supply of labour.
- all three people have increased their net income which potentially enables them to spend more money and thus potentially pay more tax in the future, perhaps in the form of VAT on their expenditures.

As you can see, from the government's point of view there is an increase in tax revenues and an increase in the income generating activity of the economy if the individual chooses to work overtime and employ a gardener compared to gardening himself.

Now let us turn our attention to the monetary factors which would increase an employee's desire to undertake additional hours at work and employ others to work for him.

The gardener will probably decide how much to charge for his services by deciding how much money he wants for himself and then adding on the cost of any tax, direct and indirect, which he must pay.

Other things being equal, the greater the difference between the after-tax income which the employee can earn and the gross cost of employing the gardener the more likely it is that the employee will undertake the overtime.

The after-tax income of the employee will also be increased if his marginal rate of tax is reduced. Similarly the gross cost of employing the gardener will be reduced if either his marginal rate of tax is reduced or the rate of VAT he must charge is reduced.

In reality, a whole series of non-monetary factors will also affect this decision. You may wish to make a second list, like the one above, of these other factors to have a more complete picture of how decisions are really made in practice.

In conclusion then:

- the lower the rate of corporation tax the more likely the employer is to increase his level of economic activity and therefore offer overtime to the employee
- the lower the rate of income tax the more likely it is that the employee will undertake extra work and employ others himself to do the jobs he does not now do for himself
- the lower the level of VAT the more likely it is that an individual will purchase services from registered traders.

The Impact of Tax Avoidance

Because of the tax implications, the decision to employ this gardener or not would be significantly affected if the gardener and employer chose (illegally) not to declare this transaction to the Inland Revenue. This illegal activity, called tax evasion, can have an important impact on an economy. The presence of tax in an economy will always induce some people to try to change the decisions made by others by 'bending' any rules that exist on what tax should be paid, when and by whom. These illegal acts cause many problems for fair tax payments in the UK economy and therefore tax laws need to exist to force people to fully declare their taxable activities to ensure fairness is achieved as much as possible.

In other cases, the way decisions are made can also lead to the same economic impact for the country (i.e. the loss of tax revenues that would otherwise be earned) but where this tax avoidance is not a primary motivation, or may not even be considered at all. The decision to eat at home or go out for a meal is one example, as is the decision to service the car at home or take it to a garage or to 'DIY' home improvements rather than using a builder. Given a little thought you will be able to think of other examples yourself. Whilst not usually thought of as a tax avoidance decision, deciding to prepare a meal at home rather than eating out effectively costs the country tax revenue and therefore could be viewed as equivalent to a tax avoidance scheme – a perfectly legal one of course. Whilst this is of course an extreme example to illustrate the point, the size of this extended 'black market' is obviously very large and needs to be carefully considered by the Chancellor when planning tax income for the country. This also illustrates the difficulty of addressing tax avoidance at a country wide level. Not all tax avoidance can be avoided whatever laws are put in place.

The personal investment decision

The financial services sector has proved to be very creative and there is a huge choice of investment vehicles for individuals who wish to save money rather than spend it. In this section we will consider the way the tax system impacts on people's savings choices. In particular we will consider ISAs, pensions and housing.

Individual Savings Accounts (ISAs)

ISAs are a new investment vehicle that were first available to investors from 5 April 1999. Prior to this time two schemes for tax exempt savings were available. First, Tax Exempt Special Savings Accounts (TESSA) allowed people to save cash with tax free interest provided the money was left in the account for 5 years. These accounts started on 1 January 1991 (ICTA1988 s 326A (3)). The maximum amount that could be deposited in a TESSA was £3,000 in the first year then £1,800 per year for the following 4 years (i.e. a maximum of £9,000 over the life of the account). These accounts ceased to be free of tax if the owner withdrew more than the interest that had accrued on the account. Anyone owning a TESSA on 5th April 1999 could continue to run the account for its full 5 year time although new accounts could not be opened.

The second tax exemption savings scheme in common operation prior to the introduction of ISAs were Personal Equity Plans (PEPs). PEPs enabled individuals to invest in equities either directly or using unitised investments (such as unit trusts). An individual could invest upto £6,000 each year in a general PEP (which invests in more than one share) or a further £3,000 in a single company PEP (only investing in one company's shares). All dividends and capital gains received from the securities held in the PEP were free of tax.

Both TESSAs and PEPs proved to be very popular and in 1997/8, for example,over 3.5 million people were using them to gain tax relief of more than £800 million.

The Chancellor announced his intention to introduce Individual Savings Accounts (ISAs) to replace TESSAs and PEPs in his first budget in July 1997.

The Chancellor's stated objective for ISAs was to maintain the total tax relief given for TESSAs and PEPs but use it to encourage people who are not currently savers to start saving. In 1999 only half of the population had savings in excess of £200, so there was clearly scope for increasing the number of savers.

The new account was available from a much wider range of institutions – even from supermarkets – as well as the usual financial institutions such as banks and building societies. ISAs were available from 6th April 1999.

The accounts have a guaranteed life of ten years. Investors who already hold TESSAs or PEPs are able to invest as much in ISAs as other savers and there is no lifetime limit on how much can be saved in the scheme. However, the maximum which can be saved in a fiscal year will be £7,000 per annum for at least the next five years. An ISA can be made up of cash, including National Savings Certificates, life insurance and stocks and shares. The account can either be of one large investment in equities (up to the full £7,000) or split between cash, shares and life insurance products. If the first option is chosen this is called a maxi-ISA. Up to £3,000 can be held as cash, up to £3,000 can be held in equities each year and up to £1,000 can be invested in life insurance (these are referred to as mini-ISAs).

In a further effort to encourage widespread use of the new account efforts have been made to minimise the restrictions on the account. As a result there is no minimum subscription amount or minimum period for which funds must be invested (unlike TESSAs). However, some providers impose additional conditions, such as notice periods prior to withdrawals, in order to offer savers higher returns.

The full accounts are available to individuals who are resident and ordinarily resident in the UK and are aged 18 or over. From the 2001 Budget 16 and 17 year olds may also invest in the cash component of a mini-ISA (ie up to £3,000 per annum). Each account is administered by a manager who can offer their own investments or other people's products. Savers are only be able to open one ISA in each fiscal year. They are able to use a single manager who offers an account which can accept the total subscription for the year or use separate managers for each component (i.e. each mini ISA can be with different managers).

Qualifying schemes will be free of income tax and capital gains tax on their investments. In addition accounts will be credited with a 10% tax credit on dividends from UK equities until 5th April 2004. This is an important concession as tax credits are no longer repaid for dividends not held in an ISA. Savers can withdraw funds from the account at any time without loss of tax relief but once the maximum amount has been subscribed in a year no further subscriptions will be allowed even if withdrawals have been made.

ISAs are therefore a good example of how the tax system is used to impact the decisions people make about their financial position. Their tax free status is used to influence the level, and type, of savings people undertake.

Personal pensions

Saving via a personal pension plan, particularly if it is a scheme to which a taxpayer's employer contributes, is extremely tax efficient. Contributions to an approved pension fund are eligible for tax relief (i.e. a deduction from their tax bill) at the taxpayer's marginal rate of tax and employer contributions are also eligible for tax relief. Investments in a pension fund are free of income tax and capital gains tax. However, apart from a tax-free lump sum that is usually paid when the pension itself starts, other income from a pension is taxed as earned income (part of your non-savings Schedule E income - as we will see later is important for personal tax computations). From 6th April 2001 a new type of pension has become available. These are called Stakeholder Pensions.

A detailed consideration of pension schemes is contained in Chapter 7.

Home ownership

Finally, we can consider the privileged tax incentives that are, or have been, available for home owners.

Prior to April 2000 the interest paid on the first £30,000 borrowed to buy the taxpayer's main or only residence attracted tax relief as part of a scheme called MIRAS (Mortgage Interest Relief at Source). In 1998/99 and 1999/2000 this was at 10%.

This proved a significant tax advantage to owning the house you lived in rather than renting it. During the 1980s homeowners could obtain this relief at their marginal rate of tax but the real tax advantage of housing is that capital growth does not give rise to a capital gains tax liability. Imagine the attitude of home owners to increases in house prices if a quarter or more of the increase had to be paid in tax when moving. A detailed consideration of the taxation of the capital gains on living accommodation is contained in Chapter 7.

Because of the privileged tax position of housing people have often been persuaded to commit more of their wealth to their main residence than would otherwise be the case. Remember the case of Hobnobs and Jaffa Cakes in the section on fiscal neutrality? The distorting effects of taxing Hobnobs and not Jaffa Cakes made buying units of Jaffa Cakes relatively more attractive. Likewise, the tax advantages of owning a house over other forms of investment create a propensity to hold wealth in property.

Before the current removal of interest relief the tax legislation may also have encouraged some individuals to move house or to borrow more when they moved house.

If a loan was raised, perhaps to buy a car, no tax relief was usually available on the interest paid on the loan (although some loans do get relief – we'll see how this works in Chapter 4). But if an individual moved house and retained capital from the sale of the house to buy a car, thus increasing the amount of the mortgage needed to purchase the new house, the same total amount will have been borrowed but, provided it was less than £30,000, all of it was eligible for tax relief.

The Conservative governments of the late 1980s and early 1990s interfered in the operation of the housing market on a number of occasions by amending the tax laws. In the 1988 budget the Chancellor announced a change from mortgage interest relief being applicable to the individuals buying the property to its being applied to the property. If two individuals, who were not married, bought a house before this change they were each eligible for relief on interest on a mortgage up to a maximum of £30,000. Hence two people who were not married could claim relief on a loan of up to £60,000 compared to a married couple who could get maximum relief of only £30,000. The Chancellor could have made the change in the law immediate by, for example, only allowing the higher relief if the contract had been signed by the end of that day, as is typical for other tax changes. However, he allowed a delay of nearly six months and so fuelled an already buoyant housing market by providing an incentive for multiple purchasers to complete quickly, thus increasing demand. This delay has been blamed for some of the increase in house prices in 1988, thus making worse the subsequent slump.

In 1992 the government attempted to exploit this behaviour impact again by abolishing stamp duty on house purchases under £250,000 for a limited period of eight months, in an attempt to boost the failing housing market. This effort was successful before the reintroduction of stamp duty on all property purchased above £60,000 in August 1992. In the 2000 Budget stamp duty on expensive houses was raised to 3% for properties costing over £250,000 and 4% for those costing over £500,000. (From 2% and 3% respectively in 1999/2000). As only 5% of all house transactions are over £250,000 these increases will not affect many people but does add to the overall progressivity of the tax system in the UK.

The tax advantage of owning your own home was largely removed from 6th April 2000 when the mortgage interest relief scheme described above was scrapped. At present there are few tax advantages linked to home ownership, but they may well be used again if behaviour impacts are considered necessary or with a change in government policy on home ownership. A key remaining advantage of having wealth in property in which you live still exists, however, in the form of a capital gains tax exemption for any gains received on selling your home. This concession does not appear to be threatened at present. We will examine it in more detail in Chapter 7.

Tax and the business investment decision

Businesses grow by incurring expenditure now in order to increase revenue in the future. There are often a number of ways in which this investment can be undertaken. For example, business might invest in fixed assets or in training costs to prepare its workforce for new technologies. One of the features that marks a successful business team from an unsuccessful one is of course the ability to determine which of these expenditures will lead to the best future revenue receipts.

When businesses undertake investment appraisal analysis they are encouraged to evaluate the cash flows associated with the project. Cash flows are however, influenced by tax in reality, but as we will see the tax treatment of the cash flows depends on the nature of the cash flow.

In this section we discuss the distortions that the tax system creates when a company is evaluating a project with a life of several years.

Investment in long-term projects and fiscal neutrality

There are a number of techniques used by companies to evaluate a potential capital project. We will confine ourselves to a consideration of discounted cash flow techniques using the net present value method. There are a large number of books which explain this method very well. The basic principle is that all cash flows are stated at their value today, termed their present value, by discounting them at the company's cost of capital. An example might help to explain the technique.

A company is considering investing £10,000 in a project which will generate a cash flow of £6,000 for two years starting one year after the initial investment. The company's after-tax cost of capital is 12%. A company's cost of capital might be the company's cost of debt. The after-tax rate is used because interest payments are tax deductible and should be included in the evaluation calculation.

You need to undertake the following calculation in order to calculate the net present value.

Year	Cash flow £	Discount factor 12%	Present value £
0	(10,000)	1	(10,000)
1	6,000	0.8929	5,357
2	6,000	0.7972	4,783
		Net present value	140

Because the net present value is positive, other things being equal, the theory tells us that the investment should be undertaken. Projects which generate a negative net present value should normally be rejected.

Notes on above example

- payments of cash are cash outflows and are shown as negative numbers
- the discount factor for each year is calculated by using the formula:

$$\frac{1}{(1+r)^t}$$

where r is the discount factor expressed as a decimal, that is 12% is written as 0.12, and t is the number of the year in which the cash flow arose
- the first cash flow, usually a cash outflow, is deemed to take place immediately and hence is recorded as occurring in year 0 and is already stated at its present value
- cash flows are deemed to arise at the end of the year in which they are recorded and so need to be discounted in full for that year.

From this example we can generate a simple test for fiscal neutrality. A tax is fiscally neutral if the decision about whether to undertake the investment is the same using the before-tax and after-tax cash flows. Capital allowances (a reduction in the tax bill) may be available when a business purchases fixed assets as we will see in Chapter 6. As an aside, it is interesting to note that at present in the UK the capital allowances available are independent of the method of payment for the assets.

Which of the following are cash flows?

(a) payment of wages
(b) purchase of fixed assets
(c) allocation of fixed overheads
(d) rent paid
(e) depreciation
(f) tax paid on profits.

Feedback

Wages paid, rent paid and tax paid on profits are all cash flows as they have an immediate effect on the cash resources of the business. The allocation of fixed overheads and depreciation are accounting activities which do not have an effect on the cash resources of the business and so are not cash flows.

It is likely that the purchase of fixed assets will result in a cash flow; even an exchange of shares in return for assets would eventually have cash flow implications when dividends are paid. If assets are bought using credit the cash flows will be the payments required by the terms of the credit agreements. Of course if the assets are bought for cash the purchase price will be a cash flow.

When a business increases its level of activity it may also need to increase its investment in working capital. This increase is calculated by adding the increase in stock to the increase in debtors and deducting the increase in creditors to find the net increase. In general this increase is deemed to take place during the first year rather than immediately. There is often an assumption that the increase in working capital which takes place at the beginning of a project will be accompanied by a corresponding decrease in working capital during the final year of the project.

You now know all that you need to know about calculating a project's net present value and we can turn our attention to the impact of taxation on investment appraisal.

The only way for a tax system to be fiscally neutral for business investment is if tax is charged on positive cash flows at the same time as the cash flow arises, and tax relief should be available for cash outflows at the time the cash payment is made. If this situation exists, the rate of tax is 't' and if the before-tax net present value is £B then the after-tax cash flows will be £$B(1 - t)$. Provided the rate of tax is less than 100% and if B is positive, then $B(1 - t)$ will also be positive. Equally if B is negative then $B(1 - t)$ will be negative. This means that so long as projects which give a positive net present value are accepted regardless of the numerical value of the net present value the before-tax decision will be the same as the after-tax decision and the system is fiscally neutral.

A government which taxes cash flows in this way is effectively going into partnership with its taxpayers. Profits and losses are shared between the business and the government in a predetermined ratio.

The impact of a time lag in the taxation of cash flows on investment appraisal

At present the UK corporation tax system does not tax cash flows. Instead profits are taxed and the tax is due nine months after the end of the accounting period (although large companies have to pay their tax bills on a more frequent basis). We will use an activity to help to determine the effect of such a delay for small and medium sized companies.

Activity

Alrewas plc wishes to evaluate an investment opportunity. After an initial cash outflow of £10,000, which is fully deductible for tax purposes, there are cash inflows of £4,000 a year for each of the next five years. Tax is paid and reclaimed on the cash flows, at a rate of 20%, one year after the cash flow. Calculate the before-tax and after-tax net present value of the project. What would the after-tax net present value of the project have been if tax was paid in the year in which the cash flow arose? The company has a cost of capital of 10%.

Feedback

Year	Cash flow £	Tax paid £	Discount factor 10%	Before-tax PV £	After-tax PV £
0	(10,000)		1	(10,000)	(10,000)
1	4,000	2,000	0.9091	3,636	5,455
2	4,000	(800)	0.8264	3,306	2,644
3	4,000	(800)	0.7513	3,005	2,404
4	4,000	(800)	0.6830	2,732	2,186
5	4,000	(800)	0.6209	2,484	1,987
6		(800)	0.5645		(452)
				5,163	4,224

The before-tax net present value of the project is £5,163. The after-tax net present value of the project is £4,224. Both calculations support the decision to proceed with the project.

The after-tax net present value of the project if tax is paid and relief received without any time delay is £5,163 × (1 − 0.2) = £4,130. This is lower than the after-tax net present value of the project with a time lag. Although the company had to wait for a year to receive the benefit of the tax relief on the initial expenditure this was more than compensated for by the delay in payment of tax on the profits.

Hence it would be possible for a tax system which taxed cash flows with a time lag to lead to a positive after-tax net present value although the before-tax net present value was negative. It is not possible for the reverse situation to arise since for a project to be acceptable the positive cash flows must be greater than the cash outflows. This situation means that a delay in the payment of tax may lead companies to accept projects which otherwise would have been rejected. In reality, most large companies pay tax during the year on that year's profits so this position would not normally occur in practice other than for small and medium sized corporation taxpayers.

The impact of the UK corporation tax system on investment appraisal

The UK corporation tax system does not tax cash flows, neither does it simply tax accounting profits (those you will see in a company's annual reports and accounts). The system is something of a hybrid with some accounting adjustments, such as depreciation, being ignored for tax purposes and other expenses taxed on the accruals basis. In addition, there is a nine-month gap for all but large companies between the end of the accounting period and the payment of tax. We will examine the operation of corporation tax in more detail in chapter 9.

Expenditure on a new project may be on any of the following items:

- land and buildings
- plant and machinery
- working capital
- advertising
- staff training.

You can probably think of more examples but let us consider the tax treatment of each of these types of expenditure.

There is no tax relief on expenditure on land and buildings except for industrial buildings such as factories and warehouses which are eligible for industrial buildings allowances. We will consider the industrial buildings allowance in some detail in Chapter 5. Generally the allowance given is equal to 4% of the cost of the industrial building for the first 25 years of the building's life.

Expenditure on plant and machinery is likely to qualify for a writing down allowance of 25% of the reducing balance each year. Again we will consider the allowances available for expenditure on plant and machinery in detail in Chapter 5.

Expenditure on working capital, that is unsold stock and money invested in debtors which has yet to be realised, is not eligible for any tax relief (although a stock relief used to be given in the UK on changes in stock holdings over a year).

The costs of advertising and staff training is likely to be considered expenditure wholly and exclusively for the purpose of trade and so is fully deductible for tax purposes. Once again we will consider allowable expenses in Chapter 5.

Even before we have looked at the details we will cover later in the book you can see that there is a wide variety of tax treatments of expenditure incurred to set up a new project.

In the light of the tax treatment of different items of expenditure it seems unlikely that any move towards fiscal neutrality is feasible. However, the lower the rate of business tax the smaller the distortions caused by the tax system. The UK rate of company tax is one of the lowest in Europe, which inevitably helps UK businesses to be competitive even if the UK tax system is distortive in the ways we have started to describe above.

You may even consider that the present bias in the tax system is advantageous as it discriminates against projects which require investment in fixed and current assets in favour of labour intensive projects.

Summary

In this chapter we have considered some of the distortions which exist in the current tax system. We have considered the distortions caused by both income and expenditure taxes for both individuals and companies. We have seen that lower marginal rates of tax are less likely to lead to distortions than high marginal rates of tax. In order to achieve low marginal rates of tax it will be necessary to levy the tax on as much income or expenditure as possible. For example, if VAT was extended to include food, children's clothing, books and newspapers it would be possible to reduce the rate of VAT and still generate the same amount of revenue for the government.

We can conclude that a broad tax base and low marginal rates of tax lead to fewer distortions than a narrow tax base with high marginal rates of tax.

Project areas and Discussion questions

There are so many interesting projects contained within the material of this chapter it is hard to choose just one or two. A topical area is that of the disincentive to work shared by many single parents who simply cannot afford to work. An evaluation of the Chancellor's Working Family Tax Credit systems or the Children/Child Tax Credit systems would prove to be an interesting project in this area.

An evaluation of the effectiveness of offering accelerated depreciation for tax purposes called first-year allowances to small- and medium-sized but not large businesses would be a good topic for a dissertation. For example, examination of the impact of 100% first year allowances for information technology equipment may be of interest.

An investigation into the likely impact of ISAs on savings patterns would also make a good topic for a dissertation.

An examination of the impact of marginal tax rates on employee decisions to work or not to work may be an interesting area for a project.

Further Reading

James, S. and Nobes, C. (1999) *The Economics of Taxation: 1999/2000 Edition*, Chapter 4, Prentice Hall: Hemel Hempstead.

3 Principles of taxation

Introduction

The history of tax and the current administration of tax was discussed in Chapter 1. In Chapter 2 some of the ways in which the system of taxation can distort the decision-making process of individuals and businesses were explored. In this chapter we will develop the ideas introduced in Chapters 1 and 2. We will consider further impacts of tax systems in general on the behaviour of individuals and businesses, introducing you to a number of important economic terms that relate to the management of the tax system. We will then identify the desirable characteristics of a tax system that underpin their design. Once we have done this we will evaluate a number of bases of taxation to illustrate the application of this theory in practice.

At the end of this chapter you will be able to:

- discuss the concept of the incidence of taxation
- discuss the concept of the excess burden of taxation
- discuss the concept of economic rent
- identify the disincentive effects of taxation
- state and discuss the five desirable characteristics of a tax system
- state the range of tax bases which are available and discuss the merits and limitations of each tax base.

The incidence of taxation

The tax system affects many people – both directly and indirectly. The formal incidence of tax falls on those who must actually pay the tax while the effective incidence of tax falls on those whose wealth is reduced in any way by the tax.

While it is not usually difficult to identify the formal incidence of tax it is, in practice, often impossible to identify the full effective incidence of tax.

To illustrate this problem consider the cost of a newspaper. Currently VAT is not levied on the sale of newspapers. If it were introduced the formal incidence of VAT would fall on the people who buy newspapers. The effective incidence is likely to fall not only on the purchasers but also on the newspaper proprietors, their distributors and the retailers who sell newspapers. Other things being equal, it is likely that the volume of sales of newspapers would fall leading to reduced profits for the newspapers, their distributors and the retailers. In addition, in order to reduce the impact of the tax on the volume of sales the newspaper proprietors, their distributors and retailers may not pass on the full amount of the VAT to their readers but may reduce their profit margins instead.

Tax wedges

In the case of indirect taxes the tax wedge is the difference between the marginal cost of producing a good and the marginal benefit from consumption. In the UK then the tax wedge is equal to the VAT and/or customs duty levied on a sale. An item which is sold for £100 before VAT has a marginal benefit from consumption of £117.50 (£100 plus VAT at 17.5%), because this is what the purchaser is prepared to pay for it, and a marginal cost of producing the good of £100 since this is the price at which the seller is prepared to manufacture the good. Hence the tax wedge is £17.50, the amount of VAT which is due from the consumer.

In the case of an income tax system the tax wedge can be said to be the difference between the marginal value of leisure sacrificed by a worker and the marginal value to society of another hour of work.

In the case of taxes on unearned income the tax wedge is the difference between the gross and net after-tax rates of return.

Activity

Determine the variables which make up the tax wedge when a trader employs a new worker.

Feedback

The tax wedge will be equal to the difference between the total cost of the worker to the employer and the after-tax salary of the employee.

This difference will be made up of four elements: the income tax which is levied on the employee's salary, the employee's national insurance contributions, the employer's national insurance contribution, and finally the value of any business tax relief which will be available to the employer with respect to the cost of employing the extra member of staff.

The distorting effect of taxation is not really dependent on the formal incidence of tax, rather it is dependent on the size of the tax wedge. For example, it is not as important to draw a distinction between employer and employee national insurance but the total amount of national insurance which must be paid. The total payment will determine the distortion effect.

The larger the tax wedge the greater the potential for distortions. A system of taxation will probably be less distortive if it contains many small distortions rather than one or two large distortions.

The ultimate payer of tax

The concept of the incidence of taxation is concerned with the question of who ultimately pays the tax. Look back to Chapter 2 to the activity where the gardener considers how much to charge for his labour. When determining his hourly rate the gardener decided how much money he wanted in exchange for his work and then added on the amount of tax which would be levied on him if he undertook the job, thus effectively passing the burden of his income tax liability on to his employer.

In theory the burden of indirect taxes, like VAT, falls on the final consumer. Yet there is evidence that manufacturers absorb some of the burden of VAT, rather than passing it on in full to their customers, either by not charging as much as they should with the tax included or by offering special sales deals. For example, many traders offered to fit double glazing free of VAT for some time after VAT was extended to double glazing, thus absorbing the burden of taxation themselves.

Crowding out

The concept of the incidence of taxation is also concerned with the transfer of resources from the private sector to the public sector. Suppose, for example, that the government decides to stimulate the economy by increasing the number of employees in the public sector. It will achieve this in two ways: firstly, taxes may increase, moving resources from the private sector and therefore reducing the level of activity in this sector and making more money available for employment in the public sector. Secondly, the government may borrow money to finance its expansion, causing interest rates to rise and deterring the private sector from investing in new projects which now do not give an adequate return. This strategy then will cause a shrinking in the private sector which will reduce the size of the tax base and lead to an increase in the rates of tax needed to maintain the level of tax raised. This phenomenon is termed crowding out.

The excess burden of taxation

The substitution distortion

We have already spent some time in Chapter 2 considering the distortive effect of taxation, including the concept of substitution distortion whereby individuals consume one item rather than another because of the effect of taxation.

This substitution distortion is also called the excess burden of taxation. The burden of tax caused by a government transferring spending power from the taxpayer to the state is not, in itself, inefficient but if it is done in such a way as to affect the economic choices of the taxpayer the cost to the taxpayer is the excess burden of taxation. For example, as the then Chancellor Norman Lamont explained in his first budget of 1993, VAT was not then charged on domestic fuel but was levied on the costs of insulating a home. This distortion might have been influencing taxpayers to consume more energy to heat their homes rather than spending money on insulating their property. In an effort to remove this distortion, and to raise more revenue, the Chancellor later extended the scope of VAT to domestic fuel, thus taxing both commodities on the same basis. In the 2000 Budget this reversal was then extended further. New measures were introduced to extend the reduced rate of VAT to installation of energy saving materials in the home. The bias was now in the favour of energy saving activity rather than energy consuming activity.

There are other examples of taxes that cause a distortion in the economic decisions made by a country's citizens. For a number of historical examples look again at Chapter 1. You should also look at Chapter 2 and find out the effect that the marginal rate of income tax has on an employee's decision about working over-time. In addition, look back to Chapter 2 for examples of the way in which taxes can distort the capital investment decisions of businesses. Investment projects which have a positive net present value before tax can have a negative net present value after tax if the tax system is not fiscally neutral. If this happens the company may choose to use its money in some other way than would have been the case without the effect of taxation. Suppose that the company decides to distribute the funds they would have used for the investment to its shareholders. If this happens the shareholders suffer a loss equal to the before-tax net present value of the project. The community generally will have lost the benefit of the expenditure planned by the company. This may have been for the consumption of goods or services from other businesses, causing other businesses to lose orders, with the knock-on impact to their profitability also. The total number of jobs may also fall (or at least not rise as may have resulted from the new investment). Finally the government has lost tax because the project was not undertaken.

The income distortion

The income distortion is the transfer of wealth from the taxpayer to the govern-ment. The income distortion then reduces the amount that the taxpayer can consume. Of course, all incidences of tax create at least some income distortion when viewed in isolation from the rest of the tax system.

A lump-sum tax

The degree of income distortion will be dependent on the average rate of tax. The greater the average rate of tax the greater the income distortion. The degree of the substitution distortion will be dependent on the marginal rate of tax. It is argued by economists that a lump-sum tax where an individual pays a given amount of tax regardless of the amount of work which he undertakes would eliminate the substitu-tion distortion when individuals decide whether to work harder or enjoy more leisure time.

If a lump-sum tax were to be introduced then a taxpayer's marginal rate of tax would be zero.

A lump-sum tax would be likely to affect the behaviour of individuals. The benefit of working for an extra hour will increase because there is no increase in taxation and so more work is likely to be undertaken. This does not mean that the lump-sum tax is not distortionary; it simply illustrates the distortions which exist in the tax system which prevails today.

To achieve this reduction in the distortive affect by a lump-sum tax the amount of a lump-sum tax paid by an individual must be independent of characteristics which the individual can influence. For example, a tax which increases with the educa-tional and vocational qualifications of the individual is not a lump-sum tax because it may have a distortive effect on the decisions made by individuals about their education and training.

While the lump-sum tax approach has some advantageous impacts, its use would not be without knock-on effects. For example, if only members of the workforce paid the lump-sum tax, there may be a distortionary effect as low paid individuals may be deterred from joining or remaining in the workforce.

The excess burden of taxation, and the distortions to economic decisions that result from the incidence of taxation, are therefore important considerations for the Government in making choices on the best way to develop the tax system.

Economic rent

Economic rent is the amount that a factor of production earns over and above what could be earned if it was put to its next best use. Some economists argue that economic rent should be subject to taxation. This section discusses the importance of economic rent in an economy.

The taxation of land

The first asset to be considered this way was land. Since there is only a finite amount of land it is a (relatively) scare resource. Consider the use of farm land. The difference between the value of the crops and the cost of cultivating the land to grow the crops is the economic rent where there is no alternative use for the land.

However, there are often other uses for land other than farming it, such as for building houses or industrial buildings. Land with planning permission for construction is worth more than land without such consent as an alternative use for the land has been approved. Under a system which taxes economic rent the increase in value brought about by the granting of planning permission should be taxable. Because planning permission is often difficult to obtain and local authorities only allow limited development in an area, land with such permission can be very valuable. In theory, it is feasible to tax such gains because landowners will still be better off by developing the land provided the tax is at a lower rate than 100%.

A tax of this kind has been tried on several occasions, the last one being the Development Land Tax which was abolished in the early 1980s. In practice landowners, when faced with a tax of this type, often choose to 'wait and see' rather than realise the gain immediately, in the hope that the tax will be abolished. To date this strategy has proved to be successful.

The economic rent of other assets

There are other assets whose value is enhanced because of the actions of governments. Recent examples of this has been the granting of the television franchises, where companies were invited to bid for the right to broadcast in a region, and the issuing of licenses for mobile telephone networks. Some companies lost their television franchises and have had to find a new role for themselves as independent producers. Other companies bid so much for their franchise that it seems doubtful that they will earn even reasonable profits from their investment in the short-term. These franchise payments can therefore be considered to be a tax on economic rents.

An economic rent on housing

Now consider a homeowner. The economic rent of his or her home is the amount which the property could be let at on the open market – the alternative use to living in the property themselves.

In an income based tax system where income received is subject to taxation then a tax liability could be made to arise on the value of this economic rent. This would effectively treat a homeowner as both tenant and landlord. The payment of a notional rent has no tax consequences for the tenant in an income tax system but the notional rent received by the landlord would be taxable in the same way as any other income is taxable. In practice, of course, it may be difficult to persuade homeowners to pay tax on income which they have not, in fact, received.

If a tax system based on expenditure is in force the notional income received by the landlord has no tax consequences but the notional rent paid by the tenant would be subject to an expenditure tax. Once again in reality, it is unlikely that such a tax would be accepted by the electorate.

Under an expenditure tax system it would also be theoretically possible that the homeowner would have to pay an expenditure tax when the property is acquired. In practice the barrier to home ownership that such a tax would create is likely to be unacceptable in the UK.

In reality, whilst economic rent is therefore identifiable, taxing it is difficult to achieve directly as where no actual transaction occurs it is difficult extract tax. The notion of economic rent is however important in the problem of developing effective tax systems as influencing economic decisions between alternatives is an important part of the way the economy is developed and managed.

The desirable characteristics of a system of taxation

Adam Smith, the originating author and founding father of tax economics, produced a series of books in 1776, called *The Wealth of Nations*, which offered four desirable characteristics for a tax system (book V, Ch II, pt II 'of Taxes'). A system of tax he suggests should be:

- *Equitable*: it should be seen to be fair in its impact on all individuals. They should contribute 'as nearly as possible in proportion to their respective abilities'.
- *Certain*: taxpayers should be able to determine what they are actually paying so that the political system can more accurately reflect the preferences of individuals.
- *Convenient*: it should be easy and inexpensive to administer and for the contributor to pay it.
- *Economically efficient*: it should not have an impact on the allocation of resources and it should 'take out and keep out of the pockets of people as little as possible over and above what it brings into the public treasury of state'.

These four characteristics have become known as 'The Canons of Taxation'. Other writers have added further characteristics to this list. A common addition is *flexibility*. This suggests the system should be established in such a way as to be able to cope with changing economic circumstances over time.

A problem with desirable characteristic lists, as given above, is that their authors usually do not prioritise the desirable characteristics. Should we allocate each of the characteristics equal weight or are some more important than others? Are some of the characteristics so important that any successful system of tax must have them? Perhaps we should consider each of these characteristics before attempting to answer these questions.

Equity

A tax which is not seen to be fair is usually resented by the individuals called upon to pay it. The most recent example of a tax which failed, at least in part because it was seen to be unfair, was the community charge (or poll tax). The introduction of VAT on domestic fuel, which is generally considered to be a basic necessity of life, is probably also seen to be unfair because the elderly, the unemployed and families with young children spend a relatively higher proportion of their income on heating than parts of the population with higher disposable incomes. This introduction of VAT therefore affects parts of the population who are less able to bear the extra burden more than those that are. There are two measures of the fairness of a tax system – horizontal equity and vertical equity:

- a tax system is horizontally equitable if taxpayers with equal taxable capacity bear the same tax
- a tax system has vertical equity if those whose need is greater suffer less tax.

We have two problems of definition when considering horizontal equity. Firstly, how will we identify taxpayers with equal taxable capacity? Two individuals doing the same job for the same money with the same personal circumstances are likely to have the same taxable capacity in most tax systems, but how do you compare the taxable capacity of an individual who has earned income with another, who is not working but has substantial wealth, to achieve equity? Equally, an individual who prefers to spend his leisure time drinking incurs a greater tax liability because of excise duty on alcohol than an individual who spends the same amount of money on trips to the theatre, regardless of their relative taxable capacities.

Secondly, consider the matter of the tax to be paid by individuals with the same taxable capacity. Suppose we consider two individuals with the same lifetime income, one of whom earns the same amount for each year of his working life of 40 years while the other earns 20 times as much for only two years of her working life. Under a progressive tax system the first taxpayer will pay less tax than the second. Hence, for a tax to have full horizontal equity it should be based on the lifetime income of the taxpayer not on incomes from year to year. This approach is likely to prove difficult, or impossible, to operate in practice and raises new difficulties. For example, how should individuals with different lifespans be taxed? Women, for example, have a longer life expectancy than men. If income is to be spread over a taxpayer's lifetime should women pay less tax than men on their taxable capacity because they will need to support themselves for more years?

What about vertical equity? Achieving this is also difficult in reality. To implement a tax system with vertical equity we must first decide who, in principle, should pay tax at the higher rate. Then we must decide how much higher that rate should be than the basic rate paid by other taxpayers, and finally we must devise a tax system which achieves these objectives.

An individual may be considered to have a greater ability to pay or to have a higher level of economic well-being or to receive more benefits from government spending. Any of these criteria might be used to identify individuals who should pay the higher rate of taxation. However, which, or which combination, of these criteria should be used? Even if the criteria to be used are agreed there will still be difficulties involved in measuring ability to pay, economic well-being or benefits received.

Suppose two individuals undertake the same job but the first chooses to work only the basic hours and spends more leisure time in their garden while the second chooses to work overtime each week. If income alone is used to determine economic well-being then the second individual will pay more tax than the first. But both employees had the same opportunity to earn extra money so is it really fair that one of them should pay more tax than the other? If we consider the ability to earn an income, instead of what is actually earned, then both will pay the same amount of tax.

So if we are to use the ability to pay as our criteria we must first decide whether we will use actual income or potential income. In practice of course it is actual income which is taxed because of the practical difficulties of measuring potential income. But even if we tax the actual income of taxpayers we may still have problems with vertical equity. Suppose two individuals have the same income but the first saves money in order to provide for retirement while the second spends money as it is earned and depends on the state for support in old age. The first individual will pay tax on the return earned on the savings and so will pay more tax in total than the second individual, while the second receives more benefits from the state. Can this be considered to be equitable? It is unlikely that, put this way, the first individual will agree at least.

Some argue that tax paid should relate to the benefit received as a way to achieve vertical equity. That is, that those who benefit most from the services provided by the government should pay the most tax. This approach is occasionally used in the UK. For example, only those individuals who have a television are required to contribute to the cost of the BBC by way of the licence fee – a sort of tax as it is a compulsory levy on owning a TV . However, this is a crude measure of benefit. There is no way of evaluating how much benefit a taxpayer derives from watching BBC programmes. In addition, the tax is difficult to collect and necessitates the use of a database of all addresses in the UK and detector vans to ensure compliance with the tax (i.e. is it economically efficient?).

There are relatively few services which can be taxed in this way. For example, defence or law and order are often quoted as benefits which are impossible for a citizen to choose whether to enjoy or not (called public goods). It is often undesirable for other services to be withheld from citizens who do not contribute to their cost, even if it were feasible. For example, there was a time when homeowners and businesses could subscribe to the fire service in the same way as a motorist can choose to join the AA or the RAC today. However, if a non-subscriber suffered a fire and the fire services did not provide their services it was possible that the fire would have spread to neighbours who had paid to have their property protected. In addition it is likely to be unacceptable to the community as a whole that some members of society are not helped by the fire services when they are in need. Nowadays, this service is therefore provided largely as a public good.

Road tolls are another way of taxing users rather than the whole population. However, road tolls are likely to lead to economic inefficiency because some road users may make an alternative travel choice rather than use the road and pay the toll, creating a substitution distortion thus leading to an inefficient allocation of resources.

It therefore seems difficult to imagine that a significant amount of tax could be raised on the basis of assessing, and taxing, benefit received.

Utilitarians argue that a tax system will be fair if individuals make an equal sacrifice of utility. They undertake an analysis of individuals' utilities and then set tax rates so that the marginal utility of income, which is the loss in utility from taking a pound of income away from an individual, is the same for all individuals. It is then argued that taking a pound away from a rich individual causes him or her a lower loss of welfare than taking a pound away from a less well off individual. This leads to the conclusion that a tax system should be progressive (the richer will pay more than the poorer to balance the losses in utility), although it does not help us to decide just how progressive the system should be. However, we have already discussed the problems created by high marginal rates of tax on work effort in Chapter 2 and the impact this could have for society as a whole and this makes utilitarianism a less attractive argument.

This concept of fairness is extremely complex and we have done little more than introduce the subject in this section, however, it is an important concept that must be considered when examining any tax system.

Certainty

For a tax system to be politically accountable the Government must legislate for all changes in taxation and the government must regularly offer itself to the electorate to gain a mandate for its policies.

For a tax system to be politically accountable the country's citizens need to be fully informed about the incidence of tax. Hence taxes where the incidence is clear are to be preferred over taxes where there is disagreement and uncertainty about the ultimate payer of the tax. If this criterion is used then corporation tax is a poor tax because it is unclear whether the shareholders or consumers bear the ultimate burden of the tax. It is also argued by some economists that individuals are more aware of how much income tax they pay than how much VAT they pay, making income taxes more certain than VAT.

In addition, the tax consequences of any financial transaction should be known in advance of the transaction being undertaken. In practice this is not always the case in the UK.

The Inland Revenue Code of Practice contains details about the information and advice that taxpayers can expect to obtain from the Inland Revenue. The Inland Revenue will give:

- answers to questions about a taxpayer's rights and obligations under the legislation relating to direct taxation
- information to help a taxpayer complete his return or claim reliefs, repayments or make an appeal
- information about their interpretation of tax law where the Revenue has a settled view and disclosure would not assist in tax avoidance or evasion
- post-transaction rulings where the tax treatment of a particular transaction was in doubt. Note that the Revenue will normally consider themselves bound by a post-transaction ruling
- their interpretation of legislation passed in recent Finance Acts
- advice on double taxation agreements
- advice on whether someone is employed or self-employed
- advice on Statements of Practice and Extra-Statutory Concessions
- advice on other areas concerning matters of major public interest in an industry or in the financial sector.

The Inland Revenue will not give help with tax planning or advice on transactions designed to avoid or reduce the tax charge which might otherwise be expected to arise.

Convenience

The costs of administering the tax system include not only the direct costs incurred by government but also the compliance costs of the taxpayer. Compliance costs are the costs which are imposed on a taxpayer when he or she attempts to comply with a given tax. These will include costs such as the need to keep records for tax purposes, costs of employing tax related staff, and so on. Some commentators estimate that the compliance costs are five times as big as the direct costs for some types of tax. There is a current trend towards measuring and planning for the full costs of tax imposition (direct and indirect). This includes changes to tax rules in the last few years directly aiming to reduce some of the compliance costs on sole traders and partnerships, however, the burden of complying with rules for PAYE, VAT and capital gains tax should not be underestimated when you are thinking about ways in which the tax system could be developed.

Economic efficiency

A tax system is seen to be economically efficient if it does not distort the economic decisions which are made by individuals. We have already discussed the concept of economic efficiency in some detail in Chapters 1 and 2. In the early part of this chapter we have identified substitution distortions and income distortions and concluded that a lump-sum tax has a reduced substitution distortion effect. In Chapter 2 we also considered both the income distortion effect and the substitution distortion effect of an expenditure tax, namely VAT.

Other examples of tax induced distortions are easy to find. For example, take planning for retirement. An individual who invests funds in an approved pension fund obtains tax relief on contributions and the pension fund itself is exempt from both income and capital gains tax. This contrasts with an individual who proposes to finance retirement in some other way, perhaps by investing in a valuable asset such as a famous painting or perhaps property – with the aim of selling the items for gain in the future to provide a source of retirement money. For these assets, the tax situation may be very different. No relief is available in the current UK tax system for funds initially invested in the valuable asset that is being purchased to fund retirement and capital gains tax will be levied when the asset is sold.

Sometimes the distortions are intended by Government in order to affect individuals' behaviour. Such taxes are termed corrective taxes. The example above of pensions may be considered a corrective tax as the tax advantages of investing in a pension rather than other assets will encourage people to save for their old age where they might not otherwise make such arrangements. Another example is the subsidy which is sometimes paid to employers who provide jobs to individuals who have been unemployed for a long time.

We also have a number of examples of the impact that announcements have on people's behaviour. For example, if people believe that the duty on cigarettes will be increased in the budget they may purchase more cigarettes in the days before the budget in anticipation of an increase in tax.

A further issue of efficiency relates to the administration of taxation. The more a tax costs to administer (creating returns, checking returns, chasing non payment etc.) the less of the money raised by the tax is available to the Government. It is not possible to have a 100% efficient collection system where some non-compliance will occur (to achieve the equity aim at least – some administrative effort must be incurred to ensure all pay who should pay) but this administration cost should be as little as possible to achieve the best possible economic efficiency.

Flexibility

A flexible tax is one which changes, or can be changed, easily in response to changes in the economic cycle. A key aim of many Governments is to reduce the fluctuations in economic activities caused by the economic cycle as this is often seem as good for an economy. A flexible tax, designed properly, can have a stabilising effect on the economy. For example, it can cause money to be taken out of a growing economy to keep it's growth at a manageable level, and reduce the amount of money that is taken out of the economy when it enters a recession to soften any downward spiral effect.

Therefore, in times of recession a government might be content to see its receipts fall and increase its borrowing in order to give the economy a boost while during boom years a government might be happy to see its receipts increase, thus moderating the boom.

The modern income tax system is a good example of a relatively flexible tax system. When incomes rise the amount of tax raised increases without any direct action from the government and equally when income falls the amount of tax collected also falls. Because of the stepped progressive nature of the UK income tax system the percentage change in the tax collected is greater than the percentage change in wages. If wages increase by, say, 10% in a year income taxes will increase by more than 10% over the same period without a need for a change in the legislation and without a protest from taxpayers, who accept that if their salaries increase their tax liability should also increase. Taxes will increase by a greater percentage than wages because marginal rates of tax are higher than average rates of tax for most income tax payers on the UK.

Another example of a tax which changes automatically is stamp duty on houses. On all house purchases over £60,000 (£150,000 in some areas) a tax (called stamp duty) is due on the transfer of the property as part of its sale (currently set at 1%). If the house value at sale exceeds £250,000 this tax rises to 3%. It rises to 4% for values over £500,000. The amount of this tax collected therefore increases both as the number of houses sold increases and as the value of houses sold increases.

In practice, there is often a time lag between the decision to take some fiscal action, the implementation of the policy and the full impact of the tax on the economy. For example, during the 1980s there was great pressure from environmentalists to reduce the lead emissions from petrol. In the late 1980s the duty on unleaded petrol was reduced to make it more attractive to use than leaded petrol. Demand for unleaded petrol increased as a result of the changes but there was a time delay while information about unleaded petrol was disseminated throughout the population and car owners arranged to have their engines modified. Ultimately, however, this has now resulted in almost no new cars being sold which, if petrol driven, do not use unleaded fuel.

The time lag for other changes may be shorter but any delay can cause instability.

For example, if the government is faced with a severe recession it might expand the economy by borrowing in order to avoid high unemployment. This expansion might turn a recovery into a boom, leading to demands for cutbacks which might, once again, lead to recession. This is the 'boom and bust' cycle for which many UK governments have been criticised in the past.

In practice, also, maintaining the flexibility in the system by changing the rates of direct taxation can be difficult to achieve, generating much political debate about the 'fairness' of each proposal. In addition, the government of the day regularly makes commitments to refrain from increasing taxes. However, increasing employee national insurance contributions by 1% from 1994/95, or the more recent widening of the benefits on which national insurance contributions are due, did not seem to cause the political argument that increasing income tax by 1% would have done, despite the fact that both changes would have had the same effect on a taxpayer on average earnings. This lesson appears to have been learned by the current Chancellor who has repeated this strategy in the 2002 Budget and added a further 1% to national insurance contributions.

Smith's Canons revisited

Now that we have spent some time discussing each of Smith's characteristics (plus flexibility) we can attempt to rank them by importance.

In recent years two particular taxes proposed and supported by the government have failed: the community charge (or poll tax) and the proposed increase in VAT on domestic fuel from 8% to the full rate of 17.5%. The community charge replaced domestic rates in April 1990, and was itself replaced in April 1993 by the current council tax. If we consider each of these taxes and try to identify the reasons for their failure we may be able to identify characteristics which a tax should have in order to be successful in the UK.

The community charge replaced domestic rates, a long–established but unpopular tax as the primary form of local taxation for provision of many local services (like schools, roads, police, fire service etc.). Rather than levy local tax solely on home-owners as the rates did, the community charge was levied on virtually all individuals over 18 years of age. The supporters of the community charge argued that it increased certainty (at least political accountability) by making the individuals who were eligible to vote in local government elections responsible for paying for their elected council's expenditure proposals. Opponents of the community charge claimed that the tax was unfair because the majority of individuals were required to pay the same amount of tax regardless of their personal circumstances (i.e. vertically inequitable). Some individuals, including students and the unemployed, were able to pay a reduced amount but little relief was available for the majority of taxpayers. In practice the tax proved to be difficult to collect with many people simply disap-pearing from official records to avoid having to pay the tax. In addition to the administrative problems, protests about the unfairness of the community charge (e.g. the Poll Tax riots) continued until it was replaced with the council tax.

The increase in VAT on domestic fuel was proposed in the spring budget of 1993. In April 1994 VAT was levied on domestic fuel at 8% and towards the end of 1994 the Chancellor attempted to introduce the legislation needed to increase the rate from 8% to 17.5%. In the event the House of Commons defeated the motion and the Chancellor was forced to abandon his proposal. The defeat occurred despite measures announced in the budget to protect many of the less well off in society from the increase in VAT. These measures including substantial increases in the state pension as well as increases above inflation to a number of other state benefits.

The opponents of the tax argued that heating and lighting were essential for everybody, and not a luxury, and so should not be taxed at the full rate despite the presence of any compensatory benefits. They successfully argued that in general people on lower incomes spend proportionately more of their income on gas and electricity and so the increase would affect the poorest people in society disproportionately (again an issue of equity).

It would appear then that the community charge failed because it was difficult to collect and was considered to be unfair because it was regressive. The increase in VAT on domestic fuel was seen to be regressive and therefore unfair. Perhaps then the most important characteristic of a good tax system, in the UK at least, is that it should be, and be seen to be, fair making equity is the most important to get right – assuming the others are not ignored too of course.

Activity

Consider what arguments may be raised by a Government proposal to increase income tax or national insurance contributions by 1%. Which is likely to be more acceptable when considering the desirable characteristics of a good tax system?

Alternative tax bases

A considerable amount of debate has been generated by the question of the tax base, or other method, which should be used to determine an individual's contribution to public funds. The five desirable characteristics of a good tax system should equip you to evaluate the following tax bases. We have already discussed two ways of allocating the tax burden, the benefit theory of income tax and the ability to pay. In this section we will consider three alternatives for applying this allocation in reality, the tax bases of:

● wealth (or capital)
● income
● expenditure.

Wealth

Chapter 1 provided a history of wealth taxes. These types of taxes are among the oldest forms of taxation because wealth is, in some ways, easier to tax than income. A wealth tax would replace taxes on unearned income (such as savings or dividends) and capital gains and is effectively a tax based on the ability to pay, which was considered earlier in this chapter, rather than on benefit received. A tax on wealth is useful as a tool for redistributing wealth if this is a key goal of a government. However, there are a number of difficulties which arise when trying to value wealth which can make wealth taxes costly to administer.

Activity

List some of the things that may contribute to an individual's wealth.

Feedback

You have probably included some tangible assets in your list like land and buildings. Other assets include shares and securities and the market value of a business run by the individual. But for many people the present value of their future earnings and the present value of their pension fund are their most valuable assets. Did you include this? Look back to Chapter 2 for an explanation of the present value technique. The present value of an individual's future earnings is the estimated positive cash flows arising from employment throughout their working life, restated in present value terms. The courts already take account of potential earnings when awarding damages in many legal cases. However, we live in a rapidly changing world in which an individual may be faced with redundancy, retraining and second or even third careers during his or her working life. In practice it does not seem feasible to value the future earnings of every citizen for tax purposes. Since future pension rights are generally dependent on earned income it would also be difficult to value the future pension of every citizen.

In practice then a wealth tax is a tax on (capital) assets. However, individuals who do not use a pension fund, for whatever reason, may accumulate assets in order to provide for old age and a wealth tax which is levied on assets but not pension rights will be inequitable.

In addition, assets may provide additional benefits to their owner such as power and influence. For example, a wealthy individual is likely to be able to borrow money at a lower rate than is available to most citizens because they can influence the lending decision in ways others may not be able to. It would be extremely difficult to ascribe a value to these economic benefits.

Finally, a wealth tax is likely to be expensive to administer compared to other tax bases, although property taxes, like the council tax, have proven relatively cheap to collect. The difficulties of a wealth tax are probably too great to enable it to be introduced in the industrialised world. However, a tax on expenditure may serve as a surrogate since it effectively taxes an individual's standard of living, as we will see later in this section.

Although a full wealth tax may be impractical for the reasons we have just examined, there are two taxes in the UK which could be considered to be, partly at least, wealth taxes namely capital gains tax and inheritance tax. Together these taxes provide the Exchequer with less than 1% of its total revenue and are predicted to only contribute £4.8 billion in 2001/02. This is only about half of the average proportion of total revenue which is raised by wealth taxes in other OECD countries, suggesting the UK makes proportionally little use of wealth taxes in its overall tax system.

The Conservative party, when in power, argued that these two taxes, in common with other wealth taxes, discourage entrepreneurship and thus restrict economic growth. This view is not substantiated by a recent study of OECD countries which suggests that wealth taxes do not significantly affect the level of economic activity of a country.

One of the purposes of capital gains tax in the UK is to reduce tax avoidance. This is commonly the excuse for at least some form of wealth taxes in many countries. Tax could be avoided if a taxpayer was able to increase their total wealth in a form other than income such as by owning shares which gain value over time. For example, if you owned your own company you could either pay yourself a wage or you could instead issue new shares to yourself each year and sell them periodically to achieve the same increase in your total wealth. Without a tax on selling these shares you would be able to keep more of your wealth gain than for the same result paid as a wage on which income tax would normally be paid. In the UK at present, taxpayers pay tax on their net chargeable gains in excess of the annual exemption limit, which is £7,700 for 2002/03, at either 10%, 20% or 40%. As a result there is relatively little incentive to realise capital gains rather than taxable income (although this incentive has increased again recently with the use of taper relief to reduce the effective rates of capital gains taxation as we shall see in later chapters). If capital gains tax is abolished it is likely that other measures will have to be introduced to restrict the scope for converting income into capital gains in order to limit the potential loss of income tax.

Inheritance tax does not serve the same purpose because it is almost entirely avoidable by taxpayers who undertake effective tax planning and are not unfortunate enough to die unexpectedly. However, there are a number of arguments in favour of an inheritance tax remaining a part of the UK's tax system. Firstly, there is no evidence that a tax on inheritance affects individuals' incentive to work so its distortive effects in this area are less of an issue than other taxes. Secondly, it is argued that one role of the tax system is to facilitate a fair balance of wealth between the better off and the poorer in society. An inheritance tax is probably one of the best ways of achieving this redistribution of wealth aim.

Income

Income is used as the major tax base throughout the world. However, this does not mean that the application of an income tax is without difficulties or that it is the best tax base to use in all cases. Our first problem arises when we try to define income to be taxed.

Hicks(1939) defined income as the maximum value which "a man can consume during a period and still expect to be as well off at the end of the period as he was at the beginning". Hence if a tax system which taxes income is to be equitable it must allow for the erosion of the capital base caused by inflation i.e. some value will be lost of the capital base each year just related to price increases. In times of inflation some of the income generated must be retained within the business in order to maintain the level of the capital base. This sounds very reasonable but there are a number of difficulties which have deterred the Inland Revenue from implementing such a system. These problems include:

● Determining how the value of the capital base should be measured.
● The use of the word 'expect' in the definition. It does not tell how much an individual can consume with certainty, only what he can consume and expect to maintain his capital base. It does not help us to determine how to tax unpre-

dicted profits, or losses.

Hicks provided a number of different definitions of income but himself claimed little usefulness for his definitions of income describing them as 'bad tools, which break in our hands'. Governments are generally reluctant to allow inflation to become an integral part of the tax system. At the moment some personal allowances and tax limits are increased in line with the increase in the retail price index unless the Chancellor elects to either freeze them or increase them by some other amount. Governments are reluctant to extend indexation for fear that it will fuel inflation.

In 1978 the Meade Committee report on *The Structure and Reform of Direct Taxation* considered a comprehensive income tax – i.e. one that could exist as the only form of taxation in the UK removing the need for capital and expenditure taxes.

A comprehensive income tax is a tax which is levied on comprehensive income, which is equal to the amount which an individual could consume without diminishing the value of his wealth. This can be restated in terms of actual events so that comprehensive income is equal to the amount which is consumed plus/(less) any increase/(decrease) in the value of the individual's wealth.

This type of income would result in all the difficulties described in the section on a wealth tax as it links income tax to measures of wealth instead. Meade rejected the comprehensive income tax, claiming that it was impracticable to introduce all the measures which would be necessary to adjust for inflation and supported the introduction of an expenditure tax.

Activity

Explain why the use of a comprehensive income tax might result in undesirable impacts on the economy of the country that introduces it.

Expenditure

Having found problems with taxes on wealth and income as sole tax bases, let us finally consider expenditure taxes. An expenditure, or consumption, tax taxes what an individual takes out of the economy in a given period, unlike an income tax which taxes what is contributed to society. With an expenditure tax there is no need to value wealth, which we have already concluded is difficult to do acceptably. The tax is only levied when the taxpayer spends money not on what wealth they hold on to. All income is also therefore free of expenditure tax. Since an expenditure tax also does not tax the return on an investment there is an encouragement to save provided that investors will save more if they can obtain a higher return.

An expenditure tax can incorporate personal allowances and varying rates of tax exactly as an income tax does. Hence it is possible for an expenditure tax to be progressive and to take account of a taxpayer's personal circumstances if it is considered desirable.

What percentage must an expenditure tax be levied at to replace an income tax of say 23% and leaving the taxpayer with the same level of after tax value?

Feedback

If we ignore the time value of money an expenditure tax of 29.87% is the equivalent of an income tax of 23%. However, because expenditure usually takes place after income is received the expenditure tax should be somewhat higher than this to compensate for the time lag between income and expenditure.

In addition, because savings are not taxed directly under an expenditure tax, the tax base will be somewhat narrower and so the expenditure tax will have to increase even more.

There are a number of ways of operating an expenditure tax system. The Meade Committee offered four alternatives mostly measuring expenditure as a residual from gains in income or wealth to avoid the impracticality of tracking actual expenditure.

- A *tax on value added*. This could operate in the same way as VAT (see later in the book for details of how VAT works). Note though that VAT is not strictly an expenditure tax, but an indirect tax. Look back to Chapter 1 for a discussion of indirect taxation. An expenditure tax will have to recognise an individual's personal circumstances which is something that a tax like VAT cannot do.
- A *tax on income with 100% capital allowances*. In Chapter 5 you will find out how a system of capital allowances can operate but capital allowances allow for expenditure on capital assets to be allowed for without tax. Of course only a taxpayer could benefit from this system; a business with accumulated losses would not pay tax and so could not benefit immediately from an allowance for capital expenditure.
- A *tax on all income apart from investment income*. Earlier in this chapter we reviewed the equity of taxing investment income differently from earned income.
- A *tax on consumption expenditure but not capital expenditure*. It was this system which was recommended by the Committee and we shall spend a little time considering how it would work in practice.

The Committee considered two forms of expenditure tax: a universal expenditure tax which is described below, and a two-tier expenditure tax which would collect a basic rate of tax through a system of VAT and higher rates of tax would be collected from taxpayers under a system such as the universal expenditure tax. This second system would be somewhat like our system of tax deducted at source where certain payments, such as interest, are paid after deduction of the basic rate of income tax, which is described in Chapter 1, and higher rate taxpayers are required to account for any additional tax payable on the receipt.

Under a universal expenditure tax a taxpayer's consumption expenditure would be calculated by adding the taxpayer's total realised income to any capital receipts, including the sale of capital assets and any amounts borrowed and deducting any expenditure which is not for the purposes of consumption including expenditure on capital assets and amounts repaid. Then tax could be levied on consumption expenditure at a number of rates if desired.

Expenditure taxes, particularly in the form of value added tax as the first option above, have become popular with governments everywhere in recent years.

Income and expenditure compared

Income is used as a tax base almost everywhere but expenditure taxes are becoming more popular as a way of raising revenue. There are a number of reasons for preferring an expenditure tax to an income tax:

- It can be argued that it is fairer to tax consumption, that is the value of goods and services which an individual takes out of society, than to tax the contribution that he or she makes to a society in the form of either work effort or capital supplied. Remember that the difference between income and consumption is equal to savings. However, the individual who saves will eventually use savings for consumption and thus has merely deferred the expenditure tax rather than avoided it. Of course, it may be the beneficiaries of an individual's estate who use the savings for consumption at a later stage pay the tax rather than the individual who earned the income in the first place, but eventually the expenditure tax will be paid.
- An expenditure tax does not discriminate against individuals who defer their expenditure by saving. An income tax does discriminate against individuals who save in order to undertake consumption in the future by taxing the return on savings as part of their measure of income.
- The evidence is that savings are relatively inelastic. That is, the amount that is saved is not dependent on the return available. Hence an expenditure tax would not seriously distort the savings decision.

However, there are a number of potential disadvantages of an expenditure tax which make an income tax look more attractive in practice than may otherwise be the case:

- Because the return on savings is not subject to an expenditure tax it seems likely that the level of an expenditure tax will have to be higher than its equivalent income tax. This may prove to be a disincentive to work. In Chapter 2 we discussed how taxpayers behave when the rate of income tax is increased. People have become adept at valuing their work effort in terms of goods and services rather than money. This is important in times of inflation when people know that a certain increase in salary is necessary simply to maintain a given standard of living. Prices can be thought of in terms of how many hours an individual on average wages must work in order to earn enough to buy the goods or services. If this is indeed how individuals think about the relationship between work and consumption then an increase in an expenditure tax will have a similar effect to an increase in an income tax. Hence an expenditure tax can still distort the decision to undertake extra work and does not resolve this distortion.
- Individuals who save in order to consume later are subject to uncertainty

because they cannot be sure of the tax they must pay when they spend their savings. This uncertainty is not present in an income tax system.

- An expenditure tax still does not account for the privileges which accrue to those with wealth, such as being offered goods at reduced prices because of past patronage. This could lead to inequity concerns which we have seen can alone create significant implementation problems

- Individuals usually have a changing pattern of income and expenditure over their lifetime. Many individuals spend more than they earn in the early years of their adult life and save in the middle years in order for expenditure to exceed income once again in retirement. This pattern may mean that individuals incur the greatest tax burden in years when their income is least able to provide for their needs.

UK Taxation System

To conclude this chapter we can briefly review how the theory of bases that can be taxed is directly translated into fact in the UK's tax system. In reality a mixture of income, wealth and expenditure taxes are used to try and minimise their individual limitations, create maximum flexibility in the system and address each of the other desirable characteristics of a good tax system, to the degree this is possible in reality.

As we saw in the section on how the UK raises its revenue, the key taxes in operation in the UK at present are:

1. Income tax – direct tax on income base payable by individuals
2. Corporation tax – direct tax on income base payable by companies
3. VAT – indirect tax on expenditure base payable by all
4. Capital Gains tax – direct tax on capital asset sales/wealth payable by all
5. Inheritance tax – direct tax on wealth/capital asset transfers payable by individuals
6. Stamp Duty – direct tax on capital/wealth transfers payable by all
7. Duties (Various) – indirect taxes on expenditure payable by all.

The bulk of the rest of this book, in conjunction with the web site, reviews some of the above taxes in detail. (see the website for discussion of inheritance tax, stamp duty and other taxes) It illustrates how the detailed rules are applied in practice at the present time.

As we examine the detail of the current rules for each tax, consider what we have learned so far about the impacts of taxation on economic decision, and the desirable characteristics of a good tax system and ask yourself to what degree the UK's current tax system is affective in achieving these goals. You will see we are good in some areas and not in others and hence the need for constant reappraisal of the tax system and regular adjustments to its operation

Summary

In this chapter we have probably raised as many questions for you as we have given answers. We began by attempting to identify the individual who actually suffers a loss in his or her wealth because of the requirement to pay tax. We found that the actual incidence of tax was often difficult to determine and that it was often different from the formal incidence. We then spent some time discussing some of the limitations of the existing tax system before identifying desirable characteristics of taxation. We then evaluated the feasibility of using wealth, income and expenditure as a dominant tax base before concluding with a brief summary of how the theory of tax bases is applied in current UK practice.

Project areas

There are many interesting questions which are inspired by the material dealt with in this chapter. However, it is important that you carefully consider to what extent any hypothesis which you may wish to examine is, in fact, testable. For example, the question of the funding of higher education is topical. A fascinating question is 'Should a graduate tax be used to fund higher education?' It would be possible to generate a discussion on the theoretical aspects of the question but it is difficult to see how you would undertake the necessary empirical work.

Other questions you may consider for a project includes the influence of tax wedges on consumer behaviour, how other countries can operate without a balance of income, wealth and expenditure taxes, or the extent to which a particular tax, or tax system, achieves one or more of Adam Smith's desirable characteristics.

For other project ideas see the website for this textbook.

Discussion questions

Question 1. Is a lump-sum tax feasible?

Question 2. What corrective taxes, if any, would you like to introduce?

Question 3. Do you think parents should pay more or less tax than childless individuals?

Question 4. If a government wished to provide funding to increase the level of fitness of the population would it be better to provide subsidised facilities such as leisure centres or to give tax relief on the cost of getting and keeping fit, such as health club memberships?

Question 5. To what degree does the current UK tax system fulfill the characteristics of a desirable tax system?

Further Reading

The Economics of Taxation: 1999/2000 Edition – James, S. and Nobes, C. (1999) Prentice Hall: Hemel Hempstead.

Value and Capital, – Hicks J.R. (1939) Oxford University Press: Oxford, UK (2nd Edition, 1974).

The Structure and Reform of Direct Taxation, – Meade Committee Report (1978), IFS/Allen and Unwin: London.

An inquiry in the Nature and Causes of the Wealth of Nations – Smith, Adam (1776), Ward, Lock & Co. Ltd: London, UK. (The World Library 1812 reprint).

4 Personal taxation

Introduction

In the first three chapters we examined the history of the UK tax system, outlined its modern administration, looked at some of the economics of taxation and discussed some of the ways taxes affect decisions made by people. This foundation provides us with the background we need to now examine the current tax system in detail. This chapter also introduces the personal income tax computation and explains the various elements that go into its make-up. Chapters 5, 6 and 7 then review the sources of income in more detail and show you how to calculate the right values to enter into the respective parts of the income tax computation. Chapter 8 then introduces you to capital gains tax – a different tax, but one that is also paid by individuals.

Throughout these chapters the focus is on taxation of the individual, either as an employed person, or as a self employed person (as a sole trader). We will review how the tax system operates for companies in Chapter 9.

In the UK individuals pay tax on their income for a fiscal year. The fiscal year runs from 6th April to the following 5th April(the reason for these odd dates was described in chapter 1). The legislation uses a system of schedules to determine the specific rules for taxing each source of income.

In recent years there have been a number of major changes to the way in which individuals are taxed. For example, at the end of the 1980s independent taxation (full, separate taxation of men and women) was introduced while self-assessment for personal taxation was introduced from 6th April 1996. We will consider both of these important changes later in this chapter.

In this chapter you will learn how to calculate the amount of an individual's income that is currently subject to income tax and learn how to determine the amount of any reliefs and allowances that are available to a taxpayer. Once you have deducted the allowances and reliefs from the taxable income you will learn how to compute a taxpayer's tax liability.

At the end of this chapter you will be able to:

- list income which is exempt from income tax
- describe the Schedules and Cases under which individuals pay income tax
- calculate the allowances and reliefs available to an individual
- describe the system of national insurance and calculate any national insurance contributions payable by both employers and employees
- prepare a simple personal tax computation for individuals
- describe the system of self-assessment for individuals
- offer basic income tax planning advice to individuals and members of a family unit.

The tax computation

A tax computation for an individual can be set out in the following way.

Laying out answers to exam questions in the same way as this proforma will help ensure you include all the necessary stages in your computations and are able to apply the figures in the correct order. You are strongly advised to learn, and then follow, this proforma each time you do a personal tax computation.

Thomas Lester's income tax computation for 2002/03.

	Dividends £	Non-savings £	Savings £	Total £
Income:				
Schedule A				
(Taxable Income from property)		500		500
Schedule D (Case I or II)				
(Taxable Income from self employment)		33,000		33,000
Bank interest received (gross)			1,000	1,000
Building Society Interest (gross)			1,000	1,000
Schedule F				
(gross dividends from UK companies)	500			500
Total Income	500	33,500	2,000	36,000
Less charges on income (gross)		(500)		(500)
Statutory Total Income	500	33,000	2,000	35,500
Less Personal Allowances		(4,615)		(4,615)
Total Taxable Income	500	28,385	2,000	30,885

Tax Due:

		£
Non savings income	1,920 @ 10%	192.00
	28,385 – 1,920 @ 22%	5,822.30
Savings income	1,515 @ 20%	303.00
	485 @ 40%	194.00
Dividend income	500 @ 32.5%	162.50
	30,885	
Tax Borne		6,673.80
Add tax withheld on charges	500 @ 22%	110.00
Tax Liability		6,783.80
Less tax deducted at source, tax credits and other income tax already paid		
Bank and Building Society Interest	2,000 @ 20%	(400.00)
Dividends	500 @ 10%	(50.00)
Tax Payable		£6,333.80

In this chapter you will find out how to produce a tax computation like this one given the basic facts of a tax payer's situation. As we will see later on, Thomas is entirely self employed (you will see he has Schedule D income, that relates to income from self employment, but no schedule E income – income from employment). If he was an employee, or earned income from both sources during the tax year, you would just need to add another line for Schedule E in the aggregation (top) part of the computation.

Income

A tax computation is really split into two parts. The first part aggregates a taxpayer's taxable income from all sources. The second part then calculates the tax due on this total taxable income. The way in which a particular source of income is taxed depends on the Schedule under which it is assessed. Let us look at the key elements of this computation quickly before going into more detail.

- *Investment income or savings income*
  Most investment income is paid to its recipient after deduction of tax at source. Chapter 1 explained why this is done. The bank deposit interest and the building society interest usually have had tax deducted at 20%. So if the gross interest is £100 the net interest received is £80 or if the interest received is £80 the gross interest must be $80 \times 100/80 = 100$ (this process is called 'grossing up' and is an important part of the tax computation calculation). The gross income received is included in the aggregation part of a tax computation and then a deduction made equal to the tax deducted at source at the end of the computation when you calculate how much tax is payable now. This process ensures that tax already paid is not payable again in the tax computation but that the correct total of taxable income is calculated. This is necessary to ensure we calculate the correct rates of tax in the second part of the computation.
- *Charges*
  Charges are payments made by the taxpayer that are eligible for tax relief. Charges are either paid net of basic rate tax (as illustrated here) or gross. The taxpayer here actually paid £390 as a charge.
- *Income tax rates*
  Non-savings income is taxed at 10% for the first £1,920 of taxable income. The next £27,980 (to £29,900 of taxable income) is taxed at 22% and any income above this is taxed at 40%. Savings income is taxed at 10%, 20% and 40% and dividend income is taxed at 10% or 32.5%. Later in the chapter we will examine exactly how these different rates are applied. Note for now however that separate columns are used in the income aggregation part of the computation so that we can determine separate totals for each of these types of income to enable us to apply these different rates in the second part of the computation.
- *Personal allowances*
  Every individual is entitled to a certain amount of income each year before they have to start paying income tax. This amount alters most years, it needs to be deducted from total income figure (after any charges) to get the total *taxable* income.
- *Tax borne*
  Tax borne is the amount of tax that the taxpayer is liable for from his income.

- *Tax liability*
  The tax liability is equal to the tax borne together with any tax retained on the charges paid. This is the total amount of tax which the taxpayer is responsible for paying to the Inland Revenue in the tax year (both directly and via deductions at source).
- *Tax payable*
  The tax payable is equal to the tax liability less the tax which has already been deducted at source from income received by the taxpayer. The tax payable is the amount that must be paid to the Inland Revenue directly.

Note that whilst the taxable income part of the calculation is always rounded *down* to the nearest pound, for the tax due part of the calculation you should always use figures calculated *to the nearest penny*. This is important to ensure you do not get rounding errors in your tax computation.

The schedular system of income tax

Income is taxed using a schedular system. It is important to identify which Schedule and Case any particular income stream is taxed under because each Schedule and Case has its own rules which deal with the following:

- the income to be taxed
- allowable deductions, if any, from the income
- the basis of assessment
- the date on which tax should be paid.

With the exception of the basis of assessment the list is fairly self-explanatory. The basis of assessment is used to identify the income to be taxed in a fiscal year, such as which dates mark the beginning and end of the year in question (if not 5th and 6th April). We will consider the basis of assessment for each Schedule and Case as we introduce them in this chapter.

The legislation for the taxation under all of the Schedules and Cases is contained in the Income and Corporation Taxes Act 1988 (ICTA 1988).

The current UK Schedular system for determining tax liability is as follows:

Schedule A income from UK property
Schedule D income from a trade or profession, interest where tax is not deducted at source, interest from foreign securities and other foreign possessions.
Schedule E Income from employment or office
Schedule F Income from UK dividends and other distributions from UK companies.

You will note that Schedules B and C appears to have been missed out. These did exist at one time but are no longer used as we discussed in chapter 1.

These schedules are split up further into more specific rules. These separate rules of each Schedule what are referred to as 'Cases'. We will look at the major Cases of Schedules D and E in this book.

We will look at each of the Schedules and Cases in turn. In this chapter we will determine the aggregated income which is subject to tax, the expenses which can be set against the income for tax purposes and the date on which tax must be paid. In later chapters some of the Schedules and Cases will be considered in more detail to illustrate further details of how these figures are arrived at in practice. Specifically Schedule D Cases I and II will form the subject matter of Chapter 5 and 6 while Schedule A, Schedule D Case VI together with Schedule E will be dealt with in Chapter 7.

First we will discuss the differences between tax raised by direct assessment and tax deducted at source and consider a number of the bases of assessment which are used.

Direct assessment and income taxed at source

Income which is taxed by direct assessment is paid gross, while income taxed at source is paid to the recipient after deduction of tax. The procedure by which some income is paid to the recipient net of tax was introduced at the beginning of the 19th century as an anti-avoidance measure. This is effective as the payer of the income is then made partly responsible for the tax due not just the recipient. The following income is taxed at source:

- interest paid by UK companies to individuals (e.g. on loans)
- interest on bank deposit accounts paid to individuals (companies receive their interest gross)
- interest paid on building society accounts
- income from deeds of covenant
- income from trusts, settlements and the estates of deceased persons
- patent royalties (but not copyright royalties)
- annuities.

From 6th April 1998 interest on government stocks has been paid gross unless the gilt holder elected to receive the interest net of lower rate tax.

Most income taxed at source has tax deducted at the lower rate of 20% (i.e. the recipient only gets 80% of the gross amount due to them). An exception is patent royalties which are paid net of basic rate tax of 22%.

Activity

Linda has £1,000 deposited in a building society account paying 4% interest, credited annually on 31st December each year.

How much interest will be credited to Linda's account in the tax year.

Feedback

Linda's account will be credited with £32 (£1000 × 4% × 80%) made up of £40 gross interest less £8 (£40 × 20%) tax deducted at source.

Income assessed under Schedule E is paid under the PAYE (Pay-As-You-Earn scheme), that is, the tax due on the income of employees is deducted before the payment is made to the employee. Although this deduction is made, this income is still technically taxed by direct assessment rather than taxed at source because the personal circumstances of the taxpayer are used to determine the amount of tax which should be deducted by the employer for the Inland Revenue. Normal tax deductions at source (e.g. building society interest) are just normally made at a flat rate of 20% irrespective to the circumstances of the taxpayer.

If individuals who are not liable to income tax, perhaps because their income is less than the personal allowances (tax free income) they are entitled to, receive income which has been taxed at source they can reclaim the tax which has been deducted.

This has not always been the case. Until 1991/92 tax was deducted at source from interest paid on building society accounts and could not be claimed back by non-taxpayers. When independent taxation was introduced married women with unused personal allowances were able to reclaim tax which had been deducted at source on all types of investment income apart from building society accounts. Building societies believed, the evidence suggests correctly, that women with incomes that did not fully 'use up' their personal allowances would transfer their savings to accounts where they could reclaim the tax deducted at source. This led the building societies to successfully lobby the government for a change in the law.

Rates of tax

To determine the rate of tax to be paid on particular income it is necessary to classify the income into various types. The three main types are savings, non-savings and dividend incomes. This is why Thomas Lester's tax computation had three columns for calculating the taxable income.

For the current fiscal year the following rates of tax apply to non-savings taxable income.

Tax Band	£	Rate (Non-savings)	Maximum amount payable in band
Starting Rate	0–1,920	10%	192.00
Basic Rate	1,921–29,900	22%	6155.60
Higher Rate	more than 29,900	40%	–

For savings income, any income falling into the starting rate band is taxed at 10%, income falling into the basic rate band is taxed at 20% (not 22% as above for non-savings income) and income falling into the higher rate band at 40%.

Savings income includes:

- interest from a bank account (including National Savings Bank)
- interest from a building society
- interest from gilt edged securities
- interest from debentures
- income from an annuity.

(Note that the 20% tax rate is called the lower rate of tax).

Dividend income is taxed at 10% if it falls in to the starting or basic rate bands and 32.5% if it falls into the higher rate band.

The order in which you include the different incomes in the computation can obviously therefore affect the amount of tax paid. You must therefore always calculate the bands using up non-savings income first, the savings income and finally dividends. This means dividends should be considered a "top slice" of anyone's income.

Also note that charges and personal allowances should be deducted from non-savings income totals first and if not fully used up, next from savings income and finally from dividends.

Look back to the example computation at the start of this chapter to see how these rates have been applied to Thomas' income.

The first time you meet these bands and rates rules it can be confusing, so try the following activities to test your understanding of these rules.

Activity

Calculate the income tax due on taxable incomes of:

(a) £2,000
(b) £10,000
(c) £40,000

(Assume none of this income comes from savings or dividends.)

Feedback

(a) £1,920 @ 10% =   £192.00
     £2,000 – 1,920@22%=   £ 17.60
                                           £209.60

(b) £1,920 @ 10% =   £192.00
     £10,000 – 1,920 @ 22% =   £1,777.60
                                           £1,969.60

(c) £1,920 @ 10% =   £192.00
     29,900 – 1,920 @ 22% =   £6,155.60
     40,000 – 29,900 @ 40%   £4,040.00
                                           £10,387.60

Savings income

Since 1996/97 a distinction has been drawn between savings and non-savings income for calculating tax due. Savings income is treated as being the middle slice of income, so you allocate this income to the tax bands after you have used up the non-savings income. Any savings income which falls within the basic rate band is taxed at 20% rather than 22%.

Activity

Calculate the income tax liability for an individual with taxable savings income of £1,000 and taxable non-savings income of:

(a) £1,000

(b) £20,000

(c) £50,000

Feedback

			£
(a) Non-savings income			
£1,000 @ 10%	=		100.00
Savings income			
£1,920 – 1,000 @ 10%	=		92.00
£1,000 – (1,920 – 1,000) @ 20%	=		16.00
			208.00
(b) Non-savings income			
£1,920 @ 10%	=		192.00
£20,000 – 1,920 @ 22%	=		3,977.60
Savings income			
£1,000 @ 20%	=		200.00
			4,369.60
(c) Non-savings income			
£1,920 @ 10%	=		192.00
£29,900 – 1,920 @ 22%	=		6,155.60
£50,000 – 29,900 @ 40%	=		8,040.00
Savings income			
£1,000 @ 40%	=		400.00
			14,787.60

Note that in each case different rates of tax apply to at least some of the savings income as it fits into different tax bands for each example. In the first case some savings income can still be taxed at 10% as the starting rate band is not filled by non-savings income. The remainder of the savings income then falls into the basic rate based and is taxed at 20%.

In the second case all of the starting rate, and part of the basic rate band is used up by non-savings income so the savings income uses up more of the basic rate band and is all taxed at 20%.

In the final case the non-savings income uses all of the starting and basic rate bands so the savings income is taxed at the higher rate of 40%.

Remember that Linda has £1,000 deposited in a building society paying 4% interest. We calculated that Linda was credited with £32 interest in the tax year. Can you now determine how much tax she will have to pay if she is:

(a)   a basic rate taxpayer (i.e. her next £1 of income will fall into the basic rate band)
(b)   a higher rate taxpayer (i.e. her next £1 of income will fall into the higher rate band)
(c)   a non-taxpayer (i.e. she does not have to pay tax as her next £1 does not bring her above the tax free income level for the year).

Feedback

(a)   Linda's account will be credited with £32 (£1,000 × 4% × 80%) made up of £40 gross interest less £8 (£40 × 20%) tax deducted at source. The tax withheld will exactly meet the additional tax of £8 that Linda will suffer as a result of the (gross) interest received.

(b)   Again £32 will be credited to Linda's account but this time Linda will be required to pay additional tax of £8. The total increase in her tax bill as a result of this interest received would now be £16 (£40 × 40%) and this will be only partly satisfied by the tax deducted at source leaving her £8 (£16 – £8) still to pay. You will note this extra is automatically included in her tax payable using the method shown for Thomas Lester. This is one reason the use of the proforma given is so important.

(c)   As a non-taxpayer Linda could have elected to have interest credited to her account without any tax being withheld. This is done by writing to the Building Society to declare she is not a tax payer. In this case £40 will be credited to her account and there will be no tax consequences. If Linda does not make the necessary election only £32 will be credited to her account and she can obtain a tax repayment of the tax deducted at source £8 by writing to the Inland Revenue.

It may help you to understand this activity if you create a basic tax computation for Linda assuming she just has this income source.

Dividend Income

Before 6th April, 1999 income from UK company dividends was treated exactly the same way as savings income. Since this time however, dividends have been subject to their own special tax rules. They are now treated as a third 'slice', of a person's income. If you receive any dividend income from UK shares it will be taxed at 10% if it falls into the starting, or basic, rate bands, or 32.5% if it falls into the higher rate band. This 10% rate for dividends is often referred to as the 'Schedule F ordinary rate'. We will look at Schedule F rules later in more detail. This schedule describes how dividends from UK companies is taxed. (Note – dividends from non-UK companies are not treated the same way and should be added to non-savings income not dividend income if the tax payer gets any overseas company dividends)

Dividends are included in tax computations at their gross value – just like we have already discussed for bank or building society interest. They are treated in the taxpayer's computation as if 10% had been deducted by the company – although no deductions are actually made. This represents the imputed tax the company pays in corporation tax on their profits. The gross dividend therefore equals the dividend actually received × 100/90. For example a dividend of £1,440 will be included in a tax computation at £1,600 (£1,440 × 100/90). The corporation tax that is paid by a UK company therefore forms part of the income of the recipient of their dividends (their Schedule F incomes). However, as it is paid by the company on behalf of the taxpayer, it is called a 'tax credit' and can normally be credited against the tax due amount in the tax computation as tax already paid from their total income (see the end of the Thomas Lester example again to see this illustrated). The tax credit is therefore worth one ninth of the value of the dividend.

Activity

Pat has the following income for the tax year:

	£
Income from his business	19,600
Dividends	900
Income from property	1,000

Pat claims the correct personal allowance for this year.
Calculate Pat's income tax payable for this year (assuming he is less than 65 years of age - meaning his personal allowance is just the standard amount).

Feedback

	Non-savings £	Dividends £	Total £
Schedule D	19,600		19,600
Dividends 900 × 100/90		1,000	1,000
Schedule A	1,000		
			1,000
Statutory total income	20,600	1,000	21,600
Less: Personal allowance	(4,615)		(4,615)
Taxable income	15,985	1,000	16,985
Tax due:			
Non-savings income:			£
1,920 @ 10%			192.00
15,985 – 1,920 @ 22%			3,094.30
Dividend income:			
1,000 @ 10%			100.00
Tax borne/tax liability			3,386.30
Less: tax credit from UK dividends			
1,000 × 10%			100.00
Tax payable			3,286.30

Activity

How would your answer to the previous activity differ if Pat had £33,195 income from his business?

Feedback

	Non-savings £	Dividends £	Total £
Schedule D Case I	33,195		33,195
Dividends 900 × 100/90		1,000	1,000
Schedule A	1,000		1,000
Statutory total income	34,195	1,000	35,195
Less: Personal allowance	(4,615)		(4,615)
Taxable income	29,580	1,000	30,580

Income tax due:	£
Non-Savings income	
1,920.00 @10%	192.00
29,580 – 1,920 @ 22%	6085.60
Dividend income	
29,900 – 29,580 @ 10%	32.00
30,580 – 29,900 @ 32.5%	221.00
Tax Borne	6,530.20
(tax withheld on charges and tax credit for dividends as before)	

Notice that £680 of Pat's income is taxed at 32.5%. Because the top slice of Pat's income is dividend income where it exists in a computation, the £680 taxed at 32.5% is deemed to be dividend income. The remaining £320 (£1,000 – £680) of dividend income falls in the basic rate band and this is taxed at 10%.

We will return to the taxation of dividends in more detail later in this chapter.

Basis of assessment

The basis of assessment is the way in which income is allocated to fiscal years for tax purposes. For example, currently employees are taxed on income which is paid to them during the fiscal year, i.e. the basis of assessment is actual income received during the fiscal year. This is not the only basis of assessment which could be used however. An alternative would be to tax income which is earned during the fiscal year (whether actually received or not). For most employees this would make no difference but for those who receive performance-related bonuses which are paid in the fiscal year after the one in which they were earned the tax on the bonus would be payable before the bonus was actually received. For self-employed people, and for companies, the basis of assessment is linked to their business year (i.e. the period for which they produce accounts). We will see how this operates in practice in the relevant later chapters.

Statutory total income

An individual's income from all sources during the tax year, as determined under the Schedules and Cases, is termed his or her statutory total income. The individual's taxable income is equal to his or her statutory total income less the single person's allowance and reliefs.

Exempt income

The legislation specifically exempts certain income from income tax. You should be aware of the most significant exemptions which are:

- the first £70 interest from National Savings Bank ordinary accounts (ICTA 1988 s325)
- the increase in the value of national savings certificates
- premium bond prizes, betting winnings and other competition prizes
- gifts
- interest from Individual Savings Accounts (ISAs) and Tax Exempt Special Savings Accounts (TESSAs)
- any income from a Personal Equity Plan (PEP)
- some social security benefits, including child benefit and housing benefit
- save-as-you-earn (SAYE) bonuses
- shares allotted to employees under approved profit sharing schemes (ICTA 1988 ss 135–137)
- educational grants and scholarships
- statutory redundancy pay, pay in lieu of notice and some other payments up to a maximum of £30,000 made when an employment is terminated (ICTA 1988 ss90, 148, 188, 579 & 580). (Note: The excess received on termination is taxable as for other Schedule E income).
- payments made by employers to employees for death in service or in respect of disability sustained at work (e.g. personal injury payments)
- lump sums received from approved pension schemes.

Income which is not specifically exempt is potentially subject to income tax under the schedular system, which is dealt with in the next section.

Residence, Ordinary Residence and Domicile

UK tax paid by an individual or by a company is influenced by the residence or domicile of the taxpayer.

It would be useful therefore to briefly consider the concept of residence, ordinary residence and domicile before looking at the income schedules in further detail.

The terms residence and ordinary residence are not defined in the legislation but can be determined from various court rulings. The Inland Revenue has published a guidance booklet *Residents and NonResidents – liability to tax in the UK* (IR20, December 1999). In general a person cannot be resident for part of a tax year. He or she is either resident, or not resident, for the entire year of assessment. The only exception occurs when an individual either leaves the UK for permanent residence abroad or comes to the UK in order to take up permanent residence (under Statutory Concession A11). Under these circumstances the tax year is split and the UK tax liability will only apply to the part of the year for which you were a UK resident.

An individual is deemed to be resident in the UK if he or she:

- Spends more than 183 days in the UK in the tax year.
- Having been a resident has left the UK for permanent residence abroad but returns to the UK for periods which equal an average (over a five year period) of 91 days or more in the tax year. However, Statement of Practice 2/91 provides that 'any days spent in the UK because of exceptional circumstances beyond an individual's control (such as illness) are excluded from the calculation'.

A taxpayer is ordinarily resident if the UK is normally their country of residence. A taxpayer may therefore be resident, but not ordinarily resident, or ordinarily resident but not resident, or both resident and ordinarily resident in any tax year. A British citizen who has been ordinarily resident in the UK but who leaves to live abroad is deemed to be resident during his or her absence unless he can prove otherwise (ICTA 1988 s334).

The 2002 Budget confirmed that a review of residence and domicile rules in relation to tax is currently underway (check the website for the latest on this issue).

Activity

Which of the following individuals will be considered to be resident or ordinarily resident in the UK for 2001/02?

- William was born in Texas and lived in the USA until he moved to the UK on 12th June 2002 where he remained until 18th April 2003 when he moved to Canada.
- Patrick was born in New Zealand and moved to the UK in 1990. He went to Australia on 12th June 2002 and returned to the UK, where he intends to live permanently, on 18th April 2003.
- John was born in the UK and lived in the UK until 10th January 2002 when he moved to Germany, until 18th April 2003 when he returned to live permanently in the UK.

Feedback

William spent at least 183 days in the UK during 2002/03 and hence is resident for the fiscal year but is not ordinarily resident as this is not his normal country of residence.

Patrick does not spend 183 days in the UK during 2002/03. However, he is ordinarily resident in the UK and does spend part of the fiscal year in the UK and hence he is both resident and ordinarily resident in the UK in 2002/03.

John is absent from the UK for the whole of the fiscal year and hence cannot be resident in the UK. However, he is ordinarily resident for 2002/03.

An individual has a domicile of origin from the moment of birth. It is usually the domicile of their father but may be the domicile of their mother under some circumstances. An individual who is under 16 years old will change a domicile if the person to whom they are dependent changes their domicile. An individual aged 16 or over may choose a domicile. To do this the individual must maintain a physical presence in the country concerned and must have evidence that he or she has an intention to remain there permanently or indefinitely. You can only have one domicile at any one time, although it may be possible to be resident of more than one country.

If you are a resident in the UK you will be liable for UK tax on all your earned income wherever it arises. If you pay tax to another government however, you may be able to get a reduction in your tax bill for those payments so you do not have to pay tax twice on that income.

Where you are resident in the UK in a tax year but are not ordinarily resident or domiciled here the Inland Revenue will usually only ask you to pay UK tax on income you bring into the UK from overseas (see IR 20 for further details).

Schedule A

All income from UK land and property is taxed using Schedule A rules. This includes income from furnished lettings and letting caravans and houseboats on permanent moorings. Individuals, whether residents of the UK or not in the fiscal year are taxed on any annual profits or gains related to UK based land or property. Taxable profits are calculated by deducting total allowable expenses from total income from land and property. The basis of assessment is the accrued income for the fiscal year. This basis of assessment is usually the accrued basis (i.e. as for the accounting for these incomes and expenses in a business) for all items other than short lease premiums. This basis was changed in 1995/6 from the actual basis.

The rules for determining allowable expenses are the same as for Schedule D Case I which is used to tax trading income. That is, the accruals basis will be used unless the income from property is very low, when the cash basis may be allowed. We will examine these in detail in Chapter 5.

Activity

Mary lets a house in London. Rent was £4,800 a year until 30th September 2002 when it was increased to £5,400. Rent is payable a month in advance on the first of the month. The rent due on 1st April 2003 was not received until 10th April 2003. Mary incurred allowable expenses of £1,000 during the year to 5th April 2003.

Determine Mary's Schedule A assessment for 2002/03.

Feedback

Income for 2002/03 using the accruals basis is:

$$6 \times £400 + 6 \times £450 = £5,100$$

Notice that it does not matter that one payment due in the fiscal year was actually paid in the following year, that is the point of the accruals basis.

Hence the Schedule A assessment is £4,100 (£5,100 – £1,000). This is the figure you should put in Mary's tax computation.

(Note: strictly the income should be calculated on the daily basis but this monthly basis is usually acceptable).

Further details on Schedule A can be found in chapter 7.

Schedule D

In order to determine the profits or gains which are taxed under Schedule D it is necessary to determine whether or not the taxpayer is resident in the UK in the fiscal year. We explained these rules above. Individuals who are resident in the UK in the fiscal year are taxed under this Schedule on any annual profits or gains arising or accruing from any trade, profession or vocation regardless of the location of the activity.

Individuals who are not resident in the UK in the fiscal year are still subject to UK tax on the annual profits or gains arising or accruing from any property located in the UK and from any trade, profession or vocation carried on in the UK.

In addition, tax is charged on non-residents under Schedule D on all interest of money, annuities and other annual profits or gains not charged under Schedule A or E, and not specifically exempted from tax (ICTA 1988 s18(1)).

Tax under Schedule D is charged under the Cases set out below. Schedule D Cases I and II are considered in more detail in Chapters 5 and 6.

(Note: see IR20, available from the Inland Revenue website, for more details).

Case I

Profits from trades are taxed under Schedule D Case I (ICTA 1988 s18(3)). The normal basis of assessment for Case I is the current year basis. Under the current year basis the basis period for a year of assessment is normally the 12 months to the accounting date ended in the fiscal year. However, there are a number of circumstances in which this simple rule cannot be applied, especially in the early years of trading, the final years of trading or years in which a business changes its accounting date. The rules which apply in most of these circumstances will be discussed in detail in Chapter 5. Expenses which are wholly and exclusively for the purpose of the trade are allowable deductions using the accruals basis.

Case II

Profits from professions or vocations are taxed under Schedule D Case II (ICTA 1988 s18(3)). The basis of assessment and calculation of allowable expenses are the same as for Schedule D Case I.

Case III

Interest received which has not had tax deducted from it at source is taxed under Schedule D Case III (ICTA 1988 s18(3)). Interest on the following is taxed under Schedule D Case III:

- National Savings Bank accounts other than the first £70 on National Savings Bank ordinary accounts which is exempt
- 3½% War Loan
- Government stocks held on the National Savings Stock Register
- Loans between individuals.

The income assessable in a fiscal year is the interest arising within the year of assessment without any deductions (ICTA 1988 s64). Note therefore, that the accruals basis is not used.

Note that for companies, bank interest is also taxed as part of Case III as they receive their interest gross. For individuals, their interest is paid net of tax and so is treated as a separate category of income as we saw in the Thomas Lester example at the start of this chapter.

Activity

Elizabeth opened a National Savings Bank investment account in 1990. Interest is credited on 31st December each year, interest in recent years has been:

	£
31st December 1999	240
31st December 2000	300
31st December 2001	360
31st December 2002	310

Determine Elizabeth's Schedule C Case III assessment for 2002/03.

Feedback

The assessment is the interest arising in the fiscal year. Hence the Schedule D Case III assessment for 2002/03 is £310.

Case IV

Interest received from foreign securities is taxed under Schedule D Case IV (ICTA 1988 s18(3)). Foreign securities include debentures. The basis of assessment is the same as for Schedule D Case III (ICTA 1988 s65(1)).

Taxpayers who are resident but not ordinarily resident and/or not domiciled in the UK pay tax only on the amount remitted to the UK (ICTA 1988 s65(5)). Other taxpayers are liable to tax on the income arising from the securities.

Case V

Income from foreign possessions is taxed under Schedule D Case V. Such income includes dividends, rents, business profits and pensions but excludes income consisting of emoluments of any office or employment (ICTA 1988 s18(3)). The basis of assessment is the same as for Schedule D Case IV.

Case VI

Schedule D Case VI is used to tax annual profits or gains not falling under any other Case of Schedule D and not charged by virtue of Schedule A, C or E (ICTA 1988 s18(3)). In particular income from casual commissions, enterprise allowance payments, some capital sums from the sale of patent rights and post cessation receipts from a business are taxed under Schedule D Case VI. The basis of assessment is the profits or gains arising in the tax year.

We will return to examine Schedule D Cases I and II in more detail in Chapters 5 and 6.

Schedule E

Income from an office or employment is taxed under Schedule E (ICTA 1988 s19). This includes salaries, bonuses, tips, benefits in kind and UK pensions. The basis of assessment is the actual income paid during the fiscal year. As we discussed earlier in this chapter, tax is collected under the PAYE (Pay As You Earn) system; however, any additional tax is due 14 days after the issue of an assessment. There are in fact three Cases for Schedule E depending on the residence of the taxpayer, the employer and the place of work.

Case I

Schedule E Case I assesses emoluments for any year of assessment in which the person holding the office or employment is both resident and ordinarily resident in the UK (ICTA 1988 s19(1)).

Where the duties of an office or employment are performed wholly outside the UK and the emoluments from the office or employment are foreign emoluments, the emoluments are exempted from Schedule E Case I (ICTA 1988 s192(2)).

Foreign emoluments are defined as the emoluments of a person not domiciled in the UK from an office or employment under or with any person, body of persons or partnership resident outside, and not resident in, the UK. However, these are not taken to include the emoluments of a person resident in the UK from an office or employment under or with a person, body of persons or partnership resident in the Republic of Ireland (ICTA 1988 s192(1)).

Case II

Income from an office or employment for duties performed in the UK when the employee is either not resident or is resident, but not ordinarily resident in the UK, is taxed under Case II (ICTA 1988 s19(1)). Foreign emoluments are dealt with as described under Schedule E Case III below. Where possible the PAYE system is used otherwise tax is collected directly from the taxpayer, usually in four instalments.

Case III

The following income is taxed under Schedule E Case III:

- Foreign emoluments earned wholly abroad by an employee who is either resident and ordinarily resident or resident but not ordinarily resident in the UK. The basis of assessment is the remittance basis, that is only income which is brought into the UK is assessed (ICTA 1988 s19(1)). Tax is collected after the end of the tax year.
- Every annuity, pension or stipend payable by the Crown or out of the public revenue of the UK.
- Any pension which is paid otherwise than by, or on behalf of, a person outside the UK (ICTA 1988 s19(3)).
- Any pension or annuity which is payable in the UK by or through any public department, officer or agent of a government of a territory other than the UK, to a person who has been employed in relevant service outside the UK in respect of that service. A territory is any country which forms part of Her Majesty's dominions. Relevant service means in the service of the Crown or service under the government of a territory.
- Any pension or annuity which is payable to the widow, child, relative or dependant of any such person as is mentioned above. The person in receipt of the pension or annuity is chargeable to tax as a person resident in the UK (ICTA 1988 s19(4)).

If the emoluments from an office or employment, other than pensions, would fall in a year of assessment in which a person does not hold the office or employment, special rules apply. If the person has not yet held the office or employment the emoluments are treated as emoluments for the first year of assessment in which the office or employment is held. If the office or employment is no longer held by the person the emoluments are treated as emoluments for the last year of assessment in which the office or employment was held (ICTA 1988 s19(1)(4A)).

We examine Schedule E in more detail in Chapter 7.

Schedule F

Dividends and other distributions from UK companies are taxed under Schedule F. All distributions which are not specifically excluded are taxed as if they were a dividend to help reduce an obvious tax avoidance strategy. Income tax is levied on the gross dividend (i.e. the aggregate of the distribution received and the related tax credit) (ICTA 1988 s20). Lower rate and basic rate taxpayers are subject to tax at 10% on their dividends which means that the tax credit exactly equals the tax due on the dividend so that no further tax liability arises. Higher rate taxpayers are taxed at 32.5% on the aggregate of their dividends and the related tax credit. Like other taxpayers they are able to use the tax credit to reduce their tax liability.

Activity

Colin received a dividend of £1,800 from his share holding in Galifrey plc. Determine the amount which would be included in Colin's tax computation for the dividend.

Feedback

The dividend of £2,000 (£1800 × 100/90) will be included in Colin's tax computation. This is made up of the dividend of £1,800 and the tax credit of £200 (£2,000 × 10%).

Since 6th April 1999 individuals, including those holding Personal Equity Plans and ISAs, and other tax exempt recipients of UK company dividends, such as Pension Funds have not been able to reclaim the tax credit attached to dividends received from UK companies even though they are not taxpayers.

However, shareholders will be able to use tax credits to satisfy all or part of the tax liability arising from the receipt of dividends in the way described earlier in this chapter.

Summary of Income Tax Schedules

This activity will help test your knowledge of the basics of UK income tax schedules we have discussed so far in this book.

Activity

Identify the Schedule and Case under which each of the following incomes are taxed:

(a) earnings from working part time in a pub
(b) earnings from appearing on television
(c) extra payments to an employee for undertaking a job which is more difficult than his normal job
(d) dividends paid to an individual who is the managing director of the company.

Feedback

Earnings received in the situations described in (a) and (c) are taxed under Schedule E since they are earnings from employment.

The situation in (b) is a little more complicated. If the taxpayer had a contract of service, as might be the case of a presenter who is required to appear in a programme on a fixed number of occasions during the period of the contract, then the income will be taxed under Schedule E. However, if the contract is for services, as might be the case of an expert who is asked to appear on a programme to give his expert opinion on only a few occasions, the income will be taxed under Schedule D Case I. Look again at the way income is taxed under each of these schedules and think about the differences in the ways in which employees and self-employed individuals are taxed. We will consider these differences in detail in Chapter 5 and 7.

The dividends paid in (d) are taxed under Schedule F. The relationship of the shareholder to the company is not relevant as dividends are received in their capacity as a shareholder, not as an employee of the company.

The distinctions between tax Schedules and Cases are important because the different rules that will apply to a tax payer having income classified under one Schedule or another can have a significant impact on the overall amount of tax they then have to pay.

Personal allowances and reliefs

Individuals are eligible to claim one or more tax related allowances which are deducted from their total income to give their taxable income. The way in which allowances have changed in the latter half of this century offers a fascinating insight into our family life. Until the Second World War a man on average income did not suffer income tax because his personal allowances were greater than his total income. At that time a family man would have been able to claim a married man's allowance, which was substantially higher than the single personal allowance, in order to reflect the costs of supporting a wife who did not work (whether or not she actually worked). In addition, he received allowances if he had children. The reverse was largely not however, true for a woman who was married such was the nature of the tax system at the time

A family was seen as a single tax unit until as recently as 1990, and that unit was focused on the husband. A married woman was not entitled to a personal allowance but her husband could claim the wife's earned income relief, which was of the same value as the single personal allowance against the family's total income. As its name suggests the relief was only available for earned income; a wife's investment income was taxed at her husband's marginal rate of tax even if she did not work. This, of course, was a ridiculous situation from an equity perspective.

Until the 1970s fathers also received tax allowances for any children in the family. However, these allowances were withdrawn and there was a compensatory increase in child benefit which was paid each week to mothers. This change was welcomed by almost everyone, especially groups concerned with child poverty. It was believed that the allowance was more likely to benefit the children if it was paid to the mother and it was paid regardless of the employment status of the husband, thus providing some much needed income in times of unemployment. However, many people appear to have forgotten the transfer from allowances to benefit in the 1970s. Now the benefit is not always increased in line with inflation and there are pressure groups who campaign for the restriction of child benefit to families on relatively low incomes. The recent 'innovation' of the Working Family and Children's Tax Credit systems in part returns to the principles of the old system. Time will tell if they are more successful.

There are numerous examples of the Inland Revenue's unusual attitude towards married women until the end of the 1980s. Until 1990 tax returns were completed by the husband and he was expected to make a return of both his own and his wife's earned and unearned income. Until recently if a married woman overpaid tax the Revenue sent any repayment due to her husband and all communications from the Revenue were addressed to the husband regardless of whether the husband or wife had initiated the correspondence. For many couples this arrangement was merely irritating but for others it was a source of great distress. Many women, for a variety of reasons, did not wish their husbands to know about either their earnings, or their savings, or both. However, for a small group of taxpayers there were some advantages to the system. If a husband had insufficient income to enable him to use his personal allowances he could apply the reliefs to his wife's income since, from the Revenue's point of view, her income was deemed to be his. In effect this meant that if a family consisted of a working wife and a husband with little or no income a personal allowance and a married man's allowance could be claimed whereas if the situation reversed and the husband worked while the wife had no income, only the married man's allowance could be claimed.

At the end of the 1960s two schemes were introduced which were intended to reflect the changing role of women, especially professional women, in society. One of the schemes was intended to offer women some measure of privacy in their tax affairs. It enabled women to complete their own tax returns and enter into correspondence with the Revenue themselves. The personal allowances available to the couple were then split between the husband and wife in proportion to their income. Of course, a curious taxpayer could easily deduce their spouse's total income from the amount of the allowances they received. The total tax paid by the couple was unchanged by this election (ICTA 1988 s283).

The second scheme was likely to be used by couples to reduce their total tax bill. The husband had to relinquish his married man's allowance and claim only the single person's allowance. In return his wife's liability to tax on her earned income was calculated without reference to his total income, enabling the couple to use the basic rate band twice, once in each tax computation. This election was only worth making if the couple were higher rate taxpayers and the wife had sufficient earned income to save more tax by using the basic rate of tax rather than her husband's marginal rate, then was lost by her husband in forgoing the married man's allowance (ICTA 1988 s287).

Pressure grew during the 1980s for the reformation of the taxation of the family unit from two sources. Women demanded independence in tax matters, but perhaps even more importantly it became apparent that many couples were better off living together than getting married, especially if they had children and a mortgage. Consider a couple with two children with only the father working and a mortgage of £70,000. If the couple were married they could claim only the married couple's allowance together with tax relief on the interest paid on the first £30,000 of the mortgage. If the couple were not married they could each claim the single person's allowance and an additional personal allowance by claiming that each parent was responsible for one child. In addition both children were entitled to a single personal allowance. The mother could take the father to court and apply for maintenance payments for herself and their children which would provide them with sufficient income to utilise the personal allowances. Of course the mother and the children also had a basic rate tax band and if the father was a higher rate taxpayer more main-tenance could be paid in order to save him tax at high rates. Finally the couple could each claim tax relief on the interest paid on £30,000 of the mortgage. You can see that it was possible for a couple who were not married to be several thousand pounds a year better off than a couple who were married. This was clearly nonsensical for a government which claimed to be the champion of the family. From 6th April 1990 a system of independent taxation was introduced which taxed individuals rather than family units.

Chancellor Gordon Brown continued this process in his March 1998 budget by granting the additional personal allowance to women in circumstances under which, in the past, only men have been eligible.

From April 2000 the removal of many of these allowances from the tax system (including mortgage interest relief, married couples allowance etc) has rebalanced the overall impact on society.

In this section we will now review the allowances and reliefs currently available to UK income tax payers.

Personal allowance (PA)

Every person (whatever age they are) who is UK resident is entitled to a personal allowance of at least £4,615 (£4,535 in 2001/02). This includes children and married as well as single people (ICTA 1988 s257). This amount may be increased if the tax payer is in receipt of the age allowance as we discuss in the next section. There is provision in statute for the personal allowance to increase in line with infla-tion each year, unless Parliament opt to waive the provision for a particular year (ICTA 1988 S257C).

Increases in personal allowances benefit less well off taxpayers proportionately more than better off taxpayers and are therefore useful as redistribution tools.

Age allowance (AA)

This allowance is available to a person aged 65 or over at any time during the tax year instead of the ordinary personal allowance (ICTA 1988 s257(2)). The age allowance is £6,100 for 2002/03 (2001/02: £5,990). If the person is 75 or over then this rate is increased to £6,370 (2001/02: £6,260). If the person's statutory total income exceeds £17,900 the age allowance is reduced by £1 for each £2 of income over £17,900 until the personal allowance has been reduced to the level of the normal personal allowance (ICTA 1988 s257(5)).

An individual who dies during the tax year in which they would have reached their 65th or 75th birthday is treated as if they had reached that age during the year (ICTA 1988 s257(4)).

Activity

Calculate the current personal allowance available to each of the following taxpayers.

Name	Date of birth	Statutory total income
Paul	10th January 1938	£14,000
John	18th April 1927	£18,500

Feedback

Paul
Paul will be 65 on 10th January 2003 and so will be able to claim the age allowance of £6,100.

John
John will be 75 on 18th April 2002. John's statutory total income exceeds £17,900 and so the age allowance is reduced to £6,070 (£6,370 – ½ × (18,500 – 17,900).

Blind person's allowance (BPA)

This allowance is given to taxpayers who are registered as blind with their local authority. The allowance is £1,480 for 2002/03 (£1,450 in 2001/02) and is available in addition to their personal allowance. If the blind person has insufficient income to use the allowance in full the excess may be transferred to their spouse (ICTA 1988 s265).

Married couple's allowance (MCA)

The married couple's allowance, along with a number of other tax reducers, finally ceased for most people from 6th April 2000. The only people still able to claim the MCA are those where at least one partner was at least 65 at the start of that year (i.e. 6th April 2000). For anyone in this category the allowance is now restricted to 10% of the annual amount available for the allowance but the maximum annual amount available has risen to £5,465 to those over 65 (£5,365 for 2001/02) and £5,535 for those over 75 (£5,435 for 2001/02) at the start of the 2000/01 tax year when the MCA ceased to exist. These amounts can be reduced, however, down to the minimum of £2,110 if the husband's STI exceeds £17,900 (note, despite the existence of independent taxation, that the wife's STI is not taken into account for reducing the MCA). This works in the same way as illustrated above for the Age

Allowance with any excess left of the income restriction after reducing the age allowance to be deducted from the MCA (subject again to the minimum amount of £2,110 being available irrespective of the STI level).

This allowance is deducted from tax borne, rather than included where the personal allowance is given in the tax computation. This is necessary to ensure only 10% of the relevant figure is given despite the individual's marginal tax rate. In Thomas Lester's case, had he been entitled to a married couples allowance, 10% of the correct rate would have been deducted after calculating his tax borne figure and before determining his tax liability.

For all other individuals the MCA has been replaced by a new credit system from April 2001. This credit system, called the Children's Tax Credit, is related to the number of children you have living with you. We discuss this new scheme below.

Activity

Determine the allowances which are available to each of the following taxpayers in 2002/03.

- Tony aged 70 has statutory total income of £12,000 and his wife Cherie aged 69 has statutory total income of £8,000.
- John aged 60 has statutory total income of £2,000 and his wife Norma aged 69 who has statutory total income of £25,000.
- Denis aged 79 has statutory total income of £19,000 and his wife Margaret aged 71 has statutory total income of £8,000.

Feedback

Tony and Cherie
Since both Tony and Cherie are aged over 65 but not over 75 they will each be entitled to a personal allowance of £6,100. In addition Tony will be able to claim a married couples allowance of £5,465.

John and Norma
John will be entitled to the normal personal allowance of £4,615. This will give him taxable income of £Nil and £2,615 (£4,615 – £2,000) of his potentially available allowance will be lost.

John will also be able to claim a married couple's allowance of £5,465 because Norma (as the older partner) was aged over 65 at the time the MCA ceased. This will be given as a tax reducer against Norma's income (as John has no taxable income after deducting his personal allowance and can give the deduction to his wife) but will not be restricted because John's statutory total income does not exceed the income limit.

Norma is aged over 65 and is therefore entitled to the higher personal allowance of £6,100. Her allowance will be reduced by the lower of:

- £1,485 (£6,100 – 4,615) and
- £3,550 ((£25,000 – 17,900) × ½)

Hence Norma will be entitled to a personal allowance £4,615 only.

Denis and Margaret

Denis is aged over 75 but his income exceeds the income limit by £1,100 (£19,000 – £17,900).

The personal allowance will be reduced by the lower of:

- £1,755 (£6,370 – £4,615)
- £550 ((19,000 – 17,900) × ½)

Thus Denis will get a personal allowance of £5,820 (i.e. £6,370 – 550).

Denis will also be able to claim a married couple's allowance of £5,535. As he has taken his full deduction against his personal allowance for his excess earnings over the £17,900 there is no further deduction to his MCA.

Had full deduction not been taken the further deduction would have to be taken against his MCA down to at worst £2,110. For example, had his STI been £22,000 his personal allowance would have been reduced to £4,615 leaving an extra £295 [((22,000 – 17,900) × ½) – £1,755] to be deducted from his MCA).

Margaret will be able to claim a personal allowance of £6,100 because her statutory total income does not exceed the income limit.

A quirk of this reduction in the age allowances is that people falling into this 'high-earning' category suffer higher than normal effective marginal tax ratio. Examine the following Activity to see this illustrated.

Activity

Calculate the marginal rate of tax of a single person aged 70 with statutory total income of £18,500.

Feedback

The easiest way of tackling a question like this is to calculate the tax paid firstly for a taxpayer with statutory total income of £18,500 and then for a taxpayer with statutory total income of £18,508.

	£	£
Statutory total income	18,500	18,508
Less personal allowance		
£6,100 – (18,500 – 17,900)/2	(5,800)	
£6,100 – (18,508 – 17,900)/2		(5,796)
Taxable income	12,700	12,712

Hence an increase of £8 in statutory total income leads to an increase of £12 in taxable income. The marginal rate of tax in both situations is 22% (assuming the income is non-savings income). Hence the extra £8 of income results in an extra £2.64 (£12 × 22%) of tax which is an effective marginal rate of tax of 33% (£2.64/£8).

Joanna is married to Simon. Joanna is 55 years old. Simon is 69 years old and registered blind. Calculate the allowances available to Joanna and Simon in the current fiscal year.

Feedback

Simon will be able to claim the age allowance of £6,100, subject to reduction if he has substantial income (i.e. over £17,900), and the blind person's allowance of £1,480. In addition, he will be able to claim the married couple's allowance of a maximum of £5,465 as he was over 65 years of age at the start of the 2000/01 tax year. Joanna will be able to claim a personal allowance of £4,615 only.

Children's Tax Credit

The tax reducers lost from 6th April 2000 (such as MCA) were replaced from 6th April 2001 with a new credit called the Children's Tax Credit. Beware, this is not a credit in the same way as the tax credit on a dividend. This credit also operates as a tax reducer (i.e. put in the calculation *after* you have determined tax borne) like those allowances it replaced. This was introduced in the Finance Act 1999 (s.30 and sch 3). For the tax year 2002/03 it has been set at £5,290 (2001/02: £5,200) at a rate of 10% (i.e. maximum debit against tax due of £529; equivalent to £10.17 per week). It will apply where the claimant has at least one child under the age of 16 living with them in the year of assessment.

It does not matter whether the child is the claimant's by birth or, if the parent is married to the claimant, if they choose for their partner to receive the credit. They can also choose to take half the credit each. The Children's Tax Credit can not be claimed by a taxpayer who is also claiming MCA. If a claimant is still entitled to MCA it must be given up if this new credit is to be claimed.

To recognise the extra costs of a new born child an extra credit claimable for the first year of a child's life, called the 'Baby rate'. This extra credit this year will be worth the same amount again as the credit for older children – i.e. £1,049 (£10,490 x 10%) can be claimed by the family of a child less than one year of age.

For higher rate tax payers the Children's Tax Credit will be reduced by £2 for every £3 of income earned over the higher rate band amount. This equates to losing £1 of the credit for every £15 extra income earned.

From April 2003 this credit will be replaced by the new Child Tax Credit and Working Tax Credit systems. The new Child Tax Credit, as announced in the 2002 Budget will combine with Child Benefit, to provide for the first child, £54.25 per week to all families on incomes less than £13,000 a year while all families with incomes less than £50,000 a year are guaranteed £26.50 per week.

Working Family Tax Credit (WFTC)

From the 5th October 1999 a new tax 'credit' has been available to some working families. This 'credit' is also not like the credit received with dividend payments but instead is like the Family Credit system, which it in fact replaces, which is a benefit paid directly to its recipients. Details of this new credit are therefore provided here only for consistency but they do not form part of an individual's tax computation like dividend credits do. Do not let the name confuse you into using these figures incorrectly.

From 6th April 2000 this credit is administered by the Inland Revenue but paid to recipients via their employers as part of their wages or salaries. Only the self-employed (or non-earning partners who are given the right to collect the credit instead of their earning partners) will get the credit paid to them directly.

The WFTC is given to any family (which includes couples with children as well as lone parents) who:

- have at least one child
- work at least 16 hours a week
- are resident in the UK, and entitled to work here
- have savings of £8,000 or less.

If the claimant has more than £3,000 in savings, they will also loose £1 of credit per week for every £250 extra they have saved between £3,000 and £8,000.

The WFTC is worth a basic amount of £60.00 per week for 2002/03 (2001/02: £59.00). However, this basic amount is increased by £11.65 per week (June 2001/02: £11.45) if at least one partner, or the lone parent, works more than 30 hours a week.

An extra credit is available for each child in the family:

| | £/week | | |
	2002/03	2001/02 (from June 2000)	Increase
under 16	26.45	26.00	0.45
16–18	27.20	26.75	0.45
Disabled child credit (from October 2000)	30.50	30.00	0.50

The disabled child credit is a further credit available if one of the children in the family is registered as disabled.

There is also a child care tax credit available for children aged up to 15 (16 if the child has a disability) worth up to 70% of the eligible child care costs up to a maximum of £135 per week for one child or £200 per week for two or more. This means it is worth £94.50 per week for one child or £140 for two or more. This credit is also restricted on the basis of earnings, but restrictions vary on the basis of particular circumstances.

The total credit available will be the sum total of the four parts outlined above (basic amount, 30 hour extra credit, child based extra credit and child care credit).

If the income of the family (after tax and NIC) is above £94.50 per week the total credit is reduced by 55p for each £1 over the £94.50 earned.

The WFTC is not a permanent award, but lasts for 26 weeks at a time, just as Family Credit used to. At this point recipients can re-apply and may continue to receive the credit if they are still entitled to it.

The WFTC will be replaced from April 2003 by the new Child Tax redit and Working Tax Credit systems, like the children's tax credit. The new Working Tax Credit is currently planned to provide a guaranteed income from full time work for those aged 25 and over (without children or a disability) of £183 per week for couples and £154 per week for single people.

Disabled Person's Tax Credit (DPTC)

The DPTC was introduced at the same time as the WFTC, this time to replace Disability Working Allowance. Its function is to help people with an illness or disability who are in work. Like the WFTC it is now paid to employees directly via their employers. DPTC is available to individuals with an illness or disability who work at least 16 hours a week, are residents in the UK (and entitled to work here), have savings of £16,000 or less and receive one of number of other benefits at present that qualify them for this new credit.

Again like WFTC the amount of credit available is based on four parts

- a basic credit of £62.10 per week (2001/02: £61.05) if single person or £92.80 (2001/02: £91.25) if a lone parent or couple
- an extra credit if the recipient or partner works more than 30 hours a week of £11.65 (2001/02: £11.45)
- a tax credit for each child (same as WFTC above with the exception that the disabled child tax credit of £30.50 is available for the whole of the year)
- child care tax credit (as for WFTC).

The available DPTC is also reduced like the WFTC if the working person earns more than £94.50 per week (£73.50 per week if the person is single). The reduction is also 55p for every £1 earned over the weekly limit. The DPTC also normally lasts 26 weeks at a time.

The DPTC is also reduced, like the WFTC, if the claimant has savings of more than £3,000 at the point they make the claim. The same reduction in the credit of £1 per week for each £250 savings over £3,000, also applied to them.

Charges on income

A charge on income is a recurring, legally enforceable, liability of the taxpayer of a type which income tax law allows as a deduction from the payer's total income calculating their statutory total income (TMA 1970 s8(8)).

The following payments are eligible to be treated as charges:

- payments of eligible interest
- payments made for proper commercial reasons in connection with the individual's trade, profession or vocation
- copyright royalties.
- patent royalties

Most charges are paid after deduction of basic rate tax, while copyright royalties and eligible loan interest are paid gross.

Tax relief is given on charges at the taxpayer's marginal rate of tax. To achieve this all charges must be shown gross in the Statutory Total Income part of the tax computation and then relief will automatically be given at the taxpayer's marginal rate of tax. This procedure is followed regardless of whether a charge is actually paid net or gross (i.e. charges paid net must be grossed up in the tax computation).

If a charge has been paid net of basic rate tax the amount of tax retained must be added to the taxpayer's tax borne in order to determine the correct tax liability.

If you are performing the tax computation for someone *receiving* a charge payment (e.g. they are paid a copyright royalty) you need to include the gross amount received as part of the non-savings income. If the charge was received net of tax then the tax already suffered should be deducted from the tax liability at the end of the computation.

Activity

Catherine has non-savings income of £15,000 in 2002/03.
    She pays an annual charge of £500 gross (eg a copyright royalty payment).
    Calculate her tax liability for the tax year.

Feedback

		£	£
Total income			15,000
Less: charge on income			(500)
Statutory total income			14,500
Less: personal allowance			(4,615)
Taxable income			9,885
Tax due	£1,920 @ 10%		192.00
	7,965 @ 22%		1,752.30
	9,885		
Tax borne			1,944.30
Add tax deducted on charges			Nil
Tax liability			1,944.30

Note – as the charge is paid gross no tax needs to be added back to determine the tax liability as she has paid it all over already. In practice, this line can normally be left out in the tax computation therefore.

How would your answer have differed if the charge Catherine had paid had been a patent royalty the charge net (i.e. would have been paid net of basic rate tax)?

Feedback

Catherine will have paid over to the patent owner during the year a charge of £390 (£500 × 78%) this time (i.e. withholding £110 as the relevant tax due on the charge). The payment must be shown gross in the Statutory Total Income calculation and then, as tax had been withheld which really forms part of the payment, it must be added to the tax borne to get the full tax liability for the year.

	£
Total income	15,000
Less: charge on income	
390 × 100/78	(500)
Statutory total income	14,500
Less: personal allowance	(4,615)
Taxable income	9,885
Tax borne (as before)	1,944.30
Add tax deducted on charges	
500 × 22%	110
Tax liability	2,054.30

In this example, the total of charges actually paid and tax liability is £2,444.30 in both cases (i.e. £1,944.30 + £500 or £2,054.30 + £390). Hence Catherine's income after tax charges is the same regardless of whether the charge is paid net or gross. This is not always the case however, as the taxpayer actually receives relief for the charge at their marginal tax rate even though they only withhold basic rate tax on a net paid charge. This means they save money on the charge if they are a higher rate taxpayer. The next activity illustrates how this works.

Activity

Michelle has non-savings income of £37,000 and pays an annual charge of £390 (net).

By calculating Michelle's tax liability with and without the annual charge determine how much the charge has effectively cost Michelle.

	With the charge £	Without the charge £
Total income:	37,000	37,000
Less: charge £390 × 100/78	500	–
Statutory total income	36,500	37,000
Less: personal allowance	(4,615)	(4,615)
Taxable income	31,885	32,385
Tax due:		
1,920 @ 10%	192.00	192.00
27,980 @ 22%	6,155.60	6,155.60
1,985 @ 40%	794.00	
2,485 @ 40%		994.00
Tax borne	7,141.60	7,341.60
Add tax deducted on charge	110.00	Nil
Tax liability	7,251.60	7,341.60

Michelle's tax liability is reduced by £90 (£7,341.60 – £7,251.60) by paying the charge. Michelle pays the charge net of tax at 22% yet gets relief at 40% (her marginal rate) resulting in a saving of £90 (18% × £500) on the charge payment.

Activity

Paulette has non-savings income of £5,500 in this year and pays an annual charge of £390 (net).

By calculating Paulette's tax liability with and without the annual charge, determine how much the charge has effectively cost Paulette.

Feedback

	With the charge £	Without the charge £
Total income	5,500	5,500
Less: charge £390 × 100/78	(500)	–
Statutory total income	5,000	5,500
Less: personal allowance	(4,615)	(4,615)
Taxable Income	385	885
Tax due		
385 @ 10%	38.50	
585 @ 10%		88.50
Add tax deducted on charge		
500 × 22%	110.00	
Tax liability	148.50	88.50

Paulette's tax liability is increased by £60 (£148.50 – £88.50). Paulette pays the charge net of tax at 22% yet gets relief only at 10% (her marginal rate) resulting in a extra cost of £60 (12% × £500).

Activity

David has non-savings income of £3,000 in this year and pays an annual charge of £390 (net).

By calculating David's tax liability with and without the annual charge, determine how much the charge has effectively cost David.

Feedback

	With the charge £	Without the charge £
Total income	3,000	3,000
Less: charge £390 × 100/78	(500)	–
Statutory total income	2,500	3,000
Less: personal allowance	(2,500)	(3,000)
Taxable income	Nil	Nil
Tax borne	Nil	Nil
Add tax deducted on charge		
500 × 22%	110	
Tax liability	110	Nil

David's tax liability is increased by £110 because he effectively claims 22% tax relief when paying the charge but is not entitled to tax relief because he is a non-taxpayer. Hence the charge effectively cost David a total of £500 (£390 + £110).

The Inland Revenue will recover the tax liability by making an S350 assessment on David for £110 (i.e. they will expect him to pay this amount once he has completed his tax return).

This is a factor of paying the charge net of a fixed rate (basic rate) irrespective of the marginal rate of tax of the payer. Does this sound fair to you? Probably not – but this is how it works as most people paying charges are taxpayers.

Notice that calculation in all these examples is carried out using the same rules. The effective cost of the charge is correctly determined in each example by following the same rules.

Payments of eligible interest

Eligible interest is treated as a charge for tax calculations. It is paid gross by the payer. The relief is therefore available at the taxpayer's marginal rate of tax just as for other charges.

Examples of eligible interest include:

- *Loans to purchase plant and machinery.* The loan must be used to purchase plant and machinery for which capital allowances are available (these rules will be discussed in Chapter 6). The relief is available to partners or (Schedule E) employees. The relief is available for a maximum of three years from the end of the tax year in which the loan was taken out. If the asset is used partly for non-business purposes the relief is proportionately reduced (ICTA 1988 s359). (Note that interest on loans to purchase plant machinery is an allowable deduction for a self-employed person for tax purposes which is why they are not allowed this treatment for their eligible interest. We will meet these in the next chapter.) Until 6 April 2002, this category of eligible interest also included loans for cars used for business purposes. This is no longer available due to the introduction of the new tax system for business use of cars and company cars (see Chapter 7).
- *Loans to pay inheritance tax.* The loan must be used by personal representatives to pay inheritance tax before a grant of representation. The relief is only available for 12 months from the payment of the tax (ICTA 1988 s364).
- *Loans to acquire an interest in a close company.* The loan must be used to acquire ordinary share capital or to make a loan. The borrower must either, together with his associates, hold more than 5% of the ordinary share capital or hold some of the ordinary share capital and work for the greater part of the time in the management of the company. If any capital is repaid by the company the loan is deemed to have been reduced by this amount and the relief is accordingly reduced (ICTA 1988 ss360, 360A & 363).
- *Loans to invest in an employee-controlled company.* The loan must be used to acquire ordinary shares either before, or within 12 months of, a company first becoming employee controlled. The company must be a UK unquoted trading company or the holding company of a trading group. A company is employee controlled if at least 50% of the issued ordinary share capital and voting power is owned by employees or their spouses. If one employee owns more than 10% of the shares he or she is deemed to own 10% when testing to see if the 50% rule is satisfied. Once again if any capital is repaid the relief will be reduced (ICTA 1988 ss361 & 363).

- *Loans to acquire an interest in a partnership.* The loan must be used to either purchase a share in a partnership or introduce capital into a partnership or make a loan to a partnership to use wholly and exclusively for business purposes. The claimant must be a member of the partnership throughout the time during which interest is claimed. Limited partners are not eligible for this relief (ICTA 1988 ss362 & 363).
- *Loans to buy annuity.* Tax relief is available for interest on up to £30,000 of a loan used by an elderly person to buy a life annuity secured on their home. This was previously part of the MIRAS scheme and the rate remains at 23% for the current tax year (despite the fall of the basic rate to 22%). This relief is only available however, for loans taken out before 9 March 1999. Beware of this unusual rate of relief if you are faced with a question on this topic.

Prior to 6th April 2000, individuals were given a tax deduction for the interest on the first £30,000 of the mortgage related to the purchase of their main home. This relief was called Mortgage Interest Relief at Source or MIRAS. This relief ceased to be available from the 6th April 2000. This removed one of the tax benefits for owning rather than renting your main residence. In the 1999 Budget speech announcing this proposal the Chancellor explained this move as to remove this distortion in the housing market and make the tax system fairer.

Copyright and patent royalties

Copyright royalties are paid gross, unless the recipient is non-resident when they are paid net and the tax withheld is paid to the Inland Revenue (ICTA ss349(1) & 536).

Patent royalties are paid net of basic rate tax and the tax withheld is paid to the Inland Revenue (ICTA s349(1)).

Note the difference between these two royalty types to ensure you correctly handle the charge in an exam.

Donations to charity

The 2000 Budget (as announced in the 9th November 1999 pre-budget statement) introduced big changes to the tax relief available on charitable donations paid by individuals. Prior to 6th April 2000 only one off large payments (£250 or more – a scheme called Gift Aid) or payments made via a deed of covenant were eligible for tax relief. The rules for companies donating to charities is now different. We will look at this in chapter 9.

From 6th April 2000 *all* payments to charities by individuals, however small and however regular, will be eligible for tax relief at the basic rate under revised Gift Aid rules (i.e. you pay them after deducting tax at the basic rate). Deeds of covenant will therefore disappear for charity donations. All donations will now be made via the new Gift Aid rules. All that is now necessary is that the donor gives to the charity a Gift Aid declaration (a simple form, or even an oral statement, saying that they are giving money to the charity, which the charity can send to the Inland Revenue to get back the tax paid by the taxpayer related to the donations).

To be eligible to pay charitable donations net of tax the donor must have paid at least the amount in tax on their taxable income that the Inland Revenue will be asked for by the charity. Where a taxpayer does not do this the Revenue will ask the taxpayer to pay back the money the charity claims from the Inland Revenue.

A payroll giving scheme was set up in the FA 1986. The scheme applies to employees who pay tax under the PAYE scheme and whose employer runs a scheme, which is approved by the Board of the Inland Revenue, which operates by withholding sums from them (ICTA 1988 s202(1) & (3)).

Tax relief is given to the taxpayer when making Gift Aid donations by increasing their basic rate band by the gross amount of the gift. This process ensures that relief is given at higher rates to taxpayers who are higher rate taxpayers (as their higher rate band starts at a higher taxable income). To illustrate how this works in practice, if you made a £100 donation to the charity, your payment will actually be worth £128.21 (£100 x 100/78) to the charity as it is able to reclaim the basic rate tax you will have paid on earning this donation. A charitable gift paid under these Gift Aid rules does not need to appear in the taxpayer's tax computation however, adjustments to that computation may need to be made under certain circumstances. The following activity illustration shows you how this may occur.

Activity

In this tax year Andrew, an employee, makes a Gift Aid donation of £1000 (net) to his favourite charity. What would his income tax computation be if his only income was non-savings income of:

a) 29,000
b) 6,000
c) 38,000

Feedback

Andrew's payment, grosses up to £1,282.05 (£1,000 x 100/78). The charity collects the extra £282.05 from the Inland Revenue via the Gift Aid scheme.

a)	£
Schedule E	29,000
Less personal allowance	(4,615)
	24,385
Tax due:	
1,920 @ 10%	192.00
22,465 @ 22%	4,942.30
	5,134.30

Nothing else needs to be done in this case as Andrew's income easily covers the reclaiming of the £282.05 from the Inland Revenue. He also is a basic rate taxpayer so no higher rate band adjustment is needed.

b)

	£
Schedule E	6,000
Less personal allowance	(4,615)
	1,385
Tax due:	
1,385 @ 10%	138.50

In this case Andrew is not paying enough tax to cover the £282.05 that the charity reclaims on his donation. He will therefore need to pay another £143.55 (£282.05 – £138.50) to the Inland Revenue as extra income tax.

c)

	£
Schedule E	38,000
Less personal allowance	(4,615)
	33,385
Tax due:	
1,920 @ 10%	192.00
(29,900 + 1,282–1,920) @ 22%	6,437.64
(33,385 – 31,182) @ 40%	881.20
	7,510.84

In this case Andrew's basic rate band is extended by the gross amount of his charitable donation so that he receives relief for this payment at the higher rate. This means £1,282.05 extra of his income is taxed at 22% instead of at 40% as would normally be the case, saving him £230.77 (18% x £1,282.05) in tax. This, added to the tax witheld on this net donation means he gets relief at 40% on the whole donation (£230.77 + £282.05 = £512.82 = 40% x £1282.05).

One quirk of the new scheme is that, if the donor to the charity is entitled to receive age-related allowances, their statutory total income is deemed to be reduced by any Gift Aid payments they may have made. This deduction is only for determining their age allowance however, it does not actually reduce their statutory total income in the computation.

The employer pays the sums withheld to an agent, who is approved by the Board, and the agent pays them to a charity or charities. Alternatively the employer may pay the sums directly to the charity or charities (ICTA 1988 s202(4)). The sums must constitute gifts by the employee to the charity or charities concerned, must not be paid by the employee under a covenant, and must fulfil any conditions set out in the terms of the scheme concerned (ICTA 1988 s202(6). The maximum that could be donated under the payroll giving scheme by an employee in 1999/2000 was £1,200 (ICTA 1988 s202(7)). This maximum amount was removed by the 2000 Budget and from the same date, April 2000, the Government will also donate an extra 10% for all payroll donations given for the next three years.

Provided that all the conditions of the scheme are met the sums withheld are treated as expenses of the employee incurred in the year in which they were paid (ICTA 1988 s202(2)). This effectively means that the employee is given tax relief for the donations made.

National insurance contributions

As we saw in Chapter 1 national insurance was introduced in 1948, largely in order to provide for retirement pensions, unemployment and sickness benefit.

Initially national insurance was payable at a flat rate by both employees and employers. The intention was for the payment to represent an insurance payment rather than to tax people on the basis of an ability to pay. Thus the burden of the tax fell heaviest on the lowest paid, hence the tax was regressive.

Over the next few years the amount which each contributor had to pay increased as social security expenditure grew. By 1961 the flat rate contribution was seen to be too great a burden on the lowest paid and earnings-related contributions were introduced. By 1975 the entire national insurance contribution was earnings related. Although national insurance is now assessed on a percentage basis there is an upper limit above which employees do not pay any extra national insurance (although from April 2003 employees will be required to pay 1% national insurance contribution on incomes over this limit). Hence the tax is still regressionary, that is taxpayers on low incomes can pay a greater percentage of their income in national insurance contributions than taxpayers on higher incomes, and leads to some rather strange marginal rates of tax as we saw in Chapter 2.

Until 2000/01 neither employee nor employer national insurance contributions were payable on most benefits in kind, making provisions of benefits in kind a tax efficient form of remuneration. This situation has now changed. Employers only are required to pay Class 1A contributions on most benefits in kind they give to their employees. For example, if an employee has a company car and/or fuel for private motoring the employer must pay Class 1A contributions, at 11.8% of the car and fuel scales.

National Insurance Contributions are collected by the Inland Revenue (via an Executive Agency called the Contributions Agency – http://www.inland revenue.gov/nic). The PAYE system is used for employees to collect these payments, but direct payment must be made by those who are self-employed.

A record is kept of an individual's national insurance contributions during their lifetime and gaps in contributions can lead to a loss of benefits, so national insurance still has some of the characteristics of an insurance scheme.

Unlike income tax, that is charged on a taxpayer's income for the year, and collected monthly under PAYE, national insurance contributions are calculated according to the employee's income for the payment period. Hence, if a taxpayer works for a number of months during the year and then has no income for the rest of the year he or she may be able to reclaim some of the income tax already paid, but no repayment of national insurance is possible. UK income tax is termed a cumulative tax system because unused allowances accumulate, national insurance is a non-cumulative tax because payments are only due in periods when payment thresholds are exceeded, irrespective of other earnings in the year.

There are four main classes of national insurance contributions. Class 1 are paid by both employees, (primary contributions), and employers, (secondary contributions). Classes 2 and 4 are paid by the self-employed. Class 3 payments are made on a voluntary basis, by self-employed or employed, in order to maintain rights to some state benefits which they may other wise not be entitled to receive.

Employees over pensionable age (i.e. 65 now) are not required to make further national insurance contributions. However, the employer's contribution, at the non-contracted out rate, is still payable.

National insurance contributions for the current year are:

Class 1

Pay per week	Employee	Employer
Below £89.00 (employee lower earnings threshold)	0%	0%
£89–£585 (employees lower earnings threshold to upper earnings limit or UEL)	10%	–
£89–£585 (employers LEL to employees UEL)	–	11.8%
£586 or more	0%	11.8%

If the employee is a member of a contracted out occupational pension scheme (either salary related or money purchase type – see Chapter 7 for more details) employee contributions on earnings between the upper and lower limit per week reduces to 8.4% (i.e. a reduction of 1.6%). The employer's contribution is reduced by 3.5% if the employee has a pension scheme based on their final salary or by 1% if the pension scheme is a money purchase scheme. The employer's reductions only apply up to the employees UEL when the normal rate of 11.8% becomes applicable again.

Class 1 contributions are based on the employee's gross pay without deducting pension contributions.

Because directors may be able to influence the timing of their remuneration package their Class I national insurance contributions are always calculated on an annual basis. The annual limits are calculated by multiplying the weekly limits by 52.

Activity

Calculate the primary and secondary Class 1 contributions of:

- Matthew who earns £60 per week and is not contracted out.
- Mark who earns £200 per week and is contracted out on a final salary scheme.
- Luke who earns £500 per week and is contracted out on a money purchase scheme.
- John who is a company director, earns £400 per week, receives an annual bonus of £10,000 in the year and is not contracted out.

Feedback

Matthew
Matthew does not pay primary Class 1 contributions because his earnings are less than the employees lower earnings threshold of £89. Similarly his employer does not pay secondary Class 1 contributions because his earnings are below the employers earnings threshold also now of £89.

Mark
Mark pays $(200 - 89) \times 8.4\% = £9.32$ per week and his employer pays $(200 - 89) \times 8.3\% = £9.21$.

Luke
Luke pays $(500 - 89) \times 8.4\% = £34.52$ per week and his employer pays $(500 - 89) \times 10.8\% = £43.38$.

John
John receives an annual income of £30,800 (£400 × 52 + £10,000) and pays annual primary Class 1 contributions of $£30,800 - (89 \times 52) \times 10\% = £2,617.20$. His employer will pay $£30,800 - (89 \times 52) \times 11.8\% = £3,088.29$.

Class 1A

Benefits in kind (non-cash rewards related to an employment) are usually not chargeable to Class 1 contributions for employees; instead they give rise to a Class 1A contribution for employers (*not* employees). The value used to determine how much the contribution will be is the same as calculated for Schedule E benefit in kind on which the employee pays income tax. We will see how this is determined in Chapter 7 in more detail. Class 1A contributions are paid at the same rates by employers as for normal Class 1 contributions (i.e. 11.8%).

Class 2

The self-employed pay national insurance contributions of £2.00 per week for the current tax year provided their annual profits are at least £4,025. If it is below this level they are exempted from these contributions.

Class 3

Anyone can pay voluntary contributions of £6.85 per week to maintain rights to some state benefits that they might otherwise lose, for example, because their earnings are too low to pay other contributions.

Class 4

In addition to Class 2 and maybe Class 3 contributions, the self-employed pay 7.0%, of their profits between lower and upper limits, which are £4,615 and £30,420 for this tax year. Profits above the upper limit are not subject to further national insurance contributions.

For Class 4 national insurance contribution purposes profits are the taxable profits under Schedule D Case I and II less capital allowances, trading losses and trade charges on income. Class 4 contributions are paid in two instalments on 31st January in the tax year and on 31st July following it (the same point at which income tax is due for self-assessed purposes).

Activity

Simon, who is self-employed, has taxable income from his business of £20,000 for this tax year. Calculate his national insurance contributions for the tax year.

Andrew, who is also self-employed, has taxable business income of £40,000 for this tax year. Calculate his national insurance contributions for the tax year.

Feedback

Simon
Simon will pay Class 2 national insurance contributions of £104.00 (£2.00 × 52) and Class 4 contributions of £1,076.95 (7% × (£20,000 − £4,615)).

Andrew
Andrew will also pay Class 2 contributions of £104.00. His Class 4 contributions will be £1,806.35 (7% × (£30,420 − £4,615)). He is not required to make further contributions on the extra £9,580 (£40,000 − £30,420) of his profits.

Benefits Received

Taxpayers making Class 1 national insurance contributions at the higher rate are eligible to receive unemployment benefit and earnings related state pension which Class 2 and Class 4 contributors are ineligible to receive.

A full basic pension is paid to individuals who, for at least nine out of every ten years of their deemed working life, have paid at least the equivalent of the lower earnings limit contribution for the whole year. The deemed working life is from 16 to 65 for a man and from 16 to 60 for a woman although the retirement age for men and women will be equalised in due course

Impact of National Insurance Contributions

As we have seen in Chapter 2, national insurance contributions are levied on earned income alongside income tax. This provides a distortion in the tax system between earned income and investment income. A taxpayer with taxable income of less than £30,420 will have a marginal rate of tax of 32% on earned income but between 10–22% on unearned income (depending on whether is is dividend or savings income). This anomaly may encourage shareholder/directors of family businesses to draw relatively low salaries and pay dividends in order to reduce national insurance contributions.

Activity

Rosemary owns all the share capital of the company in which she works full time. Rosemary wishes to extract all of the after tax profits of the company. The profits adjusted for tax, before her director's salary, were £50,000 in the accounting year ended 31st March 2003. Rosemary does not receive any benefits in kind from the company and that she has no other income and suffers no charges on income.

Calculate Rosemary's total tax and national insurance liability if she draws the maximum salary possible (i.e. to reduce the profits of the business to zero). How would Rosemary's position change if she did not draw a salary and instead all of the profits were paid out as dividends to her?

Feedback

The before tax cost to the company of paying a salary to Rosemary is the amount of her gross salary together with the employer's national insurance contributions. We know from the question that the total cost to the company of paying the salary will be £50,000. We can find the amount of Rosemary's salary by solving the following equation:

$$\text{Salary} + 11.8\% \,(\text{Salary} - 4{,}615) = £50{,}000$$

This means her salary = £45,209.81

Now we can find Rosemary's tax liability by determining her income tax liability and Class I employee national insurance contributions.

Rosemary's income tax computation for 2002/03

	£
Salary	45,209
Less personal allowance	(4,615)
Taxable income	40,594
Tax Due:	
£1,920 @ 10%	192.00
27,980 @ 22%	6,155.60
£10,694 @ 40%	4,277.60
40,594	
Tax liability	10,625.20

Class 1 national insurance contributions are $((£585 - 89) \times 52) \times 10\% = £2{,}579.20$

Hence Rosemary's salary suffers total deductions of £13,204.40 (£10,625.20 + £2,579.20). The company has suffered total deductions of £4,788.55 (11.8% of £45,209 – £4,628). Hence the total tax payable by the company and Rosemary is £17,992.95 (£13,204.40 + £4,788.55).

If Rosemary does not draw a salary but receives the profits of the company by way of dividends, the tax position will be rather different. The payment of dividends does not have national insurance implications for either the company or Rosemary. However, now that the company has made a profit a liability to corporation tax equal to 19% of the taxable profit will arise (i.e. £9,500). Dividends are paid to shareholders with a tax credit of 10%. Rosemary will therefore receive a dividend of £40,500 together with a tax credit of £4,500.

Rosemary's income tax computation for 2002/03.

	£
Gross dividend (40,000 × 100/90)	45,000.00
Less personal allowance	(4,615.00)
Taxable income	40,385.00
Tax Due:	
£29,900 × 10%	2,990.00
£10,485 × 32.5%	3,407.62
Tax liability	6,397.62
Less credit on dividend	4,500.00
Tax payable	1,897.62

(Remember that dividends are deemed to be the top slice of income and are taxed at 10% unless the income falls into the higher rate tax band when they are taxed at 32.5%).

Hence the total tax payable by the company and Rosemary is:

	£
Income tax payable	1,897.62
Corporation tax payable	9,500.00
Tax payable	11,397.62

As you can see the way in which profits are extracted from a company can have a dramatic effect on the total tax liability. However, it is important that before such decisions are made that any non-tax considerations are taken into account. A decision based solely on tax consequences may not be in the best interests of the company, or the directors, in the long term. There also may be other restrictions on such payouts based on the motive of the company (e.g. IR35 rules, see Chapter 7).

In practice there are usually benefits in taking some salary from a company. For example, if Class 1 national insurance contributions are paid a range of benefits including pensions, sickness benefit and maternity pay become available. In addition, pension contributions can only be made out of earned income (e.g. salary) not investment income (e.g. dividends).

2002 Budget Changes

In the 2002 Budget the Chancellor announced new rules that will apply to National Insurance Contributions from April 2003 – part of his scheme to provide more money for the National Health Service. Class 1 employee rates will rise by 1% (to 11% or 9.4%). In an important change to the current philosophy, this extra payment will be due on all the employees earnings – even those above the upper threshold (£585 this year).

An extra 1% will also be added to all employer's contributions raising their normal rate to 12.8% (applicable also to Class 1A and 1B contributions). Class 4 contributions will also suffer the same 1% rise (from 7% this year to 8% next year) to equalise, as far as possible, the impact on employees, employers and the self-employed.

As you might expect, this announcement was not universally welcomed.

Basic Income tax planning points for couples

If one married partner's marginal rate of tax is lower than the other's it is tax efficient to shift income from the higher rate payer to the lower rate payer. There are broadly two ways of doing this. Firstly, investments held in the higher payer's name could be transferred to the lower payer. (There is no capital gains tax liability arising from a transfer between spouses as we will see in the capital gains chapter). These investments might include shares in a family business, in which case dividends paid on the shares would be taxed at the lower rate.

The second opportunity for shifting income from the high rate taxpayer to the low rate taxpayer is where a business is being run by one or both of the spouses. For example, it is possible to pay a wage to a spouse who deals with telephone calls and paperwork for the business. The alternative is to set up in business as a partnership in which case the other spouse can be allocated a share of the profits. A similar strategy can be adopted with adult children with low marginal rates of tax. If a partnership is established then it is the responsibility of the partners to agree the profit-sharing ratio and the Inland Revenue will not challenge such an agreement. However, if a relative is employed by a sole trader, partnership or company the Inland Revenue may wish to be satisfied that the payment is wholly and exclusively for the purpose of trade. In the case of *Copeman* v *Flood* (1941) a farmer employed his son and daughter as directors of the company and they each received a salary of £2,600. The son was aged 24 and had some business experience but the daughter was only 17 and unable to carry out the duties of a director. Both did undertake some duties for the company. It was held that the entire salary was not an expense incurred wholly and exclusively for business purposes. The Commissioners were asked to decide how much of the payments should be allowable based on the actual work carried out by the son and daughter.

Summary

This chapter has provided you with the framework which will enable you to apply the legislation discussed in later chapters.

In order to calculate an individual's tax liability it is necessary to undertake a number of steps:

- Identify each source of income for a taxpayer.

- Determine the Schedule and Case which is used to calculate the taxable income for each source of income.
- Use the rules of the Schedule and Case to determine the basis of assessment for each source of income.
- Calculate the income which is assessable and determine any deductions from that income which are allowed for tax purposes. This will enable you to calculate the taxable income from each source of income.
- Determine all the allowances and reliefs which the taxpayer can claim. To do this you must know their age, whether or not the taxpayer is married, and details of any charges on income paid.
- Now you can calculate the tax liability of a taxpayer.

You should now be able to review the example personal tax computation we presented at the start of this chapter to check that you understand how this figure of Tax Payable has been reached.

The possibilities for tax planning for families were also discussed in this chapter. You should be able to suggest ways in which a married couple can legitimately minimise the amount of tax they pay. Strategies you should be aware of include:

- transferring income-earning assets to the spouse with the lowest marginal rate of tax
- employing members of the family in a family business or admitting them to a partnership in order to take advantage of their low marginal rates of tax.

The legislation which relates to national insurance contributions was also discussed in this chapter, enabling you to calculate the national insurance liability of any individual or employer.

You are now able to progress to the next four chapters, which build on the foundations which have been laid in this chapter to provide you with further details of how to perform personal tax computations.

Project areas and Discussion questions

You may have noticed that we do not use letters B and C in the current UK tax schedular system. Both of these schedules did exist at some time however. See what you can find out about them, how they operated and when and why they were removed from the UK tax system.

Questions

Question 1. (based on ACCA December 1990).
Independent taxation of husband and wife includes the following features:

(a) A personal allowance is given to everyone.
(b) A separate income tax computation is made for each spouse and each spouse is entitled to a basic rate band (currently £27,980).

(c) A separate exemption for capital gains is available for each spouse (currently £7,700).

These rules present opportunities to reduce the direct tax burden on married couples.

Required

(a) Set out in general terms the strategy to be followed to maximise the benefits of the system.
(b) Describe the basic steps to be taken to achieve those benefits.

Question 2. Janet and Dave have lived together for two years. Janet earned £26,000 during 2002/03 on which she already paid £5,000 via PAYE. She also received an annual bonus of £3,000 in August 2002 for the year ended on the previous 31st March. She received income of £2,500 in interest payments from a Building Society account she owns in her own name. She also received £60 interest from her National Savings Bank ordinary account and £1,000 winnings from her premium bonds. Janet owns a cottage in North Yorkshire which she let from 1st October 2002 at an annual rent of £8,000 payable quarterly in advance. Her allowable expenses on the property for the year amounted to £1,000.

Dave earned a salary of £27,500 in the tax year 2002/03 on which his employer deducted £5,200 in PAYE. He also had some investment income of £3,000 net from a bank deposit account and received dividends of £5,760 from his share profits (all UK shares). Dave also paid a patent royalty of £312 in the tax year for a project he is planning to turn into a business in the future.

Required Compute Janet and Dave's tax payable for 2002/03.

5 Business taxation

Introduction

In this chapter and the next we will study the taxation of unincorporated businesses, focussing on taxation of sole-traders. In practice, unincorporated businesses are not treated as separate taxable entities for tax purposes. Rather, the schedular rules are used to calculate the taxable income under Schedule D Case I and II. In the case of a sole trader the taxable income is then included in the taxpayer's tax computation.

At the end of this chapter you will be able to:

- state the badges of trade and use them to identify trading activities
- adjust business profits for tax purposes
- apply the opening year rules to new businesses
- apply the closing year rules on the cessation of a business

The next chapter will complete discussion of this topic by examining the tax treatment of capital assets (capital allowances) and what happens with trading losses incurred by unincorporated businesses.

Introduction to Schedule D Cases I and II

Look back to Chapter 4 to find out how income which is taxed by direct assessment is assessed for tax purposes. Such income is taxed under one or other of the tax Schedules. The basis of assessment that applies, and other rules to determine how much tax will be due on the income, depends on which Schedule the income is assessed under. Income from a trade is assessed under Schedule D Case I and income from a vocation or profession is taxed under Schedule D Case II. There are some small differences in the way that the tax due is calculated under these two Cases, but for our purposes we can treat them as being the same. This chapter will examine these cases. We will focus on sole-traders however, many of the rules also equally apply to partners as the other form of unincorporated business structure. We will not discuss partnership tax in more detail in this book however.

There are nearly three and a half million people, or 13% of the workforce, who are taxed under Schedule D Case I or II. While some Schedule D Case I and II taxpayers run large businesses many are running relatively small undertakings. In general, sole traders and partners are assessed on the profits which arise in the accounting period which ends in the fiscal year.

Before any assessment under Schedule D Case I can be calculated it is first necessary to demonstrate that trading is actually taking place.

In this chapter we will review the badges of trade which are used to determine this. Once the existence of trading has been established you will need to undertake a number of steps in order to determine the Schedule D Case I assessment for a fiscal year. These are:

1. determine which accounts will form the basis period for the fiscal year
2. adjust the accounting profits in order to derive the taxable profits, that is the Schedule D Case I or II assessments.

In order to determine the Schedule D Case I assessment, you will need to establish the tax implications of any investment in fixed assets. Finally, you will need to be able to deal with any Schedule D Case I losses which arise. These latter two parts of the computation are dealt with in chapter 6.

Once the final Schedule D assessment has been calculated for the sole trader you can add this amount to their tax computation as part of their aggregated income to determine their statutory total income. The Thomas Lester example in Chapter 4 showed you how this would occur.

Identification of trading activities

It is very important to determine whether a receipt was trading income or not. Before 1965, if a receipt was not deemed to be trading income then it was likely to be a capital gain and so was not taxable. Since 1965 capital gains have been taxable in the UK but until 1988 capital gains were taxed at 30%. This rate was usually lower than the taxpayer's marginal rate of tax.

Today the distinction is less important because capital gains are taxed at the taxpayer's marginal rate of tax and so much of the tax saving that may have occurred due to the classification of the income has been reduced. However, it is still necessary to differentiate between a trade and a hobby. For example, if you bought and sold a limited number of works of art, at what point would this go from being a hobby (on which you may have to pay capital gains tax if you sold anything for more than you bought it for) to being a trade (which is subject to income tax rules). For most of us hobbies cost money rather than make money; the Inland Revenue will not give us tax relief on any losses related to hobbies, however, relief is often available for losses incurred during the course of trading meaning this classification is important.

The legislation does not define trading although the TA 1988 s832(1) states that it 'includes every trade, manufacture, adventure, or concern in the nature of a trade'. We must therefore look to case law for guidance in determining whether trading is, in fact, taking place.

The Royal Commission on the Taxation of Profits and Income (1955: Cmd 9474) suggested that there were six 'badges' which can help to determine whether or not a transaction is, in fact, trading. None of the badges offer a conclusive test of trading although some are stronger than others. If trading is taking place it is likely that there will be evidence of the existence of more than one 'badge'. The Inland Revenue will, however, review these tests in deciding whether a claim made by a taxpayer to be trading, or not, is in fact correct in their opinion. If they disagree they may challenge the taxpayer.

Badges of trade

The six badges of trade are:

- *The subject matter of the transaction.* If the property which forms the subject matter of the transaction does not provide either direct income or enjoyment to the owner, it is likely that the transaction will be deemed to be trading. It seems unlikely that commodities or manufactured articles which are normally the subject of trading will form the subject of an investment rather than a trade. For example, in *Rutledge v IRC* (1929) the taxpayer bought one million rolls of toilet paper from a bankrupt German firm for £1,000 while in Berlin on business. The rolls were sent to the UK and the taxpayer endeavoured to sell them. Eventually he found a buyer who bought the whole quantity for £12,000, affording him a considerable profit. The transaction was held to be 'in the nature of a trade' largely because of the quantity of the goods involved. Hence even a single transaction can be seen to be trading.

    In contrast in *IRC v Reinhold* (1953) the taxpayer was not held to be trading. He had bought four houses within two years intending to sell them. The Court of Session stated that 'heritable property is not an uncommon subject of investment' and hence the taxpayer was not trading.

    In the recent case of *Mason v Morton* (1986) the taxpayer bought land intending to develop it but in fact sold it. The taxpayer was held not to be trading, confirming that land can be held for investment purposes even though it does not yield an income.

- *The frequency of similar transactions.* Although a single transaction can be considered to be trading the repeated undertaking of transactions in the same subject matter is more likely to indicate that trading is being conducted.

    In *Pickford v Quirke* (1927) the taxpayers formed a syndicate to buy and resell cotton mills. There were four such transactions. The membership of the syndicate was not identical for each transaction. It was held that any one transaction would not have constituted trading but the four taken together did.

- *The circumstances responsible for the realisation.* There is a presumption that trading is not occurring if the property is disposed of to raise money for an emergency. Other circumstances which indicate that trading is not taking place include sales by executors of the deceased's property and sales by liquidators and receivers of the assets of an insolvent company.

    In the case of *The Hudson's Bay Company v Stevens* (1909) the taxpayer company had sold off a large quantity of land over a number of years which it had acquired in return for the surrender of its charter. The company was held not to be trading, the court offering the following explanation: 'The company are doing no more than an ordinary landowner does who is minded to sell from time to time as purchasers offer, portions suitable for building of an estate which has devolved upon him from his ancestors.'

- *Supplementary work on or in connection with the property realised.* Trading is more likely to be taking place if either work is done on the property to make it more marketable, or an organisation is set up to sell it. The courts decided that if there is an organised effort to obtain profit there is a source of taxable income but in the absence of such effort the presumption will be that trading is not taking place.

    In *Cape Brandy Syndicate v IRC* (1927) a group of accountants bought 3,000 casks of Cape brandy, blended it with French brandy, recasked it and sold it in lots over the next 18 months. They were held to be trading because they did not simply buy an article which they thought was cheap and then resold it. The syndicate bought the brandy intending to transport it, modify its character and recask it so as to enable it to be sold in smaller quantities.

- *The motive of the transaction.* There is some evidence of trading taking place if the objective of undertaking the transaction is to make a profit. However, even in the absence of a motive to make a profit it may still be concluded that trading is taking place. The subject matter of the transaction may be crucial.

    In *Wisdom* v *Chamberlain* (1968) the taxpayer, a well-known comedian, bought silver bullion as a hedge against the anticipated devaluation of the pound. It was held that the taxpayer had undertaken an 'adventure in the nature of a trade' when he realised a profit three months later because the transaction was entered into on a short-term basis with the sole intention of making a profit from the purchase and sale of a commodity.

- *The length of ownership.* The presumption is that the shorter the period of ownership the more likely it is that trading is taking place. However, this is a weak badge of trade because the short period of ownership can often be discounted by the taxpayer, perhaps by demonstrating a need for cash at the time of the sale. Hence there are many exceptions from this as a universal rule.

Other factors which might be considered when deciding whether trading is taking place are:

- the source of finance for the transaction
- the circumstances surrounding the acquisition of the asset
- whether the subject matter of transaction is in any way related to trades and other activities carried on by the taxpayer.

In conclusion we will consider the case of *Edwards* v *Bairstow and Harrison* (1956) who were selling secondhand plant but claimed that they were not trading. In deciding that the appellants were trading Lord Radcliffe said:

> It is said that there was no organisation for the purposes of the transaction. But in fact there was organisation, as much of it as the transaction required. It is true that the plant was not advertised for sale, though advertisements asking for plant were answered by the respondents. But why should they incur the cost of advertising if they judged that they could achieve the sale of plant without it? It is said that no work had been done on the maturing of the asset to be sold. But such replacement and renovation as were needed were in fact carried out, and I can see no reason why a dealer should do more work in making his plant saleable than the purposes of sale require. It is said that neither of the respondents had any special skill from his normal activities which placed him in an advantageous position for the purposes of this transaction. It may be so, though one of them was the employee of a spinning firm. In any case the members of a commercial community do not need much instruction in the principles and possibility of dealing, and I think that, given the opportunity, the existence or non-existence of special skill is of no significance whatever. It is said finally, that the purchase and sale of plant lent itself to capital, rather than commercial, transactions. I am not sure that I understand what this is intended to mean. If it means that at the relevant period there was no market for secondhand plant in which deals could take place, there is no

finding to that effect and all the facts that are recited seem to be against the contention. If it means anything else, it is merely an attempt to describe the conclusion which the respondents would wish to see arrived at on the whole case.

There remains the fact which was the original ground of the earlier Commissioners' decision – 'this was an isolated case'. But, as we know, that circumstance does not prevent a transaction which bears the badges of trade from being in truth an adventure in the nature of trade. The true question in such cases is whether the operations constitute an adventure of that kind, not whether they, by themselves or they in conjunction with other operations, constitute the operator a person who carries on a trade. Dealing is essentially a trading adventure, and the respondents' operations were nothing but a deal or deals in plant and machinery.

Activity

Stirling Hill is a vintage motor car enthusiast. On 1st January 2002 he took out a loan of £40,000 at a fixed rate of interest of 10%, and spent £30,000 on having a workshop built. This was completed on 31st March 2002, when a further £8,000 was spent on tools and equipment. On 6th April 2002, Stirling bought a dilapidated vintage motor car for £3,000, and proceeded to restore it at a cost of £7,000 in spare parts. The restoration was completed on 30th June 2002. Unfortunately, Stirling was made redundant on 15th September 2002, and was forced to sell the motor car for £25,000. Not being able to find further employment, Stirling proceeded to buy three more dilapidated vintage motor cars on 15th October 2002 for £4,000 each. The restoration of these was completed on 28th February 2003 at a cost of £7,000 per motor car, and two of them were immediately sold for a total of £50,000. On 31st March 2003 Stirling obtained employment elsewhere in the country, so he immediately sold the workshop for £25,000, and repaid the loan of £40,000. Stirling personally retained the tools and equipment, which were worth £4,500, and the unsold vintage motor car which was valued at £25,000.

You are required to:

(a) Briefly discuss the criteria which would be used by the courts in deciding whether or not Stirling will be treated as carrying on an adventure in the nature of a trade in respect of his vintage motor car activities.

(b) Explain whether or not you would consider Stirling to be carrying on an adventure in the nature of a trade.

(based on ACCA Tax Planning Dec 94)

Feedback

(a) To answer this part of the question you need to discuss the six badges of trade set out above.

(b) The acquisition and disposal of the first car, taken in isolation, is unlikely to be deemed to be trading because:

- Vintage cars are often owned and restored by individuals in order to derive enjoyment and/or as investments.
- The length of ownership after the restoration work is completed does not suggest trading is taking place.

- The circumstances surrounding the sale of the car suggests that the disposal was a forced sale rather than trading.

However, the loan taken out to build and equip the workshop and help to finance the acquisition of the car might be taken to be a sign that trading is taking place.

The acquisition and disposal of the next three cars is likely to be treated as an adventure in the nature of a trade because:

- Stirling devoted the whole of his time to the activity.
- There were three acquisitions and disposals.
- Two of the cars were sold as soon as their restoration was completed.

If, as seems likely, Stirling Hill is deemed to be trading it is now necessary to determine whether the first transaction will be deemed to be trading as a result of the subsequent transactions. To decide this we need to refer to case law. In the case mentioned above of *Pickford* v *Quirke* (1927) the taxpayer bought a mill and sold all the assets. This would normally be treated as a capital transaction but the taxpayer carried on to asset strip a total of four mills. The courts decided that the taxpayer was trading and that the three later transactions could be taken into account when deciding whether the first transaction was trading.

In the case of *Leach* v *Pogson* (1962) the taxpayer set up 30 driving schools which were then sold. Again the courts decided that the 29 later transactions could be taken into account when deciding whether the first transaction was trading and hence the taxpayers were trading.

Finally, in the case of *Taylor* v *Good* (1974) the taxpayer bought a country house, intending to live in the house. The taxpayer's wife refused to live in the house and obtained planning permission to build 90 houses on the land. He then sold the property to a property developer having owned the property for about four years.

The courts decided that the transactions undertaken to enable the taxpayer to sell the property at a profit were not enough to make the first transaction, the acquisition of the property, to be trading.

On balance it seems likely that Stirling Hill will be taken to be trading on all his transactions.

Adjustment of profits

Now that you are able to identify trading activities from 'hobbies' you need to be able to calculate the taxable profits that may then fall due from any trading transactions. Taxable profits are made up of the difference between trading receipts and allowable expenses during a period of assessment.

In order to calculate the taxable profits you will need to:

- determine which accounting period will form the basis of assessment for the fiscal year
- identify taxable income and allowable expenditure which relates to the basis period.

In this section we will discuss the recognition of income and expenditure in general terms. Then we will determine what are trading receipts that need to form part of the trading income to be taxed and finally we will consider allowable expenses that can be deducted from trading income.

Recognition of income and expenditure

Clearly it is important to determine in which period income and expenditure will be recognised. Unfortunately there is no tax legislation to help us and in practice the taxpayer must agree a basis with the Inland Revenue.

There are three acceptable ways of recognising income and expenditure:

- The earnings (or accruals), basis where the normal accounting principles are used, for example the accruals and realisation concepts apply. Stock must be valued at the lower of cost (using FIFO) and market value. Work in progress is usually valued using absorption costing although marginal costing can be used. Most taxpayers use the earnings basis.
- The cash basis, where income and expenditure are only recognised when the related cash flow occurs. The Inland Revenue is usually reluctant to allow the cash basis to be used because of the potential to manipulate the profit figure. However, some taxpayers, such as barristers, who cannot sue for their fees, and authors, who only earn their royalties when they are received, are usually allowed to use the cash basis. The Finance Act 1998 provided that professional businesses would be required to use the earnings basis for profits assessed from 1999/2000 onwards. The profits which might escape tax by this change will be subject to a catch up charge.
- The conventional or bills delivered basis, where only bills received or issued are used. Solicitors are usually allowed to use the bills receivable basis after they have been self-employed for three years provided that they agree to invoice clients regularly.

Once a basis is agreed it will continue to be used unless the taxpayer elects to use an alternative basis. Of course, if the taxpayer wishes to change they must first obtain Inland Revenue approval.

We will now look in detail at the calculation of the Schedule D Case I income.

Trading receipts

A receipt is a trading receipt if it is a payment for services or goods. Payments made on a voluntary basis for some personal quality of the taxpayer are not deemed to be trading receipts. In *Murray v Goodhews* (1976), Watneys paid ex gratia lump sum payments to landlords of public houses when they terminated tied tenancies, partly as an acknowledgement of the good relationship they had with their tenant and partly to preserve their good name. These sums were held not to be trading receipts in the hands of the landlords since the amounts of the payments had no connection with the profits earned or barrelage taken by any house nor was it linked with future trading relations between Watneys and the taxpayer.

However, in *McGowan v Brown and Cousins* (1977), the taxpayer, an estate agent, received a low fee for acquiring property for a company in the expectation that he would be retained to deal with letting the property. The company paid the taxpayer £2,500 as compensation when they retained another agent to deal with the lettings. The payment was held to be a trading receipt despite the lack of a legal obligation to pay it.

The receipt must be income not capital. This distinction has proved difficult to draw in practice and a number of tests have been developed over a long period of time to indicate which is which. Perhaps the most obvious test is to determine if the asset is part of the fixed capital or is part of working capital of the business. The difficulty is that whether an asset is an item from stock in trade or a capital asset depends on the type of business being carried on. You will have looked at this distinction if you have taken any basic accounting courses and will have seen how difficult this can be determine at times to.

Another test which can be applied is the 'trees and fruit' test, where the tree is considered to be the capital producing the fruit which is income.

This test may result in a payment being divided into capital and revenue parts as in the case of *London and Thames Haven Oil Wharves v Attwooll* (1967) where £100,000 compensation was paid after a tanker crashed into a jetty, causing serious damage. The sum was split into a capital sum which was intended to be used to rebuild the jetty and a revenue receipt which was compensation for loss of income due to the accident.

A number of other receipts may also be considered to be trading receipts because they are seen to be compensation for loss of revenue earnings. These include receipts which relate to:

- Restrictions on commercial activities.
- Restrictions on the short-term use of commercial assets, although a receipt relating to a permanent restriction is deemed to be capital.
- Cancellations of commercial contracts or connections which are relatively small compared to the size of the business. Receipts which are compensation for contracts which are large compared to the size of the business are deemed to be capital.
- Appropriations of unclaimed deposits and advances.
- The sale of information. This receipt is covered by statute (TA 1988 ss530 and 531) unlike the four above which have been decided by means of case law. Provided that the vendor continues to trade after the sale the receipt will be treated as a trading receipt.
- A trade debt which has been deducted as a trading expense and is subsequently cancelled is treated as a trade receipt (TA 1988 s94).

Goods disposed of other than in the ordinary course of business must be accounted for, at market value, as a trading receipt. In *Sharkey v Wernher* (1956) the taxpayer who ran a stud farm as a business also raced horses as a hobby. She transferred five horses from her stud farm to her racing stables and recorded the cost of breeding the horses as a receipt of the stud farm. The Revenue argued that the market value of the horses should be entered in the accounts. It was held that horses which were transferred from the stud farm to her racing stable must be entered in the accounts as a receipt at their market value rather than their cost. The rule derived from this case applies to all goods taken by owners for their own use as well as goods they give to others.

The rule is also applied if goods are sold at less than their market value. However, provided that the disposal can be shown to have been made for genuine commercial reasons the rule in *Sharkey v Wernher* does not apply and a trader may make a disposal at whatever value he chooses.

Additionally the rule applies to traders only. It does not apply to professional persons. In *Mason v Innes* (1967) the novelist Hammond Innes gave the manuscript of *The Doomed Oasis* to his father. The writer had deducted allowable travelling expenses from his income which had been incurred while researching the book. The Inland Revenue wanted to assess the writer on the market value of the script. Lord Denning, the Master of the Rolls, said:

> 'Suppose an artist paints a picture of his mother and gives it to her. He does not receive a penny for it. Is he to pay tax on the value of it? It is unthinkable. Suppose he paints a picture which he does not like when he has finished it and destroys it. Is he liable to pay tax on the value of it? Clearly not. These instances ... show that ... *Sharkey* v *Wernher* does not apply to professional men.'

Deductible expenses

For expenditure to be an allowable deduction from income it must satisfy three criteria. It must be a revenue item. It must be incurred *wholly and exclusively* for the purposes of the trade, profession or vocation. Finally it must not be specifically disallowed as a deductible expense by statute.

The following sums are specifically disallowed as deductions when calculating the Schedule D Case I or Case II profits:

- Any expenses which are not *wholly and exclusively* incurred for the purposes of the trade, profession or vocation.
- Any payment for the maintenance of the trader, his or her family or accommodation and any payments made for any domestic or private purposes distinct from the purposes of the trade, profession or vocation.
- The rent of the whole or any part of any dwelling-house or domestic offices. However, if some part of the accommodation is used for the purposes of the trade, profession or vocation then any rent which is *bona fide* paid for that part of the accommodation up to a maximum of two-thirds of the total rent will be allowable.
- The excess of the amount actually expended for any amount spent on repairs of premises or for the supply, repairs or alterations of any assets employed for the purposes of the trade, profession or vocation.
- Any loss which is not connected with or arising out of the trade, profession or vocation.
- Any capital employed in improvement of premises occupied for the purposes of the trade, profession or vocation.
- Any debts, except bad debts, which have proved to be such, and doubtful debts to the extent that they are respectively estimated to be bad. This means provisions for bad debts are usually not allowable.
- Any sum recoverable under an insurance or contract of indemnity.
- Expenditure incurred for private rather than business purposes.
- Any annuity or other annual payment (other than interest) payable out of the profits or gains.
- Any interest paid to a person not resident in the UK if and so far as it is interest at more than a reasonable commercial rate.
- Any royalty or other sum paid in respect of the user of a patent.
- Most expenditure on hospitality is disallowed but any entertainment of *bona fide* employees is allowed without limit.
- Gifts are generally disallowed but gifts to customers costing less than £50 which carry a conspicuous advertisement for the business are allowed provided they are not food, drink, vouchers or tobacco (ICTA 1988 s74). This amount was increased in the 2001 Budget from £10 in previous years. Gifts to employees are

allowed; there will be a taxable benefit in this for the recipients, however, as we will see in Chapter 7.

However, some of the expenses which are included in the above list may be allowed if it is in the normal course of the taxpayer's business to make such provision.

There are a number of areas of difficulty with this legislation. Some of it has been dealt with through further legislation – for instance, renting business property by means of a lease is dealt with by TA 1988 s87. Other problems have been addressed by the development of case law, for instance the distinction between capital and revenue expenditure.

By extra-statutory concession small gifts to local charities made for trading purposes are deductible. Also by extra-statutory concession relief is available for trade receipts and trade debts, the proceeds of which cannot be remitted to the UK.

In a Press Release the Inland Revenue announced that living expenses incurred during business visits abroad, excluding expenses attributable to holidays taken as part of the same trip, are deductible in computing profits of the trade.

Expenditure on a training course for the proprietor of a business which is intended to provide new expertise, knowledge or skills brings into existence an intangible asset of enduring benefit to the business and is capital expenditure. However, if attendance is to update expertise, knowledge or skills already possessed the expenditure is normally regarded as revenue expenditure.

The incidental costs of obtaining finance by means of a qualifying loan or the issue of qualifying loan stock or a qualifying security and the incidental costs of obtaining finance by those means shall be treated as expenses of management and are deductible (ICTA 1988 s77(1)). That is if the interest paid on a loan is tax deductible then the incidental costs of obtaining finance are also deductible.

A qualifying loan and qualifying loan stock is defined as a loan or loan stock, the interest on which is deductible in computing, for tax purposes, the profits or gains of the person by whom the incidental costs in question are incurred. A qualifying security is any deep discount security in respect of which the income elements are deductible in computing the total profits of the company by which the incidental costs in question are incurred (ICTA 1988 s77(2)).

The incidental costs of obtaining finance means expenditure on fees, commissions, advertising, printing and other incidental matters but not including stamp duty being expenditure wholly and exclusively incurred for the purpose of obtaining the finance (whether or not it is in fact obtained), or of providing security for it or of repaying it (ICTA 1988 s77(6)).

Note that sums paid in consequence of, or for obtaining protection against, losses resulting from changes in the rate of exchange between different currencies or for the cost of repaying a loan or loan stock or a qualifying security so far as attributable to its being repayable at a premium or to its having been obtained or issued at a discount are not deductible expenses for tax purposes (ICTA 1988 s77(7)).

Charges and Interest
Look back to Chapter 4 to see how charges are dealt with. Charges paid are disallowed in the Schedule D Case I computation because they are relieved in the personal tax computation. Hence interest paid on long-term loans which are charges are disallowed. Interest paid on other types of loans including overdrafts, credit cards and hire purchase agreements will be allowable provided they satisfy the wholly and exclusively rule. However, interest paid on overdue tax is not an allowable expense.

Fines and Theft

Any payments made which are held to be contrary to public policy such as fines and penalties are disallowable. However, in practice deductions for parking fines incurred by employees parking the employer's cars during the course of their employer's business are usually allowed, although such fines incurred by directors and proprietors are never allowed.

Similarly if a business suffers from a theft by a member of staff the loss will be an allowable expense but a misappropriation by a director or proprietor will not be deductible (*Curtis v J & G Oldfield* (1933)).

The 2002 Budget announced that the law is to be amended also so that no deduction against UK tax can be made after 1 April 2002, for any payments, such as bribes, made overseas that would be a criminal payment if made in the UK.

Capital Expenditure and Revenue income expenditure

The law is consistent in its treatment of revenue income and expenditure. The tests that were used to determine whether a receipt was capital or revenue are also used to test whether expenditure is capital or revenue. However, in the case of *Lawson v Johnson Matthey plc* (1992) a payment of £50 million was made as part of a deal with the Bank of England in order to save the banking subsidiary from a threat of insolvency. Despite the size and one-off nature of the payment it was allowed as revenue expenditure.

This distinction between capital and revenue expenditure has become more important in recent years with the phasing out of many 100% first-year allowances on capital expenditure particularly for larger businesses. Now, if expenditure is deemed to be capital, the taxpayer can only claim a maximum 40% first year allowance in the year in which the expenditure is incurred. This problem does still exist, however, for small businesses who can currently obtain 100% allowances against certain capital expenditure.

Amounts spent on repairs to an asset will generally be allowable for tax purposes but amounts spent on improvements will be disallowed, although they may be eligible for capital allowances. In general the normal accounting principles are used as guidance when differentiating between revenue and capital expenditure but case law has been used to decide marginal cases.

You need to know some of the details of the main cases in order to be able to identify revenue and capital expenditure. We will begin by contrasting the decisions made in the cases of *Law Shipping Co Ltd* v *IRC* (1924) and *Odeon Associated Theatres LW v Jones* (1972) which both concern the cost of making good dilapidations which existed at the time of acquisition. We will then contrast the cases of *Samuel Jones & Co (Devondale) Ltd* v *CIR* (1951) and *Brown v Burnley Football and Athletic Co Ltd* (1980) to differentiate between repairing and replacing assets.

The first area of difficulty involves expenditure which is incurred to renovate assets soon after they were acquired. In *Law Shipping Co Ltd* v *IRC* (1924) a ship, which was built in 1906, was bought in December 1919 for £97,000. The ship was ready to sail with freight booked at the time of purchase. The periodical survey of the ship was then considerably overdue and an exemption from the survey had to be obtained. The ship was granted a Lloyd's Certificate for a single voyage to enable it to be taken into dock to undergo its survey. The purchaser had to spend £51,558 on repairs. It was agreed that the expense of keeping a ship, which is employed in trade, in proper repair is an expense necessary for the purpose of trade, even if that expense is deferred. In fact had the purchaser's predecessors undertaken the repairs they would have been able to set the costs against their income for tax purposes. However, the accumulation of repairs represented by the expenditure was an accumulation which extended partly over a period during which the ship was employed, not in the purchaser's trade, but in that of the purchaser's predecessors.

A ship which is dilapidated is worth less than a ship which has been well maintained and is in good condition. The condition of the ship at the time of the sale was reflected in the price paid. The value of the ship was presumably increased by the repairs undertaken and hence some of the cost of the repairs should be treated as capital expenditure since they increased the value of a capital asset.

It was held that most of the expenditure was incurred because of the poor state of repair of the vessel when it was bought and this amount was disallowed but £12,000 of the expenditure was allowed for post-acquisition repairs.

In the contrasting case of *Odeon Associated Theatres Ltd* v *Jones* (1972) a cinema had been bought which was in a fairly dilapidated condition after the Second World War. The cinema was used for a number of years by its new owners before it was refurbished. All of the refurbishment expenditure was allowed despite the poor condition of the cinema when it was bought.

There are some essential differences between the two cases which led to the differing conclusions. When the cinema was bought the purchase price was not reduced to reflect the condition of the property which was both usable and used immediately after purchase. In the *Law Shipping* case the purchase price did reflect the condition of the ship which was not seaworthy immediately after purchase. Finally the Court of Appeal decided that the costs of refurbishment were deductible expenses in accordance with accounting principles.

The second area which has depended on case law for clarification concerns the question of repair or replacement. That is, has an asset been repaired or replaced? In the case of *Samuel Jones & Co (Devondale) Ltd* v *CIR* (1951) expenditure on a new chimney to replace the existing one was allowable because the chimney was held to be a subsidiary part of the factory.

In the case of *Brown* v *Burnley Football and Athletic Co Ltd* (1980) the football club replaced a wooden spectators' stand with a concrete structure which also provided additional accommodation. The expenditure was disallowed because the entire stand, which was held not to be part of a larger asset, but a distinct and separate part of the club, was replaced.

Professional Charges

When considering whether legal and professional charges are allowable we need to look first at the status of the item to which they relate. For example, fees and charges incurred in respect of capital assets and non-trading items are not deductible.

Activity

For each of the following legal and professional charges decide whether they are allowable deductions for the purposes of Schedule D Case I:

1. Charges incurred in issuing shares.
2. Charges incurred when obtaining a long (more than 50 years) lease.
3. Charges for trade debt collection.
4. Charges incurred with respect to an action for breach of contract.

Feedback

The first two charges would be disallowable because they relate to non-revenue items. The third charges would be allowable and the fourth charges would be allowable provided that the contract has the quality of revenue and not capital.

However, it is not possible to classify all legal and professional charges using this rule. For example, the normal fees for preparing accounts and agreeing tax liabilities are allowable while legal fees incurred during tax appeals are not deductible regardless of the outcome of the appeal. However, accountancy expenses incurred due to an Inland Revenue investigation will be allowable provided that taxable profits for earlier years are not increased and if an increase is made to the taxable profits of the year under review this does not lead to interest charges or penalties.

Payments to Employees

Payments to employees will usually be allowable deductions for employers provided that they are in the interest of the business.

For example, the travelling expenses of your employees incurred when travelling to work are disallowable (if you compensated them for these costs) but travelling expenses they incur in the course of your business are deductible from your profits if you reimburse your employees. This seemingly simple ruling is still open to dispute. For example, it may not be easy to decide exactly where an individual employee's work commences. Recently there was a report in The Guardian about a taxpayer who is the only employee, and major shareholder, of a company which designs oil platforms who was in dispute with the Inland Revenue over travel and accommodation expenses. The company paid for its employee to travel, often hundreds of miles, in order to work. Now, as we will see in Chapter 6, an employee's expenses paid by their employer are taxable benefits unless they are wholly, exclusively and necessarily incurred in the performance of employment duties (TA 1988 s198). The Inland Revenue argued that the taxpayer's costs in getting to the area and arranging a place to stay merely enabled him to be available for work each day. This means that the costs of travel and accommodation are private expenses, paid by the company, which are therefore taxable benefits. However, if the taxpayer had been taxed under Schedule D Case I, as a sole trader, the expenses would have been an allowable deduction because the expense was incurred wholly and exclusively (no necessarily requirement this time) for the purpose of the business. Indeed, employees of large companies who receive similar payments are not taxed on them because there is a presumption that they are based at the company's offices so that the expenses are incurred in the course of their duties because they are travelling between sites.

The following week the same newspaper reported that an accountant in Wiltshire had a client in similar circumstances. The accountant successfully claimed the payments as allowable deductions by quoting from a Revenue Statement of 13th February 1981 which exempts construction workers from tax on their expenses and then went on to argue that it would contravene the Taxpayers' Charter to limit the concession to one particular industry. The accountant concluded his statement by saying that individual tax inspectors are prepared to operate this concession.

Wholly and Exclusively rule

As we stated at the start of our examination of deductible expenses, only expenditure which is *wholly and exclusively* for the purposes of business will be deductible. There are two situations in which businesses risk falling foul of this requirement. The first is when a payment is held to be too remote from the business for it to be considered to be *wholly and exclusively* for the purposes of business. The second is when expenditure has two purposes, one business and the other private, the expenditure is likely to fail the 'wholly and exclusively' test and be disallowable because of a duality of purpose.

When deciding whether subscriptions and donations are allowed we can use the 'wholly and exclusively' rule. For example, trade subscriptions are likely to be allowable while donations to a charity will probably only be allowable if they are relatively small and to local charities. Subscriptions and donations to political parties are usually disallowable but in the case of *Morgan* v *Tate and Lyle Ltd* (1954) a political donation to the Conservative Party was allowed because it was made in order to resist the nationalisation of the sugar industry proposed by the Labour Party which would have led to the cessation of the business.

Any appropriations from the business, including a salary or interest on capital paid to the owner, are disallowable.

In *Caillebotte* v *Quinn* (1975) the taxpayer, a self-employed carpenter, claimed the difference between the cost of eating at home, 10p, and the cost of eating in a cafe, 40p, for those days when he was working away from home. It was held that the expenditure was disallowable because he ate to live as well as to work and so the expenditure was tainted by the private purpose. There have been a number of other cases testing this legislation, such as in *Mackinlay* v *Arthur Young McClelland Moores & Co* (1990) where the House of Lords ruled that removal costs paid to two partners to move house were disallowable. It was accepted that the partnership benefited from the move because the partners were able to work at different offices but that there was duality of purpose. The House of Lords also confirmed that the rules for sole traders also apply to unincorporated partnerships.

Business and Personal Use

Although it is not possible to split a purpose into a business and a personal purpose, it may be possible to split a payment and allow the business portion as a deductible expense. The most widespread example of this is the treatment of expenses relating to a car which is used for both business and pleasure. The proportion of business miles compared to total miles determines the proportion of the expenses such as servicing, insurance and petrol which is an allowable deduction. As you have already seen section 74 of ICTA 1988 enables taxpayers who undertake all, or part, of their business from their own home to deduct part of the costs of running the house from their Schedule D Case I profits.

Lease Premiums

If a taxpayer leases premises he or she is likely to pay a premium when the lease is granted as well as a rent. A part of the premium paid will be allowed as a deductible expense for tax purposes. The lessee can claim the amount on which the landlord is assessed spread over the life of the lease. Hence in order to determine the relief available you need to determine the Schedule A assessment on the lease premium which is dealt with in Chapter 7. Look at the activity 'Amanda' in Chapter 7 to see how the Schedule A assessment is determined.

Pre-trading Expenses

Expenditure can only be a deductible expense from trading income if it is incurred on or after the date on which the business commences to trade. However, expenses incurred in the seven years prior to this date will be treated as a loss which arises in the year of commencement (TA 1988 s401). This may seem rather strange to you. However, as you will see in the next section, trading profits in the first period of accounts are likely to be taxed more than once. Conversely, then, an expense incurred in the same period is likely to be eligible for tax relief more than once. By allowing the expenditure as a loss rather than a trading expense this multiple relief is avoided.

Pro forma for the adjustment of trading profits

You can now identify taxable revenues and allowable deductions for Schedule D Case I purposes and you are able to allocate these revenues and expenses to periods of account. Finally you will find it helpful to use this pro forma to undertake the adjustment of profits to the Schedule D Case I assessment (Note: figures are for illustration only).

Computation of the Schedule D Case I assessment

	£	£
Net profit per accounts		20,000
Add expenditure in the accounts which is not deductible under Schedule D Case I	3,000	
income taxable under Schedule D Case I not directly credited to the P & L account	1,000	4,000
		24,000
Less income in the accounts which is not taxable under Schedule D Case I	2,000	
expenditure not in the accounts which is deductible under Schedule D Case I	3,000	5,000
Schedule D Case I income		19,000

Activity

Monica's profit and loss account for the year to 31st August 2002 is as follows:

Note			£
Sales			100,000
Less: Cost of sales			40,000
Gross profit			60,000
Add: Bank interest		500	
Profit from sales of plant		300	
Rental income		1,000	1,800
			61,800
Less: Rent and rates		3,000	
Insurance		1,000	
Heating, lighting and power		1,500	
Repairs and renewals	(a)	1,500	
Telephone	(b)	400	
Motor expenses	(c)	500	
Bad debts	(d)	200	
Wages and salaries	(e)	20,000	
Legal fees	(f)	300	
Sundry expenses		1,000	
Interest on a credit card		100	
Depreciation		3,000	32,500
Net Profit			29,300

Notes:
(a) This figure includes £1,000 spent on furnishing a new showroom and £200 redecorating the reception area.
(b) Monica has agreed with the Inspector that 30% of the telephone cost relate to private use.
(c) Monica has agreed with the Inspector that 20% of the motor expenses relate to private use.
(d) Bad debts is made up of £120 trade debt written off and £80 increase in the provision for bad debts.
(e) This figure includes drawings of £8,000.
(f) The legal fees related to the purchase of plant and machinery.

You are required: to determine the adjusted profit for Schedule D Case I for the year to 31st August 2002.

Feedback

	£	£
Net profit per the accounts		29,300
Add: Disallowed expenditure		
Drawings	8,000	
Capital expenditure	1,000	
Telephone 400 × 30%	120	
Motor expenses 500 × 20%	100	
General provision for bad debts	80	
Legal fees	300	
Depreciation	3,000	12,600
		41,900
Less: Non-trading income		
Rental income	1,000	
Bank	500	
Profit from sales of plant	300	(1,800)
Schedule D Case I profit		40,100

Activity

Roger Riviere

Roger Riviere is a self-employed wholesale clothing distributor who commenced trading on 1st July 1997. His summarised accounts for the year ended 30th June 2002 are:

	£	£
Sales (1)		400,000
Opening stock (2)	40,000	
Purchases	224,000	
	264,000	
Closing stock (2)	(32,000)	232,000
Gross profit		168,000
Wages and national insurance (3)		52,605
Rent and business rates		31,140
Repairs and renewals (4)		3,490
Miscellaneous expenses (5)		665
Taxation (Roger's income tax)		15,590
Bad debts (6)		820
Legal expenses (7)		1,060
Depreciation		570
Loss on sale of office furniture		60
Transport costs		4,250
Interest (8)		990
Motor car running expenses (Roger's car) (9)		2,000
Lighting and heating		1,250
Sundry expenses (all allowable)		710
Relocation expenditure (10)		2,400
Net profit		50,400

Figures in brackets refer to notes to the accounts.
Notes to accounts:

1. Sales include £500 reimbursed by Roger's family for clothing taken from stock. This reimbursement represented cost price.
2. Stock. The basis of both opening and closing stock valuations was 'lower of cost or market value' less a contingency reserve of 50%.
3. Wages. Included in wages are Roger's drawing of £50 per week, his national insurance contributions of £320 for the year and wages and national insurance contributions in respect of his wife totalling £11,750. His wife worked full-time in the business as a secretary.
4. Repairs and renewals. The charge includes £3,000 for fitting protective covers over the factory windows and doors to prevent burglary.

5.

Miscellaneous expenses	£
Theft of money by employee	65
Political donation to Green Party	100
Gifts of 100 'Riviere' calendars	500
	665

6.

Bad debts:	£	£
Trade debt written off		720
Loan to former employee written off		250
Provision for bad debts (2% of debtors)	450	
Less: Opening provision	(600)	
		(150)
		820

7.

Legal expenses:	£
Defending action in respect of alleged faulty goods	330
Costs in connection with lease of new larger premises	250
Successful appeal against previous year's income tax assessment	200
Defending Roger in connection with speeding offence	190
Debt collection	90
	(1,060)

8.   Interest

	£
Bank overdraft interest (business account)	1,020
Interest on overdue tax	130
Interest credited on National Savings Bank ordinary account (see note 11)	(160)
	990

9. Motor car running expenses. The Inland Revenue have agreed that one-third of Roger's mileage is private. Included in the charge is £65 for a speeding fine incurred by Roger whilst delivering goods to a customer.

10. Relocation expenditure. The expenditure was incurred in transferring the business to a new and larger premises.

11. National Savings Bank, ordinary account. The account had been opened on 1st May 1997 and interest had been credited as follows:

	£
31st December 2001	110
31st December 2002	160
31st December 2003	180

The following information is provided:

1. Capital allowances for the year to 30th June 2002 are £480.
2. Roger was born on 8th April 1968 and always pays the maximum permitted personal pension contribution.

You are required:

(a) to prepare a profit adjustment in respect of the accounting period to 30th June 2002 showing the Schedule Case I adjusted profit.

(13 marks)

(b) To calculate the Class 4 national insurance contributions payable for 2002/03 (using the data provided)

(1 mark)

(c) To prepare an estimate for Roger of the income tax payable for 2002/03 and to advise him when the tax will become due for payment.

(8 marks)
(Total: 22 marks)

(based on ACCA Tax Framework Pilot Paper)

Feedback

(a) **Roger Riviere**

Profit adjustment statement year ended 30th June 2002

	£	£
Net profit per accounts		50,400
(1) Sales – Goods for own use	333	
(3) Wages – Roger's drawings	2,600	
Roger's NIC	320	
(4) Repairs and renewals		
Capital cost of fitting covers	3,000	
(5) Miscellaneous:		
Political donation	100	
Taxation	15,590	
(6) Bad debts:		
Loan to former employee	250	
(7) Legal expenses:		
Cost in connection with lease of		
new and larger premises	250	
Cost in connection tax appeal	200	
Defending Roger in connection		
with speeding offence	190	
Depreciation	570	
Loss on sale of office furniture	60	
(8) Interest		
Interest on overdue tax	130	
(9) Motor car running expenses		
Fine	65	
1/3 of remaining expenses	645	

(10) Re-location expenditure	2,400	
		26,703

Less		
Capital allowances	480	
(2) Stock – (difference increased by 50%)	8,000	
(6) Bad Debts – Reduction in general provision	150	
(8) NSB interest (not taxed under schedule D Case I)	160	(8,790)
Schedule D Case I profit		68,313

(b) Class 4 National insurance contributions
7% × (£30,420 – £4,615) = £1,806.35 (maximum payable)

(c) Roger Riviere
Computation of income tax liability 2002/03

	Savings £	Non-savings £	Total £
Adjusted Schedule Case I profit		68,313	68,313
Personal pension contributions			
(17.5% × 68,313)		(11,954)	(11,954)
		56,359	56,359
Bank interest (180 – 70)	110		110
Statutory Total Income	110	56,359	56,359
Personal allowance		(4,615)	(4,615)
Taxable income	110	51,744	51,854

Tax Due:		
Non-savings:	1,920 @ 10%	192.00
	27,980 @ 22%	6,155.60
	21,844 @ 40%	8,737.60
Savings	110 @ 40%	44.00
Tax due/liability		15,129.20

Workings
1. Goods taken for Roger's own use must be included at the selling price less cost of sales.

	£
Sales £500 × 400/240	833
Less cost of sales	500
Profit	333

Basis of assessment

Tax is raised for individuals for fiscal years (6 April to following 5 April). These are called 'Assessment Years'. For employed people it is easy to assign their income to these periods to calculate their income tax liability. For self-employed people paying tax under Schedule D Case I or II, however, this is not quite so easy because their income is based on their accounts, as we have just seen in the previous section. Accounts are produced in periods usually, but not always, of twelve months in length. These periods may start and finish at different point during the year to the fiscal year, as suits the business. To perform tax computations for self-employed people we therefore need rules for how to allocate their income to tax years.

In this section we will discuss how these rules operate in the UK at present. These rules are called the 'current year basis' and were introduced in 1998/99 for all unincorporated businesses as part of the self-assessment regime.

Current year basis

As was mentioned in Chapter 4, the normal basis of assessment for unincorporated businesses at present is the current year basis. Under the current year regime the general rule is that the profits arising in the tax year will be assessed in the tax year (ICTA 1988 s60(1)). This is sometimes termed the actual basis because the actual profits arising in the tax year form the basis of assessment for the tax year. In particular, the profits in the tax year in which the business commenced will be taxed on the actual basis (ICTA 1988 s61(1)). However, if a sole trader or partnership uses an annual accounting date which is not 5th April the basis of assessment of a fiscal year will be the 12 months to the accounting date which falls in the fiscal year (ICTA 1988 s60(2)). Since few businesses will use 5th April as an accounting date the accounting period ended in the fiscal year will normally form the basis period for the fiscal year.

Activity

For each of the following annual accounting dates state the fiscal year for which they will form the basis period.

(a) 30th June 2000
(b) 31st August 1999
(c) 30th November 2002
(d) 31st January 2001
(e) 31st March 2004
(f) 30th April 1999.

Feedback

The fiscal years for which these accounts form the basis period are:

(a) 2000/01
(b) 1999/00
(c) 2002/03
(d) 2000/01
(e) 2003/04
(f) 1999/00

There are some circumstances in which the normal basis of assessment cannot be applied. These usually fall in the opening and closing years of a business trading or when the business decides to change its accounting date. We will consider each of these circumstances now.

Assessments in the early years of trading

The basis of assessment for the commencement year, that is the fiscal year in which the taxpayer begins to trade, is the profits which arose in the fiscal year (ICTA 1988 s61 (1)) – an actual basis calculation .

If, in the second fiscal year, the accounting date falling in that year is less than 12 months from the commencement date, the basis of assessment is the profits arising in the first 12 months of trading (ICTA 1988 s61 (2)). If the accounting date falling in that year is at least 12 months from the commencement date the basis of assessment is the profits arising in the 12 months to the accounting date (ICTA 1988 s62 (2)). If the first period of account is so long that there is no accounting date in the second year of assessment the basis of assessment is the profits arising in the fiscal year (ICTA 1988 s61 (2)).

The basis of assessment in the third fiscal year will be the period of account ending in the year provided that the second fiscal year contains an accounting date. If this is not the case the basis of assessment is the profits arising in the 12 months to the accounting date in the third year.

All subsequent years, apart from the year of cessation, will be taxed on the current year basis (ICTA s60 (3)).

The following diagram illustrates these rules.

Current Year Opening Rules

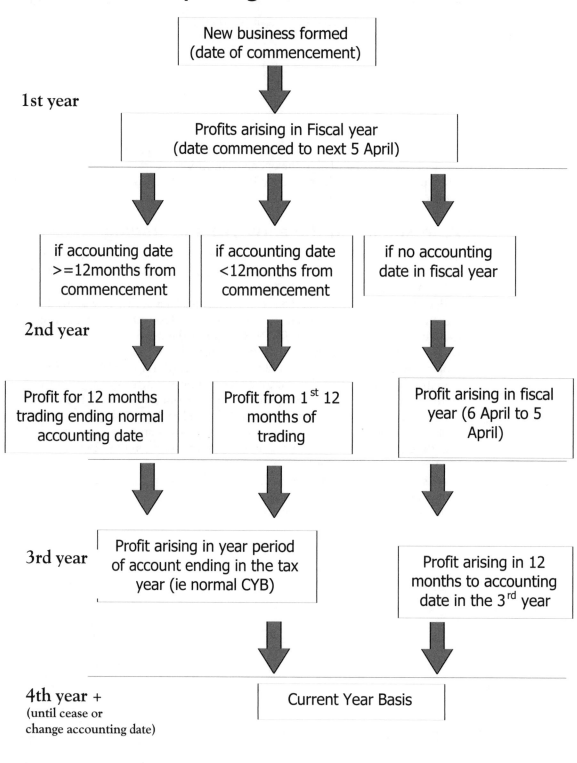

It is likely that some profits will be taxed more than once in the early years of trading. Overlap profits are the amount of profits or gains which are included in the computations for two successive years of assessment (ICTA 1988 s63A (5)). The overlap period is the number of days in the period in which overlap profits arose (ICTA 1988 s63A (5)). We will look at what is done with these double taxed profits later in this section.

Activity

Daniel, Peter, Laura and Rachel graduated in June 2000 from Birmingham Business School and they each decided to become self-employed. From the following details identify the basis periods for each of them for their first four years of assessment.

- Daniel began to trade on 1st July 2000 and drew up accounts to 5th April 2001 and 5th April thereafter.
- Peter also began to trade on 1st July 2000 but drew up accounts to 30th June 2001 and 30th June thereafter.
- Laura also began to trade on 1st July 2000 but elected to draw up accounts to 31st May 2001and 31st May thereafter.
- Rachel didn't begin to trade until 1st January 2001 and then produced accounts to 30th April 2002 and 30th April thereafter.

Feedback

Daniel

Fiscal year	Basis period	Explanation
2000/01	9 months to 5/4/01	Actual basis for year of commencement
2001/02	year to 5/4/02	12 months to the accounting date
2002/03	year to 5/4/03	12 months following previous basis period (CYB)
2003/04	year to 5/4/04	12 months following previous basis period(CYB)

Peter

Fiscal year	Basis period	Explanation
2000/01	9 months to 5/4/01	Actual basis for year of commencement
2001/02	year to 30/6/01	12 months to the accounting date
2002/03	year to 30/6/02	12 months following previous basis period (CYB)
2003/04	year to 30/6/03	12 months following previous basis period (CYB)

Laura

Fiscal year	Basis period	Explanation
2000/01	9 months to 5/4/01	Actual basis for year of commencement
2001/02	year to 30/6/01	First 12 months
2002/03	12 months to 31/5/02	12 months to the accounting date
2003/04	12 months to 31/5/03	12 months following previous basis period (CYB)

Rachel

Fiscal year	Basis period	Explanation
2000/01	3 months to 5/4/01	Actual basis for year of commencement
2001/02	year to 5/4/02	Actual basis
2002/03	year to 30/4/02	12 months to the accounting date
2003/04	year to 30/4/03	12 months following previous basis period

These four examples illustrate most of the possibilities in the early years of trading. All profits used to calculate Schedule D Case I and II income should be apportioned to the relevant basis periods using the rules outlined above. Strictly speaking, calculations should be performed on the basis of the number of days in the period, however, the Inland Revenue will usually accept a 'nearest month' calculation provided this is the same calculation each year.

Activity

For each of Daniel, Peter, Laura and Rachel calculate the overlap periods, if any.

Feedback

Daniel
No period forms part of the basis period of more than one year of assessment and hence Daniel does not have an overlap period.

Peter
The nine-month period from 1st July 2000 to 5th April 2001 is part of the basis period for 2000/01 and 2001/02 and hence is an overlap period. To calculate the overlap profits find 9/12 of the profits for the year to 30th June 2001.

Laura
Like Peter the nine-month period from 1st July 2000 to 5th April 2001 is part of the basis period for 2000/01 and 2001/02 and hence is an overlap period. In addition the month of June 2001 is part of the basis period for 2001/02 and 2002/03 hence is also an overlap period.

Rachel
The 11-month period from 1st May 2001 to 5th April 2002 is part of the basis period for 2001/02 and 2002/03 and hence is an overlap period.

Assessments in the closing years of trading

Where a sole trader or partnership ceases to trade in a year of assessment other than the commencement year, the basis period for the year of cessation will begin immediately after the end of the basis period for the preceding year of assessment and end on the date on which the business is permanently discontinued (ICTA 1988 s63). This rule applies even if the final accounting period is less than 12 months long.

If a business only trades for a few years and a particular year of assessment falls under both the opening year rules and the closing year rules, the closing year rules takes precedence.

Before you can determine the basis periods in the year of cessation you need to know one more thing. If a business has more than one accounting date in the fiscal year the legislation treats the latest of the accounting dates as the accounting date for tax purposes (ICTA 1988 s60(5)).

Activity

Kathy had been in business for many years, making up accounts to 30th April, when she ceased to trade on 31st March 2003. Her adjusted profits for the final three accounting periods were:

	£
Year ended 30.4.01	42,000
Year ended 30.4.02	44,000
Period ended 31.3.03	40,000

Calculate the Schedule D Case I assessments for the final two years of assessment.

Feedback

The final year of assessment is 2002/03 and hence the penultimate year of assessment is 2001/02.

Fiscal year	Basis period	Schedule D Case I assessment
2001/02	year to 30.4.02	£42,000
2002/03	23 months from 1.5.01 to 31.3.03	£84,000 (£44,000 + £40,000)

Activity

Toby began trading on 1st August 1998 and made up accounts to 31st July each year.
State the basis periods for his last two years if he ceases to trade with the following set of accounts (assuming the closing year rules do not change):

(a) 6 months to 31st January 1999
(b) year to 31st July 1999
(c) year to 31st July 2010
(d) 10 months to 30th June 2010
(e) 21 months to 30th April 2010.

Feedback

(a) Because trade begins and ceases in 1998/99 the basis period for 98/99 is the only set of accounts of the business, that is the six months to 31st January 1999.

(b) The business ceases to trade in the second year of assessment. Hence the basis periods are:

1998/99	Actual	1.8.98–5.4.99
1999/00	Actual	6.4.98–31.7.99
(c) 2009/10	Current year	y/e 31.7.09
2010/11	End of previous basis period to date of cessation	1.8.09–31.7.10
(d) 2009/10	Current year	y/e 31.7.09
2010/11	End of previous basis period to date of cessation	1.8.09–30.6.10
(e) 2009/10	12 months to normal accounting date	y/e 31.7.09
2010/11	End of previous basis period to date of cessation	1.8.09–30.4.10

Relief for overlap profits

Remember that under the current year rules the basis of assessment in which the business ceases to trade is the final accounting period. Because some profits are taxed more than once in the opening years the Inland Revenue gives some relief by way of overlap relief. There are two situations in which overlap relief can be claimed. Relief can be claimed in the fiscal year in which the business changes its accounting date provided that this results in the assessment of a period which is more than 12 months long. The details of this relief are beyond the scope of this text. The second occasion on which relief can be claimed is the fiscal year in which the business ceases to trade. If the business does change its accounting date and claims overlap relief, any unused relief can be carried forward to be used when the business ceases to trade (ICTA 1988 s63A(3)). When overlap relief is given in the year of cessation the maximum relief is equal to the overlap profits.

Activity

Jim commenced trading on 1st January 1997 and made up accounts to 31st December each year. He ceased to trade on 31st December 2002. His tax adjusted profits are:

Period	Assessment	£
y/e 31.12.97	48,000	
y/e 31.12.98	24,000	
y/e 31.12.99	36,000	
y/e 31.12.00	40,000	
y/e 31.12.01	36,000	
y/e 31.12.02	48,000	

Feedback

The assessments are:

Fiscal year	Basis period	Assessment £	Note
96/97	1.1.97–5.4.97	12,000	(i)
97/98	y/e 31.12.97	48,000	(ii)
98/99	y/e 31.12.98	24,000	
99/00	y/e 31.12.99	36,000	
00/01	y/e 31.12.00	40,000	
01/02	y/e 31.12.01	36,000	
02/03	y/e 31.12.02	36,000	(iii)

Notes
(i)   The profits are time apportioned £48,000 × 3/12.
(ii) The overlap profits are £12,000 (3/12 × £48,000).
(iii) The taxable profits of £48,000 are reduced by the overlap profits of
      £12,000.

You can now determine the Schedule D Case I assessment for a fiscal year. Now you need to be able to calculate the capital allowances available for a fiscal year.

Change of Accounting Date

Once a business is established it will normally produce accounts on an annual basis. This matches well with the rules you have learned so far for determining what tax is due on these accounts each year as we have assumed most accounting periods will be exactly twelve months long. Although this is normal, it is not required and a business may change it's accounting date at any time, and for a variety of reasons. If it does this it will create at least one accounting period that will not be twelve months long. In this section we review how this situation should be handled for tax purposes.

When a trader wishes to change their accounting date they must inform the Inland Revenue. This must be by the end of the January following the tax year in which the change was made (e.g. by 31 January 2004 if you change your accounting date for the 2002/03 tax year). No change of accounting date is allowed for tax purposes that creates a period of longer than eighteen months. Also, no change of accounting date should normally have been made in the previous five years (although a second change can be possible if it can be justified on commercial, rather than tax saving, grounds).

When a business changes its accounting date it will therefore result in one of the following for any tax year:

a) at least one accounting period of less than twelve months
b) an accounting period of more than twelve months
c) no accounting period in the fiscal year.

We will review how the tax computation is affected in each of these cases.

a) Short Period of Account

If a change in accounting dates produces a short accounting 'year' in the tax year, the basis period for that year becomes the twelve months to the new accounting date. This will create overlap profits for the common part the period that now falls into both fiscal years. This should be added to any overlap profits created when the business started and carried forward for later relief.

b) Long Period of Account

If a change of accounting date produces a long period of account (i.e. more than the usual twelve months) the basis period for that year ends on the new accounting date running from the start of the old basis period (i.e. it will exceed twelve months long).

There will not be any overlap profits in this situation to worry about but more than twelve months of profits are taxed in one fiscal year. To compensate for this the business can use up any overlap profits it is carrying equivalent to the length of the extra period beyond twelve months (i.e. if the long period is the maximum allowed eighteen months, the business can get back six months worth of any overlap profits it is carrying forward).

Activity

Cedric has overlap profits of 6 months totalling £6,800 from the opening years of his business. In the 2002/03 tax year he decides to move his normal accounting date from 1 September each year to 1 December. How will this affect his tax computations assuming his taxable profits are as follows:

Year to 1 September 2001	£63,100
Fifteen months to 1 December 2002	£98,200

Feedback

His profits for the 2001/02 year will be as normal – i.e. (1.9.00 – 30.8.01) £63,100. The change in accounting date produces a long period in fiscal year 2002/03 of fifteen months (1.9.01 to 30.11.02) for a taxable profit of £98,200. This can however be reduced by three months of the six months of overlap profits he is carrying forward, worth £3,400 (3/6 × £6,800) leaving a Schedule D Case I taxable profit for the year of £94,800 (£98,200 – £3,400).

The remaining unrelieved overlap profits of £3,400 (3/6 × £6,800) are carried forward for relief later. This may be when the business ceases or if Cedric decides to change his accounting date again in the future.

c) No Accounting Period in the Fiscal Year

If the change of accounting date results in no accounting year end in the fiscal year then an artificial basis period is used by deducting twelve months from the new accounting date. The basis period in the missing fiscal year is then determined by this artificial date.

This will create overlap profits with those that were assessed in the previous fiscal year. Overlap profits created this way are added to any brought forward from before just as explained for short periods of account as above.

Summary

This chapter looks at Schedule D Cases I and II. It outlines how to distinguish between a trading activity and an activity which is carried out as a non-trading activity, maybe as a hobby. It outlines how the 'Badges of Trade' are used in practice for this assessment given we have no legal definition for trading. As accounting profits for the business are the foundations for Schedule D Cases I and II assessments, it then focuses on how to adjust the accounting figures to arrive at amounts that will be acceptable for the tax computation. This involves manipulation of both receipts and expenses from the accounts. A detailed worked example is then provided to illustrate these principles in practice.

This chapter concludes with an examination of the basis of assessment for these cases. This includes looking at how the normal rules differ, during the opening and closing few years of a business existence and what happens when the accounting date is moved.

Question

See end of Chapter 6 for questions on Schedule D Case I and II tax computations.

6 Capital Allowances and Trading Losses

Introduction

This chapter continues the subject discussed in Chapter 5 – the taxation of unincorporated businesses. In this chapter we examine how the tax treatment for capital assets is applied as capital allowances. We will also examine how trading losses are treated for unincorporated businesses.

At the end of this chapter you will be able to:

- undertake capital allowance computations
- calculate the tax payable, or repayable, when an unincorporated business incurs trading losses
- offer simple tax planning advice to sole traders.

This chapter concludes with a number of examination style questions that can be used to test your knowledge of this chapter and chapter 5.

Capital allowances

You will remember that we saw the last chapter that depreciation is not an allowable expense for tax purposes. Tax relief for capital expenditure is instead given by means of capital allowances This ensures consistent treatment of capital assets for tax purposes, rather than allowing multiple possible treatments if accounting depreciation policies were used in tax computations. It also allows for special tax treatment of particular assets, asset groups or types of company as Government policy may require. We will see how the current special treatments are applied in this section.

The legislation relating to capital allowances is contained in the Capital Allowances Act 2001 (CAA 2001) which became applicable for chargeable periods ending on or after 1st April 2001 for corporation tax and 6th April 2001 for income tax. Capital allowances are available to businesses on certain capital expenditures. Under the old rules capital allowances were deducted from the Schedule D Case I income of individuals. Under the new, current year basis rules, capital allowances are an allowable expense for tax purposes. This measure has brought the rules for income tax in line with corporation tax. Capital allowances continue to be an allowable deduction when calculating the Schedule D Case I income of a company.

Capital allowances are given for years of assessment These match the accounting year of the business in usual years of operation. In other years where the accounting period is not twelve months long the available capital allowances must be reduced/expanded to the same length as the accounting period.

As we will see in Chapter 9, the chargeable periods for companies are calculated differently to unincorporated businesses. A company can not have a tax year of more than twelve months as an unincorporated business can under some circumstances (such as when it changes its accounting date).

The basis period for a year of assessment is used to determine the fiscal year in which additions and disposals will be incorporated into the capital allowances computation.

The capital allowances given each year are a fixed percentage of the value of the capital asset, or pool of assets, in question. They are usually given on a reducing balance basis. The annual amount of capital allowances allowable as deductions from Schedule D Case I profits are called writing down allowances (WDA). Writing down allowances are not available in the year in which a business ceases to trade. However, balancing allowances or charges are calculated instead. We will examine both the usual procedure for capital allowances and the treatment of balancing allowances or charges in this section.

For expenditure on capital assets to be eligible for capital allowances they must fall into one of these categories:

- plant and machinery
- industrial buildings
- patents
- know-how, and
- agricultural buildings and works.

The first two categories are the most common and so we will concentrate on these in this chapter. The others will be commented upon at the end of this section.

Plant and machinery

The CAA 2001 does not contain a definition of plant and machinery and so it is necessary to look to case law for guidance.

There has been a considerable amount of case law on the subject. One of the most important is *Yarmouth v France* (1887) in which the status of a horse was questioned. Lindley LJ concluded:

> There is no definition of plant in the Act: but in its original sense, it includes whatever apparatus is used by a businessman for carrying on his business, not his stock-in-trade which he buys or makes for sale; but all goods and chattels, fixed or moveable, live or dead, which he keeps for permanent employment in his business.

A number of subsequent cases refined the definition. In *Wimpey International Ltd v Warland* (1988) three types of asset were excluded from the definition of plant and machinery:

- assets which are not used for carrying on the business
- assets with a useful life of less than two years
- assets which form part of the setting in which the business was carried on, as opposed to assets actively used in the business.

This judgment is the result of a number of earlier cases. In would be useful for us to review some of the more interesting ones.

The last requirement is referred to as the 'function v setting' test and has generated a considerable number of cases as it can be a difficult test to apply in reality. In *CIR v Barclay Curle & Co* (1969) the costs of building a dry dock was held to be expenditure on plant and machinery because the dock played an active part in the operation of the company's trade. In *Cooke v Beach Station Caravans Ltd* (1974) the costs of excavating and installing a swimming pool were held to be expenditure on plant and machinery because the swimming pool performed a function, that of giving buoyancy and enjoyment to the swimmers.

In *Benson v Yard Arm Club* (1978) a ship which was being used as a floating restaurant was held to be ineligible for capital allowances because it failed the functional test. However, in *CIR v Scottish and Newcastle Breweries Ltd* (1982) it was held that light fittings, decor and murals performed the function of creating an atmosphere and so were plant. In contrast, in *Wimpey International Ltd v Warland* (1988) a raised floor was held not to be plant as it was considered setting, despite making the restaurant attractive to customers.

In another case, *Carr v Sayer* (1992), quarantine kennels were held not to be plant despite being purpose built.

In the case of *Brown v Burnley Football and Athletic Co Ltd* (1980) expenditure on a new stand was held not to be plant because it did not perform a direct function in the business, just provided the setting. You will remember from the last chapter that Burnley Football and Athletic Co Ltd had also failed to claim the expenditure as a repair because the entire stand was replaced. Today such expenditure would be allowed under the special provisions stated below.

The following expenditure is automatically deemed to be plant and machinery:

- expenditure on equipment in order to comply with fire regulations for a building occupied by the trader
- expenditure on thermal insulation in an industrial building
- expenditure in order to comply with statutory safety requirements for sports grounds
- expenditure on computer software.

In order to claim capital allowances a person carrying on a trade must incur capital expenditure on the provision of machinery or plant wholly and exclusively for the purposes of the trade and the machinery or plant belongs to him. The extent to which assets can be described as plant and machinery is highlighted in *Munby v Furlong* (1977) when a barrister successfully argued that his law library was plant because it was the apparatus used for carrying on his business.

For each chargeable period, apart from a period which ends with the cessation of trade, for which the qualifying expenditure exceeds any disposal value, a writing down allowance is available equal to 25% of the excess. This means that approximately 95% of the value of each asset is relieved over eight years. This allowance is reduced proportionately for short basis periods and extended for long basis periods.

First-year allowances

In his first budget, in July 1997, the Chancellor reintroduced first-year allowances for small - and medium-sized companies and those business which would be designated small - or medium-sized if they were incorporated. A business qualifies for the new allowance if in the current or previous year it meets two out of the three criteria set out in the Companies Act 1985. The criteria are:

- turnover must not exceed £11.2m
- total assets must not exceed £5.6m
- total number of employees must not exceed 250.

Qualifying expenditure in the 12 months to 1st July 1998 attracted a first-year allowance of 50% of the cost of the asset. Qualifying expenditure from then on has attracted a first-year allowance of 40% of the cost of the asset. Initially, this allowance was available for the twelve months between 1st July 1998 and 1st July 1999. It was then extended to 1st July 2000 and in the 2000 Budget was turned into a permanent allowance.

The first year allowance will not be available for expenditure on plant and machinery for leasing, cars, ships and railway assets. Qualifying expenditure on assets which are deemed to be long-life assets were eligible for a 12% first-year allowance in the 12 months to 1st July 1998 only. This has not been extended as for other plant and machinery.

A normal writing down allowance is not available in the same year as the first-year allowance. As the first year allowance is more than is normally available for an annual writing down allowance, the first year allowance therefore takes priority. However, unlike normal capital allowances, they are not scaled to the length of the accounting period when it is not the usual 12 months long. The full, standard, first year allowance rate is claimed irrespective of the length of the accounting period.

Capital allowances pro forma

As we discussed in Chapter 4 in relation to the overall personal tax computation, if you know the way to lay out a capital allowances computation you will be able to calculate the capital allowances for a business with relative ease. Note that this is the way we have laid out the answers to activities in this section and try to use it wherever you do a capital allowance calculation.

Capital allowances on the general pool for plant and machinery (numbers given are just for illustration).

		Pool	Allowances
Written down value b/f		100,000	
Additions not qualifying for a FYA		10,000	
		110,000	
Disposals		20,000	
		90,000	
Written down allowance (90,000 × 25%)		(22,500)	22,500
		67,500	
Additions qualifying for a FYA			
Plant	10,000		
FYA 40%	(4,000)	6,000	4,000
Written down value c/f		73,500	
Allowances for the tax year			26,500

With the exception of cars costing more than £12,000, leased assets, long-life assets and assets with a private use element, all qualifying capital expenditure is aggregated into a pool from which the disposal value is deducted and the writing down allowance is then calculated. This means that usually items of capital expenditure are not treated separately for capital allowance calculations. The taxpayer may also be able to elect for some assets to be de-pooled. We will study how these exceptions are handled in practice, later in this section. We will first examine how the general pool is applied.

Take note of the order in which adjustments are made the value of the capital allowance pool in the above proforma. This order matters to ensure you calculate the correct writing down allowances each year.

Note that additions not receiving first year allowances, and disposals are dealt with before this year's main writing down allowance calculation is performed. This order implies that a full year's allowance is given in the year of acquisition of a capital asset, and none in the year of disposal – both irrespective of when the assets were bought or sold in the year.

The disposal value removed from the pool when as asset is disposed of is equal to the lower of the net proceeds of disposal, including any insurance money received, and the capital expenditure incurred on the acquisition of the machinery or plant.

All or part of the writing down allowance entitlement for any given year can be waived by the taxpayer. Any amount waived simply has the effect of increasing the balance of qualifying expenditure which is eligible for capital allowances in future years. Clearly it is usually in the interest of the business to claim tax relief as quickly as possible but this may not always be the case such as if the business makes a loss that year. Rather than adding to this loss, the business may decide instead to carry forward their capital allowances to use up against profit in later years.

Activity

List reasons that might lead a business to waive or reduce their writing down allowance claim for a tax year.

Feedback

A business might waive the writing down allowance on the following occasions:

- if taxable profits would be reduced to such an extent that it would not be possible for the taxpayer to use all of his or her personal allowances
- if the taxpayer believed that his or her marginal rate of tax would increase significantly in future years.

Activity

Mulder, a small sole trader, prepares accounts to 31st December annually.
His general pool of unrelieved expenditure on plant and machinery brought forward on 1st January 2002 was £20,000.

During the year to 31st December 2002 the following transactions took place.

			£
31st March	Bought	Plant	8,000
31st August	Bought	Plant	20,000
31st October	Sold	Plant	5,000 (originally cost £10,000)

Calculate the capital allowances for the year ended 31st December 2002.

Feedback

		Pool	Allowances
Written down value b/f		20,000	
Sale/proceeds		(5,000)	
		15,000	
WDA 25%		(3,750)	3,750
		11,250	
Additions qualifying for a FYA			
Plant (31.3 and 31.8)	28,000		
FYA 40%	(12,000)	16,000	12,000
Written down value c/f		27,250	
Total allowances for year			15,750

100% First Year allowances

As part of a range of measures to support wider use of the Internet and related technologies the Chancellor announced several new capital allowance rule changes in the 2000 Budget. For three years starting 1st April 2000, 100% first year allowances will be available for investments in information and communication technologies by small enterprises (i.e. not available to medium or large businesses). These will include purchases of computers, software and internet-enabled mobile phones.

The 100% first year allowances means all of the cost of these capital purchases can be taken as a tax relief in the year in which they are purchased. This means that these capital purchases will have the same impact on total tax due as revenue expenditure items.

Activity

Philip, who runs a small printing business, buys a computer and software costing £2,500 on 1st May 2002. He also purchased a delivery van for £5,500 on 19th June 2002. His normal accounting year runs to 1st July each year and the brought forward written down value of his capital assets at 1st July 2001 was £15,000. No other purchases or sales of assets occurred in the year. Calculate the capital allowances available to Philip for 2002/03.

Feedback

	Pool (£)	Allowances (£)
Written down value b/f	15,000	
WDA 25%	(3,750)	3,750
Additions qualifying for FYA		
Computer and software 2,500		
FYA (100%) (2,500)	–	2,500
Delivery van 5,500		
FYA (40%) (2,200)	3,300	2,200
Written down value c/f	14,550	
Allowances for tax year		8,450

In the 2001 Budget the Chancellor also extended this 100% first year allowance availability to energy-saving plant and machinery by businesses of any size. For expenditures on certain plant and machinery on or after 1st April 2001 (for companies) or 6th April 2001 (for individual tax payers) products on a designated list will attract 100% allowances in their year of purchase. To see this list you should visit the Department of Environment, Transport and Regions website at http://www.eca.gov.uk. The arrangements under which these rules are operated is called the Enhanced Capital Allowances Scheme.

The scheme will apply initially to the following types of technology:-

- boilers and add ons
- motors
- variable speed drives
- refrigeration equipment
- thermal screens
- lighting
- pipe insulation.

As part of the 2002 Budget, five new categories have been added to this list:

- heat pumps
- radiant and warm air heaters
- solar heaters
- energy efficient refrigeration equipment
- compressor equipment

The scheme applies if these assets are being used in a person's business, and from 17 April 2002 also if they are hired let or leased out for other people's use. Associated costs can also be added to the allowed additions to be claimed, such as installation costs or transportation costs.

If only part of an asset purchased falls into this ECA scheme then the value of that part can be claimed at 100% as a first year allowance and the remainder should be added to the plant and machinery pool and treated as normal.

A further 100% allowance was made available as part of the 2001 Budget on conversions of certain types of property into flats. The conditions that have to be met for these allowances to apply are:

- that the property must have been built before the start of 1980;
- the money is spent on renovating or converting space that is underused or vacant (for at least a year) above shops or other commercial premises;
- the property must not be more than five floors high;
- not part of an extension to the property.

There are also restrictions on what the flats can be used for after conversion. These include that they can only be for short term letting, have separate access to the shop/ground floor premises, be no bigger than four rooms (plus bathroom and kitchen) and not be a high value flat (as determined by the notional rent that could be earned as given in the Finance Bill Sch 19). The flat must also be let to someone unconnected with the person who received the allowances. This allowance is clearly targeted at urban regeneration.

Further extensions to this category of capital allowances were given in the 2002 Budget. They are now also applicable to business expenditure on new (registered after 12 April, 2002) low emission cars (i.e. electric cars or ones that emit not more than 120g/km of carbon dioxide) and on plant and machinery purchased to refuel natural gas or hydrogen fueled vehicles. These new enhanced allowances are available whether these assets are purchased outright, leased or hired.

Long-life assets

The 1996 budget contained proposals to reduce the writing down allowances from 25% to 6% for expenditure on plant and machinery with a working life of more than 25 years. These assets are called long-life assets. This reduced percentage applies to expenditure incurred on or after 26th November 1996.

The Chancellor argued at the time that these rules will bring the tax treatment of such assets more in line with their accounting treatment. Certainly such an intention is in line with the tax treatment of depreciation in many other countries. In practice relatively few businesses have been affected by these changes as few items of plant and machinery are normally considered to have a useful life of 25 years or more.

In addition, the rules only apply to businesses spending more than £100,000 per annum on such long-life assets and the full 25% writing down allowance will continue to be available for expenditure on:

- machinery or plant in a building used wholly or mainly as, or for purposes ancillary to, a dwelling-house, retail shop, showroom, hotel or office
- sea-going ships and railway assets bought before the end of 2010. The tax treatment of expenditure in this category incurred after this date will be reviewed in due course.

In addition, expenditure on long-life assets which is below a *de minimis* limit is not be subject to these rules. The *de minimis* limit for a company will equal £100,000 divided by one plus the number of companies associated with it. The *de minimis* limit also applies to sole traders and partnerships provided that the sole trader or, in the case of a partnership, at least half the partners, devotes substantially the whole of their time to carrying on the business. However, the *de minimis* limit does not apply to expenditure on plant and machinery on which the previous owner received allowances at the reduced rate. As most small, unincorporated businesses will not spend more that £100,000 a year on long life capital assets, these special rules do not normally affect them and their long life assets are therefore in practice normally treated like all other capital assets.

Other pools and private use of assets

If the plant and machinery is only partly used for the purpose of trade the capital allowances and charges described above are reduced by the fraction A/B where A is the proportion of the time during which the asset was used for the purpose of trade while B is the total period of ownership. A separate capital allowances computation must be carried out for each asset with an element of private use. This means you should create a separate column in your proforma for assets with any private usage. Only the business use part of the total capital allowances can be claimed. See the example, Roger, below which illustrates this for you.

Leased assets are aggregated in a separate pool to the general pool (i.e. they also get their own column in the computation). The calculation of the writing down allowances is exactly as for the general pool.

Cars costing less than £12,000 also used to have their own pool. This rule was scrapped in the 2000 Budget and they now are included in the general pool for any purchases made after 6th April 2000 (individuals) or 1st April 2000 (companies).

Cars that cost more than £12,000 are termed expensive motor cars. Such cars are not usually pooled but are the subject of separate computations for each car. The writing down allowance for 'expensive' cars is limited to a maximum of:

- £3,000 or, if the period of use is only part of a year, a pro rata proportion of £3,000, and
- if the person carrying on the trade is regarded as having incurred only a part of the expenditure actually incurred on the provision of the motor car, (such as there being some private usage) a proportionate part only of £3,000 can be claimed. If the period of usage is part only of a year, that proportionate part is also proportionately reduced.

In the 2002 Budget a relaxation on the maximum writing down allowance for expensive cars was given. If the expensive car is a low emission car (emitting less than 120g/km of carbon dioxide) then for all new purchases after 17 April 2002 the maximum allowance will not apply and the full 25% of the value of the car can be claimed.

When the car is disposed of the balancing allowance or charge is calculated in the normal way (see later in this section) and is reduced if there is a private use element as described above.

Cars also do not receive first year allowances.

Activity

Roger has traded for many years making up accounts to 31st December each year. On 31st August 2001 he bought a car for £20,000 and agreed with the Inland Revenue that it was used 75% of the time for business purposes. He sold the car on 28th February 2003 for £12,000. Determine the capital allowances which can be claimed on the car.

Feedback

The capital allowances computation is:

	Expensive car £	Allowances £
2001/02		
Acquisition	20,000	
WDA	3,000 × 75%	2,250
WDV c/f	17,000	
2002/03		
Proceeds	(12,000)	
	5,000	
Balancing allowance	(5,000) × 75%	3,750

The maximum writing down allowance is £3,000 and this is the amount by which the tax written down value is reduced by. However, because the car is only used 75% for business purposes, Roger can only claim 75% of the allowance.

This means that £750 (£3,000 × 25%) of the writing down allowance is permanently lost, but note the running balance of the car's written down value is reduced by the full writing down allowance, even though only the business part can be claimed.

There are also restrictions on the tax relief available if an expensive car is hired rather than bought. If a car, which cost more than £12,000 when new, is hired the expenditure allowed for tax purposes equals the cost when new reduced in the proportion which £12,000 together with one half of the excess bears to the cost when new. Hence the maximum allowable deduction from profits when leasing an expensive car is

$$\frac{£12,000 + \frac{1}{2}(P - £12,000)}{P} \times R$$

where P is the cost of the car when new and R is the annual rental cost.

Short-life assets

The taxpayer may elect for certain machinery and plant to be treated as a short-life asset and de-pooled (i.e. given its own pool like expensive cars above) in order for the balancing allowance to be claimed when the asset is disposed of. This is a useful concession as it means the full allowances for the asset can be claimed rather than the taxpayer having to settle for only 25% of it, on a reducing balance, each year as part of the normal pool of plant and machinery.

The election must be made not more than two years after the end of the chargeable period, or its basis period, in which the capital expenditure was incurred and is irrevocable. However, if the asset is not disposed of in a chargeable period ending on or before the fourth anniversary of the end of the chargeable period in which the cost of the asset was first recorded then the tax written down value of the asset is transferred into the general pool at the beginning of the next chargeable period. From then on it will receive the normal treatment for other capital assets and the advantage of gaining a balancing allowance (if applicable) early is lost.

Activity

Scully prepares accounts to 30th June each year. The balance on her general pool of qualified expenditure at 1st July 2000 is £10,000.

On 30th March 2001 she bought two machines for £4,000 each. Scully made a short-life election for both the machines. One machine was sold for £500 on 30th April 2003 and the other was not sold for several years.

Calculate the capital allowances for the years ended: 30th June 2001 to 30th June 2006.

Feedback

		Pool £	Short-life assets 1 £	Short-life assets 2 £	Allowances £
Y/e 30.6.2001					
WDV b/f @ 1.7.2000		10,000			
WDA 25%		(2,500)			2,500
		7,500			
Machine 1					
Cost	£4,000				
FYA 40%	(1,600)		2,400		1,600
Machine 2					
Cost	£4,000				
FYA 40%	(1,600)			2,400	1,600
					5,700
Y/e 30.6.2002					
WDV b/f @ 1.7.2001		7,500	2,400	2,400	
WDA 25%		(1,875)	(600)	(600)	3,075
Y/e 30.6.2003					
WDV b/f @ 1.7.02		5,625	1,800	1,800	
Disposal proceeds			(500)		
			1,300		
Balancing allowance					1,300
WDA 25%		(1,406)		(450)	1,856
					3,156
Y/e 30.6.04					
WDV b/f @ 1.7.03		4,219		1,350	
WDA 25%		(1,054)		(338)	1,392
Y/e 30.6.05					
WDV b/f @ 1.7.04		3,165		1,012	
WDA 25%		(791)		(253)	1,044
Y/e 30.6.06					
WDV b/f @ 1.7.05		2,374		759	
Transfer of short life asset to qualifying pool		759		(759)	
		3,133			
WDA 25%		(783)			
		2,350			

Note the second machine was transferred to the general pool on the fourth anniversary of the end of the period of account in which it was acquired.

The Act identifies assets which cannot be treated as short-life assets, these are:

- ships
- motor cars, and
- machinery or plant provided for leasing.

Balancing allowances or charges

In the year in which there is a cessation of trade or when a separately pooled item is sold a balancing allowance or charge will usually arise. If the balance of qualifying expenditure exceeds any disposal value a balancing allowance equal to the whole of the excess is given. If the disposal value exceeds the balance of qualifying expenditure a balancing charge equal to the excess will be levied on the taxpayer.

Activity

Catherine retired on 31st December 2002 after trading for many years. On 6th April 2002 the tax written down value of her capital allowances pool was £10,000 and of an expensive car, which was used totally for the purposes of the business, was £4,500. The car had originally cost £12,000.

Catherine sold the plant and machinery for £12,000 and the car for £3,000 when she retired. Calculate the capital allowances and charges for 2002/03.

Feedback

The capital allowances computation is:

	Pool £	Expensive Car £	Allowances £
WDV b/f	10,000	4,500	
Disposal proceeds	(12,000)	(3,000)	
	(2,000)	1,500	
Balancing allowance		(1,500)	1,500
Balancing charge	2,000		(2,000)
Net capital allowances			(500)

Industrial buildings

An industrial building is a building or structure in use for the purposes of:

- a trade carried on in a mill, factory or other similar premises, or
- a transport, dock, inland navigation, water, sewerage, electricity or hydraulic power undertaking, or
- a tunnel, bridge or toll road undertaking, or

- a trade which involves the manufacture or storage of goods or materials, or
- a trade involving working of any mine, oil well or other source of mineral deposits, or ploughing or cultivating land (other than land occupied by the person carrying on the trade) and other agricultural operations on such land, or threshing the crops of another person, or catching or taking fish or shellfish.

A building provided by a person carrying on any of these trades or undertaking for the welfare of workers employed by that person is deemed to be an industrial building.

The legislation specifically excludes from the definition of an industrial building, any building or structure in use as, or as part of, a domestic dwelling, retail shop, showroom, most hotels or office. If the non-qualify part of the building is less than 25% of the cost of the whole building then all the building remains eligible for industrial buildings allowance. If the non-qualifying part is more than 25% of the cost of the whole building then only the relevant percentage relating to the qualifying part of the building can qualify.

A writing down allowance of 4% on a straight line basis is available when the building is brought into use. In order to be eligible for a writing down allowance a person must have an interest in the qualifying building, at the end of the basis period for the chargeable period. When a building is the subject of a long lease the lessee is deemed to be the person having an interest in the building provided that both the lessor and the lessee make an election to that affect. This means the lessee would then receive the capital allowances on the building.

Expenditure incurred on preparing, cutting, tunneling or levelling land in order to prepare the land as a site for the installation of machinery or plant is treated as expenditure on an industrial building for capital allowance purposes.

The writing down allowance is reduced for short basis periods for both income tax and corporation tax purposes.

Industrial buildings and structures, including qualifying hotels and commercial buildings, located in enterprise zones are eligible for an initial allowance of 100% of the cost, including VAT, provided the site was included in the zone not more than ten years before the expenditure. There is no requirement that buildings in an enterprise zone be in use in order to claim the allowance but only the last buyer before the building is brought into use may claim the allowance.

Activity

Bob has traded for many years and makes up accounts to 30th June each year. On 1st January 1998 he bought a new factory for £100,000 which was brought into use on 1st May 1998. Determine the industrial buildings allowance available for 1999/2000, 2000/01, 2001/02 and 2002/03.

Feedback

	Building £	Allowances £
1999/2000		
Cost	100,000	
WDA 4% × Cost	(4,000)	4,000
WDV c/f	96,000	
Allowances available		4,000
2000/01		
WDA 4% × Cost	(4,000)	4,000
WDV c/f	92,000	
Allowances available		4,000
2001/02		
WDA 4% × Cost	(4,000)	4,000
WDV c/f	88,000	
Allowances available		4,000
2002/03		
WDA 4% × Cost	(4,000)	4,000
WDV c/f	84,000	
Allowances available		4,000

If the building was not in use as an industrial building on the last day of the basis period, and was not used for any other purpose, the writing down allowance is still available, provided that the period of disuse is temporary. In practice so long as the building is used as an industrial building at some time in the future the period of disuse will be considered to be temporary. However, if the building is used for a non-industrial purpose a notional writing down allowance continues to be deducted as before but no capital allowance may be claimed by the taxpayer (i.e. just as for private use of assets).

If the asset is disposed of within 25 years of the date on which the building was first used a balancing allowance or charge may arise because for full allowance will not have been used up (as 4% straight line writes off the allowance over 25 years). If there are no proceeds of disposal, or the proceeds do not exceed the residue of the expenditure immediately prior to disposal a balancing allowance equal to the excess of the residue of the expenditure over the proceeds will be given. If the proceeds do exceed the residue of expenditure a balancing charge equal to the amount by which proceeds exceed the residue of expenditure will be made. The next activity illustrates how this calculation is performed.

Activity

Ian has traded for many years and prepares accounts to 31st December each year. On 30th September 1997 he bought an industrial building for £500,000 and brought it into use immediately. He sold it on 31st March 2002 for £600,000 to Diane who makes up accounts to 30th September. Diane brought the building into use immediately. Determine the industrial building allowances available to Ian and Diane.

Feedback

Industrial building allowances are available as follows:

	Building £	Allowances £
Ian		
1997/98		
Cost	500,000	
WDA 4% × Cost	(20,000)	20,000
WDV c/f	480,000	
1998/99		
WDA 4% × Cost	(20,000)	20,000
WDV c/f	460,000	
1999/2000		
WDA 4% × Cost	(20,000)	20,000
WDV c/f	440,000	
2000/01		
WDA 4% ×	(20,000)	20,000
WDV c/f	420,000	
2001/02		
WDA 4% × Cost	(20,000)	20,000
WDV c/f	400,000	
2002/03		
Residue before sale	400,000	
Proceeds (limited to cost)	500,000	
	(100,000)	
Balancing charge	100,000	(100,000)
Diane		
2002/03		
Residue before sale	400,000	
Balancing charge	100,000	
Residue after sale	500,000	

The building has a total tax life of 25 years. Ian owned the building for 4 years six months, leaving a remaining tax life of 20 years six months when Diane bought the building.

The writing down allowance which Diane can claim for each of the next 20 years is £24,390 (£500,000/20.5). In the following year she can claim the final writing down allowance of £12,200 (£500,000 – £24,390 × 20).

Activity

Suppose that in the above activity from 30th September 1998 to 31st May 2000 Ian used the building to run an indoor market rather than using it for industrial purposes. All the other information is unchanged. Determine the industrial building allowances available to Ian and Diane.

Feedback

Industrial building allowances are available as follows:

	Building £	Allowances £
Ian		
1997/98		
Cost	500,000	
WDA 4% × Cost	(20,000)	20,000
WDV c/f	480,000	
1998/99		
Notional WDA 4% × Cost	(20,000)	
WDV c/f	460,000	
1999/2000		
Notional WDA 4% × Cost	(20,000)	
WDV c/f	440,000	
2000/01		
WDA 4% × Cost	(20,000)	20,000
WDV c/f	420,000	
2001/02		
WDA 4% × Cost	(20,000)	20,000
WDV c/f	400,000	
2002/03		
Residue before sale	400,000	
Proceeds (limited to cost)	500,000	
	(100,000)	
Balancing charge	100,000	

The balancing charge is limited to the total allowances given.

Balancing charge		(60,000)
Diane		
2002/03		
Residue before sale	400,000	
Balancing charge	60,000	
Residue after sale	460,000	

The writing down allowance which Diane can claim for each of the next 20 years is £22,439 (£460,000/20.5). In the following year she can claim the final writing down allowance of £11,220 (£460,000 – £22,439 × 20).

Patents

If patent rights are purchased a separate pool is formed on which a writing down allowance of 25% per annum on a reducing balance basis is available provided that the patent rights are used for trading purposes. The rules for balancing allowances and charges are as for the general pool for plant and machinery. If sale proceeds exceed the original cost the deduction from the pool is limited to the original cost, as for plant and machinery, but the excess of proceeds over the original cost is taxed under Schedule D Case VI.

Research and Development

Research and Development expenditure which is not capital expenditure is an allowable deduction from trading profits for tax purposes. Since 1962, scientific research expenditure which is of a capital nature has been eligible for a 100% capital allowance in the year in which the expenditure was incurred. The 2000 Budget introduced changes to these rules to encourage small and medium-sized businesses to engage in more research and development. These included introducing a new tax definition for research and development that matched the accounting definition in Statement of Standard Accounting Practice (SSAP) 13. This broadens the range of activities now eligible for tax relief. Small and medium-sized businesses who engage in research and development under the new definition, are eligible for relief at 150%. That means for every £100 they spend on research or development they can deduct £150 from their trading profit. Any disposal proceeds are deemed to be trading receipts.

The 2002 Budget has extended these generous credits to large companies. They will be entitled to 125% tax credit against their profits on all such expenditure (using the same definition as applies to smaller businesses). This credit is not available for work sub-contracted to others (unless to a University, charity or scientific research organisation), but is available on work sub-contracted to them. Where a large company sub-contracts work to an SME they are entitled to claim the extra 25% also.

Agricultural buildings and works

Capital expenditure on farmhouses, farm buildings, cottages, fences, drainage and similar works is eligible for capital allowances. A writing down allowance of 4% per annum, using the straight line basis, is available from the year in which the expenditure was incurred. This gives agricultural buildings, like industrial buildings, a 25-year tax life.

When an agricultural building is disposed of the writing down allowances in the year of sale is time apportioned for both the seller and the purchaser. For example, if the sale takes place half way through the seller's accounting period he or she will receive half of the annual allowance. If the purchaser has a different year end so that the date of the sale falls only a third of the way through their accounting period they will be entitled to two-thirds of the annual allowances. However, if the seller and buyer make a joint election a balancing allowance/charge can be calculated for the seller in the same way as it is for industrial buildings.

Trading Losses

You can now calculate the Schedule D Case I assessment and the capital allowances for any fiscal year. Finally you need to be able to deal with trading losses.

Calculating a loss is simple. You undertake the adjustments of profits which you practiced earlier in the last chapter and if this calculation produces a negative amount, you have a loss for tax purposes. Losses obviously do not generate a tax bill, but they can also be used to influence past, other present, or even future tax bills as they can be used to relieve profits earned in other periods or related to other schedules. However, a loss can only be relieved once.

A taxpayer who incurs a trading loss has a number of alternative ways of relieving the loss. Some losses are only available in particular circumstances. For example only losses incurred in the first four years of trading can be relieved under s381. Each relief has advantages and drawbacks. The taxpayer will often have to choose between receiving a rebate quickly and maximising the amount of relief which can be claimed. If tax relief is received there is a risk that the taxpayer will be left with too little income to fully utilise his or her personal allowances. If a personal allowance is not claimed during a tax year it is lost forever and so the relief has been wasted. Managing how and when tax losses are used can therefore be a complex task.

As already stated a loss is calculated using the normal Schedule D Case I adjustments of profit computation. If the adjustment results in a loss rather than a profit the assessment is taken to be nil (i.e. no tax will have to be paid) and the loss is eligible for loss relief.

The loss can be relieved by:

- carrying forward and setting against future trading profits under s385 ICTA 1988
- setting against total income of the fiscal year in which the loss arose and/or the preceding year under s380 ICTA 1988
- carrying back and setting against total income arising in the three fiscal years before the loss arose provided the loss arose in the first four years of trading under s381 ICTA 1988
- carrying forward and setting against income received from a limited company when the loss making business is incorporated under s386 ICTA 1988
- carrying back and setting against trading income of the previous three fiscal years when the business ceases to trade under s388 ICTA 1988.

We will deal with each of these relief possibilities in turn.

Section 385 ICTA 1988: carry forward of trading losses

Losses are carried forward and set against the first available profits. The losses can be carried forward without time limit but have to be relieved against profits from the same trade.

Activity

Pat has been trading for many years and makes up accounts for calendar years. Her results for recent years are as follows:

Year ended	£
31.12.00	(7,600)
31.12.01	2,500
31.12.02	10,300

Determine Pat's assessments if she claims loss relief under s385.

Feedback

	2000/01 £	2001/02 £	2002/03 £
Schedule D Case I	0	2,500	10,300
Less s385 relief	0	(2,500)	(5,100)
Taxable profit	0	0	5,200

To keep track of the loss relief it is often helpful to maintain a loss memorandum as a working paper.

Loss memorandum	£
Trading loss	7,600
Less: claim in 2001/02	(2,500)
	5,100
Claim in 2002/03 (balance)	(5,100)
	0

Once a s385 election has been made there is no flexibility: the first available profits have to be used to relieve the loss. If the taxpayer has little income from other sources this may lead to a loss of personal allowances. In calculating the extent of the trading loss for the year the trader may also wish to delay a claim for capital allowances purposes (which would normally form part of the loss calculation as was discussed earlier in this chapter) if this claim will result in no benefit to them (i.e. if not enough other income has been earned under other schedules in the year to absorb these allowances in addition to the trading loss).

There is also a delay in receiving the relief, until the year of assessment for the year in which profits are next made. As well as having potentially serious cash flow implications the relief is worth less because it is received in the future rather than now. This is particularly so if tax rates are falling because the tax rate applied to the relief is the one in force when the relief is received not when it was incurred.

In addition the law is strict about what exactly constitutes the same trade to which the loss can be applied. In *Gordon and Blair Ltd v IRC* (1962) losses incurred from the trade of brewing could not be carried forward and relieved against profits earned from bottling. Whether the same trade is being carried on is a question of degree and so the facts of each case must be considered carefully. Hence there is an element of risk in choosing to receive relief under s385.

In the absence of any other claim by the taxpayer, the Inland Revenue will automatically apply s385 to any losses.

Section 387 ICTA 1988: relieving excess trade charges

Remember that charges, regardless of the purpose for which they were incurred, are deducted from the taxpayer's income from all sources, although they are usually first set against non-savings income.

For the purpose of section 387 charges are subdivided into trade charges and non-trade charges. A trade charge is a charge which has been incurred wholly and exclusively for the purpose of the trade. Examples of common trade charges, as we saw in Chapter 4, are patent royalties and some interest payments.

When an individual has insufficient taxable income to fully relieve their charges (whether they have actually incurred a tax loss or not) relief may be available under section 387. First all the non-trading charges should be relieved against whatever income there is. Any non-trading charges which are not relieved in this way cannot be relieved in any other way. Next trade charges should be set against any remaining income. Any trade charges which are not relieved in this way can be carried forward and relieved against future trading profits in the same way as losses are relieved under section 385.

Activity

Ruth has the following income and expenditure:

	2001/02 £	2002/03 £
Schedule D Case I	2,000	30,000
Investment income	4,000	7,000
Non-trade charge (gross)	8,000	8,000
Patent royalty (gross)	10,000	10,000

Calculate Ruth's statutory total income for 2001/02 and 2002/03.

Feedback

	2001/02 £	2002/03 £
Schedule D Case I	2,000	30,000
Less loss c/f s387		10,000
	2,000	20,000
Investment income	4,000	7,000
	6,000	27,000
Less non-trade charges	6,000	8,000
		19,000
Trade charges	–	10,000
Statutory total income	Nil	9,000

Notice that £2,000 (£8,000 – 6,000) of non-trade charges cannot be relieved in 2001/02 and so relief is lost.

The trade charge unrelieved in 2001/02 is carried forward and relieved under s387 in 2002/03.

Section 380 ICTA 1988: relieving trading losses against total income

Under section 380 a trading loss can be relieved against a taxpayer's statutory total income. The loss in a basis period is the loss, for s380 purposes, of the fiscal year. If there is an overlapping period the loss is deemed to arise in the earlier of the fiscal years for which it forms the basis of assessment.

Section 380 does offer some flexibility to the taxpayer. The taxpayer can elect to use the loss in the year in which it was incurred and/or in the preceding fiscal year. However, the taxpayer cannot choose how much relief is claimed in each year; the loss must be fully relieved if there is sufficient statutory total income. Remember that statutory total income is made up of income from all sources during the tax year, as determined under the Schedules and Cases.

The loss can also, at the taxpayer's election, be set against chargeable gains for the year (under s72 Finance Act 1991). The exemption limit and capital losses brought forward from previous years are ignored for this purpose. The loss must first be relieved against any statutory total income for the year before this election can be made. The claim can only be made provided the taxpayer is still undertaking the same trade at the beginning of the tax year in which the claim is made.

We will deal with capital gains tax in detail in Chapter 8 but it might help you to attempt the activity below if you know a little about the tax now. The basis of assessment for capital gains is the fiscal year. Hence in the tax year 2002/03 taxpayers will pay tax on their chargeable gains realised between 6th April 2002 and 5th April 2003. Individuals, but not companies, are entitled to an annual exemption limit of £7,700 in 2002/03, that is the first £7,700 of chargeable gains are not subject to taxation. Individuals pay tax on their chargeable gains at the same rates as they do for savings. This means at 10% if the gains fall into the starting rate tax band(when added to the rest of their STI), 20% if it falls in to their basic rate band, or 40% if the gains fall into the higher rate band.

Any unrelieved losses after all these adjustments are not lost, instead that are then available to carry forward using the usual s385 rules.

You should also apply s380 relief to minimise the remaining tax liability. This usually means applying the relief first to non-savings income, then to savings income and finally to dividend income, where possible.

Activity

Graham has been trading as a self-employed person for many years and has the following results:

Year end	£
31st December 1999	7,000
31st December 2000	(500)
31st December 2001	(12,000)
31st December 2002	1,500

His capital gains are as follows

	£
1999/2000	1,000
2000/01	9,000
2001/02	2,000
2002/03	500

Graham receives £4,000 (gross) each year from a building society investment account. Calculate the maximum loss relief claims which can be made under s380. You may assume that the annual exemption limit for capital gains was £7,700 for all of the years.

Feedback

Assessments	1999/2000 £	2000/01 £	2001/02 £	2002/03 £
Schedule D Case I	7,000	Nil	Nil	1,500
Taxed interest	4,000	4,000	4,000	4,000
Statutory total income	11,000	4,000	4,000	5,500
Less s380 relief	(500) (i)	(4,000) (ii)	(4,000) (iii)	Nil
Statutory Total Income	10,500	Nil	Nil	5,500
Chargeable gain	1,000	9,000	2,000	500
s380 relief		(4,000) (iv)		
		5,000		
Less annual exemption	(7,700)	(7,700)	(7,700)	(7,700)
Capital Gains Tax Liability	Nil	Nil	Nil	Nil

Loss memorandum:

	£	£
Trading loss	500	12,000
s380 (i)	(500)	
(ii)		(4,000)
(iii)		(4,000)
(iv)		(4,000)

Notes on example:

(i) The loss arising in the year ended 31st December 2000 is relieved under s380 in 1999/2000.

(ii) The loss arising in the year ended 31st December 2001 is carried back and relieved under s380 in 2000/01.

(iii) The remaining loss arising in the year ended 31st December 2001 is set against statutory total income of the fiscal year 2001/02.

(iv) Graham has elected to set the balance of the unrelieved loss against his net chargeable gains of the fiscal year prior to the year in which the loss arose. By doing this he has lost £2,700 of the annual exemption limit for chargeable gains he would otherwise have used that year.

Once again the taxpayer risks losing personal allowances when making a claim under s380. In addition, if he makes the election to relieve the loss against net capital gains he risks losing at least some of the annual exemption limit (as in 2000/01 above).

However, there is more flexibility than under s385 because the taxpayer can choose which years to relieve the loss against. In addition the taxpayer can receive a cash refund immediately which might be very welcome. The loss is set off against earned income first and then investment income. Although the amount of tax paid is not affected there may be an adverse effect on the amount of pension premiums which can be eligible for tax relief.

Activity

Helen commenced trading on 1st June 2001 with 31st December as her year end. In the period to 31st December 2001 Helen incurred a loss of £12,000. In the year to 31st December 2002 the loss incurred rose to £18,000. Calculate the loss which can be relieved under s380 against other income she may have.

Feedback

Fiscal year	Basis period	Loss (£)	Notes
2001/02	1.6.2000–5.4.01	16,500	(i)
2002/03	1.1.01–31.12.01	13,500	(ii)

Notes

(i) The loss is made up of the aggregate of the loss to 31st December 2001 of £12,000 and the loss in the period 1st January 2002 and 5th April 2002 £4,500 (£18,000 × 3/12).

(ii) The loss is made up of the loss for the basis period of £18,000 less the portion of the loss which had been dealt with in 2001/02 £4,500.

Section 381 ICTA 1989: relief for losses in the early years of a trade

Under section 381 the loss is calculated by reference to basis periods. Like s380 relief, the loss cannot be double counted and so any loss in an overlap period is deemed to be a loss in the earlier fiscal year only. The loss can be carried back and set against the total income assessable in each of the three previous years starting with the earliest year first. The taxpayer cannot restrict the claim. If the loss is sufficiently large it must be set against all three years.

Activity

John worked for a company retailing menswear until 31st December 1998. On 1st January 1999 he set up his own business distributing menswear to businesses across the north of England. His Schedule E income was as follows:

Fiscal year	Income £
1995/96	7,000
1996/97	8,000
1997/98	9,000
1998/99	4,000

His trading profits/(losses) were as follows:

Accounting period	Profit/(loss)
	£
6 months to 30.6.99	(5,000)
y/e 30.6.2000	(4,000)
y/e 30.6.01	(2,000)
y/e 30.6.02	1,000

Calculate the net income tax assessment for each of the years involved assuming that claims are made under s381. To do this you need first to calculate the allowable loss for each of the fiscal years in which a loss is incurred. Then the allowable loss can be carried back and set against the Schedule E income using s381.

Feedback

The first fiscal year in which the allowable losses arise is 1998/99. Allowable losses are:

Fiscal year	Basis period	Allowable loss	Note
1998/99	1.1.99–5.4.99	(2,500)	(i)
1999/2000	1.1.99–31.12.99	(4,500)	(ii)
2000/01	1.7.99–30.6.2000	(2,000)	(iii)
2001/02	1.7.2000–30.6.01	(2,000)	(iv)

Notes

(i) Three months loss is allowable in 1998/99. Hence allowable loss is £2,500 (£5,000 × 3/6).

(ii) The loss of the first period plus six months loss from the second period less the overlap loss is allowable in 1999/2000. Hence the allowable loss is £4,500 (£5,000 + (£4,000 + 6/12) – £2,500).

(iii) The loss for the year to 30th June 2000 less the overlap loss is allowable in 2000/01. Hence the allowable loss is £2,000 (£4,000 – £2,000).

(iv) The loss for the year to 30th June 2001 is the allowable loss in 2001/02.

Now we can relieve the allowable losses. Losses are relieved in chronological order.

	1995/96 £	1996/97 £	1997/98 £	1998/99
Schedule E	7,000	8,000	9,000	4,000
s381 relief				
1998/99	(2,500)			
1999/2000		(4,500)		
2000/01			(2,000)	
2001/02				(2,000)
Assessable income	5,500	3,500	7,000	2,000

The assessable income for 1990/2000, 2000/01 and 2001/02 is zero.

Section 386 ICTA 1988: relief for losses when a business is transferred to a company

Where a business is converted into a company and the same trade is carried on after the conversion, relief can be claimed under s386 provided that the consideration is wholly or mainly made up of shares. The relief is available for the unrelieved trading losses of the unincorporated business.

The loss must be set against the first available income from the company with earned income taking priority over interest received and dividends from the company.

Section 388 ICTA 1988: terminal loss relief

When a business ceases terminal loss relief may be claimed. First, losses must be relieved using all the other available reliefs. Any losses still unrelieved can then be carried back and set against total income of the three fiscal years preceding the year in which the business ceased to trade.

As before you need to calculate the amount of loss relief before you can set it against taxable income.

The terminal loss is made up of:

- the trading loss from 6th April to the date of cessation
- the trading loss from 12 months before the date of cessation to the following 5th April
- any trading charges unrelieved in the final fiscal year;
- a proportion of the unrelieved trading charges from the penultimate fiscal year to make up 12 months' trading charges.

If the trading result is a profit in either the year of cessation or the penultimate year of trading it is taken to be zero for the purpose of the above computation.

Activity

After making a loss Helen decided to cease to trade on 30th September 2002. Helen's trading results in recent years have been:

Accounting period	Profit/(loss)
	£
y/e 31.12.98	15,000
y/e 31.12.99	12,000
y/e 31.12.2000	6,000
y/e 31.12.01	1,000
p/e 30.9.02	(9,000)

Feedback

Narrative	Loss	Notes
	£	
Trading loss:		
in year of cessation	(6,000)	(i)
proportion of penultimate fiscal year	(2,750)	(ii)
Terminal loss	8,750	

Notes

(i) Basis period for year of cessation is 6.4.02–30.9.02, a six-month period. Allowable loss is £9,000 × 6/9.

(ii) Basis period for penultimate year is 1.10.01–5.4.02, a six-month period. Allowable loss is 3/9 × £9,000 – 3/12 × 1,000.

Now that we know how much terminal loss can be claimed you need to be able to relieve the loss. Remember that the loss can be carried back and set against total income of the three fiscal years preceding the year in which the business ceased to trade, taking the later years first.

Feedback

	1998/89 £	1999/2000 £	2000/01 £	2001/02 £
Sch D Case I	15,000	12,000	6,000	1,000
s388 relief		(2,000)	(6,000)	(1,000)
Revised				
assessment	15,000	10,000	0	0

Summary

The main theme of the chapter has been to examine how capital allowances and losses are dealt with as part of Schedule D. In order to do this you need to be able to undertake the following:

- Identify trading by differentiating between hobbies, trading and capital transactions. You can also use the badges of trade to determine whether a single transaction is a trading activity (from Chapter 5).
- Determine which profits fall to be taxed in a fiscal year (from Chapter 5).
- Calculate any capital allowances which are available by using the legislation and case law to determine which allowance can be claimed and then calculate the relief which can be claimed.
- Determine the extent of any loss, identify which loss reliefs are available and explain the advantages and disadvantages of each of the reliefs.

Project areas

This chapter provides a rich source of material for projects including the:

- effectiveness of capital allowances
- impact of taxation on reported profit.

A successful project will be stated in terms of a question to be answered or a hypothesis to be tested. The areas identified above yield the following questions which would make interesting dissertation titles:

- Does increasing capital allowances lead to increased investment in plant and machinery?
- Do businesses reclassify expenditure in order to minimise the tax they pay?

Discussion question

Question 1. What tax advice would you give to two brothers planning to start a business selling and installing computer systems for dentists?

Computational questions

Question 1. (based on CIMA May 1992). The following events occurred and were reflected in the profit and loss account of Mr Jones' self employed business for its year ended 31st March 2003.

Debits

(a) Expenditure of £8,500 was incurred on the reconstruction of a roof on a secondhand warehouse which was recently purchased. This had been damaged in a fire some months before Jones acquired it.

(b) During the year a director was convicted of an embezzlement and the amount of the loss, as established in court, was £18,000.

(c) Due to a contraction of the trade, a works manager was made redundant. His statutory redundancy entitlement was £12,000 and the total gratuitous lump sum paid to him (including the £12,000) was £38,000.

(d) For the whole of the year, one of the senior managers was seconded to work full-time for a national charity. Her annual salary, included in the salaries charged in the profit and loss account, was £24,000. Also included in the salaries figure was the salary of a manager, amounting to £18,000, who was, throughout the above period, wholly engaged in working for an associated business of Jones.

(e) Costs of £24,000 were incurred in constructing a crèche to be used for employees' children. Administration costs include £8,000 in respect of the running costs of the crèche incurred during the year.

Credits

(f) £24,000 was received from an insurance company in respect of damage caused to a processing plant as a result of a fork-lift truck colliding with it. The cost of repairing the plant was £18,000 and this was credited against the repairs account. The additional £6,000 was an agreed sum paid for loss of profits while the plant was unusable and this was credited to the profit and loss account.

(g) A gain of £30,000 arose on the sale of investments. No details of the original cost or disposal price are given at this stage.

(h) Jones has included in its sales figure for the year, sales amounting to £50,000 to X Ltd, a company in which Jones has an interest. These sales have been heavily discounted and, if they had been made at the normal retail price, would have been sold for £80,000.

Required   Indicate, giving full reasons and quoting case law where appropriate, how each of the above items would be dealt with in arriving at the adjusted Schedule D Case I profit figure for the year.

You must state in your answer whether each item would be added to or subtracted from the profit shown by the profit and loss account (which is not given) or left unadjusted.

Question 2.   (based on ACCA Paper 7 June 1994, part b only).
Bill, who starts to trade on 1st April 1998 and makes up accounts to 31st March, erects a poultry house on 31st December 2000 at a cost of £30,000.

On 31st December 2002 he sells the poultry house and the land on which it stands to Ben, whose accounting date is 30th June and who started to trade on 1st July 1998. The poultry house is sold for £20,000.

Required   Show the allowances which Bill and Ben can claim for all relevant years:

(i)   assuming Bill and Ben make an election on the sale;

and

(ii)   assuming no election is made.

(5 marks)

Question 3.   (based on ACCA Paper 7 December 1994, part a only).
Joseph Kent commenced in business on 1st October 1999 as a self employed joiner making conservatories. Joseph's business qualifies as a small business for tax purposes. His tax-adjusted profits before capital allowances were as follows:

	£
Period to 31.12.2000	35,000
Year ended 31.12.2001	24,000
Year ended 31.12.2002	42,000

Capital additions and disposals were as follows:

Additions	£
1.10.99 car (1) (at valuation)	12,200
1.10.99 trailer	2,000
1.10.99 plant and machinery (not energy-saving)	8,000
1.12.2001 car (2)	13,000
Disposals	£
1.12.2001 car (1)	7,000
1.1.2001 plant and machinery (at less than cost)	2,000

Private use of cars (1) and (2) has been agreed with the Revenue at 20%. No claim is made to treat any of the assets as short-life assets. Joseph manufactured the conservatories in rented premises until 1st January 2002 when he purchased a new factory unit for £20,000 on an industrial estate (not an enterprise zone). All assets were brought into use immediately on acquisition.

Required   Calculate the taxable profits for the years 1999/2000 to 2002/03 inclusive, and the overlap profits carried forward.

(18 marks)

Question 4.   (based on ACCA Paper 7 December 1994).

Jacqueline retired from her do-it-yourself shop on 28th February 2003 after a 20-year trading period. Overlap profits on commencement were £2,000.

Her adjusted profits/loss had been agreed with the Inland Revenue as follows:

	£
Year ended 31.3.2000	6,000 profit
Year ended 31.3.01	13,000 profit
Year ended 31.3.02	8,000 profit
Period to 28.2.03	14,500 loss

Jacqueline has investment income of £6,000 for 2002/03 only. You should assume that the current basis period rules have applied throughout the life of the business.

Required

(a) Show the final taxable profits for 1999/2000, 2000/01, 2001/02 and 2002/03 after claiming terminal loss relief.

(7 marks)

(b) Identify an alternative loss relief claim, and state whether it would be better than terminal loss relief.

(4 marks)

(Note: answer available via lecturer's website)

7

Taxing income from other sources

Introduction

In Chapters 1 and 4 you read about the Schedular system which has been used to tax income for nearly 200 years. You learnt that to calculate the tax liability from the receipt of income it is necessary to identify the Schedule and Case under which the receipt is taxed. In Chapters 5 and 6 you studied Schedule D Cases I and II, which are used to tax income from trades, vocations and professions.

In this chapter you will learn about the detail the remaining Schedules. Once you have completed this chapter you will be able to prepare an individual's full tax computation. We will not consider Schedule D Cases III, IV and V in any more detail than is given in Chapter 4.

At the end of this chapter you will be able to:

- calculate an individual's taxable income under Schedule A
- state the tax treatment of income which is taxed under Schedule D Case VI and calculate an individual's taxable income under Schedule D Case VI
- state the tax treatment of emoluments from an office or employment, including benefits in kind, and calculate an individual's taxable income under Schedule E
- outline the rules which relate to pension contributions
- determine the maximum pension contribution which may be made by an individual in a fiscal year
- prepare a tax computation for an individual.

We will use the framework of the schedular system to provide a structure for this chapter starting with Schedule A briefly examining Schedule D Case IV and then focusing on Schedule E in detail.

Schedule A

All income from land and property in the UK is taxed under Schedule A. This includes property or rents, lease premiums (if the lease is for letting more than 50 years), income from rights of way or sporting rights over land or income from letting of fixed caravans or permanent moored house boats. Overseas property income is taxed under Schedule D Case V as we briefly examined in Chapter 4.

Taxable income from UK property is pooled to create one net profit or loss from all sources belonging to a taxpayer. This profit or loss is calculated in the same way as trading profits are computed under Schedule D Case I. Receiving money from UK property is even called running a 'Schedule A Business'. However, income from most Schedule A sources (all apart from furnished holiday lettings) is treated as unearned non-trading income, not earned income. A key implication of this is that it can not be used as a source of income to count towards deductible pension contributions. The rules for furnished holiday lettings are different. We will examine these later in this section.

The basis of assessment for Schedule A is the income for the fiscal year, computed using the accruals basis. However, for very small simple businesses, for example where income is only received from one property, it is likely that the cash basis will be acceptable if you wish to argue this case with the Revenue. The Schedule A accounts will include the total income from land and property in the UK, regardless of the source, less total allowable expenses. Allowable expenses include:

- expenses incurred wholly and exclusively for the purpose of the Schedule A business such as repairs, insurance, advertising, legal costs etc.
- capital allowances for plant and machinery which enable taxpayers to carry on their business if the property is an industrial or agricultural building
- rent paid by the Schedule A business to another landlord (e.g. when rental income results from sub-letting).

If the rental comes from a dwelling instead of normal capital allowances an allowance is given either on 'wear and tear' or using an alternative renewals basis. The 'wear and tear' rules allow for capital allowance to be claimed equal to 10% of the relevant receipts from furnished lettings as relief for the wear and tear of furniture and equipment provided. Relevant receipts are gross receipts less any sums for services which would normally be borne by the tenant (Statement of Practice A19). Payment of the council tax by the landlord would be an example of such a payment. Alternatively the taxpayer may elect to use the renewals basis. The renewals basis entitles the taxpayer to deduct the cost of replacing furniture. Note, however, that the initial costs of acquiring furniture are not allowable expenses if the renewals basis is chosen. These are the only capital expenditure deductions allowed for Schedule A businesses.

Activity

Andrew has a furnished house which is let for £4,800 per annum payable monthly in advance. Andrew incurred the following expenditure in 2002/03.

June 2002	Replacement of doors and windows with double glazed units. The improvement element of the expenditure was £2,000	£3,500
July 2002	Annual insurance premium runs from 1st August to 31st July (2000's premium was £600)	£900
November 2002	Redecoration	£500
June 2003	Repairs to boiler – the work was undertaken and completed in January 2003	£200

Andrew claims the 10% wear and tear allowance.

Andrew's tenant left in May 2002 without paying the rent due for May. Andrew was unable to recover the debt but he let the house to new tenants from 1st July 2002.

Determine Andrew's Schedule A assessment for 2002/03.

Feedback

	£	£
Rent due £400 × 11		4,400
Less expenses		
Doors and windows £3,500 – £2,000	1,500	
Insurance 5/12 × £600 + 7/12 × £900	775	
Redecoration	500	
Repairs to boiler	200	
Bad debt May 2001 rent	400	
Wear and tear 10% × (£4,400 – 400)	400	
		3,675
Schedule A assessment		725

Loss relief

In general losses arising under Schedule A are carried forward and set against the first available Schedule A profits in the future (ICTA 1988 s379A(1)). Where a loss arises across all a taxpayer's Schedule A business the assessment for that year will be nil. If a loss arises for one part of the business only it will be netted against any gains in other parts first however.

The following illustration will help demonstrate how these rules work in practice.

Activity

Diana owns three houses which are rented out. Her assessable income and allowable expenses for the two years to 5th April 2003 are:

	House		
	1	2	3
	£	£	£
Income			
2001/02	6,000	2,000	4,000
2002/03	4,000	4,000	5,000
Expenses			
2001/02	4,000	3,000	6,000
2002/03	3,000	1,000	6,000

Calculate Diana's Schedule A assessment for both tax years.

Feedback

	House 1 £	House 2 £	House 3 £
2001/02			
Income	6,000	2,000	4,000
Less expenses	(4,000)	(3,000)	(6,000)
	2,000	(1,000)	(2,000)
Schedule A assessment			Nil
(2,000 – 1,000 – 2,000)			
Loss c/f £1,000			
2002/03			
Income	4,000	4,000	5,000
Less expenses	(3,000)	(1,000)	(6,000)
	1,000	3,000	(1,000)
Net income			
(1,000 + 3,000 – 1,000 = 3,000)			
Schedule A assessment		£2,000	
(3,000 – 1,000 loss b/f)			

Furnished holiday lettings

A special tax position exists for furnished holiday lettings. They are assessed under Schedule A, however, the regulations which apply to Schedule D Case I are used to determine the taxable income as this income is normally treated as trading income unlike other Schedule A income. Capital allowances can therefore be claimed (i.e. instead of wear and tear allowance or renewals basis as for other dwellings), relief for the disposal of business assets is available and loss relief can be claimed under the regulations which apply to losses incurred by traders. Because these profits are treated as earned income the taxpayer can also provide for retirement by making contributions to a pension fund that include this income in their computation (see the later section in this chapter for detail on this). Relief from capital gains tax, including rollover relief, retirement relief, relief for gifts of business assets and relief for loans to traders, are also available. Note that the basis period rules for Schedule A rather than Schedule D Case I still apply to income from furnished holiday lettings despite this special treatment.

To be eligible for this advantageous treatment the accommodation must be let commercially with a view to making a profit. The property must be available for letting to the public for at least 140 days in the fiscal year and must have actually been let for 70 of those days. For at least seven months of the fiscal year, including the 70 days, the property must not normally be occupied by the same tenant for more than 31 days.

If the taxpayer owns more than one property each of which satisfies the 140 day rule, they will all be deemed to satisfy the 70 day rule providing their average number of days let is at least 70.

Leonard owned four furnished houses in a village in the Yorkshire Dales which are let as holiday homes. None of the houses is normally let to the same tenant for more than 31 consecutive days. The number of days for which each house was available for letting and actually let in 2002/03 were:

House	Days available	Days let
1	160	85
2	175	50
3	130	115
4	160	65

Determine Leonard's potential averaging claims.

Feedback

House 3 does not satisfy the 140 day rule and so cannot be included in an averaging claim.

If no averaging claim is made, only house 1 qualifies as furnished holiday accommodation.

Possible averaging claim	Average days let
House 1 and 2	67.5
House 1 and 4	75
House 2 and 4	57.5
House 1, 2 and 4	67

Averaging house 1 and 4 is beneficial because the average number of days is 75.

No other averaging claim would succeed.

The 'rent a room' scheme

If an individual lets one or more furnished rooms in his or her main residence rents received up to a limit of £4,250 in 2002/03 (unchanged from 2001/02) are exempt from tax under Schedule A. If another individual is also receiving rent from letting accommodation in the same property the limit of £4,250 will be halved. If the gross rents exceed the limit the total amount received will be taxable unless the taxpayer has elected to be taxed on the alternative basis when the gross receipts less £4,250 or £2,125 if the limit is halved, without any deductions for either expenses or capital allowances will be taxed.

Premiums on leases

When a lease is granted the lessee may have to pay a premium to the lessor. In fact, sometimes the lessor receives very little rent for the duration of the lease but has to depend on the lease premium for income from the property.

If the lease term is more than 50 years (called a long lease) then the premium is taxable as a capital gain rather than an income. If the lease is for 50 years or less (a "short lease") income tax is paid on the value of the premium less 2% of the premium for each complete year of the lease after the first year.

Written as a formula the assessable amount of the lease premium therefore equals

$$P - (P \times (L - 1) \times 2\%)$$

where P is the premium on the lease and L is the length of the lease.

Activity

Amanda granted a 21-year lease on a property on 1st January 2002 for an initial premium of £30,000 and an annual rent of £6,000 payable monthly in advance. Determine Amanda's Schedule A assessment for 2001/02 and 2002/03.

Feedback

In 2001/02 the assessment on the premium of the lease is £18,000 (£30,000 – (2% × (21 – 1) × £30,000)). The rent due in 2002/03 is £2,000 (£6,000 × 4/12). Hence the total Schedule A assessment for 2001/02 is £20,000 (£18,000 + £2,000).

In 2002/03 the Schedule A assessment will be £6,000.

The lessee on a short lease can deduct the annual equivalent of the amount of premium on which the landlord is liable to pay tax in each year of the lease. In the activity above Amanda's tenant would be able to claim a deduction of £18,000/21 = £857 in each year of the life of the lease.

Note that the above rules on premiums only apply on the granting of the lease (i.e. from landlord to lessee) not if it is subsequently assigned (i.e. from one lessee to another lessee).

In some cases the premium paid may actually be paid by the landlord to the lessee, rather than the lessee to the landlord, for example, as an inducements to the lessee to take on the lease. This is not an untypical event in commercial leasing particularly. This type of premium is usually called a "reverse premium". When a reverse premium is paid the landlord can usually either treat the payment made as an enhancement expenditure against their capital gains tax bill when they sell the property (see Chapter 8 for details on how this works in practice), or as an allowable business expense if they are a property developer or dealer. Of course, the lessee must declare the receipt of the premium as income on which they will have to pay tax (under Schedule D Case I if the property rented is used for this business, or under property rented is used for their business, or under Schedule A if it is not for commercial use).

Schedule D Case VI

Schedule D Case VI is used to tax annual profits or gains not falling under any other Case of Schedule D and not charged under Schedule A or E. The main types of income which are taxed under Schedule D Case VI are:

- income from the sale of patent rights
- commissions earned on a casual basis
- the sale of future earnings.

Any income falling into this case is taxed in the year in which it arises. It should appear as a separate line in the taxpayers annual computation.

Schedule E

The rest of this chapter will be taken up with the legislation which relates to employees. Since employees form a majority of the working population the regulations which apply to the taxation of employees is clearly very important.

Emoluments, pensions and unemployment benefit are taxed under Schedule E. Emoluments are defined as "all salaries, fees, wages, perquisites and profits whatsoever." This will therefore include any bonuses an employee may receive, tips from customers if working in the kind of business where this occurs, and also any non-cash payments received (called benefits in kind). In general income is taxed in the year of receipt.

Employment or self employment

It is not always as clear as it may seem to determine whether an individual taxpayer working with/for someone else during all, or part of a tax year is in fact employed by them (working for them) or is self-employed (working with them). This distinction matters for tax purposes as it will determine whether the taxpayer is taxed using Schedule D Case I or II rules or Schedule E rules. The total tax the taxpayer will pay on their earnings will vary, sometimes significantly , based on how the Inland Revenue agrees to classify them.

At a basic level the Inland Revenue may wish to examine the contract that describes the working relationship. If it is a contract *of* service, this would often indicate employment, and the taxpayer will be taxed under Schedule E rules. If it is a contract *for* services then this would often indicates a self employed relationship and the taxpayer will be allowed to pay tax under Schedule D Case I or II rules. As the latter usually results in lower income tax and national insurance bills, taxpayers usually try to get Schedule D status if they can.

A simple examination of the contract title is of course not sufficient and the Inland Revenue will usually also examine the content of the contract to look for the real relationship that is in existence. For example they will look at:

- who has control in the relationship
- who provides the equipment
- must further work be accepted by the taxpayer

- must the "employer" provide further work
- who is responsible for providing other staff to help the taxpayer
- who bears the financial risk involved in the contract
- who benefits from efficient management of the contract
- can the taxpayer choose when to work on the contract

This list is illustrative not exhaustive, but will give you the idea of how the Inland Revenue approaches this classification task. If the taxpayer appears to be suitably in control of the relationship, providing their own equipment, hiring their own staff, bearing the risk of the contract but benefiting from managing it well, and so on, then the Inland Revenue will probably agree this relationship is a proper self-employed relationship. If the balance follows the grantor of the contract, then it is likely the taxpayer will be classified as an employee instead.

In recent years the Inland Revenue has examined more closely the range of occupations which are taxed under Schedule E. For example, many individuals who work in television in the past were able to operate their relationships with their "employers" as if they were self-employed. In many more cases than used to be so they are now considered to be employees and therefore taxed under Schedule E rules instead of Schedule D Case I.

The taxation of so called 'personal service companies', where individuals set up companies with themselves as the only employee and with their "employer" as their only client so as to benefit from being taxed as a company rather than as an employee, has also been caught in this trap. The rules relating to this tax charge (called IR 35) have been the subject of much recent debate. While you are reading this chapter and undertaking the activities you might like to try and identify the reasons for the Revenue's tactics in wishing to have more people taxed under Schedule E.

Basis of assessment

Pensions and unemployment benefit are taxed on the accruals basis and benefits in kind are taxed when they are provided. However, in general emoluments are taxed on the receipts basis, that is, they are taxed in the fiscal year in which the date of the receipt falls.

For all employees, other than directors, the date of receipt is deemed to be the earlier of the date on which payment is made and the date on which there is an entitlement to payment. This legislation is intended to prevent employees from transferring emoluments, such as bonuses, to a fiscal year in which their marginal rate of tax is lower.

Activity

When might a taxpayer's marginal rate of tax be likely to fall?

Feedback

There are two reasons for a fall in a taxpayer's marginal rate of tax. Firstly, he or she might suffer a drop of income, or an increase in allowable deductions, which reduces his or her highest rate of tax.

Secondly, there might be, as there has been since 1979, a trend towards lower tax rates so that the tax payable falls from one year to the next even though income remains constant.

There are additional restrictions on the date of a receipt if the employee is a director who is likely to be in a position to influence the payment of an emolument. Directors' earnings are taxed in the fiscal year which contains the earliest of the following dates:

● the date of receipt as determined by the above rules for all employees
● the date when the emolument is charged in the company's accounting records
● the end of the company's period of account in which the amount arose provided that it had been determined by then
● the date on which the amount is determined if it is after the end of the company's period of account.

Allowable expenses

As we saw in Chapter 4 the basic rule is that only expenses which are *wholly, exclusively and necessarily* incurred in the performance of their duties will be allowable deductions from an employee's Schedule E income. Note that this includes an additional *'necessary'* element which is not required for Schedule D Case I or II deductions. In practice this means it is often difficult to claim expenses as a deduction from Schedule E emoluments because *'necessary'* is not always easy to prove. However, trade unions and associations sometimes negotiate special allowances, particularly for specialist equipment such as safety equipment.

As you might expect there is a substantial amount of case law which is used to identify expenditure which is an allowable deduction for the purposes of Schedule E.

In *Brown v Bullock* (1961) the employee, a bank manager, was required by his employers to join a London club. His subscription was held not to be an allowable deduction because it was not necessary for the performance of his duties.

In *Lupton v Potts* (1969) a solicitor's articled clerk was not able to claim the costs of his examination fees because the expenditure was held not to be incurred wholly and exclusively in the performance of his duties.

Some expenditure is specifically allowed as a deduction from Schedule E emoluments. This includes:

● contributions to an approved occupational pension scheme
● premiums paid to approved personal pension plans
● subscriptions to professional bodies and learned societies listed by the Inland Revenue, provided it is relevant to the duties of the employment.
● payments to charities under a payroll deductions scheme

In addition, travelling expenses incurred necessarily in the performance of the duties of the employment and capital allowances on plant and machinery necessarily provided for use in the performance of those duties are allowable deductions.

Expenditure which is incurred in order to put an employee in a position which enables him to perform his duties, for example travel expenses from home to work, are not allowable deductions. Recently the House of Lords disallowed the cost of newspapers bought by journalists arguing that buying and reading the newspapers was preparation for work rather than part of the performance of their duties.

In *Pook v Owen* (1970) a doctor was telephoned at home by the hospital where he worked as a part-time consultant. He sometimes gave instructions to staff at the hospital before travelling to work. It was held that he was travelling between sites since his work started when he answered the phone at home and so his travelling costs between his home and the hospital were allowable expenses. However, a taxpayer will not be able to claim travelling expenses from his home to work because he chooses to undertake some of his duties at home.

The rules on employees' travel and subsistence expenses were changed in 1998 to define things such as 'normal commuting' to prevent abuse of deductions for travel.

Site-based employees are allowed to set the full costs of travelling to and from sites against their Schedule E income. A 'site-based' employee is one who has no fixed place of work but who is required to perform duties at several sites by their employer. They can also obtain relief for subsistence expenses when staying at a site.

When an employee is required to attend a site other than his normal place of work, such as a client's premises, in order to perform his duties, relief is available for the total costs of the journey.

If an employee is required to work at a site for a continuous period of at least 24 months this site will be considered to be a permanent site. Note that a continuous period need not be full time. An employee may not have a normal place of work but may have a normal area in which they work. An example might be a district nurse who is required to cover a particular area but lives outside it. In this case the area would be considered to be the normal place of work.

Employees with a travelling appointment are those required to travel as an integral part of their job. They have no normal place of work and are deemed to be performing their duties as soon as they leave home. Such employees will be entitled to relief in full for their business travel.

The cost of business phone calls made using a private phone are deductible, but no line rental for that phone can be claimed. An employee cannot claim the cost of work clothes, unless they are specialist, protective equipment. If you are required to work from home however, you will usually be able to claim a part of your additional domestic bills (e.g. heating, lighting etc.).

From April 2002 an employee will also be able to claim a deduction for any underpayment from their employers on business miles driven in their own car. The 2002 Budget introduced a new entitlement to mileage rates. We will examine how this works later in this chapter.

In general, most of these expenses will be met by an employer and therefore it is not necessary to claim them as a deduction. The employer will reimburse these costs to you and deduct them as part of their own income tax, or corporation tax bill.

This is an area of tax which is complex due to a lack of clear guidelines from legislation and much case law. The 'necessary' rule, not present for sole-traders, causes many problems for employees seeking to claim tax deductions, often probably legitimately, for costs they incur in working for their employers but not fully reimbursed by them. Where many of these would be allowable for deductibility if the employee was instead self-employed, it seems a little unfair that they can not claim these same costs just because of their employment status is different. This rule is unlikely to change in the near future however, because of the substantial cost it would imply to the Government – both in terms of actual costs of having many more employee claims for deductions.

Benefits in kind assessable on all employees

In addition to receiving a wage or salary many employees receive other benefits because of their employment. These benefits may include things such as subsidised lunches, non-contributory pensions, private health care and company cars.

The tax treatment of some benefits in kind is dependent on the status (income level or office holder) of the taxpayer while the tax treatment of other benefits in kind is independent of the status of the taxpayer. We will start with the general rule for benefits in kind and consider those benefits which are assessable in the same way on all employees. Then we will turn our attention to the tax treatment of benefits given to higher paid employees and directors.

By concession, some benefits received by employees by reason of their employment are not assessed to tax under Schedule E. For example, the free coal received by miners is not chargeable to tax (Extra-statutory Concession A6). For all other benefits, the general rule is that for status independent benefits, employees are assessed on the cash equivalent of the benefit. For status dependent benefits it is actual cost of provision that becomes the benefit (or marginal cost if the benefit is provided to non-employees as well). The cash equivalent is taken to be the amount that the benefit could be sold for once the employee has received it. This rule tends to operate in favour of the employee because benefits in kind may have either no resale value, for example, a season ticket for rail travel, or a low resale value, such as the secondhand value of a suit.

Special rules for accommodation and vouchers

There are some special rules which relate to specific benefits in kind. All employees are assessed on the provision of living accommodation and vouchers.

Employees who receive cash vouchers, credit tokens or exchangeable vouchers will be assessable on the cost to the employer of providing the benefit. However, luncheon vouchers with a value of up to 15p per day are not subject to tax in the hands of the employee.

If an employee is provided with accommodation by an employer that is not job related, the employee will be assessed to tax on the annual value of the property less any contributions made by the employee to the employer for the accommodation. The annual value is taken to be the rateable value, if available, or a value estimated by the Inland Revenue if the property does not have a rateable value (Press Release 19.4.90). However, if the property is rented by the employer the employee will be assessed on the higher of the annual value and the actual rent paid.

If the accommodation either cost over £75,000 or, if acquired more than six years before it was first provided to the employee, its market value on the date it was first provided to the employee was over £75,000, a further assessment is made on the employee. The additional benefit is equal to the excess of the cost of providing the accommodation over £75,000 multiplied by the official rate. The official rate is the interest rate given by the Treasury (this rate varies periodically, but the latest rate can be found by looking at the Press Releases on the Inland Revenue website or the website for this book). The cost of providing the accommodation includes the costs of any improvements undertaken before the start of the tax year as well as the purchase price of the property.

If the accommodation provided is job related then no assessment to tax under Schedule E arises on employees other than directors, who may still incur a tax liability. Accommodation is job related if either:

- the employee is required to live in the accommodation for the proper performance of his or her duties; or
- the employment is of the kind where it is customary to provide accommodation or the accommodation is provided to enable the better performance of the employee's duties; or
- the accommodation is provided for reasons of security.

If living accommodation is provided because of a person's employment then alterations and additions to the accommodation which are of a structural nature, or repairs which would be required if the property were leased under the Landlord and Tenant Act 1985, are not assessable benefits under ICTA 1988 s154 (ICTA 1988 s155(3)).

All employees are also assessed on the amount of any loan which is written off by reason of their employment.

Authorised Mileage Rates

When an employee uses their own car for their employer's business they will usually be paid expenses. To prevent abuse of this process a limit is given to the amount of tax free expenses that can be received in this way. These rates are called the Authorised Mileage Rates (what used to be called the Fixed Profit Car Scheme). The maximum rates payable before a taxable benefit will arise are given in the table below. If they are exceeded both income tax and national insurance contribution liabilities will be created. The miles given are for business miles driven in a year.

If the rate of expense paid by an employer does not exceed these amounts no tax under Schedule E is due on these payments as a benefit in kind and neither are any NIC required.

Type of vehicle	Rate
Car or van	40p per mile on first 10,000 business miles in the year
	25p per mile on excess over 10,000 miles
Motorcycle	24p per mile
Cycle	20p per mile

Employees who do not receive any mileage allowance payments from their employers, or who receive less than the prescribed levels, will be able to claim tax relief on the difference as an allowance deduction against their Schedule E income.

A rate of up to 5p per mile can also be paid tax free to a passenger travelling in the same vehicle provided they are also travelling on business. This rate will apply to passengers in both private and company cars used for business travel.

Activity

Fred uses his own car when travelling for his employer. During the tax year he drove 8,600 business miles. How would Fred's tax computation be affected if his employer paid him the following rates for his business miles:

        a)   30p per mile

        b)   45p per mile.

Feedback

a)   This payment is below the mileage allowance rate Fred is entitled to. He would receive £2,580 (30p × 8,600 miles) from his employer but could have been paid £3,440 (40p × 8,600 miles) before a taxable benefit arose. He is able to claim a deduction of the difference (£860) against his Schedule E income.

b)   This payment is above the mileage allowance rate and so a benefit in kind is created. Fred will have to add £430 ((45p × 8600 miles) – £3,440) to his Schedule E income and will pay tax on this at his marginal rate of income tax.

Exempted benefits in kind

Some benefits in kind are specifically excluded from assessment to tax in the hands of all employees. In-house sports facilities for employees, for example, are not liable to tax.

Employees are also not assessed on the benefit of any entertainment which is provided by third parties provided that the following conditions are fulfilled:

- the entertainment was not provided, or procured, by the employer or persons connected to the employer, (Note: a list of who are connected persons can be found in the Glossary.) and
- the entertainment was not provided in recognition of services which have been or are to be performed (ICTA 1988 s155(7)).

Employees, by way of an extra-statutory concession, are not assessable on long service awards provided that they have worked for the organisation for at least 20 years, have not received a similar award within the past ten years and the cost to the employer of the award is no more than £20 per year of service.

Rewards for suggestions are taxable, but again there is an extra-statutory concession that exempts awards provided there is a formal suggestions scheme which is open to all employees and all of the following conditions are met:

- the suggestion relates to activities which are outside the scope of the employee's normal duties
- if the award is more than £25 it is only made after a decision has been taken to implement the suggestion

- awards over £25 either do not exceed 50% of the expected net financial gain during the first year after implementation or do not exceed 10% of the expected net financial gain during the first five years after implementation
- awards over £25 are shared equitably between any employees making the suggestion.

If the award exceeds £5,000 the excess is always taxable.

The costs of relocation if an employee has to move for work reasons up to a maximum of £8,000 are not taxed as a benefit in kind. If expenses of more than £8,000 are paid the employee will be assessed on the excess over £8,000 as a benefit in kind. Note that it is not necessary for a taxpayer to sell a house in order to qualify for the relief.

A nursery place at a workplace nursery is not a taxable benefit. All other forms of childcare provision, including cash or vouchers, provided by the employer are taxable.

Benefits in kind assessable on higher paid employees and directors

In addition to benefits in kind taxable on all employees, higher paid employees and directors may be required to pay extra benefits in kind if they receive certain payments. This section examines these extras.

A higher paid employee is one whose emoluments are £8,500 a year or more. Emoluments include not only salaries, commissions and fees but also reimbursed expenses and benefits in kind, valued as if the taxpayer were a higher paid employee, other than the benefit of receiving a loan to purchase a home.

A director is any person who either acts as a director or on whose instructions the directors are accustomed to act, other than a professional advisor.

If a director owns 5% or less of the company's share capital and is either a full-time working director or the company is either non-profit-making or is established for charitable purposes he or she is not subject to these rules unless he or she is also a higher paid employee.

General rule – cash equivalents

The general rule on benefits in kind is that if an employee or members of the employee's family or household, by reason of employment, receive any benefits, they are to be treated as emoluments of the employment and are chargeable to income tax under Schedule E at an amount which is equal to the cash equivalent of the benefit (ICTA 1988 s154(1)). The cash equivalent of any benefit chargeable to tax under section 154 is an amount equal to the cost of the benefit, less any contribution made by the employee to those providing the benefit (ICTA 1988 s156(1)).

Whilst this cost is usually the additional cost of the benefit to the employer, In *Pepper* v *Hart* (1992) the House of Lords decreed that cost meant the marginal cost to the provider rather than the average cost in circumstances where the benefit is also available to the non-employees. In this case the benefit received was school education provided to children of the taxpayer. They successfully argued the actual cost they should be taxed upon was only marginal cost of providing for an extra child not the full cost of that place, as education was also provided to non-employees children. This will often have the effect of substantially lowering the value of the benefit to be taxed. Of course if it is not possible to directly attribute any costs to the provision of the benefit to the taxpayer then there will be no assessable benefit.

Notice that for a benefit in kind to be taxable it is not necessary for the employer to provide it, it is simply necessary that the benefit is provided to the taxpayer or family by reason of the taxpayer's employment.

If an asset is provided for the use of a higher paid employee or a director then the assessable benefit is the annual value which is the greater of 20% of the market value of the asset when first provided as a benefit to an employee, and the rent paid by the employer if the asset was rented. If ownership of the asset is subsequently transferred to the employee the assessable benefit is the greater of:

- the excess of the current market value of the asset over the price paid by the employee;
- the excess of the market value of the asset when it was first provided to the employee over the total of the annual benefits assessed on the employee for that asset.

There are a number of exceptions to these general rules. A taxpayer is not (at least currently) assessable on the benefit of a car parking space at or near his or her place of work (ICTA 1988 s155(1A)).

Meals which are provided in the employer's canteen for the staff generally are not an assessable benefit (ICTA 1988 s155(5)).

If the employee is provided with medical treatment outside the UK when the need for the treatment arises while the employee is outside the UK for the purpose of performing duties of employment there is no assessable benefit under ICTA 1988 s154 (ICTA 1988 s155(6)). Similarly no assessable benefit arises if the employer provides insurance for the employee against the cost of such treatment (ICTA 1988 s155(6)).

Car-based benefits in kind

One of the most important benefits in kind, in terms of the number of employees receiving it, is the company car. All higher paid employees and directors are assessed on a benefit if they are provided with a company car. Company cars became widespread during the 1970s for a number of reasons. The most important was the wages legislation in force at the time which attempted to limit increases in wages. Providing cars to some employees was a way of rewarding employees despite the legislation. It then became apparent that providing company cars to employees was extremely tax efficient. The employer could deduct the full cost of providing the car and the employee suffered relatively little tax on the benefit. Finally the provision of a company car did not lead to an increase in the national insurance contributions of either employees or employers. During the 1980s the Chancellor turned his attention to the taxation of company cars and over a number of years the tax on the benefit has increased very substantially. While there may still be some tax advantages which encourage the use of company cars the benefits are lower than in the past. Employers are required to pay national insurance contributions on company cars (under Class 1A) although employees are still not required to pay national insurance contributions on the benefit.

From 1994/95 all cars were assessed on their list price. This was to prevent car manufacturers from quoting a high retail price and then offering discounts. The actual benefit in kind was then calculated based on business miles driven in that tax year, the age of the car and any contributions made to the capital cost of the car by the employee.

A major rule change related to how the benefit of using a company car was introduced in April 2002. These new rules are be based upon the emissions of the car rather than how it is used.

CO_2 in g/km	Taxable % Petrol	Diesel	CO_2 in g/km	Taxable % Petrol	Diesel	CO_2 in g/km	Taxable % Petrol	Diesel
Less than 170	15%	18%	200 to 204	22%	25%	235 to 239	29%	32%
170 to 174	16%	19%	205 to 209	23%	26%	240 to 244	30%	33%
175 to 179	17%	20%	210 to 214	24%	27%	245 to 244	30%	33%
180 to 184	18%	21%	215 to 219	25%	28%	250 to 254	32%	35%
185 to 189	19%	22%	220 to 224	26%	29%	255 to 259	33%	35%
190 to 194	20%	23%	225 to 229	27%	30%	260 to 264	34%	35%
195 to 199	21%	24%	230 to 234	28%	31%	265 and over	35%	35%

In order to use this table of course you need to know what the emissions level of your car is. For all cars registered after 1 January 1998 these can be found either:

- on the cars registration document (V5)
- from the dealer
- in car magazines (for current models only usually)
- on the Society of Motor Manufacturers and Traders' website http://www. smmt.co.uk/co2/co2search.asp

For cars registered before 1 January 1998 the following rates apply:

Engine Capacity	Rate
up to 1400 cc	15%
1401 – 2000cc	22%
over 2000cc	32%

Once you have found the emission level of your car you simply look up the percentage rate on the above tables to determine the benefit in kind for the year. This percentage is then multiplied by the list price of the car when it was new.

This system is designed to benefit people driving newer, lower emissions cars. It is designed to achieve the opposite of the old system which benefitted older, higher business mileage cars.

If an employee must make a contribution to the employer towards the cost of the car (not including insurance costs) this is deducted from the annual charge. A flat rate (£200) also applies for private use of company vans.

The tax costs of company cars will rise for at least the next two years as the 15% of levels will drop in 2003/04 to less than 160g/km and again in 2004/05 to less than 150 g/km. All the other rates will also drop the same amounts.

In addition to the charge for the benefit of the car, if the employee receives the benefit of any fuel for private use of the company car he or she is assessed on the benefit of the fuel. A table is used (as below) to determine the amount of the taxable benefit when an employee is provided with private fuel. In an effort to deter employers from providing private fuel the Chancellor in the past has increased the scale charge by more than the cost of the fuel. If the employee makes a contribution to the cost of the fuel which has been used, but does not reimburse the entire cost, the assessable benefit is not reduced. Hence, if the employee is going to make a partial contribution it is more tax efficient if he or she contributes to the cost of the car rather than to the cost of the fuel.

Fuel Benefit

	2002/03		2001/02	
Car engine capacity	Petrol (£)	Diesel (£)	Petrol (£)	Diesel (£)
0–1400 cc	2,240	2,850	1,930	2,460
1401–2000 cc	2,850	2,850	2,460	2,460
> 2000 cc	4,200	4,200	3,620	3,620

From 6 April 2003 a new emissions based charge will also apply to the fuel benefit as it does this year to the provision of the car itself. The new benefit will be determined by the rate applied to the carbon dioxide emissions of the car. This percentage will then be multiplied by a set monetary amount set for each tax year. This amount is currently proposed to be £14,400 for 2003/04. The result of these changes will mean driving low emission cars will cost less than at present, but driving higher emissions cars will be more. Unlike at present, if an employee opts out of free fuel during the year, only the proportion (pro rata) of the annual charge will be due as a benefit. Class 1A national insurance contributions for employers are also due on new fuel benefits.

Activity

Sarah, a higher paid employee, had the use of a 1600cc, petrol engined company car throughout 2002/03. The car was first registered on 1st January 2000, has an emissions rate of 220g/km of carbon dioxide and cost £14,000 new. Sarah contributed £50 per month towards the cost of the car and £30 per month towards her private fuel. Sarah drove 18,000 miles in the year of which 70% is business mileage.

Determine the benefit assessable to Sarah.

Feedback

Unlike previous years, the number of business miles driven, age and engine capacity in the the tax year no longer affect the car benefit in kind calculation. The capacity of the car is still relevant, however, if fuel is provided by the employer as it is needed to calculate the fuel change in 2002/03.

The assessable benefit is therefore

$(14,000 \times 22\%) - (£50 \times 12) = £2,480$

(Note: Last year these same figures would have produced a taxable benefit of £1,500 producing a significant increase in taxable benefit this year).

As Sarah only makes a partial contribution towards her private fuel a taxable benefit arises. This amounts to an extra taxable benefit of £2,850 in the tax year (compared to £2,460 in 2001/02).

The charges for cars given in the tables above are for full years. When the car is unavailable for part of the tax year then these rates fall pro rata to the time in the year the car was actually available to the taxpayer. Unavailable times obviously include before and after the car is available to the taxpayer, but also if the car is being repaired for at least 30 consecutive days during the year this period can also be deducted from the benefit computation. (Note that no reduction is made if you are unable to drive the car, only if the car can not be driven).

Activity

Jane, a higher paid employee, has an 1800cc, diesel engined company car which was first registered in 2001 when it had a list price of £24,000 and produces emissions of 183 g/km of carbon dioxide. Fifty per cent of Jane's mileage was for business purposes and she makes no contributions towards the cost of the car or her private fuel.

Calculate Jane's car related benefits assessable in 2002/03 if:

(a) Jane has the use of the car for the whole year and drives a total of 4,800 miles during the year.

(b) Jane has the use of the car only from 5th October 2002 and she drives 4,800 miles between 5th October 2001 and 5th April 2003.

Feedback

(a) As for Sarah above, Jane's business miles and the age of her car is no longer relevant to the computation.

The assessable car benefit is

$£24,000 \times 21\% = £5,040$.

This compares to £8,400 in 2001/02. Jane has gained from the new rules because of the relatively low emission levels of her car and the fact she drives few business miles for which she was previously penalised under the old system where more business miles driven meant reduced rates.

Her fuel benefit will be £2,850 for the year (it would have been £2,460 in 2001/02).

(b) As she only had the car for six months her car benefit rate is halved to £2,520. Note that this calculation should be done to the nearest day.

Jane's' fuel benefit will also be halved to £1,425 as this is also reduced for the shorter period she has had the car for.

Accommodation for higher paid staff

Higher paid employees who are provided with living accommodation are assessed on the benefit of the accommodation, as for all employees that we examined earlier in this chapter. They are also, however, taxed on any other expenses which are paid by the employer which relate to the accommodation, for example, the cost of heating, lighting and repairs and 20% a year of the cost of any furniture provided.

If the accommodation is job related the maximum assessment of ancillary services is 10% of the employee's net emoluments. Net emoluments is the Schedule E assessment after any allowable expenses and pension contributions but excluding the cost of any ancillary services. If the accommodation is not job related the taxpayer will be assessed on the full cost to the employer of providing any ancillary services.

A director can only claim to be living in job-related accommodation if, as well as meeting the conditions given above, he or she has an interest in less than 5% of the company and he or she is either a full-time working director or the company is non-profit-making or is a charity, unless the accommodation is provided as part of special security arrangements.

Activity

Alexandra has a house in Yeovil and normally lives there but she has been transferred to London for two years to establish a new branch of the company she works for. Her gross salary in 2002/03 is £30,000. She has been provided with a flat in Mayfair which has an annual rateable value of £1,000. In 2002/03 the company paid £5,000 in ancillary services. Alexandra made a contribution of £1,000 to these services. She also pays £3,000 a year into a pension fund. Determine Alexandra's Schedule E assessment for the tax year.

Feedback

Schedule E assessment: Alexandra

	£	£
Salary		30,000
Less pension contributions		3,000
		27,000
Accommodation benefits		
Annual value (exempt)		
Ancillary services	5,000	
Restricted to 10% of £27,000	2,700	
Less employee's contribution	1,000	1,700
Schedule E assessment		28,700

Loans to employees

If a higher paid employee or director, or a member of their family, receives a loan which was obtained because of their employment and either no interest was paid on the loan for the year or the amount of interest paid on the loan in the year is less than interest at the "official rate" the employee will be assessed, at their marginal rate of tax, on the cash equivalent of the benefit of the loan. The cash equivalent is equal to the difference between the interest paid, if any, and the interest calculated at the official rate (ICTA 1988 s160(1)). However, if the total amount of all loans does not exceed £5,000 no tax liability will arise (i.e. the benefit is therefore ignored for tax purposes). Once the loan or loans exceed £5,000 however, it is all liable for a taxable benefit calculation, not just the excess over this amount.

The amount of the loan is normally taken to be the average of the balance at the beginning of the year and the balance at the end of the year if the loan had been in existence throughout the year. Otherwise the balance on the dates on which the loan was taken out and/or repaid are used instead and only complete tax months in which the loan existed are taken into account. A tax month runs from the 6th of the month to the 5th of the following month. However, the taxpayer can make an election for interest at the official rate on the outstanding balance to be calculated on a daily basis, which is obviously more accurate. If an employee receives a loan that comes under the 'qualify loan' rules for tax deductability (e.g. a loan to buy necessary equipment to carry out their job as an employee) then no benefit will obviously arise. Loans at full commercial rates to employees where the employer is in the business of providing loans, also give rise to no taxable benefit.

Activity

Harry, a higher paid employee, has loans from his employer that have been in existence all year:

(a) A loan of £50,000 at an interest rate of 3% pa which Harry used to finance the purchase of his main residence.

(b) A loan of £1,500 to buy an annual season ticket at an interest rate of 2% pa.

(c) A personal loan of £2,000 at an interest rate of 5% which Harry used to refit the bathroom in his home.

(d) A loan of £1,800 at an interest-free rate to buy equipment he needs for his job.

Take the official rate of interest to be 5%.

Determine the benefit assessable on Harry for the tax year.

Feedback

The loan d) is qualifying and therefore does not form part of any benefit calculations.

The other loans can be totalled to calculate the total benefit arising.

		£
a)	50,000 × (5% − 3%)	1,000
b)	1,500 × (5% − 2%)	45
c)	no benefit as rate matches official rate	
		1,045

Other benefits

A number of other benefits in kind are worth mentioning because of their relative importance for large numbers of employees. The first is the mobile phone. Prior to the 1999 Budget the provision of a mobile phone to an employee was a taxable benefit in kind if any private use was allowed paid for by the company. The final charge applicable to this benefit was £200 in 1998/99. This charge no longer exists and no benefit arises from provision and use of a mobile phone.

A second benefit worth extra comment is the provision of a computer to an employee for their home use. If you are a higher paid employee then a benefit arises if any private use is made of the computer. The first £500 per annum of the benefit that would arise is exempt, however any extra benefit received is taxable at the normal rate for employer assets loaned for private as we discussed at the start of this section – namely 20% of their value when new per year.

A final special benefit you may come across is the provision of scholarships. Again, for higher paid employees, if a scholarship of any kind is made available to the employee's family the employee is taxed on the actual cost of the scholarship except when no more than 25% of the award is available because of the fact the recipient is a family member of an employee (i.e. at least 75% of the amount needs to be available to any applicant irrespective of any family ties to the giver of the scholarship).

For all other loaned asset benefits a rate of 20% of the cost when new applies each year as we saw at the start of the section on Benefits to higher paid employees.

Employment and Self-employment Revisited

You are now in a good position to review the discussion at the start of this chapter about the relative merits of being taxed under Schedule D Case I or II, as a self-employed person, or under Schedule E, as an employee.

Activity

List the main differences between the taxation of a Schedule D Case I taxpayer and a Schedule E taxpayer. Who do you think enjoys the more advantageous treatment?

Feedback

You might have written your answer using different headings but you should have noted most of the following points.

Basis of assessment
Employees are taxed on the basis of the income received in the current year while self-employed taxpayers are taxed on the taxable profits for the accounting period which ended in the fiscal year. This provides a small advantage for taxpayers with accounting dates which are early in the fiscal year, the end of April for instance, particularly in times of inflation or growth, because of the relatively long delay between earning the profits and paying tax on them.

Allowable deductions
The self-employed can claim relief for expenses which are incurred wholly and exclusively for the purpose of trade while the employed can only gain relief for expenses which are wholly, exclusively *and necessarily* incurred in the performance of their duties. It is likely therefore that the self-employed will be able to claim a larger total deduction from income than employees. For example, if an academic purchases a computer to enable him to produce teaching materials at home no deductions for the costs of the computer will be allowable. However, a freelance lecturer who takes the same action will be able to claim a capital allowance for the cost of the computer.

National insurance

The self-employed must pay both Class 2 and Class 4 national insurance contributions and yet receive fewer benefits in return for their contributions. Employees also pay national insurance contributions (under Class 1 rules) but in return become entitled to sickness benefit, maternity benefit and unemployment benefit none of which self-employed people can usually claim. The levels of national insurance contributions will usually be different for the same levels of income but these differences may not reflect the differences in benefit entitlement.

Administration

Most self-employed individuals use the services of an accountant and certainly find themselves spending some time maintaining records which are required by the tax authorities. Employees usually incur few expenses when dealing with tax matters. This difference is likely to remain despite the introduction of self-assessment. These costs are called the compliance costs of the tax system and can be heavy for self employed people with anything other than simple tax affairs.

The taxation of investments available to employees

If employees are given, or sold, the right to buy shares at a price which is lower than the quoted share price a taxable benefit arises. The employee is taxed on the difference between the market price of the shares and the aggregate of the cost, if any, of acquiring the rights and the cost of buying the shares.

If there is a change in the rights or restrictions on some of the company's shares, called a chargeable event, which causes the value of the employee's shares to rise the increase will be assessable under Schedule E. Ex-employees will also be liable to tax under Schedule E if a chargeable event occurs within seven years of their employment with the company ending. If there is a change in the rights or restrictions which affects all of the shares of the same class it is not treated as a chargeable event and no tax liability arises.

However, there are a number of special schemes which, if approved by the Inland Revenue, offer tax breaks to employees who obtain shares in the company or participate in the profits of the company.

We will start by identifying the general conditions which must be satisfied in order for an employee to subscribe to shares in the company which employs them and then consider each of the following schemes:

- approved share option schemes
- profit-sharing schemes
- employee share-ownership plans.

Approved share option schemes

If certain conditions are met, the normal liability to tax on issuing of options can be avoided for directors and employees of the company issuing the options. Where there is a genuine offer to the public of shares in a company at a fixed price or by tender and a director or employee is entitled, by reason of his or her office or employment, to an allocation of the shares, in priority to members of the public and the following conditions are satisfied:

- the total number of shares offered to employees and directors of the company is not more than 10% of the shares subject to the offer
- all persons entitled to such an allocation are entitled to it on similar terms
- persons entitled are not restricted wholly or mainly to persons who are directors or whose remuneration exceeds a particular level
- the directors and employees must pay at least the fixed price or the lowest price successfully tendered or the notional price for the shares.

then any benefit derived by the director or employee from his entitlement is not treated as an emolument of his office or employment (FA 1988 s68(1), (1A), (2) & (2A)).

If employees are given, or sold, an option to acquire shares there is a liability to tax under Schedule E when the option is exercised. Tax is levied on the difference between the market value of the shares on the date on which the option was exercised and the amount paid for the option together with the amount paid for the shares.

However, if the shares are acquired through an approved share option scheme and the option is exercised between three and ten years after the granting of the option there is no income tax liability when either the option is granted or the option is exercised (ICTA 1988 s185).

When the shares acquired through an approved share option scheme are disposed of any capital gain will be subject to capital gains tax in the normal way. You will learn how to calculate the capital gains tax liability when a taxpayer disposes of shares in Chapter 8.

If the market value of the shares when the option was received exceeds the amount paid to obtain the right together with the price at which the shares are acquired by exercising the right there may be a charge to income tax under Schedule E (ICTA 1988 s185(6)).

In order for a scheme to be approved a number of conditions must be satisfied. The current schemes available are split into two types – slightly different rules apply depending on the type of option scheme used.

a) *Savings Related Share Option Schemes* – these schemes must be made available to all employees on similar terms. A qualifying period of up to 5 years of employment for eligibility for the scheme can be used however. The company can grant employees options to buy the company's shares in either 3, 5 or 7 years time at either the price on the day of the grant of the option or at up to a price no more than 20% discounted from the day's price. The money used to buy the shares after the agreed period is up is taken from a savings fund that the company must set up for the purpose so employees will be able to buy the shares as agreed. These savings must be between £5 and £250 a month.

b) *Company Share Option Plans* – these schemes are discretionary, meaning the company can choose which directors and employees can join. No participant can be granted options under the scheme with a value of more than £30,000 as at the date they are granted. These schemes are also not available to anyone owning more than 10% of the company.

Where companies operate schemes that do not fit into these rules they will not be approved by the Inland Revenue and no special tax treatment will be given to them. Anyone receiving share options under unapproved schemes will normally have to pay income tax under Schedule E when they receive (are granted) the share options free or cheaply, and when they exercise the options may be liable to income tax on the gain they realise (difference between the option price and market value on the shares when exercised).

Enterprise Management Incentives (EMI)

In the 2000 Finance Bill, Parliament introduced a new scheme to help small businesses recruit and retain employees by offering them share options with improved tax advantages to those previously available (Clause 61 and Schedule 14). These rules were amended as part of the 2001 Budget.

For a business with gross assets of no more than £15 million, employees can be given share options worth up to £3 million as part of the EMI. This amount was previously restricted to £100,000 each for up to 15 'key' employees, but the maximum number of employees has now been removed and all employees can now qualify, not just 'key' ones. There is no income tax or national insurance to pay on the share options when issued (granted) or when they reach the point the option can be exercised (usually three years after their granting). However, when selling the shares capital gains tax will be due calculated in the normal way (taper relief applying from when the options were granted not when exercised – we will look at how this works in Chapter 8).

Unapproved share option schemes

All share options schemes operated by businesses that do not meet the approved status rules are deemed 'unapproved'. This means they currently receive no favourable tax treatments. When the options are granted national insurance liability arises (even though no money has been received by the employee).

There is currently a strong lobby for bringing more unapproved share option schemes into some form of approved status in order to lower the cost of recruiting and retaining staff. This is particularly a problem in small high tech or high growth businesses where financing may not be available to pay large salaries immediately and share options are used to give staff a stake in the future of the company. We can expect some changes in these rules in the near future.

Profit-sharing schemes

A profit-sharing scheme will be approved by the Board (become an 'approved profit shares scheme' or APS) if it is administered by trustees and the Board is satisfied that every participant in the scheme is bound in contract with the grantor:

- to permit his shares to remain in the hands of the trustees throughout the period of retention, and
- not to assign, charge or otherwise dispose of his beneficial interest in his shares during that period, and
- if he directs the trustees to transfer the ownership of his shares to him at any time before the release date, to pay to the trustees before the transfer takes place a sum equal to income tax at the basic rate on the appropriate percentage of the locked-in value of the shares at the time of the direction, and
- not to direct the trustees to dispose of his shares at any time before the release

date in any other way except by sale for the best consideration in money that can reasonably be obtained at the time of the sale or, in the case of redeemable shares in a workers' co-operative, by redemption (ICTA 1988 Sch 9 s2(2)).

All employees and directors must be eligible to participate in the scheme for it to be approved. The period of retention is the period beginning on the date on which they are appropriated to the participant and ending two years later or, if it is earlier:

- the date on which the participant ceases to be a director or employee of the company because of injury, disability or redundancy, or
- the date on which the participant reaches the age specified in the scheme, or
- the date of the participant's death, or
- in a case where the participant's shares are redeemable shares in a workers' co-operative, the date on which the participant ceases to be employed by either the co-operative or its subsidiary (ICTA 1988 Sch 10 s2).

Provided that the above conditions are fulfilled there will not be an income tax liability when the beneficial ownership of the shares passes to the participant (ICTA 1988 s186(1) & (2)).

However, the participant will be subject to tax on any dividends received in respect of the shares. In addition a charge to income tax under Schedule E will arise if the trustees become, or the participator becomes, entitled to receive a capital receipt in respect of the shares before the release date.

The number of shares that can be given to employees as part of profit sharing schemes is limited. The maximum value of shares that can be given to an employee is the higher of £3,000 or 10% of the employees salary subject to a deemed maximum of £80,000. This means that any employee earning £30,000 per annum or less can get up to £3,000 worth of shares. Over £30,000 a year they can get shares worth 10% of their salary up to £80,000.

If the trustees dispose of any of a participant's shares at any time before the release date or, if it is earlier, the date of the participant's death, then the participant shall be chargeable to income tax under Schedule E for the year of assessment in which the disposal takes place (ICTA 1988 s186(4)).

For the purposes of capital gains tax a person who is a participant in relation to an approved profit-sharing scheme shall be treated as absolutely entitled to his shares as against the trustees of the scheme (TCGA 1992 s238(1)). Hence when the shares are transferred to the participator from the trustees no capital gains tax arises but if the shares are disposed of by the participant, capital gains tax will be levied on any chargeable gain. The allowable cost is the market value of the shares when they were transferred to the employee. There is no allowable deduction for any charge to income tax (TCGA 1992 s238(2)).

The Approved Profit Sharing (APS) schemes outlined above are to stay until 31 December 2002. After this time all plans must be moved over to new schemes, particularly the new 'all employee share ownership plan'.

All employee share-ownership plans (AESOP)

In the 2000 Finance Bill, Parliament introduced a new 'all-employee share ownership plan' scheme that extends the arrangements available for share ownership schemes before 6th April 2000 (clause 47 and sch 8).

Companies are now able to promise up to three different types of share to their employees as part of a plan. These will include free shares, partnership shares (that employees must pay for) and matching shares (that employers can give to employees who choose to purchase partnership shares). Any dividends received from ownership of the shares can be reinvested into further shares (called dividend shares). There is no income tax or national insurance payable by an employee on the shares provided they hold them in the plan for at least five years. If they only hold them for three years then tax and national insurance is payable, but only on the initial value of the shares. The employer is entitled to a deduction from their corporation tax bill equal to the market value of the shares minus the employees' contribution when acquired by the trustees of the scheme on behalf of the employees.

The key features of the new plans are:

1. Up to £3,000 worth of free shares can be given to each employee each year
2. At least some of these free shares can be awarded for meeting performance targets
3. Employees can buy partnership shares from their pre-tax salary up to a maximum of £1,500 a year. These are also free of tax and national insurance
4. Employers can give employees up to two free matching shares for each partnership share the employees actually buy
5. If the shares are kept with the plan until sold by the employee then capital gains tax will be payable in the sale
6. The shares must be non-redeemable, fully paid, ordinary shares, although they can be of a special class.

The 2001 Budget added a number of small changes to this scheme. Employees who are moved around within a group of companies will not be disadvantaged by the optional 18 month qualifying period companies can impose on eligibility for the AESOP.

Pensions

An individual can derive a pension from at least three direct sources: the state pension scheme, occupational pension schemes and personal pension schemes. A fourth type of pension available to everyone, working or not, has been available since 6 April 2001. These pensions are called Stakeholder Pensions. The state pension scheme is funded from the general tax fund as discussed in Chapter 1. Contributions to the state pension scheme have no income tax consequences although state pensions, like occupational pensions and personal pensions, are taxable under schedule E when received after the pension itself starts. Both occupational pension schemes and personal pensions schemes have income tax implications and it is these we will study in this section. We will also then briefly examine the new Stakeholder Pension schemes.

A good source of information about pensions is the new Government department responsible for this area of the economy – the Department of Work and Pensions. (see their website at http://www.thepensionservice.gov.uk).

Occupational pension schemes

Occupational pension schemes are available for employees who elect to join a pension scheme set up by their employers. An employee cannot be required to join a pension scheme by his employer.

An employer has considerable scope for flexibility in setting a scheme up but for contributions by employees to be deductible for income tax purposes a scheme must be Inland Revenue approved.

In order to obtain Inland Revenue approval a scheme must meet all of the following conditions:

- the scheme is intended to provide benefits to employees or their dependents
- the employer is a contributor to the scheme
- no repayment of an employee's contribution can be made under the scheme (ICTA 1988 s590(2)).

In addition, the following conditions must be satisfied:

- any benefit for an employee is a pension on retirement at age between 60 and 75 which does not exceed one-sixtieth of the employee's final remuneration for each year of service up to a maximum of 40 years
- any benefit for an employee's widow or widower takes the form of a pension payable on the death of the employee after retirement which does not exceed two-thirds of any pension or pensions payable to the employee
- no other benefits are payable under this scheme
- a scheme may allow for an employee, on retirement, to obtain, by commutation of his pension, a lump sum not exceeding a total of 3/80ths of his final remuneration for each year of service up to a maximum of 40 years (ICTA s590(3)). The maximum that can be paid is 1.5 times the final remuneration.

Note that the maximum lump sum which can be taken is one and a half times final remuneration as this is three-eightieths up to a maximum of 40 years for each year of service.

In practice the Inland Revenue may approve schemes which do not meet all of the conditions set out above. In particular, some approved schemes offer:

- a pension of two-thirds of final salary after less than 40 years' service
- a pension for the widows of employees on death in service, or for the children or dependents of employees
- a lump sum of up to four times the employee's final remuneration plus a refund of contributions on the death in service of the employee
- benefits to be payable on retirement within ten years of the specified age, or on earlier incapacity
- benefits additional to those provided by a scheme to which the employer is a contributor (ICTA 1988 s591).

If a scheme is Inland Revenue approved:

- income from investments or deposits held for the purposes of the scheme, apart from income from shares, are exempt from income tax (ICTA 1988 s592(2))
- sums paid by an employer by way of contribution under the scheme shall be allowable deductions from Schedule D Case I or II in the chargeable period in which the sum is paid (ICTA 1988 s592(4))
- a lump sum, not paid by way of ordinary annual contribution, paid by the employer may be deemed to be an allowable deduction in either the year in which it was paid or a number of years at the Board of Inland Revenue's discretion (ICTA 1988 s592(6)

- any contribution paid under the scheme by an employee shall, up to a maximum of 15% of either the gross emoluments or the earning cap (£97,200 in 2002/03), be deductible from his Schedule E income (ICTA 1988 ss 592(7) & 592(8))
- contributions by an employer are not regarded as benefits in kind in the hands of the employee.

Clearly contributing to a pension fund is an extremely tax efficient way of saving for retirement as employees pay contributions net of basic rate tax with higher rate tax payers getting an extra adjustment via their tax codes. In the FA 1989 the Chancellor limited the tax advantages of saving via a pension fund. This was done by placing an upper limit (cap) on the earnings on which payments into an approved pension scheme can be based. In the current fiscal year the maximum earnings are £97,200 (2001/02; £95,400).

An employee is free to make additional voluntary contributions to increase his or her retirement benefits provided that his total benefits do not exceed the limits set out above and that his total contributions do not exceed 15% of gross emoluments, limited to the earnings cap (ICTA 1988 s592(8A)). Additional voluntary contributions are paid net of basic rate tax. If an employee makes additional voluntary contributions no lump sum, in commutation of a pension, shall be allowed (ICTA 1988 Sch 23 s7(2)).

Personal pension schemes

Employees can use a personal pension scheme if either their employer does not operate a pension scheme or they choose not to join their employer's occupational pension scheme. They are also used by the self-employed. Like occupational pension funds the investments bought with the premiums are free of both income tax and capital gains tax. Pensions received are treated as earned income and so are taxed under Schedule E.

A personal pension scheme must provide some or all of the following benefits (ICTA 1988 s633):

- An annuity which commences when the member of the scheme is aged between 50 and 75 years (or earlier if the member becomes incapable, through 'infirmity of body or mind of carrying on his own occupation or any occupation of a similar nature for which he is trained or fitted or if the Inland Revenue deem the member's occupation is one in which persons customarily retire before that age (ICTA 1988 s634(3)). Any annuity paid must be payable for life and may continue to be paid for up to ten years after the member's death (ICTA 1988 s634(4) & (5)). The annuity must not normally be capable of assignment or surrender.
- A lump sum, provided that the member makes an election to receive a lump sum on or before the date on which an annuity, as described above, is first payable to him or her (ICTA 1988 s635(1)). The right to payment of the lump sum must not be capable of assignment or surrender (ICTA 1988 s635(5)).
- The payment, after the death of a member, of an annuity to the surviving spouse of the member or to the member's dependents at the time of his or her death (ICTA 1988 s636 (1 & (2)).
- The payment of a lump sum on the death of the member before he or she attains

the age of 75 (ICTA 1988 s637(1)).

From 6 April 2001 contributions to a personal pension scheme up to £3,600 can be made irrespective of earnings. If you wish to make extra contributions the excess must conform with limitations based on your net relevant earnings and your age. For example, anyone under the age of 36 the maximum contribution that can be paid is 17.5% of the net relevant earnings.

Net relevant earnings equals the aggregate of earnings under Schedule D Cases I, II and income from furnished holiday lettings taxed under Schedule A or Case VI and Schedule E for the year less capital allowances, loss relief, Schedule E deductions and the excess of trade charges over other income (ICTA 1988 s623(6)) just as for occupational pension schemes. Net relevant earnings for pension calculations are limited to a maximum cap of £97,200 for 2002/03 (ICTA 1988 s640A) just as for occupational pension schemes.

In the case of individuals whose age at the beginning of the year of assessment is over 35 the relevant percentage is as follows:

Age	Relevant percentage
36–45	20
46–50	25
51–55	30
56–60	35
61 and over	40 (ICTA 1988 s640(1))

Where personal pension arrangements are made by an employee, but whose employer then also makes contributions under the arrangements, the maximum amount that may be deducted in any year of assessment has to be reduced by the amount of the employer's contributions in the year (ICTA 1988 s640(4)).

The contribution paid by a self-employed individual under approved personal pension arrangements made by him or her is made gross and is deducted from any relevant earnings of his or her for the year of assessment in which the payment is made (ICTA 1988 s639(1)). An employed taxpayer will deduct the basic tax rate from the contribution when it is paid (ICTA 1988 s639(3)). The scheme administrator may recover an amount equal to the deduction from the Board (ICTA 1988 s639(4)).

An individual who pays a contribution to an approved personal pension scheme may elect for all or part of the contribution to be treated as paid in the fiscal year preceding the year it was paid in.

Unused relief is the difference between the premiums paid to a personal pension scheme and the appropriate maximum percentage of net relevant earnings allowed. Until 6th April 2001 this could be carried forward for up to six years but the rules changed as part of the 2000 Finance Act and carrying forward of entitlement in this way will no longer be allowed (ICTA 1988 s642(1)).

In the November 1994 budget the Chancellor proposed to allow members of approved personal pension schemes to defer purchasing an annuity up until the age of 75 while withdrawing amounts during the deferral period. The amounts withdrawn should be approximately the same as an annuity which the fund could have provided. This measure was proposed in order to help individuals who retire at a time when annuity rates are very low. The ability to make withdrawals from the accumulated fund will enable taxpayers to retire and receive an income from their pension fund while waiting for annuity rates to increase.

At the moment this facility will only be available to members of personal pension schemes. However, there is pressure on the government to extend the option to individuals paying into either retirement annuity schemes, the forerunner of personal pension schemes, or occupational pensions which use a money purchase formula rather than the final salary.

Stakeholder Pension

Stakeholder Pensions are a new type of low cost pension available for contributions from 6 April 2001. Any employer who employs five or more employees must make a stakeholder scheme available to their employees by 8th October 2001 (unless they are exempt, for example, by already offering an occupational pension scheme or contribute a reasonable sum to another personal pension scheme).

This scheme for enhancing private pensions in the UK is primarily meant for people who currently do not have a good range of pension options open to them and who would therefore have to rely on the state pension for their retirement income. They are therefore targeted at people on relatively low incomes and the self-employed.

As with other pension options the schemes are contributory. You (or another person such as your employer) contribute to a plan that will enable you to build up a fund to provide you with an income stream when you retire.

These schemes differ from other pension schemes we have examined in this chapter in a number of ways. These include:

- Providers of Stakeholder pensions can only charge you a maximum of 1% of the value of the fund each year plus direct costs to manage the fund (typically 3%+).
- Extra services must be optional to the scheme unless required by law e.g. life assurance cover.
- No charges for stopping making contributions for a time or to transfer your pension to another provider.
- Contributions as little as £20 can be made which can be made weekly, monthly or at less regular intervals.
- Contributors do not have to be working or to pay contributions in their own name.

As for other pensions, you cannot draw on the money you pay into these schemes until you retire.

Like other pensions you also get tax relief on Stakeholder Pension contributions you make. This tax relief is available to everyone whether you are a taxpayer or not. Tax relief is available at your marginal rate. If you are a basic rate taxpayer for every £78 you contribute to your pension your fund actually grows by £100 with the other £22 coming directly from the Government. If you are a higher rate taxpayer therefore you only have to contribute £60 to get the £100 extra in your fund.

A restriction on contributions exists however, as for other schemes. In this case the restrictions are straightforward – a maximum of £3,600 can be contributed in the year (to include the amount you, your employer, or another person pays into your fund plus your tax relief – although not the contracted out rebate if you use the stakeholder scheme to opt out of SERPS).

As with other schemes, when you reach retirement age for your Stakeholder scheme you can take a lump sum (tax free) from the fund and then use the rest to buy an annuity. In the latter case this must be done before you reach your 75th birthday (although not necessarily when you retire).

The Pension Credit

The 2002 Budget announced details of a new credit for pensioners that was outlined in the Pre-Budget report in November 2001. This new credit is scheduled to commence in 2003 and will operate will similar aims to the new Child Tax Credit and Working Tax Credit we discussed in Chapter 4. The current plans are that this credit will boost incomes for pensioners whose income from all sources is up to £135 per week as a single person or £200 a week as a couple. Its aim is to ensure no pensioner lives on less than £100 a week (£154 a week as a couple).

Summary

In this chapter we have focused on the taxation of income from land and buildings and income from employment. Since the majority of the workforce are employees it is an important area of the study of the UK tax system. Broadly, every benefit received by reason of an employment is taxable but very few deductions are allowable. The tax treatment of individuals with gross emoluments of less than £8,500 a year is more generous than that of other employees. However, this limit has not increased for more than a decade and so more and more employees are subject to the more stringent tax regime which applies to those earning at least £8,500 a year without a commensurate increase in real incomes. There are some tax planning opportunities for employers and employees. These include the provision of benefits in kind and planning for retirement. There are also a number of special schemes such as approved share option schemes which are dealt with in this chapter.

Project areas

The taxation of rental income and income from employment provide a number of interesting areas to research. One such topic would be to undertake a comparison of the taxation of employment throughout the EU. Another interesting area of research is the question of extending the existing tax relief for workplace nurseries to all kinds of child-care costs.

A topical project would be an investigation into the provision of private versus company cars or of private fuel by employers. It would be interesting to find out how the role and use of company cars is changing in the UK as a result of the new rules or how many employers pay for their employees private fuel and whether their decisions will change as a result of the Chancellor's measures.

Discussion questions

Question 1. Income from employment, described as a contract of service, is taxed under Schedule E while income from self-employment, described as a contract for services, is taxed under Schedule D Case I. How might you decide whether an individual is employed or self-employed? (You might like to look at this issue in the context of the recent IR35 rule changes for private service companies).

Question 2. What are the advantages of income from holiday lettings being considered to be trading income?

Question 3. Is is fair to tax heavy users of vehicles more under the new emissions based rules when they need to use their cars for work?

Question 4. Is is fair to impose the extra 'necessary' rule, not present for sole-traders, on employees for deductibility of expenses from their taxable income?

Case study material

At this point in your study you should now attempt the KPMG case material you find on the website associated with this book (http://www.taxstudent.com). You have now studied enough material to be able to attempt Case Studies 1–3.

Computational questions

Question 1. (based on ACCA Taxation December 1993).

Martin was appointed sales director of Multiple Mechanics Ltd on 1st July 2002. His employment package was as follows:

1. Annual salary of £30,000 payable in equal instalments in arrears on the last day of each month.

2. A commission related to sales and payable annually shortly after the company's year end, 31st March. The commission to 31st March 2003, £2,700, was paid on 30th April 2003.

3. Company car, a Mercedes diesel 3000cc. The car was first registered on 1st August 2001 has an emission level of 243g/km of carbon dioxide and cost £30,000 when new. All running expenses, including private fuel, were to be paid for by the company but Martin was to pay the company £50 per month for private use of the car and £20 per month for private fuel, whatever the amount used. His total mileage from appointment to 5th April 2003 was 16,000, of which 1,000 were private. These mileage figures were evenly spread over the period. The fuel consumption of the car averaged 5 miles per litre, a litre costing

an average 80 pence.

4. A clothing allowance of £600 per annum payable monthly on the first day of each month.

5. A furnished flat, annual value £1,200, which was provided rent free until such time as Martin could find a suitable house in the locality, which was not until the summer of 2002. The flat had cost £120,000 in 2000 and the furniture had cost £10,000 at the same time.

Required   Show the amounts assessable under Schedule E on Martin for the tax year 2002/03.

Question 2. (based on ACCA December 1990). Maurice Thistlethwaite, aged 53, is a research chemist with Pulsating Paints Ltd. His wife Marjorie, aged 52, is a teacher with North Shires County Council. Details of their income and outgoings for the year ended 5th April 2003 are as follows.

(a) Gross salaries

Maurice	£24,407
Marjorie	£17,000

Maurice paid 5% of his salary to an approved personal pension scheme and Marjorie paid 6% of her salary to the teachers' occupational pension scheme.

(b) Pulsating Paints Ltd provided Maurice with a new 1500cc petrol-engined car costing £14,500 on 6th November 2001. This car's emission levels are 207 g/km of carbon dioxide. His total mileage from that date to 5th April 2002 was 8,000 miles of which 1,000 was on business. The company paid all running costs of the car, £1,200, including Maurice's private petrol.

(c) Maurice paid £100 to a professional body of which he was a member and Marjorie paid £60 to her teaching union. Marjorie also purchased an academic gown during the year at the request of her employer. This cost £75.

(d) Marjorie made free-standing additional voluntary contributions to a UK life assurance company of £900 (after relief for basic rate income tax). It had been agreed with the Inland Revenue that the contributions would be eligible for relief from both basic and higher rate tax.

(e) On 1st January 2000 Maurice began performing as a magician at local charities and social clubs. It had been agreed with the Inland Revenue to treat the income as trading income and adjusted profits have been agreed as follows.

Year ended 31st December 2001	£2,000
Year ended 31st December 2002	£3,000

Out of this income Maurice paid the maximum amount (based on the 2002/03 assessment only) to a personal pension scheme in February 2003.

(f) Maurice and Marjorie had joint accounts with the Barland Bank plc on which interest of £600 was paid and with the Barchester and Bognor Building Society on which interest of £4,000 was paid. No specific election on sharing this interest has been made.

(g) Investments in UK companies were held in joint names and dividends of £3,500 were received.

(h) Maurice made a payment for a patent royalty on 25th April 2002 for £250.

Required Calculate the income tax for 2002/03 of Mr and Mrs Thistlethwaite.

Question 3. (based on ACCA June 1991). Arthur owned a furnished house in a holiday resort which was available for commercial letting when not occupied by Arthur and his family. In the tax year 2002/03 it was let for the following periods, no letting to the same person exceeding 30 days.

Month	Days
April	7
May	14
June	7
July	31
August	30 – occupied by Arthur
September	14

Apart from the above periods and two weeks in April when it was being decorated, the house was available for letting throughout the tax year. The total rent received was £1,900 and the following expenditure was incurred.

	£
Insurance	550
Repairs and decorating	616
Water rates	160
Accountancy	160
Cleaning	60
Advertising	480
Replacement furniture	140

The annual allowance of 10% of rent (less water rates) has been agreed for wear and tear of furniture.

Arthur has also purchased two shops in the resort:

Shop 1. The annual rent was £3,000 on a tenant's repairing lease which expired on 24th June 2002. Arthur took advantage of the shop being empty to carry out repairs and decorating. The shop was let to another tenant on a five-year tenant's repairing lease at £4,000 per annum from 29th September 2002.

Shop 2. The shop was purchased on 10th April 2002 and required treatment for dry rot. Arthur also undertook some normal redecorating work before the shop was let on 29th September 2002 on a seven-year tenant's repairing lease at an annual rent of £6,000. A premium of £2,000 was received from the incoming tenant upon signing the lease on 29th September 2000.

The rent for both shops was due in advance on the usual quarter days which are 25th March, 24th June, 29th September and 25th December.

The following expenditure was incurred:

	Shop 1 £	Shop 2 £
Insurance	190	300
Ground rent	10	40
Repairs and decorating	3,900*	5,000
Accountancy	50	50
Advertising for tenant	100	100

Notes

*Includes £2,500 for re-roofing the shop following gale damage in February 2002. Because the roof had been badly maintained the insurance company refused to pay for the repair work. Includes £3,000 for dry rot remedial treatment. The dry rot was present when the shop was bought in April 2002.

Required Calculate the income assessable on Arthur for the current tax year from the house and both shops and show how any losses would be dealt with.

(Note: answer available via lecturer's website)

Capital gains tax

Introduction

Until capital gains tax was introduced in 1965 capital receipts were largely free of tax. This meant that receiving increases in wealth via capital value growth as opposed to income resulted in substantially less tax being paid on increases in total wealth. Much of the incentive to classify a receipt as capital rather than revenue has now been removed by the introduction and development of capital gains tax, although there are still differences between the operation of income tax and capital gains tax systems, as you will see in this chapter. During its relatively brief life capital gains tax has undergone many changes as successive Chancellors have attempted to improve the tax. Chancellor Brown was no exception: in the Finance Act 1998 he announced a major reform of the taxation of capital gains for individuals, trustees and personal representatives. You will need to know both the old and the new rules because the reforms did not affect companies. He also changed some of the rules again in the 2000 Budget and made other changes in 2002. We will consider the taxation of the capital gains of companies in the next chapter. In this chapter we focus on the basic principles of the tax and its application for individuals.

After reading this chapter you will be able to:

- describe the introduction and development of capital gains tax
- calculate the capital gains tax liability which arises as a result of a range of transactions
- describe the reliefs available to taxpayers
- discuss the use of tax planning to reduce the liability to capital gains tax.

Background to the current rules

The first modern attempt to tax capital gains was related to short term capital gains in 1962. The tax was replaced in 1965 by James Callaghan, as Labour Chancellor, by capital gains tax which was intended to tax profits which were not subject to income tax. You will remember from Chapter 3 that taxes are sometimes introduced into a tax system because they are seen to be needed to make it more fair. Capital gains tax is certainly an example of this. The proportion of direct taxation raised by capital gains tax has reduced in recent years due to the introduction of the indexation allowance (and later, taper relief). During the 1970s increases in an asset's value caused by inflation were taxed along with increases in the real value of the asset. From 1982 to 1998 (and onwards for companies) only real gains have been subject to capital gains tax and since then individuals have been entitled to discounts that cover the inflationary impacts of asset value increases.

Today capital gains tax accounts for only 2–3% of the revenue raised by direct taxation but as James Callaghan said at the time, the tax was not primarily introduced to raise income but to 'provide a background of equity and fair play'. By taxing capital gains it is also possible to reduce the incentive to manipulate the tax affairs of an individual to create capital gains rather than income.

There is no intention in the UK tax system to subject a receipt to both income tax and capital gains tax. The general rule is that if a receipt is subject to income tax no capital gains tax liability will arise although there is no legislation which actually prevents a receipt being taxed twice.

Look again at some of the legal cases in Chapter 5 which are used to determine whether trading has occurred. Some of these cases may not be brought today because if the receipt is not seen to be a trading receipt it will automatically now be dealt with as a capital receipt. Of course, there are differences between the treatment of capital gains and income despite this mutual relationship that mean they are not completely inter-changeable as far taxpayers are concerned. For example, capital gains cannot be included in the calculation of net relevant income allowable for pension contribution purposes.

The tax was not intended to be retrospective so only gains which arose after 6th April 1965 are liable to capital gains tax. There were two ways of achieving this. Firstly, the 'Budget day value' at 6th April 1965 could be substituted for the original cost of assets acquired before that date. This would enable the tax to be levied only on gains which arose after 6th April 1965. The second solution was to 'time-apportion' the gain. That is the total gain which arose throughout the period of ownership was calculated and then apportioned, on a time basis, to the periods of ownership prior to and subsequent to 6th April 1965. Only the gain which was attributable to the later period of ownership was subject to capital gains tax. In practice, the rules were sometimes more complicated than is described here but the broad principles are accurate and you are unlikely to meet this situation in a introductory tax course.

Since it was introduced there have been substantial changes to the legislation. In 1971 the liability to capital gains tax arising solely because of the taxpayer's death was abolished and in 1982 the then Chancellor, Geoffrey Howe, introduced measures which gave taxpayers some relief for inflation.

The effects of inflation

When capital gains tax was first introduced no relief was given for the effects of inflation. Broadly speaking tax was paid on the difference between the allowable costs of acquiring the asset and the disposal proceeds. This led to all increases in value, including those which were due to inflation, being taxed rather than to just the appreciation in the value of an asset. In 1985 the law was amended to give full relief, for capital gains tax purposes, for inflation. Given the various ways in which actual inflation could be measured, the decision was taken to use increases as measured by changes in the retail price index – RPI – as the measure for inflation.

In 1988 the tax was rebased so that gains before March 1982 were no longer liable to taxation. This is achieved by undertaking two computations when an asset held on 31st March 1982 is disposed of, one using the allowable cost of the asset as normal and the second using the market value of the asset on 31st March 1982. If both computations yield an indexed gain the smaller of the gains becomes chargeable. If both computations yield a loss the smaller of the two losses becomes allowable.

For disposals on or after 30th November 1993 the indexation allowance cannot be used to create (i.e. the minimum it can reduce the taxable gain to is zero) or increase a loss if one exists before the indexation allowance calculation. If one computation results in a gain and the other gives a loss then there is neither a chargeable gain nor an allowable loss (i.e. a nil assessment for capital gains tax).

Taxpayers can also make an irrevocable election for the market value on 31st March 1982 to be used instead of the actual costs for all of their assets, except quoted securities, which were held on 31st March 1982.

In 1992 there was a Consolidation Act and legislation relating to capital gains tax is now contained in the Taxation of Chargeable Gains Act 1992 (TCGA 1992).

We will examine how these rules work in practice with examples as we go through this chapter.

Taper Relief for individuals

After a period of consultation, the Chancellor announced a major reform of capital gains tax for individuals in his 1998 budget. The Chancellor claimed that the new system will be simpler to apply. It will no longer be necessary to refer to the retail prices index to calculate the chargeable gain. In the short term, the Chancellor does not believe that the changes will affect the amount of revenue raised from capital gains tax. It is not possible to predict whether the changes will affect the revenue raised in the future, however, because of the uncertainty about:

● the future rate of inflation
● the real growth in the value of assets and
● the length of time individuals will hold assets.

The new rules are intended to encourage individuals to undertake long-term investment by holding assets for relatively long periods. This will be achieved by way of a taper relief which will reduce the effective rate of tax the longer assets are held. The taper relief is significantly more generous for business assets than non-business assets to encourage investment by entrepreneurs.

For individuals indexation will not be given for periods of ownership after April 1998. Instead, taper relief will be given ranging from 5% for non-business assets held for 3 years to a rate of 75% for business assets held for at least 2 years.

The rates for business assets had been substantially reduced by the 2000 Budget. In the 2002 Budget the Chancellor again accelerated when the maximum taper relief (75%) is available for business assets. The full relief is now available to disposals after 5 April 2002 where ownership of a business asset has been for only two years. Previously the maximum relief given was 75% for asset owners for at least 4 years.

Note that the replacement of indexation allowance with taper relief after April 1998 only applies to individuals. Indexation allowance continues to be necessary for disposals of assets owned by companies.

No taper relief will be available for assets owned for less than one year for business assets and three years for non-business assets.

A liability to capital gains tax arises when a *chargeable person* makes a *chargeable disposal* of *chargeable assets*. You need to be able to define each of these terms and list exemptions to capital gains tax to understand the affect of capital gains tax.

Chargeable person

A chargeable person may be:

- *An individual who is either resident or ordinarily resident in the UK during the tax year in which the chargeable disposal occurs* (TCGA 1992 s2(1)). If the individual is resident and domiciled in the UK disposals anywhere in the world may give rise to a capital gains tax liability. If he or she is resident but non-domiciled only gains from the disposal of assets held in the UK or remitted to the UK will be within the scope of capital gains tax. If an individual is neither resident nor ordinarily resident in the UK but undertakes a trade, profession or vocation via a branch or agency based in the UK, disposals of assets used in the course of the business will be within the scope of capital gains tax. If either the trade ceases or the assets are exported there is a deemed disposal, at the market value, for capital gains tax purposes (TCGA 1992 s10(1)). Look back at Chapter 4 for a discussion of residence and domiciles in tax.

- A *personal representative*. Personal representatives are deemed to acquire the assets at the market value at the date of death. When the personal representatives make disposals a liability to capital gains tax may arise. The annual exemption limit is available to the personal representatives for the three years commencing with the year of death to set against any chargeable gains which arise when assets from the estate are disposed of (TCGA 1992 s3(7)). For these three years the treatment of chargeable gains and allowable losses will be exactly as they would have been if the testator were alive.

- A *partner in a business*. A partnership does not have a separate legal identity. When a partnership makes a chargeable disposal of partnership assets the partners are individually liable to tax in proportion to their share of the capital gain.

The legislation contains a list of exempt persons who are not therefore liable to capital gains tax on asset sales (but also therefore can not claim any losses). These are:

- charities using gains for charitable purposes
- approved superannuation funds
- local authorities
- registered friendly societies
- approved scientific research associations
- authorised unit and investment trusts.

Whilst companies also are chargeable persons for capital gains tax purposes, corporation tax is charged on their profits which includes their chargeable (capital) gains rather than companies paying separate gains tax. We will discuss the taxation of companies, including the taxation of corporate capital gains, in Chapter 9.

Chargeable disposal

The term chargeable disposal includes the sale or giving of all or part of an asset. It also includes the loss or destruction of an asset (TCGA 1992 s24), the appropriation of assets as trading stock and the receipt of a capital sum in return for the surrender of rights to assets (TCGA 1992 s22). Examples of this are the sale of rights which attach to shares when a company makes a rights issue. The chargeable disposal is deemed to take place when the title to the asset passes to its new owner.

A number of disposals are exempt disposals and do not give rise to a capital gains tax liability. These are:

- Transfers of assets on death. The assets are deemed to be acquired by their new owners at their value at the date of death.
- Transfers of assets to provide security for a loan or mortgage.
- Gifts to charities and national heritage bodies.

The taxpayer may elect for a capital sum, received by way of compensation for any kind of damage to an asset, not to be treated as a disposal provided that:

- The capital sum is wholly applied in restoring the asset, or
- The capital sum is used to restore the asset except for a part which is not reasonably required for the purpose and which is small in comparison with the whole capital sum, or
- The amount of the capital sum is small, as compared with the value of the asset (TCGA 1992 s23(1)).

In practice a capital sum is deemed to be small if it is less than 5% of the value of the asset. To obtain the relief at least 95% of the capital sum must be used to restore the asset.

If this election is made the capital sum is deducted from the allowable cost incurred prior to receiving the capital sum. It is not possible for this calculation to reduce the allowable costs to below zero (TCGA 1992 s23).

Chargeable assets

All assets are chargeable assets unless they are specifically exempted from capital gains tax. Here is a list of some of the exempt assets:

- motor vehicles (TCGA 1992 s263)
- national savings certificates, premium bonds and SAYE deposits (TCGA 1992 s121)
- foreign currency provided it was for private use (TCGA 1992 s269)
- decorations for valour unless the chargeable person purchased them (TCGA 1992 s126)
- damages for personal or professional injury (TCGA 1992 s51)
- life assurance policies when disposed of by the original beneficial owner (TCGA 1992 s210(2))
- works of art or scientific collections given for national purposes are treated as being disposed of on a no gain/no loss basis (TCGA 1992 s258(1))
- gilt-edged securities, for example Treasury loans, Treasury stocks, Exchequer loans and War loans (TCGA 1992 s115)
- qualifying corporate bonds (TCGA 1992 s115)
- the disposal of debts, other than debts on a security, by the original creditor

(TCGA 1992 s251)
- pension and annuity rights (TCGA 1992 s237)
- betting winnings (TCGA 1992 s51).
- investments held in individual savings accounts (ISAs).

In addition, in certain circumstances tangible moveable property, also called chattels, are exempt from capital gains tax and we will consider these later.

If a taxpayer disposes of exempt assets no chargeable gain, or allowable loss, arises.

The basic computation

First we will study the computation of the chargeable gain or allowable loss. Then we will illustrate how the calculation is applied in practice using a number of transactions together with the taxpayer's income liable to tax (which you will see we need to know in order to calculate the amount of capital gains tax which must be paid even though these are really separate taxes).

The pro forma for calculating the chargeable gain or allowable loss is (Note: numbers are for illustration only):

	£
Gross proceeds on disposal (or market value)	20,000
Less incidental costs of disposal	(1,000)
Net proceeds	19,000
Less allowable costs	(4,000)
Unindexed untapered gain/(loss)	15,000
Less indexation allowance	(5,000)
Indexed untapered gain	10,000
Losses	(2,000)
Net indexed untapered gain	8,000
Net tapered gain £8,000 × 70%	5,600

We will now consider each of these elements of the capital gains tax computation in turn.

Gross proceeds on disposal

In general the proceeds received from an 'arm's length' transaction are used. An arm's length transaction occurs when vendor and purchaser are not connected in any way that could affect the price agreed between them. That is, the price is one which two strangers might mutually agree. However, if the disposal is not a bargain at arm's length the consideration is deemed to be the market value of the asset regardless of the value of any consideration actually given.

Disposals to connected persons and gifts are always taken to be not at arm's length. The market value is also used if the consideration for the disposal cannot be valued.

Connected persons are defined in the TCGA 1992 as follows:

- An individual is connected to his or her spouse, siblings, direct ancestors, lineal descendants and their spouses. He or she is not connected to lateral relatives like uncles, aunts, nephews and nieces.

- Companies are connected to each other if they are under common control. A company is connected to a person if, either alone or with individuals connected to him or her, that person controls it.
- An individual is connected to his or her partners and their spouses and relatives except for acquisitions and disposals of partnership assets under *bona fide* commercial arrangement.
- A trustee is connected with the settlor of the trust, any person connected with the settlor and any close company in which either the trustee or any beneficiary of the trust is a participator. A trustee is not connected with the beneficiaries of the trust.

Sometimes a taxpayer may try to reduce tax liability by disposing of assets piecemeal to connected persons. For example, a majority shareholder may pass shares on to the next generation in a series of small gifts. If it were not for the anti-avoidance legislation this would give a lower market value than if the shares were transferred by way of one transaction.

However, if a taxpayer disposes of related assets in a series of linked transactions to connected persons the disposal proceeds for each disposal are a proportion of the value of the aggregate of the assets transferred. Transactions are deemed to be linked if they occur within six years of each other.

There are strict rules for calculating the market value of some assets. When calculating the market value no reduction is made if several assets are sold at the same time. So if a large number of shares are disposed of to a connected person no account is taken of any reduction in the share price due to the size of the disposal. For example, the market value of quoted securities is taken to be the lower of the:

- 'quarter-up': the lower of the two prices quoted in the Daily Official List plus a quarter of the difference between the two prices
- 'mid price': half way between the highest and lowest prices at which bargains were recorded on the date of disposal excluding bargains at special prices.

Incidental costs of disposal

The incidental costs of disposal include all commissions and fees which relate to the sale such as legal costs, valuation fees and the cost of advertising. These are deducted from the gross proceeds to find the net proceeds.

Allowable costs

Allowable costs include the following:

- The base cost of acquiring the asset. This will usually be the purchase price. However, there are a number of situations in which some other value will be used. For example, if the asset is inherited rather than bought, the market value at the date of death will be an allowable cost. There are other examples which we will consider later on.
- Any incidental costs of acquisition such as legal fees.
- Any capital expenditure incurred in enhancing the asset or establishing, preserving or defending title to, or a right over, an asset. For enhancement

expenditure to be allowed the benefits of the expenditure must be reflected in the state or nature of the asset at the time of disposal. There are a number of specific exclusions from this category of allowable expenses. These are the costs of repairs, maintenance and insurance and any expenditure which is either an allowable deduction for income tax purposes or was met by public grants, such as home improvement loans.

The indexation allowance

The indexation allowance is applied to all items of allowable costs (except incidental costs of disposal). The allowance is designed to compensate for the percentage increase in the retail price index from the later of March 1982 and the month in which the asset was acquired to:

- April 1998 for individuals
- the month in which the disposal took place for companies.

Hence the indexation factor for companies is:

$$\frac{(\text{RPI for month of disposal} - \text{RPI for the later of the month of acquisition and March 1982})}{\text{RPI for the later of the month of acquisition and March 1982}}$$

The retail price index figure for the appropriate months can be found in the RPI table in the rates and allowances section in Appendix A.

The indexation factor should be stated as a decimal correct to three decimal places.

For individuals the indexation factor can be found directly (without the need for the above calculation) in the second CGT table in Appendix A.

The indexation allowance is equal to the indexation factor multiplied by the allowable cost. If there is enhancement expenditure this also is indexed but from the date of the expenditure, not from the date of acquisition of the asset.

Remember from the introduction to this chapter that it is not allowable for the indexation allowance to turn an un-indexed gain into a loss or to increase an unindexed loss. If the allowable costs exceed the net proceeds a loss is deemed to have been made for capital gains tax purposes and no further indexation can be applied. If a gain before indexation exists but indexation will turn this into a loss, then a nil assessment is given instead of creating a loss.

In conclusion, the indexation allowance will be given for the period of ownership of assets by individuals between March 1982 and April 1998. Of course assets bought by individuals after 1st April 1998 will not be eligible for an indexation allowance.

Taper relief

Taper relief is used to reduce the amount of the chargeable gain which is subjected to capital gains tax. The amount of taper relief available will depend on the length of ownership of the asset between April 1998 and the date of disposal and whether the asset is a business asset or a non-business asset. Non-business assets acquired before 17th March 1998 will be given an additional deemed period of ownership of one year after April 1998 for the purposes of calculating the taper relief.

For business assets the bonus year was removed by the 2000 Budget for any sales after 5th April 2000, when the minimum period for owning an asset to get full taper relief was reduced from 10 years to 4 years. The lowest rate was reduced further in the 2002 Budget and is now set at 25% of the indexed gain after 2 years of ownership of the asset. This results in an effective tax rate on capital gains of only 10% (25% × 40%) for a higher rate tax payer. (See tables in the appendix for full taper relief details. You will need this table as we do examples in this chapter).

Activity

An antique bought for your home in June 1997 is disposed of in May 2003. How much taper relief will be available?

Feedback

An antique for your own home will, more than likely, be a non–business asset. The period of ownership between April 1998 and May 2003 is five years and one month. For the purposes of tapering relief this is taken to be six years as it is a non-business asset, made up of five complete years of ownership plus one year of deemed ownership. Hence, only 80% of the gain will be chargeable after taper relief of 20%.

Business assets

The Inland Revenue Press Release 16 (17th March 1998) defines a business asset as:

- an asset used for the purposes of a trade carried on by the individual (either alone or in partnership) or by a qualifying company of that individual
- an asset held for the purposes of a qualifying office or employment to which that individual was required to devote substantially the whole of his time
- shares in a qualifying company held by the individual.

The 2000 Finance Act (clause 66) defined the shareholdings which will be treated as business assets from 6th April 2000. Before this date the definition was narrower. These rules were amended in the 2001 Finance Act to widen them further, enabling more shares to be included as business assets. Now the following shareholdings apply as business assets:

1) all shares and securities in unlimited trading companies
2) all shares and securities in a company of any type (limited or unlimited), or associated company where the individual is an employee or officer (full-time or part-time). This was restricted to trading companies until the 2001 Finance Act. This rule only applies however, if the employee's shareholding (along with those of their connected pensions) does not exceed 10% of the voting rights (called 'having a material interest').
3) all shares and securities in a limited company where the individual is not an employee but is able to exercise at least 5% of the voting rights of the company.

Note that if holdings are now claimed as business assets, but would not have been prior to 6th April 2000 when the definition changed, it will be necessary to apportion the gain on the shares between business and non-business asset taper relief.

Activity

Susan bought a holiday cottage for her own use in January 1990 for £47,000. She sold it in January 2005 for £250,000. Calculate Susan's chargeable gain.

Feedback

April 1998 to January 2005 is 6 years. Total tapering relief is therefore 7 years as a non-business asset owned at 17 March 1998 gets the bonus year.

	£
Proceeds	250,000
Less allowable costs	(47,000)
Unindexed untapered gain	203,000
Indexation allowance	
$((162.6 - 119.5)/119.5) \times £47,000 =$	
$0.361 \times £47,000$	(16,967)
Indexed untapered gain	186,033
Tapered gain	
$£186,033 \times 75\%$	139,525

Activity

Jessica bought a business asset in February 1996 for £20,000. She sold it in May 2005 for £70,000. Calculate Jessica's chargeable gain.

Feedback

Ownership between April 98 and May 2005 is 7 years. Total tapering relief of at least 2 years is therefore achieved to reduce the taxable amount to 25% of the indexed gain.

	£
Proceeds	70,000
Less allowable costs	(20,000)
Unindexed untapered gain	50,000
Indexation allowance	
$0.078 \times 20,000$	(1,560)
Indexed untapered gain	48,440
Tapered gain	
$£48,440 \times 25\%$	£12,110

Assets used only partly as business assets

Where an asset is used partly as a business asset and partly as a non-business asset during the period to which taper relief relates the gain on disposal will be apportioned. Part of the gain will qualify for the business asset taper relief and the rest will qualify for the non-business asset taper relief. If the asset is owned for more than 10 years the split will be determined according to the use of the asset in the final 10 years of ownership.

Activity

Brian bought a holiday cottage that he used for weekends for himself and his family in June 1998. In June 2001 he decided to let it as furnished holiday accommodation and from then until it was sold in June 2008 the property qualified for treatment as trading.

How much taper relief is available?

Feedback

The property was owned for a total of 10 years made up of 3 years owned as a non-business asset and 7 years as a business asset.

Hence 3/10this of the gain will qualify for non-business asset taper relief and 7/10this of the gain will qualify for business asset taper relief.

Hence, 95% of 3/10this of the gain and 25% of 7/10this of the gain will be chargeable.

Activity

Use the data from the last activity. Suppose that Brian had paid £50,000 for the asset and it was sold for £150,000. How much of the gain is chargeable?

Feedback

The gain is £100,000 (£150,000 – £50,000)

The chargeable gain is:

	£
95% × 3/10 × £100,000	28,500
25% × 7/10 × £100,000	17,500
Chargeable gain	46,000

Activity

Use the data from the last two activities. Assume that Brian sold the cottage in June 2009. Calculate the chargeable gain.

Feedback

Now Brian has owned the property for a total of 11 years. To determine the split between business and non-business for taper relief purposes only the last 10 years of ownership is considered.

During the last 10 years, the asset was owned as a non-business asset for 2 years and as a business asset for 8 years.

Hence the chargeable gain is:

	£
100% × 2/10 × £100,000	20,000
25% × 8/10 × £100,000	20,000
Chargeable gain	40,000

Losses

If a taxpayer incurs a capital loss in a year, the loss is set against any indexed untapered gains of the same fiscal year. The loss is automatically set off against gains in the way which is most beneficial to the taxpayer. A little thought should soon convince you that this will be achieved by setting the loss against the gain which attracts the least amount of taper relief.

If a taxpayer has net losses in a fiscal year, that is losses for the year exceed indexed untapered gains, the net loss is carried forward to future fiscal years.

Losses carried forward are set against the first available gains. In that year any current year losses are deducted first. Prior year losses brought forward are then deducted. However, the brought forward losses can be restricted, if necessary, to enable the taxpayer to gain the full benefit of the annual exemption limit for capital gains that is available to individuals each year. This means the taxpayer does not have to claim all the carried forward losses at any time, they can choose how much to use up.

Losses are dealt with before taper relief for the year, but losses brought forward can only be deducted from the net gain in the year to the extent that the gain is greater than the current year's exemption. This may result in the loss of taper relief in years you bring forward losses, but this is how the system currently works.

Activity

Ewan had the following disposals in 2002/03:

	Description	Proceeds (£)	Month of disposal	Cost (£)	Month of acquisition
1	Business asset	40,000	June 2002	50,000	May 1991
2	Business asset	70,000	Feb 2003	10,000	March 1996
3	Non-business asset	100,000	February 2003	20,000	June 1990

Calculate Ewan's net chargeable gain for 2002/03.

Feedback

Business asset 1	£
Proceeds	40,000
Less cost	(50,000)
Allowable loss	(10,000)

Remember that no indexation allowance or taper relief is available when a loss has incurred.

Business asset 2 attracts taper relief of 25% as it was held for four years after March 1998 and sold after April 2002.

Non-business asset 3 attracts 5 years tapering relief (4 years actual ownership plus the bonus year as a non-business asset held at the end of March 1998).

Hence, the loss on business asset 1 will be set against the gain on non-business asset 3.

Non-business asset 3	£
Proceeds	100,000
Less cost	(20,000)
Unindexed untapered gain	80,000
Less indexation allowance	
0.283 × 20,000	(5,660)
Indexed untapered gain	74,340
Less current year loss	(10,000)
Net indexed gain	64,340
Tapered gain 64,340 × 85%	54,689

Business asset 2	£
Proceeds	70,000
Less cost	(10,000)
Unindexed untapered gain	60,000
Less indexation allowance	
0.073 × 10,000	(730)
Indexed untapered gain	59,270
Tapered gain 59,270 × 25%	14,817

The chargeable gain for the tax year is therefore £69,506 (£54,689 + £14,817). Note that if the loss had been deducted from the gain from businesses asset 2 instead of non-business asset 3 the total gain would have been £75,506 ((£49, 270 × 25%) + (£74,340 × 85%). You should always deduct the carried forward loss from the capital gain that has the higher percentage chargeable to maximise the benefit of the loss.

Activity

Gurpreet had the following disposals in 2004/05:

	Description	Month of disposal	Proceeds (£)	Cost (£)	Month of acquisition
1	Business asset	May 2004	20,000	30,000	May 1994
2	Business asset	Sept 2004	30,000	13,000	April 1998

Calculate Gurpreet's net chargeable gain for 2004/05 (assuming current year rules apply in 2004/5).

Feedback

Business asset 1

	£
Proceeds	20,000
Cost	(30,000)
Allowable loss	(10,000)

No indexation allowance or taper relief applies as a loss exists.

Business asset 2

No indexation allowance is available because the asset was bought after April 1998.

The period of ownership for taper relief purposes is 6 years (April 1998 to September 2004). The maximum relief of 25% is therefore available

	£
Proceeds	30,000
Less cost	(13,000)
Untapered gain	17,000
Less current year losses	(10,000)
Net untapered gain	7,000
Tapered gain £7,000 × 25%	1,750

Activity

Raj had the following disposals in 2003/04:

	Description	Month of disposal	Proceeds (£)	Cost (£)	Month of acquisition
1	Business asset	April 2003	30,000	10,000	Nov 1990
2	Business asset	June 2003	30,000	50,000	Sept 1994
3	Non-business asset	March 2004	20,000	15,000	May 1998

Calculate Raj's chargeable gain (assuming current year rules apply in 2003/04).

Feedback

Business asset 2	£
Proceeds	30,000
Less cost	(50,000)
Allowable loss	(20,000)

The deemed period of ownership for taper relief purposes on the non-business asset is 5 years (5 years of ownership but no bonus year as not owned at the end of March 1998).

The period of ownership for taper relief on business asset 1 is also 5 years.

The loss is set against the non-business asset first having the highest percentage charge for taper relief.

Non-business asset	£
Proceeds	20,000
Less cost	(15,000)
Untapered gain	5,000
Less loss	(5,000)
	Nil

A loss of £15,000 (£20,000 – 5,000) is still unrelieved and so it will be set off against the business asset.

Business asset 1	£
Proceeds	30,000
Less cost	(10,000)
Unindexed untapered gain	20,000
Indexation allowance	
0.251 × 10,000	(2,510)
Indexed untapered gain	17,490
Less current year loss	(15,000)
Net untapered gain	2,490
Tapered gain £2,490 × 25%	622

Activity

Molly had the following disposals of non-business assets in 2002/03.

	Description	Month of disposal	Proceeds (£)	Cost (£)	Month of acquisition
1	Non-business asset	May 2002	10,000	50,000	March 1999
2	Non-business asset	Dec 2002	20,000	17,000	May 1998

Calculate Molly's allowable loss carried forward.

Feedback

Non-business asset 1	£
Proceeds	10,000
Less cost	(50,000)
Allowable loss	(40,000)

Non-business asset 2	£
Proceeds	20,000
Less cost	(17,000)

(No indexation allowance applies)

Indexed untapered gain	3,000
Less loss	(3,000)
	Nil

A loss of £37,000 (£40,000 − £3,000) is carried forward.

Activity

Use the data from the previous activity to calculate Molly's chargeable gain in 2003/04 if she has the following disposals (assuming the current year's rules apply in 2003/04):

	Description	Month of disposal	Proceeds £	Cost £	Month of acquisition
1	Non-business asset	June 2003	40,000	10,000	Nov 1997
2	Business asset	March 2004	28,000	20,000	April 1999

Feedback

The deemed period of ownership for taper relief purposes is 6 years (5 + bonus year as owned at the end of March 1998) for the non-business asset and 4 years for the business asset.

The loss brought forward is first set against the non-business asset having the largest percentage chargeable after the taper relief.

Non-business asset	£
Proceeds	40,000
Less cost	(10,000)
Unindexed untapered gain	30,000
Indexation allowance	
$0.019 \times 10,000$	(190)
	29,810
Less loss brought forward	(29,810)
Chargeable gain	Nil

Note that it is clear that the untapered indexed gain on the disposal of the business asset will be more than £7,700 and so there is no need to restrict the amount of the loss that is offset in the above computation.

A loss of £7,190 (£37,000 − 29,810) remains unrelieved.

Business asset	£
Proceeds	28,000
Less allowable cost	(20,000)
Untapered gain	8,000
Less loss (restricted)	(300)
Net untapered gain	7,700
Tapered gain	
£7,700 × 25%	1,925

Capital loss carried forward is £6,890 (£7,190 – £300). Taper relief lost is therefore £75 (£300 × 25%) as the brought forward loss had to be considered before the taper relief was calculated.

Calculation of the capital gains tax liability

Basis of assessment

The basis of assessment for capital gains tax depends on whether the gain was made by a company or an individual.

Companies are not liable to capital gains tax, but pay corporation tax on the net chargeable gains arising in the accounting period, less unrelieved capital losses brought forward (TCGA 1992 s8(1)). Hence the basis of assessment for companies is the accounting period. The calculation of the chargeable gain or allowable loss is, however, almost the same as for individuals. In Chapter 9 you will find out how to determine the capital gains to be included in a company's corporation tax computation.

For individuals capital gains tax is charged on the chargeable gains accruing during the year of assessment after the deduction of:

- allowable losses accruing during the year, and
- any allowable losses accruing from a previous year of assessment which have not already been allowed as a deduction from chargeable gains (TCGA 1992 s2(2)).

Allowable losses cannot be carried back except on the occasion of the taxpayer's death.

A year of assessment for individual's capital gains tax runs from 6th April to the following 5th April (TCGA 1992 s288(1)). Capital gains tax is charged on a current year basis (i.e. what arises in the year of assessment). The tax is payable on the later of the 31st January following the year of assessment and 30 days of the issue of a notice of assessment (TCGA 1992 s7). Hence for disposals made in the fiscal year 2002/03 the tax is payable on 31st January 2004. In order to maximise the gap between making the disposal and paying the tax, disposals should be made as early as possible during the fiscal year (other constraints allowing).

Rate of tax

For individuals, although not companies, there is an annual exemption for each tax year. An individual can realise capital gains up to this amount each year before any liability to this tax arises. The allowance is increased in line with the increase in the RPI and rounded up to the next multiple of £100 each year (TCGA 1992 s3(3)). As we saw earlier in this chapter, the annual exemption limit operates something like personal allowances for the purposes of income tax. For 2002/03 the annual exemption limit is £7,700.

Although capital gains tax is a separate tax to income tax, the rate of tax applied to net chargeable gains in excess of this annual exemption limit depends on the income tax band the gain falls into as the very top slice of the income (i.e. after non-savings, savings and dividend incomes have all been added in to the income tax calculation). If it falls into the starting rate band it is taxed at 10%. If it falls into the basic rate band it is taxed at 20%. If it falls into the higher rate band it is taxed at 40%. This means most capital gains are taxed at the same rates as savings.

Activity

In 2002/03 James, a single person, has Schedule E income of £24,000 and net chargeable gains of £20,000. Calculate James' capital gains tax liability.

Feedback

James' capital gains tax liability is calculated as follows:

	£
Income:	
Schedule E	24,000
Less personal allowance	(4,615)
Taxable income	(19,385)
Capital gains tax:	
Chargeable gains	20,000
Less annual exemption	(7,700)
	12,300
Capital gains tax payable	
$(29,900 - 19,385) = 10,515 \times 20\%$	2,103.00
$1,785 \times 40\%$	714.00
12,300	2,817.00

Husband and wife

Capital gains tax is a little more complicated in its treatment of spouses. For most purposes a husband and wife are treated as two separate people. They each have the full annual exemption limit and each pays tax on their capital gains at either 10%, 20% or 40%. As they are treated separately it is not possible for losses to be transferred from one spouse to the other.

If an asset is jointly owned any chargeable gain, or allowable loss, will be apportioned between the husband and wife by reference to the beneficial interest of each in the asset.

Disposals between a husband and wife living together are treated on a no gain or loss basis. This is done by taking the net proceeds to be such that the chargeable gain is nil regardless of any consideration actually given.

When an asset is transferred between spouses the taper relief on the subsequent disposal of the asset will be determined by reference to the combined period of ownership of both spouses.

As usual, it is not possible to use the indexation allowance to create or increase a loss. As a result there is some complexity in the treatment of transfers between spouses.

If the spouse making the chargeable disposal acquired the asset on a no gain/no loss basis before 1st April 1982 a computation based on the March 1982 market value, as well as one using the original cost, will be made (TCGA 1992 s55 (1)). If the asset was acquired on a no gain/no loss basis after 1st April 1982 but before 30th November 1993 and the transferring spouse originally acquired the asset before 1st April 1982 the spouse making the chargeable disposal will be deemed to have held the asset at 31st March 1982 (TCGA 1992 s55 (5)). This means that a computation using the March 1982 market value should be made.

These rules obviously give great scope for tax planning. Assets can be transferred between spouses before their final disposal to make the best use of annual exemption limits and low marginal rates of tax. The legislation also offers opportunities to maximise the benefit to be obtained from capital losses.

Activity

Richard and Judy are a married couple. In May 1984, Judy bought a non-business asset for £10,000, which she gave to Richard in November 1999. Richard sold the asset for £40,000 in April 2003.

Calculate the chargeable gain that arises when Richard sold the asset.

Feedback

The transfer from Judy to Richard will be on a no gain/no loss basis.

Cost to Judy	£
Proceeds	10,000
Indexation to date of transfer	
0.828 × 10,000	8,280
Deemed cost to Richard	18,280

The deemed period of ownership is 6 years (5 years + 1 bonus year). It is the combined period of ownership that is taken into account.

When Richard sold the asset:

	£
Proceeds	40,000
Less Deemed cost	(18,280)
Untapered gain	21,720
Tapered gain 21,720 × 80%	17,376

Special Capital Gains Tax Rules

Now that you are able to calculate the capital gain on a disposal there are some special situations which you need to be able to deal with. Broadly speaking there are two potential difficulties when calculating a capital gain. Firstly, it may not be possible to use the proceeds actually received when a disposal is made and secondly, allocating allowable costs may not be straightforward.

For example, suppose an individual buys a large plot of land and then sells a small part of it. It is likely that the large plot is worth more per acre than the part sold. If the taxpayer is allowed to apportion costs by reference to the areas sold a lower chargeable gain will arise than if the cost is apportioned according to the market value of the part disposed of and the part retained. Perhaps understandably, the legislation lays down that the allowable costs are allocated according to market values when part disposals are made.

We will look at how gains on part disposals are calculated in this section, but first we examine the sale of chattels, another example of an anomaly in calculating capital gross tax, and then discuss how to handle assets held on 31st March 1982. We will conclude this section with a discussion of negligible value claims.

Chattels

Chattels are tangible, movable, property. Assets such as cars, paintings and horses are chattels. Securities and land are not chattels. Wasting chattels are chattels with an estimated remaining useful life of 50 years or less. Hence a horse, as an example, is a wasting chattel but a painting will probably not be.

Wasting chattels are usually exempt from capital gains tax. However, there are two special exceptions we must consider to this general rule. First, you will remember that cars are entirely exempt from capital gains tax anyway. Second, assets which are used during the course of a trade, profession or vocation and are eligible for capital allowances are subject to capital gains tax even if they are wasting chattels. The capital gains tax computation for such assets depends on whether an unindexed loss arises or not. If an unindexed loss arises the allowable cost is reduced by the lower of the unindexed loss and the capital allowances, including any balancing allowance or charge given for the asset. If a gain is made the rules set out next, relating to the relief available for chattels, apply as normal.

A relief is available for all chattels subject to capital gains tax which have a relatively low value. If the proceeds of sale are £6,000 or less, no capital gains tax liability will arise. This is true even if the asset was eligible for capital allowances. If the sale proceeds exceed £6,000 the chargeable gain is equal to the lower of

$$5/3 \times (\text{gross proceeds} - £6,000)$$

and the indexed gain.

It is not possible to give a benchmark of when it is no longer worth making both calculations, and so for relatively low value chattels both calculations will have to be made.

The following activities illustrate the chattel rules we have just explained.

Activity

Jack sold a valuable book in June 2002 for £6,600. He had bought the book for £100 in November 1984 in an antique shop. Calculate the chargeable gain (assuming the book is a non-business asset).

Feedback

Proceeds exceed the £6,000 minimum, therefore a calculation must be performed. As it is a chattel however, the maximum gain calculation will apply to cap any gains.

	£
Proceeds	6,600
Less cost	(100)
Unindexed untapered gain	6,500
Indexation allowance	
0.788 × 100	(79)
	6,421
Tapered gain 6,421 × 85%	5,457
5/3 × (£6,600 − £6,000) = £1,000	

The chargeable gain is the lower of £5,457 and £1,000. Hence the chargeable gain is £1,000.

If a chattel is sold for less than £6,000 any allowable loss is calculated as if the chattel had been sold for £6,000. This will have the effect of reducing or extinguishing the loss but cannot create a gain.

Wasting Assets

Not all wasting assets are chattels. Examples include registered designs and copyrights with less than 50 years to run. In such cases the allowable cost is the full original cost of the asset written down over its useful life on a straight line basis. The indexation allowance is also given on this reduced cost.

Activity

Stephen sold a registered design, a business asset, with a remaining life of 15 years for £12,000 in January 2003, which had cost £10,000 in March 1987. Calculate the chargeable gain.

Feedback

	£
Proceeds	12,000
Allowable cost	
$\quad$ 10,000 × 15/30	(5,000)
Unindexed untapered gain	7,000
Indexation allowance	
$\quad$ 0.616 × 5,000	(3,080)
Indexed untapered gain	3,920
Tapered gain	
$\quad$ £3,920 × 25%	980

Chattels for which capital allowances are available and which are used throughout their period of ownership in a trade, profession or vocation do not have their allowable cost written off.

Assets held on 31st March 1982

In the introduction to this chapter we mentioned that in 1985 capital gains tax was rebased to 31st March 1982. This means that gains which arose due to ownership of an asset before this date are no longer subject to capital gains tax.

In order to find out how much of the total gain on sale is subject to tax two computations are carried out. One computation uses the actual cost of the asset while the other uses the market value on 31st March 1982. In both cases the indexation allowance is based on the higher of the actual cost and the 31st March 1982 market value.

When the 31st March 1982 market value is used, enhancement expenditure before 31st March 1982 is excluded from the computation. This is reasonable because the March 1982 market value should already reflect the value of any such expenditure.

The actual taxable gain or loss will then be determined by the rules:

- If both calculations produce gains the chargeable gain is the lower of the two.
- If both calculations produce losses the allowable loss is the smaller of the two.
- If one calculation results in a loss and the other in a gain there is deemed to be neither a gain nor a loss.

Activity

Rex bought a holiday cottage in 1975 for £25,000. The legal and survey fees relating to the acquisition were £500. He built a garage in 1978 for £1,500. In September 1985 central heating was installed at a cost of £3,000. The house was valued at only £20,000 in March 1982 because of plans to build an industrial estate nearby but in 1983 planning permission was refused and the industrial estate was built ten miles away. In January 2003 the house was sold for £60,000. Rex had to pay estate agency fees of £1,000, £600 related to the sale and £400 related to maintenance of the property during the time it was for sale, and £300 in legal fees. Compute the chargeable gain or allowable loss.

Feedback

	Cost £	31.3.82 Value £
Gross proceeds	60,000	60,000
Less:incidental costs of disposal:		
Estate agency fees	(600)	(600)
Legal fees	(300)	(300)
Net proceeds	59,100	59,100
Less: cost 1975	(25,000)	
Costs relating to the acquisition	500)	
Enhancement cost 1978	(1,500)	
31.3.82 market value		(20,000)
Enhancement cost 1985	(3,000)	(3,000)
Unindexed untapered gain	29,100	36,100
Less indexation allowance		
On original cost:		
1.047 × £25,000	(26,175)	(26,175)
On enhancement cost 1978		
1.047 × £1,500	(1,571)	(1,571)
On enhancement cost 1985		
0.704 × £3,000	(2,112)	(2,112)
Indexed untapered gain	(758)	6,242

Because one calculation gives a loss and the other a gain there is no capital gain on disposal and so no further calculation is necessary.

Part disposals

A taxpayer may dispose of all or part of an asset. For example, he/she may dispose of one chair from a set of four. Alternatively he/she may dispose of a part share in an asset, for example selling a third interest in a painting. A part disposal may still be a chargeable disposal even if the rest of the asset is still owned by the seller. Under these circumstances special rules apply to determine how much gain may be taxable.

Only part of the allowable cost is included in the capital gains tax computation. To calculate this multiply the allowable cost which relates to the entire asset by

$$\frac{A}{A+B}$$

where A is the value of the part disposed of and B is the market value of the remainder. The amount which is eligible for the indexation allowance is similarly reduced (TCGA 1992 s42).

To some extent this legislation acts as an anti-avoidance measure. If we take the example of the chairs, a set of four valuable chairs will be worth more than the aggregate values of a single chair and a set of three and equally a set of three chairs will be worth less than three-quarters of the value of the four chairs. This leads to a lower allowable cost and indexation allowance and so a higher chargeable gain.

Activity

Susan gave a third interest in a painting of her great-grandfather, which had been commissioned at a cost of £30,000 in April 1982, to her daughter on the occasion of her 21st birthday in June 2002. The market value of the third disposed of was estimated to be £20,000. The market value of the remaining two-thirds of the painting was estimated to be £55,000. Calculate Susan's chargeable gain (assuming this is a non-business asset).

Feedback

The allowable cost using market value in June 2002 is:

$$\frac{20,000}{20,000 + 55,000} \times 30,000 = 8,000$$

	£
Proceeds (deemed to be market value)	20,000
Less allowable cost	(8,000)
Unindexed untapered gain	12,000
Less indexation allowance	
1.006 × £8,000	(8048)
Indexed untapered gain	3,952
Tapered gain £3,952 × 85%	3,359

The legislation which deals with the part disposal of small areas of land is a little different.

Provided the total amount or value of the consideration for all disposals of land made by the transferrer in the year does not exceed £20,000 if there is a transfer of land which forms part of a holding of land, and the amount or value of the consideration for the transfer does not exceed one-fifth of the market value of the holding immediately before the transfer, the transfer shall not be treated as a disposal (TCGA 1992 s242(1) & (3)). The consideration is then deducted from any allowable expenditure when computing a gain on any subsequent disposal of the holding (TCGA 1992 s242(2)).

A taxpayer can claim for a transfer of land, forming part of a holding of land, to an authority exercising or having compulsory powers to purchase the land not to be treated as a disposal. The consideration for the transfer must be small, in practice less than 5% of the market value of the holding immediately before the transfer. The transfer must not have taken any steps by advertising, or otherwise, to dispose of any part of the holding or to make his or her willingness to dispose of it known to the authority or others (TCGA 1992 s243(1) & (2)). Once again the consideration is then deducted from any allowable expenditure when computing a gain on any subsequent disposal of the holding (TCGA 1992 s243(2)).

When a subsequent disposal takes place the indexation allowance is calculated on the original cost, rather than the cost reduced by the consideration. Then a negative indexation allowance is calculated on the value of the consideration, based on the date on which the part disposal took place.

Negligible value claims

If an asset becomes effectively worthless the taxpayer can make a negligible value claim in which the asset is deemed to be sold at its then market value and immediately re-acquired at the same value. This enables the taxpayer to create a capital loss which can be relieved in the normal way. Of course, the allowable cost on any subsequent disposal is the market value at the date of the negligible value claim.

We have now considered most of the special situations which you need to be aware of. However, there are two more important ones that you need to know something about. The first is the treatment of quoted securities and the second is the treatment of houses which either have some element of private use as well as being used for other purposes or are not considered the taxpayer's principle private residence throughout the period of ownership.

Quoted securities

Special rules are needed for calculating the capital gains on the sale of quoted securities because a taxpayer may undertake many transactions in the same quoted securities and in these cases a 'matching problem' may arise. Suppose a taxpayer acquires a number of ordinary shares in a company on several different dates. When he makes a disposal it will be necessary to calculate the allowable cost of the shares. As the shares are effectively identical, but will have been purchased at different prices in all likelihood, rules are needed to determine which shares are actually being sold. This is much the same problem as arises in the valuation of stock for accounting purposes and many of the same techniques offer possible solutions, for example First-in, First-out (FIFO), Last-in, First-out (LIFO) and average cost. In addition, there are circumstances when it may be difficult to identify the appropriate allowable costs, for example when rights and bonus issues are made. Since 1985 indexed weighted average cost has been the method used as we will see.

During the relatively brief life of capital gains tax a number of strategies have been adopted to deal with this matching problem. At the same time efforts were made to reduce tax avoidance.

For example, a taxpayer may wish to realise a gain or loss without relinquishing the shares. Perhaps he will want to realise a gain to use the annual exemption limit to the full, or he may wish to realise a loss in order to set it against gains on other disposals. Without anti-avoidance legislation this could be done by selling the shares and immediately buying them back (called 'bed and breakfasting' the shares). If this is done in the same period of account for the stock exchange, normally two weeks long, the transaction costs are relatively low. However, as you will see, anti-avoidance legislation now makes this transaction unrewarding if the objective is solely to reduce any capital gains tax liability.

The legislation in this area was reformed once again by the Chancellor in his 1998 budget. In this section, we will focus on the rules that now apply to individuals. However, the operation of the Finance Act 1985 pool (called this as it was introduced by the Finance Act of 1985) will be discussed because you may be required to construct the pool prior to a disposal by an individual. The pool continues to be maintained for companies so you may also be required to construct and maintain a pool to answer a question on companies ownership of quotable securities.

First, however, you must understand the matching rules which are in force today. For any shares purchased after 5th April 1998 by individuals, individual records of each purchase must be kept to determine exactly which shares are actually sold. This is consistent with the introduction of taper relief from the same date. Taper relief can only be applied if you know how long you have owned the shares, so pooling will no longer work as it used to.

Disposals by individuals of shares and securities since 6th April 1998 are matched in the following order:

- acquisitions made on the same day
- acquisitions within the 30 days following the disposal
- acquisitions between 5th April 1998 and the date of disposal on a LIFO basis
- shares in the FA 1985 pool
- shares in the FA82 pool
- shares acquired before 6th April 1965
- shares acquired after the date of the disposal.

The last item in the list may surprise you. An investor who believes that a share price is likely to fall might sell shares that they do not actually own. This is called 'selling short' and is quite legal. The investor will be gambling that by the time settlement is due, when they must buy shares in order to complete the transaction, the price of the shares will have fallen and he will have made a profit.

Of course, securities must be matched to identical securities. If a taxpayer holds 'A' shares and 'B' shares in the same company a disposal of 'A' shares can only be matched against acquisitions of 'A' shares.

Activity

Brian sold 10,000 shares in Westmid plc on 16th August 2002.
   He acquired shares as follows:

Date acquired	No. of shares
31.3.1998	8,000 (held in the FA 1985 pool)
31.5.1998	2,000
30.6.1999	3,000
30.8.2002	2,000

How will the disposal and acquisitions be matched?

Feedback

Acquisition of 30.8.2002 is within 30 days of the disposal so this match is first.
   Then the acquisitions on 30.6.1999 and 31.5.1998 are matched using the LIFO basis.
   The final 3,000 shares are matched against the FA 1985 pool, the shares acquired on 31.3.1998.

Activity

John sold 15,000 shares in Barlloyd plc on 29th November 2002.
He acquired shares as follows:

Date	Number	
16.8.1960	2,000	
16.8.1993	1,000	(held in the FA 1985 pool)
16.8.1998	1,000	
28.11.1998	10,000	

How will the disposal and acquisitions be matched?

Feedback

The acquisitions on 28.11.1998 and 16.8.1998 are matched on a LIFO basis.
The 1,000 shares in the FA 1985 pool are then matched.
The final 2,000 shares are matched against the shares bought on 16.8.1960.

   As the policy of pooling shares for companies did not stop at 6th April 1998 they have different matching rules to those for individuals. The matching rules for companies are:

a) shares acquired on the same day
b) shares acquired in the previous nine days (earliest acquisitions first)
c) shares from the FA 1985 pool
d) shares from the 1982 holding
e) shares acquired before 6th April 1965.

If the sold shares are matched with those purchased within the last nine days then no indexation allowance can be claimed to offset any gain, even if there has been a change in the index during the period.

The composition of the FA 1985 pool

We have spoken about the Finance Act 1985 pool a number of times now. What is this and how is is made up? Each 1985 pool is made up of shares of the same class in the same company, so a person may have to maintain a number of FA 1985 pools.

An individual's FA 1985 pool includes the following securities:

- shares acquired on or after 6th April 1982 and held on the 6th April 1985
- shares acquired between 6th April 1985 and 5th April 1998.

For shares purchased after 5th April 1998 separate records of each transaction must be kept – they are not entered into the FA 85 pool.

The FA 1985 pool for companies is the same as for individuals but the relevant date is 1st April 1982/85 rather than 6th April and new acquisitions continue to be included in the FA 1985 pool.

Shares acquired between 6th April 1982 and 5th April 1985 are included in the FA 1985 pool at the cost of acquisition plus the indexation allowance for the period from the date of acquisition to April 1985 (March 1985 for companies).

The legislation describes disposals and further acquisitions of shares which change the indexed value of the pool as 'operative events'. Before each operative event is dealt with in the pool the indexed value of the pool is changed to reflect the change in the RPI from the date of the last operative event to the date of the new operative event. This increase is termed the indexed rise rather than an indexation allowance but is effectively the same thing.

The indexed rise is calculated in the same way as the indexation allowance but this time the indexation factor applied to the indexed cost of the pool is not rounded to three decimal places. (Note however, that the rounding rule does apply to the indexation factor used to first establish the pool in April 1985).

When an acquisition occurs after 5th April 1985 (and before April 1998 for individuals) the shares acquired are added to the pool at their allowable cost, which will be either their purchase price, or their market value on the date of acquisition. When a disposal takes place the proportion of shares disposed of is used to find the proportion of the indexed cost which should be deducted from the net proceeds. No further indexation allowance is available as the pool has already been indexed of course.

Activity

Nancy undertakes the following transactions in ordinary shares of XYZ plc:

	Number of shares	Value (£)
2 January 1983 bought	1,000	2,200
6 January 1985 bought	1,500	4,000
6 January 1988 bought	500	1,800
15 May 2002 sold	1,000	7,000

Calculate the chargeable gain.

Feedback

First, we must set up the FA 1985 pool as the shares were purchased before April 1998.

	Number of shares	Cost £	Indexed pool
2nd January 1983	1,000	2,200	2,200
4th January 1985	1,500	4,000	4,000
	2,500		6,200
Indexation allowance			
$\frac{94.8 - 82.6}{82.6} = 0.148$			
$0.148 \times 2,200$			326
$\frac{94.8 - 91.2}{91.2} = 0.039$			
$0.039 \times 4,000$			156
		6,200	6,682
Indexed rise			
$\frac{103.3 - 94.8}{94.8} \times 6,682$			599
Acquisition	500	1,800	1,800
	3,000	8,000	9,081
Indexed rise to April 1998			
$0.574 \times 9,081$			5,212
			14,293
Disposal	(1,000)		
Proportion applicable to sale			
1,000/3000		(2,667)	(4,764)
	2,000	5,333	9,529

Now we can calculate the applicable gain:

	£
Proceeds	7,000
Less cost	(2,667)
Unindexed untapered gain	4,333
Less indexation allowance	
(4,764 – 2,667)	(2,097)
Indexed gain	2,236
Tapered gain £2,236 × 85%	1,900

You might want to note that what we have referred to as the FA 1985 pool is elsewhere sometimes called the Section 104 holding (which comes from section 104 of TCGA 1992 which is the legal basis for the principles we are showing here).

The composition of the 1982 holding

You also need to be aware of a second pooling of shares. All shares of the same class and same company acquired between 6th April 1965 and 5th April 1982 (31st March for companies) are pooled at their allowable cost in the 1982 holding. Any subsequent disposal has an allowable cost which is taken to be a proportion of the cost of the pool. An indexation allowance calculated from April 1982 until the date of the disposal is also available to companies, for the April 1998 plus taper relief beyond that for individuals – as normal.

Activity

Robert undertakes the following transactions in shares of ABC plc:

	Number of shares	Value (£)
5th June 1975 bought	1,000	2,000
10th November 1979 bought	1,000	3,000
4th July 1981 bought	1,000	4,000
10th July 2002 sold	2,000	18,000

The market value per share on 31st March 1982 was £4.50. Calculate the chargeable gain.

Feedback

First, find the value of the 1982 holding.

	Number of shares	Cost (£)
5th June 1975	1,000	2,000
10th November 1979	1,000	3,000
4th July 1981	1,000	4,000
	3,000	9,000

Then calculate the gain:

	Pool cost (£)	31st March 1982 market value (£)
Proceeds	18,000	18,000
Less pool cost		
$\dfrac{2,000}{3,000} \times 9,000$	(6,000)	
31st March 1982 value		
$2,000 \times 4.5$		(9,000)
Unindexed gain	12,000	9,000
Indexation allowance to April 98		
$1.047 \times 9,000$	(9,423)	(9,000)
Indexed untapered gain	2,577	Nil

Robert's chargeable gain is therefore Nil under the normal rules for capital gains computations for assets held at the end of March 1982.

Bonus issues and share splits

An investor's share holdings can change for a variety of reasons other than simply buying and selling shares. The simplest reason is probably a bonus issue whereby some of a company's reserves are capitalised and shareholders receive extra shares in proportion to their existing holding.

Another simple situation, for capital gains tax purposes at least, occurs when there is a stock split so that one old share is replaced by, for example, two new shares.

More complex situations include rights issues, takeovers and mergers and capital distributions. We will consider each of these in turn.

In these situations no change to the value of the holding has occurred. The change instead is to the number of shares held. All that is needed is to increase the number purchased at each time purchases, prior to the bonus issue or share split, were made.

Activity

Ruth has had the following transactions in shares in LMN plc.

	Number of shares	Value (£)
4th June 1972 purchased	1,000	900
10th June 1982 purchased	600	1,000
14th June 1989 purchased	400	1,000
2nd January 1990 bonus issue of one for two		
10th September 2002 sale of	2,000	6,000

The market value on 31st March 1982 was £1.20 per share. Calculate the chargeable gain.

Feedback

The first step is to set up the FA 1985 pool and then the 1982 holding. Then the disposal can be dealt with.

FA 1985 pool	Number of shares	Cost £	Indexed pool
10th June 1982	600	1,000	1,000
Indexation allowance			
$\dfrac{94.8 - 81.9}{81.9} \times 0.158$			
0.158×1000			158
Value at 6 April 1985			1,158
Indexed rise			
$\dfrac{115.4 - 94.8}{94.8} \times 1,158$			252
			1,410
Addition June 1989	400	1,000	1,000
	1,000	2,000	2,410
Bonus issue			
January 1990	500		
	1,500		
Indexed rise			
$0.409 \times 2,410$			986
			3,396
Disposal			
September 2002	(1,500)	(2,000)	(3,396)

The 1982 holding	Number of shares	Cost (£)	31.3.82 Value (£)
Acquisition 4th June 1972	1,000	900	1,200
Bonus issue 2nd January 1990	500		
	1,500	900	1,200

To calculate the chargeable gain it is necessary to undertake two computations, one dealing with the disposal from the FA 1985 pool and the second dealing with the disposal from the 1982 holding.

FA 1985 pool	£
Proceeds	4,500
$6,000 \times \dfrac{1,500}{2,000}$	
Less cost	(2,000)
Unindexed untapered gain	2,500
Less indexation allowance (3,396 – 2,000)	(1,396)
Indexed untapered gain	1,104
Tapered gain £1,104 × 85%	938

1982 holding	Cost £	31.3.82 Value (£)
Proceeds		
$6,000 \times \dfrac{500}{2,000}$	1,500	1,500
Less cost		
$900 \times \dfrac{500}{1,500}$	(300)	
31.3.82 value $1,200 \times \dfrac{500}{1,500}$	—	(400)
Unindexed untapered gain	1,200	1,100
Less indexation allowance		
1.047 × 400	(419)	(419)
Indexed untapered gain	781	681
Tapered gain 781 or 681 ×85%	663	578

The chargeable gain is therefore the lower gain, i.e. £578. The total chargeable gain is £1,516 (£938 + £578).

How would your answer to the previous activity have been altered if Ruth had not sold shares until June 2004?

Feedback

The deemed period of ownership for the purposes of taper relief is 7 years (6 years + 1 year).

The balance on the FA 1985 Pool is unchanged at cost £2,000 and indexed cost £3,396. Hence, we can move straight to the capital gains tax calculation:

FA 1985 Pool	£
Proceeds $£6,000 \times \dfrac{1,500}{2,000}$	4,500
Less cost of FA 1985 Pool	(2,000)
	2,500
Less indexation allowance	(1,396)
Indexed untapered gain as before	1,104
Tapered gain £1,104 × 75%	828

1982 Holding	£
Indexed untapered gain as before	681
Tapered gain £681 × 75%	511

The total chargeable gain is £1,339 (£828 + £511).

Rights issues

When a rights issue is made existing shareholders are given the right to subscribe to new shares at what is supposed to be an attractive price. Because money is exchanged for the new shares in a rights issue we need to amend the cost of the shares this time. For the purposes of capital gains tax rights issues are aggregated with the shares which conveyed the rights. This is illustrated in the next activity.

When the indexation allowance is calculated expenditure on a rights issue is deemed to be made on the date of the rights issue. If the rights are sold rather than exercised the proceeds are treated as a capital distribution and the rules relating to capital distributions are used to calculate any chargeable gain.

Suppose that in the above example Ruth had taken up a one for two rights issue at a cost of £1 per share on January 1990 rather than receiving a bonus issue. Calculate the chargeable gain on the subsequent disposal in September 2002.

Feedback

Ruth's transactions are now:

	Number of shares	Value (£)
4th June 1972 purchased	1,000	800
10th June 1982 purchased	600	1,000
14th June 1989 purchased	400	1,000
2nd January 1990 rights issue		
of one for two	1,000	1,000
10th September 2002 sale of	2,000	6,000

The market value on 31st March 1982 was £1.20 per share.

As before we will first set up the FA 1985 pool and the 1982 holding before dealing with the disposal.

FA 1985 pool 10th June 1982	Number of shares	Cost £	Indexed pool £
As before to the	600	1,000	1,410
Addition June 1989	400	1,000	1,000
	1,000	2,000	2,410
Indexed rise			
$\dfrac{119.5 - 115.4}{115.4} \times 2,410$			86
			2,496
Rights issue			
January 1990	500	500	500
	1,500	2,500	2,996
Indexed rise			
0.361 £2,996			1,082
			4,078
Disposal			
September 2002	(1,500)	(2,500)	(4,078)

The 1982 holding	Number of shares	Cost £	31.3.82 Value (£)
Acquisition 4th June 1972	1,000	900	1,200
Rights issue 2nd January 1990	500	500	500
	1,500	1,400	1,700

Once again to calculate the chargeable gain it is necessary to undertake two computations, one dealing with the disposal from the FA 1985 pool and the second dealing with the disposal from the 1982 holding.

FA 1985 pool	£
Proceeds	4,500
$£6,000 \times \dfrac{1,500}{2,000}$	
Less cost	(2,500)
Unindexed untapered gain	2,000
Less index allowance (4,078 – 2500)	(1,578)
Indexed untapered gain	422
Tapered gain 422 × 85%	358

	Cost £	31.3.82 Value (£)
Proceeds $£6,000 \times \dfrac{500}{2,000}$	1,500	1,500
Less cost $£900 \times \dfrac{500}{1,500}$	(300)	
$31.3.82 \times £1.2 \times \dfrac{500}{1,500}$		(400)
Less cost of rights $£500 \times \dfrac{500}{1,500}$	(167)	(167)
Unindexed gain	1,033	933
Less indexation allowance		
$1.047 \times £400$	(419)	(419)
0.361×167	(60)	(60)
Indexed untapered gain	554	454
Tapered gain 554 or 454 × 85%	470	385

The chargeable gain on the disposal from the 1982 holding is therefore £385 as the lower of the two gains.

The total chargeable gain is £743 (£358 + £385).

Capital distributions

A capital distribution is a repayment of share capital rather than a dividend which is paid from income.

A capital distribution is treated as a part disposal for capital gains tax purposes. Provided it has a value of more than 5% of the value of the shares the normal part disposal rules apply which we examined earlier in the chapter.

However, if the capital distribution is 5% or less than the value of shares the distribution can be deducted from the allowable cost of the shares. This has the effect of deferring any gain until a future disposal occurs. The Inland Revenue are able to exercise their discretion when applying this rule if, for example, they suspect tax avoidance is being deliberately entered into, although the taxpayer may appeal if the deduction is disallowed.

If a deduction is made from the allowable cost, when a subsequent disposal is made, the indexation allowance is calculated in two parts. Firstly, the full indexation allowance based on the original allowable cost is calculated. Secondly, an allowance based on the deduction indexed from the date of the small disposal to the date of the subsequent disposal is calculated. The indexation allowance used for the subsequent disposal is the first allowance less the second allowance. Remember of course that the indexation allowance for individuals was frozen on 6th April 1998.

Reorganisations

During a reorganisation new shares and possibly debentures are exchanged for the original shareholding. If the exchange is for only one class of securities, for example ordinary shares, there is no difficulty. The allowable cost of the original holding becomes the allowable cost of the new holding.

If shares are exchanged for more than one class of securities, such as ordinary shares and debentures, it is necessary to apportion the allowable cost of the original securities to the new holdings. If all the new securities are quoted the allowable cost is split in proportion to their market values on the first day on which they are quoted after the reorganisation.

Takeovers and mergers

The way in which share exchanges which occur during a takeover or merger are valued is exactly as you might expect from reading the sections on reorganisations and capital distributions.

New shares and securities received in exchange for existing holdings do not lead to a capital gains tax liability. Their allowable cost is derived from the allowable cost of the original holding as described in the section on reorganisations. If new capital is introduced it is an allowable cost. If part of the consideration is in the form of cash a capital distribution is deemed to have taken place and the procedure described in the section on capital distributions is followed.

Private residences and capital gains tax

An individual's only, or main residence (termed their 'principal private residence'), including grounds of up to 5,000 square metres, is exempted from capital gains tax provided that he or she has occupied the whole of the residence throughout the period of ownership.

This exemption has helped to contribute to the attitude of homeowners to any increase in the value of their property. Homeowners are in a unique position to become highly geared, with loans of up to 100% (or even more in some cases)of the value of the house available at times during the boom in house prices in the 1980s. This meant that even a small increase in the value of houses could generate a nice tax-free increase in the value of the owner's equity. This has led to a sense of economic well-being when the price of houses goes up among the more than 65% of households who own their own homes. Few people however, see increases in house prices in the same light as increases in other commodities such as cars or furniture. Imagine, for a moment, the impact of applying capital gains tax to principal private residences. Increases in value would no longer be seen as beneficial because of the large amount of tax which may be payable each time an individual moves. There is some pressure on the government to levy tax on the gains made by homeowners but it is hard to imagine a government accepting the level of unpopularity which would surely be the result and therefore we can probably expect no change in this area in the near future.

There are some restrictions to this generous rule you should be aware of however. For example a husband and wife can claim only one principal private residence between them unless they are legally separated. If you own more than one property, and live in them both at any time, you must elect (tell the Inland Revenue in writing) which is your principal private residence. The sale of the other will be subject to capital gains tax under the rules explained below. This implies you can only have a principal private residence at any one time. If you fail to notify the Inland Revenue of your wishes they will decide for you based on their interpretation of the facts (i.e. where it appears you were living at different times). You must tell the Revenue which is your principal private residence within two years of moving in.

Another key restriction occurs if the taxpayer has not occupied the residence throughout their period of ownership a capital gains tax liability may arise. To calculate the proportion of the gain which is exempt from capital gains tax multiply the total gain, calculated in the normal way, by:

$$\frac{\text{Period of deemed occupation since 31st March 1982}}{\text{Total period of ownership since 31st March 1982}}$$

Remember that capital gains which arose prior to 31st March 1982 are no longer taxable.

Provided that the residence was the taxpayer's principal private residence at any time during his period of ownership, the last 36 months of ownership are deemed to be a period of occupation even if the taxpayer nominates another property to be his principal private residence during this period. This measure is designed to help taxpayers who have moved house and are trying to sell their old house and may otherwise be caught by the capital gains tax rules.

There are a number of other occasions on which a period of absence can be treated as a period of deemed occupation provided that the property both before and after the period of absence, although not necessarily immediately before or immediately after, was occupied as the taxpayer's principal private residence. The periods of deemed occupation are not affected if the property is actually let during them or not.

The periods of deemed occupation are:

- any periods of absence totalling up to three years
- any periods during which the taxpayer was required to live abroad in order to fulfill employment duties
- any periods totalling up to four years during which the taxpayer was required to work elsewhere in the UK in order to fulfill employment duties.

Strictly each period of absence should be followed by a period of occupation. However, as an extra-statutory concession, if a taxpayer's employment requires him to work in the UK immediately followed by a period of working abroad or vice versa the periods will still be allowed as periods of deemed occupation. To try and make these complicated rules clearer we will illustrate them with the following example.

Activity

John bought a house on 1st January 1982 for £30,000. He lived in the house until 30th June 1984 when he obtained work in another part of the country. The house was let until he returned on 1st April 1988. On 1st May 1993 he went to work abroad until 1st May 1998 when he returned to the UK and moved in with his friend. The house was sold on 1st January 2003 for £120,000. John incurred fees and costs of £5,000 relating to the sale. The house was estimated to be worth £45,000 on 31st March 1982.

Feedback

It is first necessary to calculate the proportions of exempt and chargeable months to the period of ownership since 31st March 1982. The total period of ownership is 252 months (21 years from 1.1.82 to 1.1.2003).

Period	Exempt months	Chargeable months
1.1.82–31.3.82	3	0
1.4.82–30.6.84 (occupied)	27	0
1.7.84–31.3.88 (working away in UK <4 years)	45	0
1.4.84–30.4.93 (occupied)	61	0
1.5.93–31.12.99 (see below)	0	80
1.1.2000–1.1.2003 (last 36 months)	36	0
	172	80

The period from 1st May 1993 to 31st December 1999 is not exempt because the absence was not followed by a period of owner occupation. Had he re-occupied the house after this period instead of moving in with his friend, even for a short time, the period 1st May 1993 to when he moved out would also have been exempted under the working away rules, and the normal principal private residence exemption.

Now the chargeable gain can be calculated:

	£
Gross proceeds	120,000
Incidental costs of disposal	5,000
Net proceeds	115,000
Less 31.3.82 value	45,000
Unindexed untapered gain	70,000
Less indexation allowance	
$1.047 \times £45,000$	47,115
Private residence exemption:	22,885
$172/252 \times 22,885$	15,620
Indexed gain	7,265
Tapered gain £7,265 × 85%	6,175

(No computation based on cost needs to be done because it would clearly produce a higher gain.)

Taxpayers living in job-related accommodation will be able to claim any residence which they own as a principal private residence provided that they intend to occupy it as their main residence in due course. Look back to Chapter 7 for a definition of job-related accommodation.

Lettings

If a lodger lives with a family sharing living accommodation and eating with them there is no liability to capital gains tax. However, if part or all of a property is let for residential purposes, the principal private residence exemption may extend to gains which relate to the period of letting.

This relief is available if:

- the owner is absent and lets the property during a period which is not considered a deemed period of occupation

- only part of the property is let.

The relief available is the lowest of:

- the gain accruing during the letting period
- £40,000
- the total gain which is exempt under the principal private residence provisions.

However, this relief cannot turn a gain into an allowable loss for capital gains tax purposes.

Business Use

If part of the residence is used wholly for business purposes the gain which is attributable to the use of that part is taxable. This is an important point to bear in mind when deciding whether to claim that part of a residence is used exclusively for business purposes, perhaps an office or a workshop. In the short term it may be possible to set some expenses against income for income tax purposes but it may give rise to a substantial liability for capital gains tax purposes in the future.

Reliefs from capital gains tax

As you have already seen capital gains tax is largely intended to create a fair and equitable system of tax and to limit the incentives to create a capital receipt rather than a revenue receipt. However, there are a number of situations when relief is available to mitigate the impact of capital gains tax. For example, the profit on the sale of a taxpayer's principal private residence is exempt from capital gains tax.

There are also special reliefs available on retirement from a business. These recognise the fact that taxpayers often provide for retirement by investing in the growth of the business rather than contributing to a pension fund.

Businesses often sell an asset intending to replace it with another. For example, a business may move to new premises and thus sell existing land and buildings in order to purchase new property. Rollover relief (which defers capital gains tax due) may be available if the proceeds from a sale of assets are invested in new assets. You may consider this to be entirely reasonable since, although a liability to capital gains tax has arisen because of the sale, the business is clearly no better off and probably needs the money it has raised from the sale to buy the new asset. In reality the taxpayer has simply exchanged one asset for another. Such a favourable tax treatment will also encourage a business to reinvest their money into other businesses assets rather than to take it out of the economy. This is good for an entrepreneurial society.

If the new asset is a depreciating asset then the taxpayer may claim holdover relief rather than rollover relief.

If a taxpayer makes a chargeable disposal for less than the market value of the asset then, providing both the donor and the beneficiary make an election, some or all of the chargeable gain can be deferred and transferred to the beneficiary by means of gift relief. This enables assets to be passed from one generation to the next without a capital gains tax liability arising.

In each of these situations the amount of taper relief depends on the period of ownership of the replacement asset.

We will consider each of these reliefs in turn.

Retirement relief

Relief from capital gains tax is given in any case where a material disposal of business assets is made by an individual who, at the time of the disposal, has at least reached the age of 50 or has retired on the grounds of ill-health below the age of 50 (TCGA 1992 s163(1)). Note that if the individual is 50 or over they can claim retirement relief when selling their business regardless of whether they actually cease work and retire. A person will be treated as having retired on the grounds of ill-health if the Board are satisfied that they have ceased to be engaged in and, by reason of ill-health, is incapable of engaging in, work of the kind which they previously undertook and is likely to remain permanently so incapable (TCGA 1992 Sch 6 s3(1)).

Retirement relief is given after the indexation allowance but before taper relief. Taper relief can then be used to further reduce any gain left.

A disposal of business assets is:

- a disposal of the whole or part of a business, or
- a disposal of one or more assets used in the business until it ceased to be carried on, or
- a disposal of shares or securities of a company (TCGA 1992 s163(2)).

In order to claim the relief the business must be owned, throughout the 12 months prior to the disposal, by:

- the individual making the disposal, or
- a trading company which is the individual's 'personal company', in which he works full time in a managerial or technical capacity, or
- a trading company which is a member of a trading group of which the holding company is the individual's personal company, and that individual works full time, in a managerial or technical capacity, in one of the companies in the group (TCGA 1992 s163(3) & (4) & (5) & Sch 6 1(2)).

A company is an individual's personal company if he exercises at least 5% of the voting rights in the company (TCGA 1992 Sch 6 1(2)).

Additionally, in order to claim retirement relief, when the disposal is of one or more assets, the disposal must take place within one year after the date on which the business ceased to trade (TCGA 1992 Sch 6 s1(2)).

The chargeable gain is equal to excess of the appropriate proportion of the gains of the disposal over the maximum relief available (TCGA 1992 Sch 6 s7(1)).

The appropriate proportion is found by dividing the company's chargeable business assets by the company's chargeable assets. Both valuations should take place immediately before the disposal takes place (TCGA 1992 Sch 6 s7(2)).

Every asset is a chargeable asset apart from assets which would not have given rise to a chargeable gain if they had been disposed of immediately before the date of disposal (TCGA 1992 Sch 6 s7(3)). In practice stock, debtors, cash, motor cars and items of plant and machinery which cost less than £6,000 are the main examples of assets which are not chargeable assets.

Similarly if there is a qualifying disposal of the shares or securities of a holding company the chargeable gain is equal to the excess of the appropriate proportion of the gains of the disposal over the maximum relief available (TCGA 1992 Sch 6 s8(1)).

A chargeable business asset is an asset, including goodwill but not including shares or securities or other assets held as investments, which is used for the purposes of the trade (TCGA 1992 Sch 6 s12(2)). In practice shares and securities and assets which are held for investment purposes are not chargeable business assets. Only part of any gain which related to chargeable business assets can receive retirement relief (see the example on the next page that illustrates this point).

If the conditions outlined above are met throughout the ten-year period prior to the date of disposal the maximum retirement relief that can be claimed in 2002/03 is the first £50,000 of the gain and one half (50%) of any gain on the next £150,000. If the conditions are met for only a proportion of the ten-year period the limits are reduced proportionately. Since in order to claim the relief the conditions must have been met for at least one year the smallest possible proportion is 10% (TCGA 1992 Sch 6 s13(1)).

If the individual has met the conditions for retirement relief in two businesses one after the other within the ten-year period prior to the disposal, the two periods of involvement can be added together for the purposes of determining the maximum relief available, provided the time between the involvement in the two businesses is not more than two years (TCGA 1992 Sch 6 s14(2)).

Strictly relief can only be claimed for two or more businesses if the final qualifying business had been undertaken for at least a year. In April 1994 the Inland Revenue announced an extra statutory concession. From 14th April 1994 taxpayers will not have to satisfy this requirement in order to add together several periods of business activity provided that all of the other conditions have been met (Statement of Practice U5).

Activity

Rupert, a company director, owns 50% of the ordinary share capital of Eco Ltd. He retired on his 60th birthday, 12th June 2002. Rupert had bought the shares in 1980 for £100,000 and sold them on 12th June 2002 for £800,000. The March 1982 value of the shares was £250,000. On the date the shares were sold the company had the following assets:

	£
Goodwill	100,000
Plant (cost £600,000)	300,000
Premises (cost £400,000)	600,000
Investments	100,000
Net current assets	500,000
	1,600,000

Calculate Rupert's chargeable gain.

Feedback

The chargeable business assets are goodwill, plant and premises with an aggregate value of £1,000,000. The chargeable assets are equal to the chargeable business assets plus the investments giving a total value of £1,100,000.

Because the March 1982 valuation is higher than the original cost it is only necessary to undertake one calculation using the March 1982 value in order to give the smallest gain.

	£	£
Proceeds		800,000
Less March 1982 valuation		(250,000)
Unindexed untapered gain		550,000
Less indexation allowance		
1.047 × £250,000		(261,750)
		288,250
Less retirement relief		
Exempt amount	50,000	
$50\% \times £\left(200,000 \times \dfrac{1,000,000}{1,100,000} - 50,000\right)$	65,909	
		(115,909)
Indexed untapered gain		172,341
Tapered gain	£172,341 × 25%	43,085

Where gains eligible for retirement relief are not fully relieved by retirement relief, the relief will be applied in such a way that the maximum possible taper relief can be obtained.

As part of his reform of capital gains tax the Chancellor began to phase out retirement relief from 6th April 1999. The relief has gradually withdrawn over a five-year period by reducing the relief thresholds. The maximum thresholds over this period are:

Year	100% relief on gains up to (£)	50% relief on balance of gains up to (£)
1998/99	250,000	1,000,000
1999/00	200,000	800,000
2000/01	150,000	600,000
2001/02	100,000	400,000
2002/03	50,000	200,000

As you can see from the table, the relief will be fully withdrawn on 6th April 2003.

The Chancellor reasons that retirement relief will no longer be necessary because it will be replaced by taper relief. However, there is a fundamental difference between retirement relief and taper relief. Retirement relief is given as monetary limits, that is businesses sold for a relatively small capital gain will escape capital gains tax altogether while businesses sold for a gain of over £1 million will be taxed at the higher rate of tax, in the main.

In contrast tapering relief is given as a percentage reduction of the gain. Thus, all taxpayers will be assessed on a percentage of their gains in the future.

Rollover relief

If the consideration that a taxpayer obtains for the disposal of assets used for the purposes of the trade is used, by the taxpayer, to acquire other assets which are also used only for the purpose of the trade rollover relief may be available (TCGA 1992 s152(1)). Both the old and the new assets must fall into one of the following classes (Note: it does not matter if they fall into different categories.):

- Class 1:
    - any land or building or part of a building used only for the purpose of trade
    - fixed plant or machinery which does not form part of a building
- Class 2:
    - ships, aircraft and hovercraft
- Class 3:
    - satellites, space stations and spacecraft
- Class 4:
    - goodwill
- Class 5:
    - milk quotas and potato quotas
- Class 6:
    - ewe and suckler cow premium quotas (TCGA 1992 s155).
- Class 7:
    - fish quota

In order to claim the relief the new assets must be acquired between 12 months before and three years after the disposal of the old assets (TCGA 1992 s152(4)). It is also not necessary for the old and new assets to be used in the same business.

If rollover relief is claimed the chargeable gain is deducted from the allowable cost of the new asset. If the total proceeds from the sale of the old asset are reinvested in the new asset full relief will be given. However, if some of the proceeds are not reinvested then a chargeable gain equal to the lower of the chargeable gain before rollover relief and the amount which has not been reinvested will be subject to capital gains tax immediately.

Remember that taper relief on the second disposal will be based on the length of ownership of the second asset. This may mean losing the relief you would have received on gains due on the first asset.

Activity

Mike bought a factory in March 1987 for £500,000 and sold it for £1,000,000 in September 2002. He bought a ship in November 2002 for £850,000. Determine any chargeable gain that arises on the sale of the factory assuming that rollover relief is claimed and compute the base cost of the ship bought in November 2002.

Feedback

Disposal of factory	£
Proceeds	1,000,000
Less allowable cost	(500,000)
Unindexed gain	500,000
Indexation allowance	
0.616 × £500,000	(308,000)
Indexed gain	192,000
Less amount not reinvested	
£1,000,000 – £850,000	(150,000)
Gain eligible to be rolled over	42,000
The chargeable gain is £150,000	
Base cost of the ship	
Cost	850,000
Less rolled over gain	(42,000)
Base cost of the ship	808,000

Activity

Using the data from the previous example determine the chargeable gain arising when Mike sells the ship in June 2005 for £1 million.

Feedback

The period of ownership of a ship for the purposes of taper relief is 3 years.

	£
Proceeds	1,000,000
Less allowable cost	(808,000)
Untapered gain	192,000
Tapered gain £192,000 × 25%	48,000

Holdover relief

Rollover relief cannot be claimed if the replacement asset is depreciable. That is if it is, or within the next 10 years will become, a wasting asset. Remember that a wasting asset has a life of 50 years or less and so holdover relief is going to apply to any replacement asset with a life of 60 years or less. Plant and machinery is always treated as a depreciating asset while land and buildings are never treated as depreciating assets.

Holdover relief is available instead of rollover relief if the proceeds are reinvested in a depreciable asset. The relief is given by reducing the amount of the chargeable gain and making a reduction of the same amount in the expenditure allowable in respect of the replacement asset (TCGA 1992 s154(1)).

The held-over gain gives rise to a chargeable gain on the earlier of:

- the date on which the taxpayer disposes of the replacement asset
- the date on which the replacement asset ceases to be used for the purposes of a trade carried on by the taxpayer
- ten years after the date of the acquisition of the replacement asset (TCGA 1992 s154(2)).

If, before the held-over gain crystallised, the replacement asset is itself replaced by an asset which is not a depreciating asset then some or all of the held-over gain can be transferred to the new asset (TCGA 1992 s154(4) & (5)). Taper relief is applied to the original gain before it is deferred. There is no further entitlement to relief for the time the gain 'held-over'. For the new asset the usual rules then apply.

Activity

May bought a workshop in February 1972 for £25,000 and ran a business making and selling soft furnishings. In July 1981 she sold the premises for £40,000 and in August 1981 she bought plant for £50,000 to use in the new premises she was renting. In January 1984 May bought a new workshop for £35,000 and in October 2002 she sold the machinery for £80,000. The March 1982 value of the plant was £55,000. Determine May's chargeable gains on each of the transactions.

Feedback

July 1981 disposal	£
Proceeds	40,000
Less allowable costs	(25,000)
Gain	15,000

The entire proceeds of £40,000 were reinvested in plant and so the £15,000 gain can be held over.

January 1984 purchase
When the workshop, not a depreciating asset, was bought part of the held-over gain could be rolled over to the new workshop.

The £5,000 not eligible to be rolled over will continue to be held over until the charge crystallises 10 years after acquisition in August 1991.

	£
Total gain held over	15,000
Less proceeds not reinvested £40,000 – £35,000	(5,000)
Gain eligible to be rolled over	10,000

August 1991

The held-over gain of £5,000 crystallised and was chargeable to capital gains tax in 1991/92.

October 2002 disposal	Cost £	1982 market value £
Proceeds	80,000	80,000
Less cost	(50,000)	
1982 market value		(55,000)
Unindexed gain	30,000	25,000
Less indexation allowance		
1.047 × £55,000	(57,585)	(57,585)
Loss	Nil	Nil

Since it is not possible to create a loss using the indexation allowance the chargeable gain is nil.

Incorporation Relief

At present holdover relief is also available were a business and all its assets (other than cash) are transferred to a company in exchange for shares in that new company (TCGA 1992, 5162). This relief is referred to as Incorporation Relief. Prior to 5 April 2002 this relief was mandatory for gains after any retirement relief was applied (if applicable). From this date however, incorporations can be made without application of this relief if the taxpayer so elects. This may be in their favour if they wish to use up allowances or release gains at the new low taper relief levels.

If a taxpayer wishes to do this they must normally inform the Inland Revenue of their decision no later than the second anniversary of the 31 January following the tax year in which the transfer occurs.

Gift relief

Gift relief is available if an individual makes a disposal, otherwise than as a bargain at arm's length (i.e. 'give' it away at less than its true value), of a qualifying asset and both the transferrer and the transferee elect for the transferrer's gain to be reduced to nil. If the election is made the transferee is deemed to acquire the asset at its market value less the gain which would otherwise have arisen (before any taper relief is applied). If the transferee provides some consideration the deferred gain is equal to the gain less any excess of the consideration over the allowable costs, excluding the indexation allowance. This deferred gain is termed the held-over gain (TCGA 1992 s165(1) & (4)).

For the purposes of gift relief an asset is a qualifying asset if:

- it is, or is an interest in, an asset used for the purposes of a trade, profession or vocation carried on by:
  - the transferrer, or
  - his or her personal company, or
  - a member of a trading group of which the holding company is his or her personal company or
- it is shares or securities of a trading company, or of the holding company of a trading group, and either:
  - the shares are neither quoted on a recognised stock exchange nor dealt with in the Unlisted Securities Market, or
  - it is the transferrer's personal company (TCGA 1992 s165(2)).

If the taxpayer makes a disposal by way of a gift to a charity or for national purposes, or for a consideration which would give rise to an allowable loss, then the disposal and acquisition shall be treated as being made for such consideration as to secure that neither a gain nor a loss accrues on the disposal. The recipient of the asset is deemed to have acquired the asset at the same time and for the same consideration as the donor of the gift (TCGA 1992 s257(2)).

A gift is deemed to be for national purposes if it is made to the National Gallery, the British Museum, the National Trust or universities, among others (IHTA 1984 Sch 3).

It should be noted that no gift relief is available for any transfers of shares or securities to a company by individuals or trustees after 9th November 1999.

Activity

Alan sold a small paper recycling plant to his daughter Sarah on 30th May 2002. The plant had a market value of £300,000 but Alan sold it to Sarah for £100,000 and claimed gift relief. Alan had bought the business in May 1982 for £50,000. Sarah intends to sell the business in April 2004 and believes that she will be able to obtain a price of £400,000. Determine Alan's chargeable gain and advise Sarah on the amount of any chargeable gain she will be assessed on when she sells the business.

Feedback

Sarah's period of ownership for taper relief purposes is 1 year.

	£
Alan	
Deemed proceeds	300,000
Less allowable cost	(50,000)
Unindexed gain	250,000
Less indexation allowance	
0.992 × £50,000	(49,600)
Indexed untapered gain	200,400
Less gain held over	
£200,400 − (£100,000 − £50,000)	(150,400)
Untapered gain	50,000
Tapered gain £50,000 × 50%	25,000
Sarah	
Proceeds	400,000
Less allowable cost £300,000 − £150,400	(149,600)
Untapered gain	250,400
Tapered gain £250,400 × 50%	125,200

Alan's chargeable gain is £25,000 while Sarah's chargeable gain will be £125,200 if she sells the business as planned.

If both retirement relief and gift relief are available retirement relief must be deducted first. Any gain remaining can be held over.

Tax planning

Capital gains tax is a tax which is amenable to tax planning because the timing of events is often within the control of the taxpayer. Tax planning is also an important issue because it is possible to incur a significant capital gains tax liability if good advice is not taken.

Consider the disposal of a company on retirement. The taxpayer can sell either the shares of the company or the business's assets and wind the company up.

If the assets are sold a capital gains tax liability will accrue to the company. When the company is then liquidated the taxpayer will incur a second capital gains tax liability on the gain received on the shares. The taxpayer may be able to use retirement relief to mitigate the second charge but the total amount of tax paid is obviously likely to be relatively high.

If the shares are sold then only the gain on the shares will be taxable and once again the retirement relief can be used to mitigate the charge.

However, for a number of reasons the purchaser may rather buy the assets than the shares. If the company is sold the purchaser also acquires the liabilities and obligations of the company whereas acquiring the assets is more straightforward.

These factors, together with many more, will become part of the negotiations which are entered into before the business is sold.

Regardless of whether the assets or the shares are disposed of there are a number of points to be borne in mind when disposing of a business. For example, if the taxpayer is married ensure that both the spouses have an interest in the business so that each can claim retirement relief.

In general, capital disposals should be made as early as possible in the fiscal year in order to delay the payment of tax as much as possible. An individual or married couple should try to fully utilise their annual exemption limit each year since if it is not used it cannot be carried forward.

If at all possible losses should not be wasted by being set against current gains which would otherwise have benefited from the annual exemption limit.

It is important to obtain good tax advice before making a large disposal so that any exemptions and reliefs available can be claimed.

Summary

Capital gains tax was introduced in 1965. In the early years there were many changes in the legislation which were needed to correct fundamental flaws in the original legislation. One of the most important developments was the introduction of the indexation allowance. Of course this also significantly reduced the amount of tax which was collected but it might be argued that it made the tax 'fairer' which seems to be one of the most important characteristics of capital gains tax. Now that the indexation allowance is frozen and taper relief has been introduced, the question of whether the tax is fair must be raised again.

Taxpayers, both individuals and companies, pay tax on their chargeable gains. However, there is considerable scope for tax planning as the taxpayer can often choose the date on which to make the disposal. There are a number of reliefs which are available to taxpayers including relief on a principal private residence and retirement relief, rollover relief, holdover relief, incorporation relief and gift relief. Remember also that gains on assets held in pension funds and personal equity plans are not subject to income tax or capital gains tax. These reliefs, together with the annual exemption limit, enable most individuals to avoid any liability to capital gains tax.

Project areas

Because of the introduction of the new CGT regime, there is great scope for dissertations on the subject of capital gains tax. A survey of holders of chargeable assets, especially chargeable business assets, to determine if the change will affect their decision to hold or sell might be interesting. A comparison of the taxation of capital gains in more than one country is likely to be interesting. The question of whether capital gains tax is a fair tax is always worth asking. You might like to consider whether encouraging individuals to hold business assets for longer periods of time is a good idea.

Discussion topic

It is sometimes possible for individuals to arrange their affairs in order to have receipts taxed as income rather than a capital gain and vice versa. For example, directors planning to sell a family company could either pay themselves high salaries taxable under Schedule E or take relatively low salaries thus increasing the funds retained in the business, leading to a higher value for their shares when the company is sold. List the taxation consequences of making this decision and discuss the circumstances in which income may be preferable to capital gains.

Case Study materials

Having completed this chapter successfully you should now review KPMG Case Study 6 from the website (http://www.taxstudent.com). This case will illustrate for you the application of the material you have learned in this chapter using the same family you met at the end of Chapter 7.

Computational questions

Question 1.   (based on ACCA June 1990).

(a)   Adrienne sold 2,000 ordinary shares in The Paramount Printing Company plc, a quoted company, on 4th August 2002 for £18,000. She had bought ordinary shares in the company on the following dates.

	Number of shares	Cost £
12th April 1970	1,500	4,000
1st May 1988	1,500	5,000

The value of each of the shares on 31st March 1982 was £4.

No election has been made or is to be made to have all pre-March 1982 acquisitions rebased to March 1982.

Required   Calculate, before annual exemption, the capital gain assessable on Adrienne in 2002/03.

(b)   James purchased a house in Oxford, 'Millhouse', on 1st July 1986 and took up immediate residence. The house cost £50,000. On 1st January 1987 he went to work and live in the United States where he stayed until 30th June 1989. On 1st July 1989 James returned to the UK to work for his United States employers in

Scotland where it was necessary for him to occupy rented accommodation. On 1st July 1990 his mother became seriously ill and James resigned from his job to go and live with her. His mother died on 30th September 1991 leaving her house to James. James decided to continue to live in his mother's house and finally sold 'Millhouse' on 30th June 2002 for £200,000. The value of the house on 31st March 1982 was £75,000.

Required   Calculate, before annual exemption, the capital gain assessable on James in 2002/03.

Question 2.   (based on ACCA December 1988).

(a) Arthur bought 300 hectares of land to be used in his business for £120,000 on 1st February 1988. On 1st July 2002 he sold 50 hectares of the land for £40,000. On 1st July 2002 the value of the remaining 250 hectares was £187,500.

Required   Calculate Arthur's capital gain in 2002/03 (before annual exemption).

(b) Margaret sold her holiday home, which had never been her main residence, on 6th April 2002 for £65,000. She had purchased the home on 6th April 1971 for £3,000. The following amounts of enhancement expenditure were incurred:

6th October 1975	Central heating system	£1,000
6th May 1985	Extension to rear of house	£4,000

The value of the house on 31st March 1982 has been agreed with the Inland Revenue as £25,000.

Required   Calculate Margaret's capital gain in 2002/03 (before annual exemption).

(c) On 3rd August 2002, her 55th birthday, Anne retired from running her nursing home and gave the business to her daughter, Jocelyn. Both Anne and Jocelyn are resident and ordinarily resident in the UK. Anne had owned the business for the previous 15 years.
    Her accountant had agreed the chargeable gain with the Inland Revenue at £200,000, before any reliefs.

Required   State the reliefs (other than annual exemption) which can be claimed and outline the effect of claiming them.

Question 3.   (based on ACCA June 1989).

(a) On 6th April 1968 Edward acquired for £5,000 a small workshop where he carried on his trade as a furniture maker. On 6th April 2001 he sold the workshop for £120,000 and moved on 10th April 2002 to smaller premises which cost £114,000. Edward was born in 1943. The market value of the workshop on 31st March 1982 was £60,000.

Required   Calculate Edward's capital gain in 2002/03 (before annual exemption), assuming that Edward makes any necessary claim to reduce his capital gain. Edward has not elected to have all pre-31st March 1982 acquisitions rebased to 31st March 1982.

(b) On 31st August 2002, his 56th birthday, Robert retired from his newsagent's business which he had owned since 1st September 1986. The sale proceeds were £425,750 and the allocation of this amount was agreed with the purchaser of the business. The relevant details are as follows.

	Cost £	Sale proceeds £
Goodwill (September 1986)	10,000	180,000
Shop premises (September 1986)	80,000	240,000
Movable fittings (April 1991)	2,000	1,500
Trading stock (July 1994)	1,500	1,750
Motor van (October 1993)	3,000	2,500
		425,750

Required   Calculate Robert's capital gain in 2002/03 (before annual exemption), arising from the disposal of the business assets. Robert has not elected to have all pre-31st March 1982 acquisitions rebased to 31st March 1982.

(c) Michelle bought an antique vase in January 1980 for £2,000 and sold it in November 2002 for £8,000. £800 sales commission was deducted from the sale price. The vase was valued at £4,000 on 31st March 1982.

Required   Calculate Michelle's gain in 2002/03 (before annual exemption). Michelle has not elected to have all pre-31st March 1982 acquisitions rebased to 31st March 1982.

(Note: answer available via lecturer's website)

Question 4.   (based on ACCA Tax Framework June 1994).

(a) On 31st July 2002, his 56th birthday, Oskar Barnack retired as sales manager of European Traders Limited and sold his 10% ordinary shareholding in the company. He had been a full-time employee of the company for 12 years. The sale of the shares on 31st July 2002 realised £550,000. Oskar inherited the shares on 1st August 1989 at a valuation of £125,000. The market values of the assets of the company at 31st July 2002 were:

	£
Land and buildings	700,000
Goodwill	300,000
Shares held as an investment	200,000
Stock	160,000
Bank and cash balances	25,000
Government securities	220,000

Calculate Oskar's chargeable gain in 2002/03, before annual exemption.

    (b) Walter purchased his business premises in October 1976 for £10,000. In May 1986 he gave them to his son Darren when the value was £50,000. The appropriate joint election for gift relief was made. The value of the premises on 31st March 1982 was £40,000. In April 2002 Darren sold the premises for £200,000.

Required Calculate the capital gain assessable on Darren in 2002/03, before annual exemption.

    (c) Calculate the capital gains assessable for 2002/03 and any losses carried forward in each of the following situations:

        (i) Marlene had capital gains for the year 2002/03 of £12,000 and capital losses for the year 2002/03 of £8,000.

        (ii) Moira had capital gains for the year 2002/03 of £12,000 and capital losses brought forward of £8,000.

        (iii) Marina had capital gains for the year 2002/03 of £3,000 and capital losses brought forward of £8,000.

        (iv) Melissa had capital gains for the year 2002/03 of £12,000, capital losses for the year 2002/03 of £8,000 and capital losses brought forward of £4,000.

(Note: answer available via lecturer's website)

9 Corporation tax

Introduction

Corporation tax is charged on the profits of companies, and the Corporation Tax Acts apply for any financial year for which Parliament so determines (ICTA 1988 s6(1)). Until 1965 companies were taxed under the income tax legislation. In 1965 a reform of the tax system led to the introduction of corporation tax. As you will learn in this chapter there are many similarities in the way in which companies are taxed under corporation tax rules compared to sole traders and partnerships who are subject to income tax, including the use of the same schedule system. However, there are some important differences in the way in which corporation tax rules apply to be aware of. At the end of this chapter you will be able to:

- describe the imputation system of taxation
- state the basis of assessment of tax for companies
- determine the profits chargeable to corporation tax
- calculate a company's corporation tax
- state the date on which the corporation tax is due
- compute the loss relief available to a company.

The liability to corporation tax

For corporation tax purposes a company is defined in the Companies Act 1985 as being either a corporate body or an unincorporated association. The definition of a company extends to organisations such as clubs and political associations which are therefore subject to corporation tax. Remember that the definition excludes part-nerships, which are subject to income tax like sole traders.

UK resident companies are liable to corporation tax on their total world-wide profits arising in an accounting period regardless of whether the profits are remitted to the UK or not (ICTA 1988 s12(1)). However, dividends received from other UK resident companies are not liable to corporation tax (ICTA 1988 s208). The capital gains of a company are not subject to capital gains tax. Instead, its capital gains are subject to corporation tax just like all their other income (ICTA 1988 s6(3)).

A company is deemed to be UK resident if it is either incorporated in the UK or if its effective management and control are exercised in the UK. A company is still deemed to be resident in the UK, even if it is no longer carrying on any busi-ness or it is being wound up outside the UK, if it was resident in the UK immedi-ately prior to it ceasing to trade or being wound up (FA 1988 s66(2)).

Non-resident companies are liable to UK corporation tax if a trade is carried on in the UK through a branch or agency. The trading profits arising, directly or indirectly, from the UK based branch or agency are liable to UK tax whether or not they arise in the UK. Income from property or rights either used by, or held by or for the branch or agency is chargeable to corporation tax, as are any chargeable gains arising from the disposal of assets which were situated in the UK (ICTA 1988 s11(1) & (2)).

The imputation system of taxation

In Chapter 3 we considered whether companies should be liable to tax given they are just collections of other taxpayers operating in business using a particular legal structure. We also reviewed the principal methods of taxing companies that are used in practice despite this possible issue. When corporation tax was first introduced the classical system was used. Under the classical system the relationship between a company and its shareholders is ignored for tax computations. A company pays tax on its profits without reference to its dividend policy and its shareholders pay tax on their dividends received without receiving any relief for the tax already paid by the company on those profits. This is a simple system but does lead to distributed profits being taxed twice, once in the hands of the company and then again in the hands of the shareholders. This is how company profits are taxed in many parts of the world, however, including in the USA.

In 1973 in the UK this problem of double taxation of distributed profits led to a switch to the imputation system under which shareholders were given a tax credit for the corporation tax which had been paid by the company. The tax credit was used to offset any liability to income tax. This is the system still in operation in the UK. If you need to, look again at the way in which dividends are included in a tax computation under Schedule F in Chapter 4 to see how these credits are applied in personal tax computations. The advantage of this system of taxation over the classical system is that the impact of double taxation on distributed profits is reduced.

For the current tax year the tax credit is set at a rate of 10%. Taxpayers receive a tax credit equal to 1/10th of any gross dividend from a UK company. Gross dividends, that is the dividend actual received together with the related tax credit received by basic rate taxpayers, are subject to income tax at a rate of 10%. This means that lower rate and basic rate taxpayers are able to use their tax credit to fully satisfy their tax liability. Higher rate taxpayers are taxed at a rate of 32.5% on their gross dividends received although of course they are able to use the tax credit to reduce the tax liability. Individual non-taxpayers are not able to reclaim the tax credit under the current tax system.

Calculation of the corporation tax payable

Company taxable income is computed under Schedule D Cases I, III, V and VI on the full amount of the profits or gains or income arising in the accounting period (whether or not received in or transmitted to the UK), after any deductions authorised by the Corporation Tax Acts (ICTA 1988 s70(1)).

In order to calculate the corporation tax payable you will need to undertake a number of steps. These are:

1. Determine the accounting period(s) which are to be assessed.
2. Adjust accounting profits for tax purposes and allocate income and allowable expenditure to the correct period.

3. Calculate the profits chargeable to corporation tax.
4. Ascertain the rate(s) at which corporation tax will be charged.

In the first section of this chapter we will review each of these stages in order.

1. Determining the accounting period to be assessed

Look for the similarities and differences between the basis of assessment for companies and unincorporated traders when reading this section. The calculations are largely the same with just a handful of changes.

Corporation tax is assessed and charged for any accounting period of a company on the full amount of the profits arising in the period, whether or not received in or transmitted to the UK, minus allowable deductions.

An accounting period of a company shall begin, for corporation tax purposes, whenever:

- the company comes within the charge to corporation tax; usually on commencing to trade
- an earlier accounting period of the company ends without the company then ceasing to be within the charge to corporation tax (ICTA 1988 s12(2)).

An accounting period of a company shall end, for the purposes of corporation tax, on the earliest of the following:

- 12 months after the beginning of the accounting period
- an accounting date of the company or, if there is a period for which the company does not make up accounts, the end of that period
- the commencement of a winding up
- the date on which the company ceases to be UK resident
- the date on which the company ceases to be liable to corporation tax (ICTA 1988 s12(3)).

Beware that you do not confuse accounting periods for tax purposes (called 'accounting periods') with the company's reporting period for accounting purposes (called 'periods of account'). Whilst these two are often the same (usually 12 months long and ending on the same day) this is not always the case. The key rule to remember is an accounting period for tax purposes cannot be more than 12 months long so if the period of accounts (for reporting purposes) is longer than 12 months it must be split up into more than one accounting period for tax calculations. If the accounting period is less than 12 months long then it becomes its own chargeable period. Be aware that this is one of the important differences between soletraders/partnerships and companies. The former can have longer tax periods as we discussed in Chapter 5.

Activity

Apply the above rules to determine the accounting periods for tax when a company changes its year end from 31st December to 31st March by having a 15-month period of accounts starting on 1st January 2003.

Feedback

The 1st January 2003 is the start of an accounting period because it is immediately after the end of the previous accounting period. Since it ends 12 months after it starts the first accounting period must run from 1st January 2003 to 31st December 2003.

The second accounting period must commence as soon as the first one finishes and so it begins on 1st January 2004. It ends at the end of the period of account which is 31st March 2004.

Try the next activity to be sure that you understand the difference between accounting periods and periods of account.

Activity

State the accounting periods for each of the following periods of account:

Blue Ltd. has a period of account for the year to 30th September 2002.
Green Ltd. has a period of account for the 6 months to 31st December 2002.
Yellow Ltd. has a period of account for the 15 months to 31st January 2003.
Pink Ltd. has a period of account for the 26 months to 31st March 2003.

Feedback

Blue Ltd.
The accounting period is the period of account, i.e. the 12 months to 30th September 2002.

Green Ltd.
Again the accounting period is the same as the period of account, i.e. the 6 months to 31st December 2002.

Yellow Ltd.
The first 12 months of the period of account forms an accounting period. The remaining 3 months of the period of account makes a second accounting period. Hence the 12 months to 31st October 2002 and the 3 months to 31st January 2003 are the accounting periods.

Pink Ltd.
The accounting periods are made up of two 12-month periods and a 2-month period, namely the 12 months to 31st January 2002, the 12 months to 31st January 2003, the 2 months to 31st March 2003.

2. Allocating profits to accounting periods

In the activity above you found that the 15-month period of account was split into two accounting periods for tax purposes, the first one 12 months long and the second one three months long. If this split happens we must then split the profits between the two periods in the following way:

- Schedule D Case I, III and VI income before capital allowances is apportioned on a time basis (ICTA 1988 s72). In our example 12/15ths would be included in the first accounting period while the remaining 3/15ths would be included in the second accounting period.
- Capital allowances, including balancing allowances and charges, are calculated for each accounting period. Writing down allowances are also reduced for short accounting periods. For companies, although a short period of account will result in an adjustment to the capital allowances available, there are never any reductions in capital allowances for private usage of assets owned by the company. Instead private use is charged on the user as a benefit in kind.
- Other income is usually allocated on an actual basis to the period to which it relates. For example, rent is allocated to the period in which it is due. Bank Interest (and other non-trading loan relationships e.g. Building Societies) however, are allocated on an accrued basis.
- Charges are allocated to the period in which they are paid.
- Chargeable gains are allocated to the period in which they are realised.

Activity

Cherry Ltd. makes up accounts for the 18 months to 31st March 2003. The company's results for the period of account are:

		£
Trading income before capital allowances		300,000
Bank interest (gross) received:	31.12.2001	1,200
	30.9.2002	1,000
	31.3.2003	1,100
Chargeable gains disposal:	31.12.2001	5,000
	6.6.2002	3,000
	31.12.2002	7,000
Charges on income paid:	31.12.2001	15,000
	31.12.2002	20,000

Calculate the chargeable profits for each of the accounting periods within the period of account.

Feedback

The period of account will be split into two accounting periods, the 12 months to 30th September 2002 and the 6 months to 31st March 2003.

The chargeable profits are:

		12 months to 30.9.2002	6 months to 31.3.2003
Trading income	12/18 × 300,000	200,000	
	6/18 × 300,000		100,000
Bank interest received		2,200	1,100
Chargeable gains		8,000	7,000
		210,200	108,100
Less charges on income		15,000	20,000
		195,200	88,100

Note – as, for tax purposes, interest received by companies is assessed on an accrued, not received, basis, you should assume the payments received on 30.9.2002 and 31.3.2003 represent all interest outstanding on those dates.

Now you need to be able to adjust the company's trading profits for tax purposes. As for income tax, the easiest way of calculating the Schedule D Case I profits is to follow the pro-forma given here. (Numbers are used in the pro forma to make it easier to follow – they do not relate to the previous example.)

Schedule D Case I adjustment of profits:

Adjustment of profits for the accounting period ended on 31st December 2002.

	£000	£000
Net profits per accounts		3,270
Add expenditure disallowed under Sch DI		530
		3,800
Less: Income not assessable under Sch DI	120	
Expenditure not included in the accounts which is an allowable deduction	180	
Capital allowances	500	
		800
Schedule D Case I income		3,000

Notice that the computation is very similar to the one prepared under the rules for income tax when looking at self-employed business taxation.

Charges are treated in the same way as they are for income tax purposes, being disallowed in the Schedule D Case I computation and relief instead given by way of a deduction from total profits. The special treatment of gifts for individual taxpayers does not apply to companies. They continue to be treated as charges on income for companies. They are paid gross by the company.

Charitable donations that are paid as part of the trading activities of the company (e.g. for public relations purposes) can, however, be deducted with other trading expenses in the Schedule D Case I calculation. These payments are not therefore treated as charges.

If the company receives a loan related to its trading activity, the interest payable, or the other debt costs, are allowed as trading expenses and can therefore be deducted from Schedule D case I income. If they give a loan, any interest received is treated as a trading receipt and is also included in the Schedule D Case calculation. Giving or receiving trade loans is referred to as a *trade loan relationship*. A company will be said to have a debt relationship if its trade loans given exceed those received, or a credit relationship if the reverse is true.

Companies are also entitled to a special credit on research and development expenditure (as defined by the normal accounting rules). If the company is a small or medium-sized company this credit is 150% of valid expenditure. For larger companies the credit is 125%. This latter case is a new credit introduced in the 2002 Budget.

3. Profits chargeable to corporation tax

Now that the Schedule D Case I income has been computed we can calculate the profits chargeable to corporation tax. Once again we will use a pro forma with numbers in it to illustrate how to do this.

Profits chargeable to corporation tax for the accounting period ended on 30th September 2002

	£000
Schedule D Case I (trading income minus capital allowances)	3,000
Schedule D Case III (net interest on non-trading relationships)	1,000
Schedule D Case V (income from foreign possessions)	500
Schedule D Case VI (miscellaneous income)	300
Schedule A (property income)	200
Taxed income (gross)	300
Chargeable gains	700
Total profits	6,000
Less charges on income (gross)	(1,000)
Profits chargeable to corporation tax (PCTCT)	5,000

You need to know a little more about some of these items before you are ready to calculate the profits chargeable to corporation tax. We will consider the relevant points in the order in which they appear in the pro forma.

Schedule D Case III

Income received under this schedule usually relates to interest from 'non-trading loan relationships' – i.e. bank and building society accounts and other interest receivable that is not to do with trading activity. This income is assessed on an accrued basis. Trading loan relationships are dealt with under Schedule D case I as we discussed above.

Note that, unlike for individuals, companies always receive interest gross from banks and building societies (no grossing up needed or 'tax deducted at source' deductions form part of the corporation tax computation). This is why it is taxed as part of this case for companies.

Any interest received or paid for non-trading loan relationships must be pooled. If the net figure is positive (debts paid are less than credits received) then the total forms part of Schedule D Case III income for the company. If a net deficit exists then it can either be set against other income for the same accounting period, surrendered as group relief if the company is part of a group, carried back against any surpluses on non-trading loan relationships in the last twelve months or carried forward to set against future non-trading profits (i.e. future PCTCT less Schedule D Case I).

Schedule D Case IV

You will notice that Schedule D Case IV is missing from the above aggregation of incomes. This is because interest from foreign securities (e.g. debentures in overseas companies) taxable under this case for individuals is taxable under Schedule D Case III for companies. Income from foreign positions is taxed under Schedule D Case V however, just as for individuals.

Schedule A

Income from land and buildings is taxed under Schedule A provided that the property is located in the UK (Schedule D Case V applies if the property is outside the UK – just as for individuals). Income includes rents due, including income from holiday lettings and furnished lettings, premiums on leases, ground rents and payments for sporting rights. As for individuals, all UK property income is combined to produce a single net Schedule A income.

Taxable income will be determined using all the Schedule D Case I rules that you are familiar with. This means that the accruals basis will be used for income and expenses including management expenses for the property will be treated as trading expenses. Because this is in line with normal accounting principles no tax adjustment will be necessary. Interest paid by a company on a loan related to UK property is dealt with under the loan relationship rules. It is not an allowable Schedule A expense. Capital allowances will be deducted to determine the Schedule A assessment.

Activity

Cyan Ltd bought a warehouse for £100,000 on 1st January 2002 and spent £5,000 having it rewired in order to obtain a fire certificate. The warehouse was let for 12 months on 1st April 2002 for a rent of £20,000 per annum paid 6 months in advance. During 2002, Cyan incurred allowable costs of £2,000.

Determine the Schedule A assessment for the year to 31st December 2002.

Feedback

	12 months to 31.12.2002 £
Income £20,000 × 9/12	15,000
Les: allowable costs	2,000
Schedule A assessment	13,000

Note that using the accruals basis the date on which rent is received or receivable is irrelevant.

The £5,000 cost of rewiring is unlikely to be an allowable deduction following the Law Shipping case (see discussion of expense deductibility in Chapter 5) because presumably the warehouse could not be let without a fire certification.

Loss relief

If a company owns several properties, the Schedule A assessment will be the aggregate of the profits and losses for all of the properties. In this way loss relief on one property is given automatically by setting against total Schedule A profits. If a loss is made in aggregate the Schedule A income is nil. The loss can then be set off against other income for the same accounting period. Any loss still unrelieved (i.e. if the business does not have enough other profits to cover the loss) can be carried forward and set against future income from any source (provided the Schedule A business is still in operation at the time) or surrendered as group relief (the latter is not covered in this book in any detail). Some restrictions to carrying forward Schedule A losses also exist if the business is taken over.

These reliefs are different to those available to individuals. Companies have more options to relieve Schedule A losses against other income than individuals can as we saw in Chapter 7.

Activity

Gold Ltd owned four shops. Income and expenditure in relation to the shops in the year to 31st March 2003 are as follows:

Y/e 31st March 2003	Shop 1	2	3	4
Income	5,000	2,000	1,000	4,000
Expenditure	4,000	3,000	4,000	3,000

Determine the Schedule A income for the two years.

Feedback

Y/e 31st March 2003		£
Income less expenditure		
Shop 1 5,000 – 4,000		1,000
Shop 2 2,000 – 3,000	(1,000)	
Shop 3 1,000 – 4,000	(3,000)	
Shop 4 4,000 – 3,000		1,000
	(4,000)	2,000

In aggregate a loss of £2,000 (2,000 – 4,000) arises giving a Schedule A income of Nil.

The loss can be relieved as described above.

Taxed income

Taxed income includes all income received net of basic and lower rate tax. Examples include interest received from a UK company (before 1 April 2001) and patent royalties but not copyright payments, gilt edged securities, bank interest or building society interest (all received gross by companies). Interest received from UK companies (before 1 April 2001) was received net of 20% tax. Patent royalties will be received net of 22% tax (23% prior to April 2000).

As part of the changes introduced by the Finance Bill 2001 all interest payments made between UK companies can be made without deduction of tax from 1 April 2001. From this date you should treat interest received from other UK companies in the same way as interest from banks – as untaxed income.

Taxed income is included in the tax computation at its gross value, that is the amount received together with the tax credit. This may be different from the amount included in the profit and loss account although figures in the accounts are usually shown gross.

The way relief is given on any tax credits received is different to sole traders. It should be netted off against tax deducted from charges and interest paid net with just the difference than being deducted from the corporation tax liability.

It is important to note that dividends received from UK companies are excluded from the tax computation because they are not subject to corporation tax, having already had tax deducted by the company issuing the dividend.

Chargeable gains

Companies are not liable to capital gains tax but their chargeable gains and allowable losses are subject to corporation tax (ICTA 1988 s6(3)). However, unlike individuals, companies do not have an annual exemption to set against their chargeable gains.

The reform of capital gains tax introduced in the 1998 Budget does not apply to companies. This means that there are a number of other differences between the way in which individuals and companies are now taxed on their capital gains:

- The indexation allowance is not frozen for disposals by companies after April 1998.
- Taper relief on chargeable gains is not available to companies.

The pro forma for calculating the chargeable gain or allowable loss is (numbers included only for illustration purposes):

	£
Gross proceeds on disposal (or market value)	12,000
Less incidental cost of disposal	(2,000)
Net proceeds	10,000
Less allowable costs	(2,500)
Unindexed gain/(loss)	7,500
Less indexation allowance	(1,000)
Indexed gain/(unindexed loss)	6,500

The indexation allowance cannot create or increase a loss, just as was the case for individuals.

Prior to April 1998, it was necessary to calculate the indexation allowance for disposals by individuals and companies. Since April 1998 the indexation allowance was frozen for individuals and so we were able to use the fixed factor given in the table in the 'Rates and Allowances' section at the end of the book to calculate the indexation allowance for disposals by individuals.

For disposals by companies you still need to know how to calculate the change in the retail price index as disposals by companies get indexation allowance right to the date of sale.

The Retail Prices Index used to calculate the indexation allowance for companies is also given in a table at the end of the book.

Remember from Chapter 8 that the indexation factor is:

$$\frac{(\text{RPI for month of disposal} - \text{RPI for the later of the month of acquisition and March 1982})}{\text{RPI for the later of the month of acquisition and March 1982}}$$

The indexation factor should be stated as a decimal correct to three decimal places.

Once you have calculated the index factor you can use it in exactly the same way as we did for individuals.

Activity

Cream Ltd sold land and buildings for £200,000 in November 2001. The property cost £50,000 when bought in December 1991. Cream Ltd spent £30,000 extending the building in June 1996.
   Calculate the chargeable gain on the property.

Feedback

	£	£
Proceeds		200,000
Less allowance costs		
Cost	50,000	
Enhancement expenditure	30,000	(80,000)
Unindexed gain		120,000
Indexation allowance		

$$\frac{173.6 - 135.7}{135.7} = 0.279$$

$0.279 \times 50,000$	13,950	

$$\frac{173.6 - 143.0}{143.0} = 0.214$$

$0.214 \times 30,000$	6,420	(20,370)
Indexed gain		99,630

Activity

Red Ltd sold a painting for £200,000 in August 2001. The painting had been bought in January 1980 for £20,000 and was valued at £30,000 in March 1982.
   Determine the chargeable gain.

Feedback

Since the March 1982 value is higher than the original cost and both computations will give a gain, we only need to determine the indexed gain using the March 1982 value.

	£
Proceeds	200,000
Less March 1982 m.v.	(30,000)
Unindexed gain	170,000
Indexation allowance	
$\dfrac{174.0 - 79.4}{79.4} = 1.191$	
$1.191 \times 30,000$	(35,730)
Indexed gain	134,270

The chargeable gain is £132,110

Quoted securities

As for individuals, special rules are needed for quoted securities because a company may undertake many transactions in the same quoted securities and in these cases a 'matching problem' may arise.

Shares which are disposed of are matched in the following order:

- shares acquired on the same day
- shares acquired in the previous nine days on a FIFO basis
- shares in the FA 1985 pool
- shares in the FA 1982 holding
- shares bought before 6th April 1965 on a LIFO basis.

Remember that the FA 1985 Pool is frozen from April 1998 for individuals but not companies. We dealt with setting up and maintaining the pool in Chapter 8. You will need to be able to make additions to the pool for companies. Look back to Chapter 8 if you are not sure how to do this.

Activity

Violet Ltd sold 2,000 shares in Superhomes plc for £50,000 in August 2001. Violet Ltd had acquired shares in Superhomes as follows:

Date	No. of shares	(£)
April 1983	500	3,000
May 1984	1,000	7,000
June 1986	1,500	12,000
September 1992	1,000	15,000

Determine Violet Ltd's chargeable gain.

Feedback

FA 1985 Pool	Date	No. of shares	Cost £	Indexed Cost £
	April 1983	500	3,000	3,000
	May 1984	1,000	7,000	7,000
		1,500	10,000	10,000

Indexation

$$\frac{94.8 - 84.3}{84.3} = 0.125$$

0.125×3000				375

$$\frac{94.8 - 89.0}{89.0} = 0.065$$

$0.065 \times 7,000$				455
Balance @ 6.4.1985		1,500	10,000	10,830

Indexation

$$\frac{97.8 - 94.8}{94.8} \times £10,830$$

				346
Acquisition June 1986		1,500	12,000	12,000
		3,000	22,000	23,176

Indexation

$$\frac{139.4 - 97.8}{97.8} \times £23,176$$

				9,849
Acquisition September 1992		1,000	15,000	15,000
		4,000	37,000	48,025

Indexation

$$\frac{174.0 - 139.4}{139.4} \times £48,025$$

				11,910
		4,000	37,000	59,935
Disposal August 2000 (50% of holding)		(2,000)	(18,500)	(29,970)
		2,000	18,500	29,965

	£
Proceeds	50,000
Less cost	(18,500)
Unindexed gain	31,500
Less indexation allowance	
29,970 – 18,500	(11,470)
Chargeable gain	20,030

The treatment of bonus issues, stock splits, right issues, take-overs and mergers and capital distributions are the same as for individuals.

Other aspects of taxation of chargeable gains

The treatment of the disposal of chattels, assets held at 31st March 1982, part disposals and negligible value claims is the same for companies as it is for individuals, subject only to the differences set out above.

The principal private residence relief legislation, retirement relief and gift relief, obviously are not available to companies.

Rollover relief and holdover relief are available to companies however, an amendment was made in the 2002 Budget for companies on some assets. These new rules apply to expenditure and receipts by companies related to intangible assets after 1 April 2002. A form of rollover relief, but not the same as normal rollover relief, will be available on realising intangible assets in the future where the proceeds are reinvested in new intangibles. This means these assets are removed from normal rollover relief rules if they are purchased after 1 April 2002 (although the company maintains the right to choose which set of rules it wishes to apply if the assets were owned on 1 April 2002).

Activity

Burgandy Ltd bought an office block to use in its business in June 1982 for £100,000. In March 2002 the company sold the building for £300,000 and at the same time bought another office block to use in its business.

Assuming that Burgandy claims rollover relief calculate the chargeable gain arising on the disposal of the office block if the replacement office block has a cost of:

(a) £380,000
(b) £280,000
(c) £180,000.

Feedback

	£
Proceeds	300,000
Less cost	100,000
Unindexed gain	200,000
Less indexation allowance	
$\dfrac{174.5 - 81.9}{81.9} = 1.131$	
1.131 × 100,000	113,100
Indexed gain	86,900

(a) Since all of the sale proceeds have been reinvested in the replacement building the entire gain be rolled-over against the cost of the new building. The allowable cost of the new building is £293,100 (£380,000 – £86,900).

(b) £20,000 of the sale proceeds have not been reinvested in the new asset and this amount will be chargeable leaving £66,900 (£86,900 – £20,000) to rollover. The allowable cost of the new building is £213,100 (£280,000 – £66,900).

(c) £120,000 of the sales proceeds have not been reinvested in the new asset and this amount exceeds the indexed gain, so the entire £86,900 is immediately chargeable and the allowable cost of the new office block is the purchase price of £180,000.

Activity

Navy Ltd sold a warehouse used exclusively for business purposes for £200,000 in November 1998 realising a chargeable gain of £50,000. The company also bought fixed plant for £240,000 in November 1998. The company elects to hold-over the gain on the warehouse against the fixed plant. How will the held-over gain be treated (assuming current tax rules still apply) if:

(a) Navy Ltd sells the fixed plant in January 2003
(b) Navy Ltd sells the fixed plant in April 2011
(c) Navy Ltd bought another warehouse for business use in December 2001 and elected to transfer the held-over gain on the fixed plant to the new warehouse which cost £220,000
(d) The new warehouse in part (c) cost £185,000.

Feedback

(a) The replacement asset is sold before the tenth anniversary of its acquisition. The allowable cost of the fixed plant is £240,000 for the purposes of determining the chargeable gain or allowable loss arising on its disposal and the gain of £50,000 crystallises.

(b) The replacement asset is still held on the tenth anniversary of its acquisition. Hence the held-over gain of £50,000 crystallises in November 2008 and will be included in the company's chargeable gain in 2008/09.

(c) Because the whole of the proceeds of the disposal of the original warehouse have been invested in the new warehouse the total held-over gain of £50,000 can be rolled over. The allowable cost of the new warehouse will be £170,000 (£220,000 – 50,000).

(d) £15,000 (£200,000 – £185,000) of the proceeds of the original warehouse were not reinvested in the new warehouse and so cannot be rolled-over. It continues to be held-over against the fixed plant and will become chargeable in November 2008 at the latest.

The remaining £35,000 (£50,000 – £15,000) of the gain is converted to a rolled-over gain.

The allowable cost of the new warehouse will be £150,000 (£185,000 – £35,000).

Activity

Bournemouth Ltd had the following results for the year ended 31st March 2003.

	£000	£000
Gross profit on trading		1,200
Investment income		300
Profit on sale of investments		200
		1,700
Less: Depreciation	100	
Directors' emoluments	150	
Patent royalties payable	30	
Audit and accountancy fees	45	
Legal costs	20	
Salaries	100	
Premium on lease written off	25	
Miscellaneous expenses	30	
		500
Net profit for year		1,200

	£000
(a) Investment income:	
Investment income comprised the following:	
Dividends from UK companies (gross)	200
Loan interest from UK company (gross- non-trading loans)	100

(b) Profit on sale of investment:

The profit on the sale of investment relates to a sale of quoted ordinary shares during the year. The chargeable gain is £150,000.

(c) Legal costs

	£000
Legal costs comprised the following expenditure:	
Costs re debt collection	5
Costs re issue of shares	12
Costs re renegotiations of directors' service agreements	3

(d) Lease premium

The lease premium written off relates to a lease taken out at the beginning of the accounting period for a warehouse for a period of 17 years. The premium paid was £25,000

(e) Capital allowances:

Capital allowances have been agreed at £50,000

Calculate the profits chargeable to corporation tax.

Feedback

First you needed to calculate the Schedule D Case I income.

Schedule D Case I	£000	£000
Net profit per accounts		1,200
Add: Depreciation	100	
Patent royalties (treat as a charge)	30	
Legal costs (not allowable)	12	
Lease premium written off	25	
		167
		1,367
Less: Investment income (dealt with elsewhere)	300	
Profit on sale of investments	200	
Capital allowances	50	
Lease premium (Working 1)	1	
		(551)
Schedule D Case I income		916

Working 1
The amount of the lease premium assessable on the landlord under Schedule A is [£25,000 – £25,000 × (17 – 1) × 2%] = £17,000. The amount which is allowable for the lessee in the accounting period ended 31st March 2003 is therefore £17,000/17 = £1,000.

Now you can calculate the profits chargeable to corporation tax.

	£
Schedule D Case I	916,000
Schedule D Case III	100,000
Chargeable gains	150,000
	1,166,000
Less charges paid: patent royalties	(30,000)
Profits chargeable to corporation tax	1,136,000

The preceding activity is intended to give you an opportunity to determine the profits chargeable to corporation tax from a profit and loss account. You can find out how to deal with the premium on a lease in the section on Schedule A in Chapter 7.

Charges paid

Just like for individuals paying income tax, charges are tax deductible payments made by the company related to trading activity. Unlike for individuals, since 1 April 2001 patent royalties are paid gross by companies if they are paid to another UK company (or an overseas company that pays UK corporation tax).

Where a charge is paid net of tax, the company must account to the Inland Revenue for the tax they have withheld. This is performed as a separate calculation to their main corporation tax computation. The tax (actually income tax) they withhold on charges is netted against any income tax that is withheld from them as recipients and the difference is paid to/reclaimed from the Inland Revenue. Since 1 April 2001 as all patent royalty and loan interest payments made to other UK companies (or other companies who pay UK corporation tax) are now paid gross you will rarely meet this computation in current year calculations.

Donations to charity can also be charges, however, they must be made gross (from 1st April 2000) if they are treated as a charge. Donations to charities which are made wholly and exclusively for the purpose of the trade are allowable deductions from the Schedule D Case I profits. Of course no payment can be both an allowable deduction from the Schedule D Case I profits and a charge, it must be used as one or the other and treated correctly in the tax computation. An example of such a donation might be a gift to an employees' welfare organisation.

The charges which are added back in the adjustments of profits computation are equal to the amount which is included in the profit and loss account. This figure will usually be determined using the accruals basis rather than the cash paid basis. The amount allowed as a charge in the calculation of profits chargeable to corporation tax is the cash paid plus any tax withheld if the charge was paid net. Hence the two figures may not be the same.

4. The rate of corporation tax payable

The rate of corporation tax is set for *financial years*, rather than the *fiscal years* of the income tax legislation. A financial year (FY) runs from 1st April to the following 31st March: the financial year 2002 runs from 1st April 2002 to 31st March 2003.

The rate of corporation tax for a financial year is set in arrears in the Finance Act (ICTA 1988 s8(5)). Hence the rate for the financial year 2002 will be set in the Finance Act 2002. In practice in recent years Chancellors have offered companies advance notice of the rates. During the mid-1980s the rate of corporation tax was reduced in stages from 52% to 35% at the same time as the first year allowances for plant and machinery were phased out. The changes were legislated for in advance. More recently in the Finance Act (No 2) 1998 the Chancellor set the rate for the financial year 1998 to 31% and the rate for the financial year 1999 to 30%. The rate has remained at 30% for financial years 2000 onwards.

Look back to Chapters 1 and 3 for a full discussion of the impact of these changes. The changes led to a broadening of the tax base, by reducing the rate of capital allowances on plant and machinery from 100% to 25%, and enabled the Chancellor to reduce the tax rates while maintaining the level of taxation raised from companies. This balance has to some extent been changed by the present Chancellor who has introduced a first year allowance for small and medium-sized businesses. However, many manufacturing companies still found themselves paying corporation tax for the first time for many years. The generous capital allowances given previously had shielded them from corporation tax entirely. Companies which did not invest heavily in plant and machinery benefited greatly from the reduction in the rate of corporation tax. Hence the move tended to benefit service industries with high labour costs and low capital investment at the expense of manufacturing industries.

In the 1996 budget the Chancellor introduced measures to reduce the capital allowances for plant and machinery with an expected useful life of at least 25 years to 6%. (We discussed the implications of these changes in Chapter 5.) The new rules will only apply to companies which spend more than £100,000 a year on such long-life assets. This limit of £100,000 must be shared equally between associated companies (irrespective of their size). For example, a company which has three associated companies will have an annual limit of £25,000 (£100,000/4).

Companies are associated with each other if either one controls the other or if both are controlled by the same person or persons, who may be individuals, partnerships or companies (ICTA 1988 s13(4)). Associated companies do not have to be UK resident.

Control for these purposes is defined as holding over 50% of the share capital or 50% of the voting power or being entitled to over 50% of the distributable income or of the net assets in a winding up (ICTA 1988 s416).

Year ends straddling 31st March

What happens to companies with year ends other than 31st March which straddle two financial years which may have different rates for corporation tax?

If the rate for the two years is the same there is no difficulty. The profits chargeable to corporation tax are taxed at the rate prevailing for the two years and only one tax computation needs to be done.

If the rate changes between the two years, however, the profits chargeable to corporation tax are apportioned to the two financial years on a time basis (ICTA 1988 s8(4)). This happened last between FY98 and FY99, when the rate of corporation tax dropped from 31% to 30%. It also happened between FY96 and FY97 when the rate fell from 33% to 31%. It has also happened for the FY02 at the starting and small companies rates.

Activity

Lilac Ltd has 30th June as a permanent accounting date. In the year to 30th June 1999, Lilac Ltd generated profits chargeable to corporation tax of £4 million. In the financial year 1998, the full rate of corporation tax was 31% while in the financial year 1999 the rate was 30%.

Calculate Lilac Ltd's tax liability for the year to 30th June 1999.

Feedback

Profits £	Tax rate %	Tax liability £
£4 million × 9/12	31	930,000
£4 million × 3/12	30	300,000
	Tax payable	1,230,000

The first nine months of the accounting period fall in the financial year 1998 and so the profits attributable to this period are taxed at 33%. The remaining three months of the accounting period fall in the financial year 1999 and so the profits attributable to this period should be taxed at only 30%.

Activity

Lemon Ltd has profits chargeable to corporation tax of £4 million for the year to 30th June 1998 and expects to have profits chargeable to corporation tax of £6 million for the year to 30th June 1999. Determine Lemon Ltd's tax liability for both these years.

Remember that the corporation tax rate was 31% for the financial years 1997 and 1998 and 30% for the financial year 1999.

Feedback

The year to 30th June 1998 falls into the financial years 1997 and 1998.

The rate of tax for both years was 31% and hence the tax for the year will be £1,240,000 (£4 million × 31%).

The year to 30th June 1999 falls into the financial years 1998 and 1999 and hence straddles a change in the rate of tax.

Profits £	Tax rate %	Tax liability £
£6 million × 9/12	31	1,395,000
£6 million × 3/12	30	450,000
	Tax liability	1,845,000

Role of Franked Investment Income (FII)

Franked investment income (FII) is made up of dividends received from another UK resident company and the related tax credit (ICTA 1988 s238(1)). You have already seen that such dividends are not subject to corporation tax and not therefore included in the PCTCT calculation. Franked investment income is important, however, as it needs to be used when determining the rate of corporation tax a company must pay.

A new 'profits' figure is used to determine this rate which is made up of profits chargeable to corporation tax plus franked investment income. To prevent confusion with other profits this amount is always referred to as 'profits' (i.e. in quotes).

Calculation of corporation tax rate

From the 1st April 2000 a new introductory rate of corporation tax has applied (s28 FA1999.) This rate is called the 'starting rate' of corporation tax and was set for FY2001 at 10%. This has fallen however, to 0% (i.e. no tax is due) for FY2002.

Where a company has 'profits' (profits chargeable to corporation tax plus franked investment income) of less than £10,000 it will pay corporation tax at the starting rate (i.e. pays no corporation tax in FY2002). Where a company has 'profits' between £10,000 and £50,000 a sliding rate will apply that results in a percentage between 0% and the current small companies rate (19%). The scale used means that the closer the 'profits' are to £50,000 the nearer the applicable rate will be to 19%.

To find the applicable rate where 'profits' fall between £10,000 and £50,000 a formula is used to reduce the tax due on PCTCT calculated at the small companies rate. This provides what is called a *marginal relief deduction*. The formula to use is:

$$\text{Fraction} \times (M - P) \times \frac{I}{P}$$

Where M is the upper limit of the band (£50,000 for FY2002), P is the 'profits' figure (PCTCT + FII) and I is the PCTCT (without FII added). The fraction figure is set for FY2002 at 1/40th.

If the company's 'profits' lie between £50,000 and £300,000 then a rate called the small companies rate of 19% will apply.

If a company's profits chargeable to corporation tax plus franked investment income exceeds £300,000, but is not more than £1,500,000, another marginal relief is available (ICTA 1988 s13(2)). This is calculated using the same formula as for the marginal relief available between £10,000 and £50,000 except now M becomes the larger upper limit of £1,500,000.

The fraction for FY 2002 is also 1/40.

If a company has other associated companies these limits must be shared between them.

This diagram may help illustrate which rate to apply to your 'profits' figure:

Test your understanding of these rules with the following activity

Activity

Holborn Ltd has profits chargeable to corporation tax of £12,000 and dividends received of £900 for their year ended 30 August 2002. Calculate Holborn's corporate tax liability.

Feedback

	£
PCTCT	12,000
FII 900 × 100/90	1,000
'Profits'	13,000

The profits lie between £10,000 and £50,000 so marginal relief applies.

	£
Corporation tax on PCTCT £12,000 × 19%	2,280.00
less tapering relief	
1/40 × £(50,000 – 13,000) × 12,000/13,000	(853.85)
Corporate tax liability	1,426.15

(effective corporate tax rate 1426.15/12,000 = 11.88%)

Activity

Ealing plc has profits chargeable to corporation tax of £290,000 and franked investment income of £40,000 for the year ended 31st March 2003. Calculate Ealing's corporation tax liability.

Feedback

	£
PCTCT	290,000
FII	40,000
Profits	330,000

The profits lie between £300,000 and £1,500,000 so marginal relief applies.

	£
Corporation tax on PCTCT £290,000 × 30%	87,700
Less tapering relief	
1/40 × £(1,500,000 – 330,000) × 290,000/330,000	(25,705)
Corporation tax liability	61,295

(effective corporate tax rate therefore of 61,295/290,000 = 21.13%)

If a company's accounting period straddles two financial years in which any of the limits change (as the small companies rate and starting rates lower in FY2002) the accounting period is split into two, the first one ending on 31st March, and the second one beginning on the 1st April and ending on the date of the end of the accounting period. The tax is calculated for each period separately. All income and expenditure is apportioned on a time basis regardless of when any payments or receipts occurred. The upper and lower limits are proportionately reduced on a time basis.

Doncaster Ltd reported profits chargeable to corporation tax of £500,000 for the accounting period ended 30th June 1994. The lower limit for the financial year 1993 was £250,000 and the upper limit was £1,250,000. The lower limit for the financial year 1994 was £300,000 and the upper limit was £1,500,000. The marginal relief fraction for both years was 1/50. Calculate the profits which will be allocated to each period and find the limits which are used to determine the rate at which the company will pay tax.

Feedback

	Financial year 1993 £	Financial year 1994 £
Lower limits	$250,000 \times 9/12$ = 187,500	$300,000 \times 3/12$ = 75,000
Upper limits	$1,250,000 \times 9/12$ = 937,500	$1,500,000 \times 3/12$ = 375,000
PCTCT	$500,000 \times 9/12$	$500,000 \times 3/12$

Nine months of the accounting period fall in the financial year 1993 while the remaining three months fall in the financial year 1994. The profits and limits for the financial years are shown above.

Now that you can calculate the profits chargeable to corporation tax and determine the rate of tax at which a company will pay tax you are able to calculate a company's corporation tax liability.

If a company has a short accounting period the upper and lower limits are reduced proportionately (ICTA 1988 s13(6)). If a company has one or more associated companies the upper and lower limits are divided by the total number of companies associated with each other (ICTA 1988 s13(3)).

Activity

Felixstow plc prepared accounts for 9 months to 31st December 2002. Felixstow has profits chargeable to corporation tax of £160,000 and franked investment income of £40,000. Felixstow has one associated company. Determine the corporation tax payable.

Feedback

	£
PCTCT	160,000
FII	40,000
'Profits'	200,000

The limits for tapering relief are reduced by a quarter because the accounting period was only 9 months long. The limits are then divided by the total number of associated companies, in this case there are two associated companies.

Hence the lower limit is £300,000 × 9/12 × 1/2 = £112,500 and the upper limit is £1,500,000 × 9/12 × 1/2 = £562,500.

	£
Corporation tax payable on PCTCT 160,000 × 30%	48,000
Less tapering relief	
1/40 × £(562,500 – 200,000) × 160,000/200,000	7,250
Corporation tax liability	40,750

Payment of corporation tax

Before July 1999

From 30th September 1993 to July 1999 corporation tax was payable 9 months after the end of the accounting period. Companies had to pay the estimated corporation tax on the due date, that is, 9 months after the end of the accounting period, even if the exact amount was not known by that date. The company then had to file complete accounts, computations, the return form (called a CT200) and any corporation tax still outstanding on the filing date, which was 12 months after the end of the accounting period (unless the period of account is more than 18 months long in which case the return is due 30 months from the start of the period of account). This system was called 'pay and file'.

The Inspector of Taxes raised an assessment if he or she believed that the filed computation understated the amount of tax which was payable. If the amount of tax paid was either late or too little the company could also be liable for interest payments or penalties or both.

After July 1999

For company accounting periods ending after July 1999 a new payment regime has been introduced. This regime is called 'self-assessment for companies'. Individuals have been self-assessed for their income since the 1996/97 tax year.

The primary difference between the old 'pay and file' system and the new self-assessment system is that no assessments will be raised by the Inland Revenue. A company will be required to perform its own tax computation and pay over the tax due according to this computation on the correct dates (these have not changed from pay and file). If the Inland Revenue wishes to query the calculations they now have up to one year from the date of filing the computation by the company to say so. If they do not query the computation within this time then the year is completed.

In conjunction with the changes to the assessment rules, companies are also now required to maintain full records of all the information they use to do their tax computation for 6 years beyond the end of the period of assessment. Companies failing to be able to produce records if asked to by the Inland Revenue in this period could now be prosecuted.

The advantage of the new scheme to the Inland Revenue is that they can operate a 'process now – check later' approach for dealing with corporate tax returns. This enables them to spread their work load throughout the year in more flexible ways then was previously the case. A disadvantage of the scheme for the company is that they now need to employ more expert help in completing their returns which increases their compliance costs.

Payment Dates

Most companies will continue to pay their corporation tax liability 9 months after their accounting period end. However, for large companies there is a new requirement also introduced from 1st July 1999, for quarterly installments of their corporation tax liability (FA 1998 S30) – called quarterly payments on account.

Companies with taxable 'profits' of more than £1.5 million (i.e. pays full corporation tax with no marginal reliefs) will be required to pay a percentage of the total tax liability in four equal payments. This percentage has risen to 100% of the tax liability over the last few years to allow companies time to adjust to the new rules.

Last day of accounting period	% of total tax liability payable by instalments
1.7.99–30.6.2000	60
1.7.200–30.6.01	72
1.7.2001–30.6.02	88
1.7.2002 onwards	100

During the transition the balance of any tax due not covered by the quarterly instalments is due on the normal due date as at present (9 months after the year end).

The actual quarterly dates on which payments should be made are calculated using the rule – the first payment is due on the 14th day of the 7th month of the accounting period, then in three further equal payments at quarterly intervals.

Activity

Calculate the corporate tax payment dates for a large company with an accounting period ending 31st December 2002.

Feedback

The due dates will be:

1st instalment –   14th July 2002
2nd instalment –   14th October 2002
3rd instalment –   14th January 2003
Final instalment –   14th April 2003

You should note that the final instalment is not due until 3 months and 14 days after the accounting period ends. This enables the company to ensure all their records have been completed for the accounting period so that a full determination of the tax due is possible.

Where accounting periods exist of less than 12 months fewer than four payments will be made. The final instalment will always be due 3 months and 14 days after the end of the accounting period. Earlier instalments are only due if the due dates of the usual gaps (six months and 13 days then 3 monthly intervals) fall before the due date for the final instalment.

This means:

Accounting period length	Instalments due
less than 3 months	final
3–6 months	first + final
6–9 months	first, second + final
9–12 months	all four instalments

Activity

Calculate the instalment dates due for a company with an accounting period of 1st January 2002 to 31st July 2002.

Feedback

Final instalment	14th November 2002
First instalment	14th July 2002 (14th day of 7th month)
Second instalment	14th October 2002 (3 months after 14th July)
Third instalment	not due (would be due 3 months after 14th October 2002 which would fall after final instalment)

Where a company has an accounting period of less than 12 months the amounts of tax due at each instalment should be calculated using the formula:

$$\frac{3 \times CTL}{n}$$

where:

- CTL is the amount of the company's total tax liability for the accounting period due for payment by instalments
- n is the number of months in the accounting period.

Note that applications of this formula will also result in a quarter of the tax due by instalments where the accounting period is 12 months long.

Where a company has reasonable grounds for believing that its total tax liability at the end of the year will be less than the total amount that will be paid based on the amounts currently being paid in instalments, then the company can adjust subsequent payments to reflect the correct liability (or make a claim for repayment if they have already paid too much).

Income tax suffered or withheld related to charges and interest

As we saw at the start of this chapter, occasionally a company may receive some of its income after tax has already been deducted, just as individuals do. This may have been at 20% or at 22% depending on the type of income involved. This is now only from a very limited number of sources however as all UK business to business relationships will occur gross (including interest and royalty payments). Where net income is received, however, it is known as taxed income or *unfranked investment income* (UFII). The gross amount of UFII needs to be included in the company's profits chargeable to corporation tax and the income tax already paid should be deducted from the corporate tax liability.

Just as a company receives income net of tax for some income types, they will also be required to withhold income tax on certain payments if they make them (mostly to individuals or non-UK based companies). In effect, the company collects the tax on behalf of the Inland Revenue and must then pay over the correct amounts to them.

To remind you, some payments can sometimes be paid net of 20% tax (mostly debenture interest and other interest – unless now paid to other companies paying UK corporation tax) changes paid will be net of basic rate tax (22%) (e.g. patent royalties – also now unless to other UK tax paying corporations). Remember that companies receive bank interest gross so it will not be included in the taxed income calculations at all.

The difference between income tax suffered and income tax withheld is payable to the Inland Revenue at the end of each quarter (31st March, 30th June, 30th September, 31st December). A fifth payment must be made if the company's accounting period ends on a different date to one of these normal quarterly dates.

The quarterly return form, called a CT61, contains lists of all income tax suffered and all income tax withheld and the balance between the two amounts (which is the amount to be paid to the Inland Revenue).

If the tax suffered on its income is more than the tax a company has withheld on its payments then the difference can be reclaimed. In practice, no requests for repayments are normally made during a year but the balance is rolled forward from one quarter to the next. If at the end of the year tax suffered exceeds tax withheld in total, this balance can then be used to reduce the company's corporation tax bill.

The compliance cost burden this placed on some companies has been lessened in the 2001 Finance Act as the need to make payments net of tax to other companies who pay UK tax has been abolished with effect from 1st April 2001. This means payments of interest or royalties between UK companies will now all be made gross. The Revenue has reserved the right to reclaim the tax from the payer that would have previously been withheld by them if it later proves to be the case that the recipient should not have received it gross (e.g. not a company that pays UK corporation tax on their profits). An interest charge, and possibly a penalty, may also be claimed in this circumstance.

Losses

Now that you are able to calculate a company's corporation tax liability you are ready to deal with the situation which arises when companies make losses.

There are a number of ways in which a loss can be relieved. Although there are some similarities between the taxation of individuals and companies when losses are made it is probably easier to treat them completely separately. Unlike the adjustment of profits for Schedule D Case I, where a little common sense might help you to find the right answer, it is necessary to learn the rules for company loss relief. One of the easiest ways of learning the rules is to use a pro forma.

There are a number of different ways of incurring a loss and a number of different reliefs which are available. Briefly these are:

- *Trading losses*. Trading losses can be: set against other income of the same accounting period, carried back and set against trading income of earlier accounting periods, carried forward and set against future trading income.
- *Non-trading losses*. These are relieved as for trading losses except against non-trading income.
- *Capital losses*. Capital losses can be set against current or first available future capital gains. (i.e. never against income). They must be claimed against the next available capital gain. As no exemption applies to companies, no restriction on the claim is necessary, as we saw for individuals.
- *Schedule A losses*. Corporate Schedule A losses were illustrated earlier in this chapter. Briefly, they are set first against non-Schedule A income and gains of the company in the same period. Any losses left over can then be carried forward to be set against future income (of any type) provided the Schedule A business is still in operation when the losses are claimed.
- *Schedule D Case VI losses*. Relievable only against other Schedule D Case VI profits in the current or future period.

We will now look in more detail at each of the reliefs available for trading losses. In each case you will be given a pro forma which will help you tackle the problems at the end of the chapter.

Loss relief by setting against future trading income (ICTA 1988 S393(1))

If a company carrying on a trade incurs a loss in the trade in an accounting period the company can claim for the loss to be set off, for the purposes of corporation tax, against trading income from the trade in future accounting periods.

If, within three years, there is both a change in the ownership of a company and a major change in the nature or conduct of a trade carried on by the company, losses incurred in an accounting period beginning prior to the change in ownership cannot be carried forward and set against trading profits earned in an accounting period ending after the change in ownership under section 393 (ICTA 1988 s768(1)). Note that for the purposes of section 768 an accounting period is deemed to end on the date of the change of ownership (ICTA 1988 s768(2)).

A major change in the nature or conduct of a trade includes a major change in the type of property dealt in or services or facilities provided in the trade or a major change in customers, outlets or markets of the trade. The Revenue may consider that such a major change has taken place even if the change is the result of a gradual process which began outside the three-year period identified above (ICTA 1988 s768(4)).

In a Statement of Practice published in 1994 the Inland Revenue offered guidance as to what would be considered to be a major change in the nature or conduct of a trade. In addition to the factors mentioned in the legislation the Revenue would consider changes in other factors such as location of business premises, suppliers, management, staff, methods of manufacture and pricing or purchasing policies to indicate that a major change may have occurred.

The following changes would be considered to be major changes:

- A company operating a dealership in saloon cars switches to operating a dealership in tractors. Such a change would be considered a major change in the type of property dealt in.
- A company owning a public house switches to operating a club in the same, but converted, premises. Such a change would be considered a major change in the services of facilities provided.
- A company fattening pigs for their owners switches to buying pigs for fattening and resale. Such a change would be considered a major change from providing a service to being a primary producer (Statement of Practice 10/91 issued in July 1994).

Provided that the company is carrying on the same trade, the trading income from the trade in future accounting periods will be reduced by the amount of the loss. Only losses which have not been relieved by carrying back to an earlier accounting period can be relieved in this way however. The loss must be set against the first available trading profits (ICTA 1988 s393(1)).

Activity

Beige Ltd incurred a trading loss of £500,000 in the year to 31st March 2002. It anticipates the following future results:

	y/e 31st March	
	2003	2004
	£	£
Trading profits	300,000	2,000,000
Bank interest received	10,000	70,000
Chargeable gains	30,000	70,000

Determine the company's profits chargeable to corporation tax for the years to 31st March 2003 and 2004.

Feedback

	y/e 31st March	
	2002	2003
	£	£
Schedule D Case I	300,000	2,000,000
Less S393(1)	(300,000)	(200,000)
	0	1,800,000
Schedule D Case III	10,000	70,000
Chargeable gains	30,000	70,000
PCTCT	40,000	1,940,000

Loss memorandum	£
Loss for year to 31.3.2002	500,000
Less S393 (I) 31.3.2003	300,000
	200,000
Less S393 (I) 31.3.2004	200,000

You will probably find the use of a loss memorandum (separate calculation note) in this way helpful in figuring out where the loss will be used.

Charges

If the charges paid in an accounting period exceed the amount of the profits against which they are deducted and include payments made wholly and exclusively for the purposes of a trade carried on by the company, the excess of those payments can be treated as a trading expense for the purpose of section 393(1) (ICTA 1988 s393(9)). This means that unrelieved trading charges can be added to any trading losses being carried forward under s393(1).

Unrelieved charges which are not wholly and exclusively for the purposes of trade, for example donations to charities, cannot be relieved under s393(1). In addition, non-trade charges can be set against any trading income for the year in which they are paid before trading charges, which can be carried forward, and relieved.

An example should help to explain this section and will also serve as a pro forma for you to use when you attempt questions yourself.

Activity

London Ltd has the following results for the three years to 31st March 2003

	Year ended		
	31.3.01	31.3.02	31.3.03
	£	£	£
Trading profit (loss)	(10,000)	6,500	6,000
Charity donations (Non trade charges)	500	500	500
Patent royalties paid (Trade charges)	800	800	800

Calculate the profits chargeable to corporation tax for each of the years concerned.

Feedback

	Year ended		
	31.3.01	31.3.02	31.3.03
	£	£	£
Schedule D Case I	Nil	6,500	6,000
Less s393(1) loss relief		(6,500)	(5,100)
non-trading charges	0	0	(500)
trading charges	0	0	(400)
PCTCT	0	0	0
Loss memorandum			
Trading loss for y/e 31.3.01			10,000
Add: unrelieved trading charges for y/e 31.3.01			800
Loss carried forward @ 1.4.01			10,800
Less s393(1) relief in y/e 31.3.02			(6,500)
			4,300
Add: unrelieved trading charges for y/e 31.3.02			800
Loss carried forward @ 1.4.02			5,100
Less s393(1) relief in y/e 31.3.03			(5,100)
			0
Add: unrelieved trading charges for y/e 31.3.03			400
Loss carried forward @ 1.4.03			400

Note the way in which a loss memorandum has been used again. It is a good way of keeping track of the way in which the loss has been relieved.

Loss relief against total profits (ICTA 1988 s393A(1))

If a company incurs a trade loss, it can may claim for the loss to be set-off against profits, before charges, from any source arising in the accounting period in which the loss arose and against the profits before non-trade charges of the 12 months immediately preceding the accounting period in which the loss is incurred. This is only allowed however, if the company was still carrying on the trade giving rise to the loss. In each period in which the loss is relieved sufficient profits should be left unrelieved to enable any trade charges paid in that year to be relieved except for the year in which the loss arose. The amount of the reduction which may be made to the profits of an accounting period falling partly before the beginning of the 12-month period cannot exceed a part of those profits which are proportionate to the part of the accounting period falling within the 12 months (ICTA 1988 s393A(1) & (2)).

Note that when within any period of three years there is both a change in the ownership of a company and a major change in the nature or conduct of a trade carried on by the company, it will not be possible to set a loss incurred by the company in an accounting period ending after the change in ownership against any profits of an accounting period beginning before the change in ownership under section 393A(1) (ICTA 1988 s768A(1)).

Relief must be claimed for the current period before any loss can be carried back to earlier periods. The carry back is on a LIFO basis, that is, the loss is carried back to more recent periods before earlier periods.

Once again an example will help you to see how the relief is calculated in practice and provide you with a pro forma to use for your own work.

Activity

Maidstone Ltd has reported the following results for the period from 1st October 2001 to 31st March 2003.

	Year to 30.9.01 £	6 months 31.3.02 £	Year to 31.3.03 £
Trading profit/(loss)	30,000	26,000	(75,000)
Charges on income:			
trade	2,000	4,000	–
non-trade	1,000	2,000	3,000

Assuming that a s393A claim is made for the loss in the year ended 31st March 2003.
   Calculate the profit chargeable to corporation tax for all the periods.

Feedback

Maidstone Ltd

	Year to 30.9.01 £	6 months 31.3.02 £	Year to 31.3.03 £
Schedule D Case I	30,000	26,000	–
Non-trade charges	(1,000)		
Trade charges	(2,000)	(4,000)	–
	27,000	22,000	–
Less s393A relief	(14,000)	(22,000)	–
PCTCT	13,000	Nil	Nil
Unrelieved non-trade charges		2,000	3,000

Loss Memorandum	£
Loss for year to 31.3.2003	75,000
Less: s393A relief	(22,000)
six month to 31.3.2002	53,000
to make up to 12 months	
y/e 30.9.01 (£30,000 – £2,000) × 6/12	(14,000)
Loss carried forward under s393(1)	37,000

Note that it would also be acceptable to carry the loss back and set against the appropriate proportion of the previous years' profit before trade charges, i.e. £15,000 (£30,000 × 6/12).

Activity

Ginger Ltd reported the following results for the four accounting periods ended on 31st March 2003.

	Year to 30.9.00 £	6 months 31.3.01 £	Year to 31.3.02 £	Year to 31.3.03 £
Trading profit/(loss)	20,000	(15,000)	30,000	(33,000)
Taxed income (gross)	3,000	2,000	3,000	3,000
Schedule A	1,000	500	1,000	1,000
Chargeable gains		1,000		5,000
Charges on income				
Patent royalties (gross)	1,000	–	1,000	1,000
Gift (gross)	500	500	500	500

Ginger Ltd had a loss brought forward at 1st October 1999 of £10,000.

Calculate the profit chargeable to corporation tax for each of the above accounting periods assuming that loss relief is claimed as early as possible.

Feedback

You need to deal with each of the three losses in the order in which they arise so that relief is given for earlier losses before later losses.

	Year to 30.9.00 £	6 months 31.3.01 £	Year to 31.3.02 £	Year to 31.3.03 £
Schedule D Case I	20,000		30,000	
Less s393(I)	(10,000)			
	10,000			
Taxable income	30,000	2,000	3,000	3,000
Schedule A	1,000	500	1,000	1,000
Chargeable gains		1,000		5,000
	14,000	3,500	34,000	9,000
Less s393A	(11,500)	(3,500)	(24,000)	(9,000)
	2,500	–	10,000	–
Less Patent royalties	(1,000)	–	(1,000)	–
Gift (gross)	(500)	–	(500)	–
PCTCT	1,000	Nil	8,500	Nil

Loss memorandum:

	£
Loss brought forward at 1.10.99	10,000
Less s393(I) y/e 30.9.00	(10,000)
	–
Loss for 6 months to 31.3.01	15,000
Less: s393A 6 months to 31.3.01	(3,500)
	11,500
s393A y/e 30.9.00	(11,500)
	–
Loss for year to 31.3.03	33,000
Less s393A y/e 31.3.03	(9,000)
	24,000
s393A y/e 31.3.02	(24,000)
	–

Note that losses are always dealt with on a FIFO basis, that is a loss from an earlier year is relieved before a loss from a later year is dealt with. If you think about this you will realise that in practice this would happen automatically, but when working an example it is possible to make mistakes.

Any unrelieved trade charges can be added to the Schedule D Case I loss arising in the final period of trading which is carried back under s393 (ICTA s393A(7)).

Change of ownership

The legislation for the relief of trading losses outlined above may not apply if there is a change of ownership between the period in which the loss was incurred and the period in which the profits it is set against are earned. This rule applies to losses carried back under s393A(1) as well as losses carried forward under s393(1).

Specifically relief will not be available if there is a change of ownership between the two periods and there is either a major change in the nature or conduct of the trade within three years before or after the change of ownership or after the change of ownership there is a considerable increase in the level of the company's trading activities which had been small or negligible at the date of the change of ownership. If the change of ownership occurs during an accounting period the period is divided into two notional accounting periods, one before and one after the change. As usual if this is done profits and losses are time-apportioned.

If the company is a 75% subsidiary of the same company before and after the change of ownership it is deemed not to be a major change of ownership and can be disregarded for the purposes of loss relief (ICTA 1988 s768).

Basic tax planning of UK resident companies

Companies which are family owned and managed may have some flexibility when remunerating the owner/managers. Paying dividends or providing benefits in kind rather than high salaries may reduce the total national insurance contributions which must be paid. For example, when employees make contributions to a pension scheme the contributions are allowable deductions for tax purposes but not for national insurance contributions. But if the contributions are made by the employer they are fully deductible for tax purposes and do not give rise to a liability to either employee or employer national insurance contributions. Hence it may be tax efficient for small companies to operate non-contributory pension schemes.

Companies may have marginal rates of tax of 0%, 19%, 23.75%, 30% or 32.75% depending on the profits chargeable to corporation tax. Ideally companies should plan their affairs so as to avoid paying tax at a marginal rate of 32.5%. While this may not be possible a little thought may help a company to save tax at the highest possible rate. For example a company may reduce its profits chargeable to corporation tax by increasing its contribution to the company pension scheme in years in which the marginal rate of tax is relatively high. Similarly it may be possible to defer a chargeable gain to a period with a lower marginal tax rate.

Summary

This chapter has provided you with the skills needed to calculate the corporation tax liability of companies which are resident in the UK.

In order to calculate a company's tax liability it is necessary to undertake a number of steps:

• identify each source of income for a company

- determine the Schedule and Case which is used to calculate the taxable income for each source of income
- using the current year basis, which applies to the income and expenditure of companies, calculate the income which is assessable and determine any deductions from that income which are allowable for tax purposes
- determine details of any charges which are paid by the company
- this will enable you to calculate the profits chargeable to corporation tax
- calculate the income tax paid
- using the small companies limits and the tapering relief equation if necessary determine the mainstream corporation tax liability.

You are also able to state the ways in which a loss can be calculated and calculate the corporation tax for periods in which a loss is incurred or relieved.

The imputation system was explained in this chapter and the effect of recent changes in the system was discussed.

You have been able to compare and contrast the taxation of companies with the taxation of individuals. You might like to list the similarities and differences and decide if the differences between the two are sufficient for one business medium to be preferred to the other. However, it is important to remember that tax is just one aspect of the environment in which businesses operate. Other considerations are at least as important, for example the benefit of limited liability and the ability to raise extra finance.

Discussion questions

Question 1. (based on CIMA May 1987).

Compare and contrast the reliefs for trading loss in both UK unincorporated businesses and UK limited companies. You are not required to deal with group relief.

Case Study materials

Having completed this chapter you can now review, and extend, your knowledge of UK Corporation Tax compliance by reading and undertaking the KPMG Tax Business School® Corporation Taxation Case Study you will find on the website for this book (http://www.taxstudent.com).

Computational questions

Question 1. (based on ACCA June 1989).

Ultimate Upholsterers Ltd is a UK resident trading company which manufactures leather upholstered chairs. It has been trading for many years. The company's results for the year ended 30th September 2002 are summarised as follows.

	£
Trading profits (as adjusted for taxation but before capital allowances)	375,000
Net dividend from UK company (29th May 2002)	18,000
Gross loan (non-trading) interest accrued (30th September 2002)	12,000
Gross debenture interest paid (31st December 2001)	10,000
Profit on sale of land	42,000
Writing down allowances on plant and machinery	49,000

The company operates from two factories, both of which meet the definition of 'industrial building' in the Capital Allowances Act. Neither building is situated in an enterprise zone. Factory 1 was first occupied by Ultimate Upholsterers Ltd on 1st October 1980 under the terms of a 25-year lease which had been acquired for £50,000. Factory 2 was purchased on 1st January 2002 for £300,000. The factory cost £150,000 on 1st January 2002 and had been used continuously as an industrial building by the previous owner (who had owned it for 8 years) until it was sold. An extension to Factory 2 was completed on 1st July 2000 at a cost of £125,000 to provide extra production facilities following increased demand for the company's products and was brought into use on 8th August 2002.

Notes

(a) The land had been purchased in March 1974 for £5,000 and sold in December 2001 for £47,000. The value in March 1982 was £10,000.

(b) The company had no losses to carry forward on 1st October 2001.

Required Calculate the corporation tax payable for the year ended 30th September 2002.

Question 2. ABC Ltd (a company with no associates) has a corporate tax liability of £1.8 million for FY 2002.

Required Calculate the due dates for installments of corporate tax ABC Ltd will have to pay and the amounts due on each of these dates if:

(a) The company has a 12 months accounting period to 31st October;

(b) The company produces accounts for 8 months to 30th June 2002 instead (assume the amount of the tax liability is not affected for the purpose of this question).

Question 3. (based on ACCA June 1990).
Unsurpassable Umbrellas Ltd is a UK resident trading company which began to trade in 1964. Accounts have always been prepared to 31st December and the summarised results for the year ended 31st December 2002 are as follows.

	£
Schedule D Case I adjusted profit	310,000
Income from property, after expenses (31.3.2002)	4,000
Bank interest received (30.9.2002)	1,900
Chargeable gain (17.3.2002)	8,200
Patent royalties (30.6.2002)	20,000
Gross debenture interest accrued (31.12.2002)	28,200
Dividend from UK company (17.2.2002)	14,000
Dividend from UK company (17.7.2002)	18,000

Notes

(a) Trading losses of £60,000 were brought forward from 2001.
(b) Income tax had been deducted from the debenture interest received.
(c) Dates in brackets are dates upon which the transactions occurred.

Required (a) Calculate the corporation tax payable for the year ended 31st December 2002.

(Note: answer available via lecturer's website)

Question 4. (based on ACCA June 1991).

Unstoppable Uniforms Ltd is a UK resident trading company which commenced in 1970. The company had always prepared accounts to 31st March but in 2001 moved to a 30th September accounting date. The company's results for the 30 months to 30 September 2002 were as follows.

	Year ended 31.3.01 £	6 months to 30.9.02 £	Year ended 30.9.03 £
Adjusted trading profit (loss)	80,000	(170,000)	900,000
Capital allowances	10,000	20,000	100,000
Building society interest accrued	4,500	5,000	2,200
Dividends from UK companies	5,000	8,000	39,000
Bank interest received	3,000	4,500	5,000
Profit on sale of shares	0	20,000	0
Patent royalties paid (gross)	2,500	5,000	5,000
Dividends paid	20,000	10,000	250,000
Donations made to charity (gross)	500	500	500

Notes

(a) The book profit on the sale of shares resulted in an indexed chargeable gain of £15,000.
(b) Capital allowances were on plant and machinery.
(c) The company had losses to carry forward on 1st April 2001.

Required

(a) Calculate the loss relief available in respect of the trading loss for the period ended 30th September 2002 and show how this loss can be utilised assuming that claims are made against the earliest available profits.

(b) Calculate the corporation tax payable for all relevant periods after utilisation of any loss relief in respect of the loss sustained in the accounting period to 30th September 2002.

(Note: answer available via lecturer's website)

10 Value added tax

Introduction

VAT (value added tax) has become an increasingly important source of income for the UK government since it was introduced in 1973. The Treasury expects to raise almost £60billion from VAT in the fiscal year 2002/03, which is easily the second highest revenue raiser for the UK Government after income tax.

At the end of this chapter you will be able to:

- state the broad principles of VAT
- state the criteria for compulsory registration and deregistration
- state the advantages and disadvantages of registration
- identify taxable supplies
- list the occasions on which input tax is irrecoverable
- state which goods are standard rated, zero rated and exempt from VAT
- state the differences in the treatment of standard rated, zero rated and exempt supplies
- describe the main characteristics of the administration of VAT including the special schemes
- state the VAT consequences of imports and exports
- describe the system for administering VAT which is operating within the EU
- discuss the difficulties of harmonisation of VAT within the EU.

Background

VAT was introduced in April 1973 partly as a consequence of the UK joining the European Union. It replaced purchase tax, which had many anomalies, and introduced three classifications of goods and services (zero-rated, exempt and standard - rate). Goods and services were taxed in accordance with their classification. When VAT was first introduced it was seen to be a relatively simple tax which was not amenable to tax planning. However, in recent years VAT has been the focus of a considerable amount of planning attention and although simple in principle, the complexity of the rules now developed from the initial basic principles make it difficult to apply in practice.

The legal basis for VAT is contained in the Value Added Tax Act (VATA 1994) and subsequent Finance Acts. VAT is administered by HM Customs and Excise who have extensive enforcement powers. The legislation covering the administration of VAT is contained in the Customs and Excise Management Act 1979 (CEMA 1979). The Commissioners of Customs and Excise are responsible to the Treasury but are appointed by the Crown (CEMA 1979 s6(1)). The Commissioners are responsible for collecting and accounting for, and otherwise managing, the revenues of Customs and Excise (CEMA 1979 s6(2)).

VAT is an indirect or expenditure tax which is borne by the final consumer, although it is charged whenever a taxable person makes a taxable supply of goods or services in the course of business (VATA 1994 s4(1)). It is a tax on turnover not on profit, like all the other taxes we have seen in this book.

A taxable person

A person is a taxable person for the purposes of VAT while he is, or is required to be, registered under the Value Added Tax Act 1994 (VATA 1994 s3(1)). As we see below, a trader is required to register for VAT once their annual turnover of a taxable supply reaches the annual registration threshold (2002/03: £55,000). However, any trader making a taxable supply, can register whatever their turnover level is.

A taxable person can be an individual or partnership, company, club, association or charity. Unlike many things to with tax, a partnership is treated as one entity for VAT purposes, not as a collection of individual taxpayers.

A taxable supply

A taxable supply includes all forms of business supply made in return for consideration (VATA 1994 s5(2)). For example, the following transfers are taxable supplies:

- Any transfer of the whole property is a supply of goods. The transfer of any undivided share of the property or the possession of goods is a supply of services. If the possession of goods is transferred either under an agreement for the sale of goods or under agreements which expressly contemplate that the property will also pass at some time in the future, which is not later than when the goods are fully paid for, it is a supply of goods (VATA 1994 Sch 4 s1(1)).
- A treatment or process applied by one person to another person's goods (VATA 1994 Sch 4 s2).
- The supply of any form of power, heat, refrigeration or ventilation (VATA 1994 Sch 4 s3).
- The grant, assignment or surrender of a major interest in land (VATA 1994 Sch 4 s4).
- The transfer of fixed assets or current assets, including transfers to the registered trader whether or not for a consideration (VATA 1994 Sch 4 s5(1) & (4))
- Business gifts are taxable supplies unless the transfer or disposal is either a gift of goods made in the course or furtherance of the business which cost the donor not more than £50 or a gift to an actual or potential customer of the business of an industrial sample in a form not ordinarily available for sale to the public (VATA 1994 Sch 4 s5(2)).
- Goods which were owned by the business and are put to any private use or are used, or made available to any person, including the registered trader, to use for a private purpose (VATA 1994 Sch 4 s5 (6)).
- Goods lent to someone outside the business or, hired to someone are a taxable supply of services.

Input and output tax

A taxable person's input tax is the VAT:

- on the supply to him or her of any goods or services
- on the acquisition by him or her of any goods from another member state
- paid or payable by him or her on the importation of any goods from a place outside the EU

provided that the goods or services are, or will be, used for the purposes of a business carried on by the taxable person (VATA 1994 s24(1)).

A taxable person's output tax is the VAT on supplies they make or on the acquisition by them of goods from another member state (VATA 1994 s24(2)).

The difference between a taxable person's input and output tax is the amount paid to the Government. We will see how this works in practice on the next page.

The tax point

The basic tax point is the date on which a supply of goods or services is treated as taking place. This is important to know for each transaction as it will determine to which return the transaction belongs.

A supply of goods will be treated as taking place if the goods are:

- to be removed; at the time of the removal
- not to be removed; at the time when they are made available to the person to whom they are supplied
- removed before it is known whether a supply will take place; at the time when it becomes certain that the supply has taken place, or, if sooner, 12 months after the removal (VATA 1994 s6(2)).

A supply of services is any taxable supply which is not a supply of goods. A supply of services will be treated as taking place at the time when the services are performed (VATA 1994 s6(3)). A trader can elect to use the basic tax point. However, if a tax invoice is issued within 14 days of the date on which the supply is deemed to have taken place the supply will be treated as taking place at the time the invoice is issued (VATA 1994 s6(5)). The Commissioners can, at the taxpayer's request, substitute a period longer than the 14 days specified in s6(6) (VATA 1994 s6(6)). For example, some companies generate all invoices at the end of the month; if this is the case then it is likely that this date will be treated as the date of supply. The deemed date of supply is termed the tax point.

The impact of VAT on registered traders and final consumers

The easiest way to illustrate the operation of VAT and its impact on registered traders and their consumers is to use an example. The following activity illustrates the cascade effect of VAT where traders effectively account for VAT on their value added.

Susan runs a small farm on which she keeps some rare breed sheep. She sells the fleeces for £200 to a local manufacturer, Country Crafts Ltd, which employs spinners and knitters to produce garments which are sold for a total of £600 to a shop, Country Clothes Ltd, which sells the clothes to members of the public for £1,000. Both Susan and Country Crafts Ltd are registered for VAT purposes. None of the above amounts include VAT which is levied at the standard rate of 17.5% on each of the transactions. Output tax is the VAT charged on the business's supplies while input tax is the VAT suffered on supplies bought by the business. Calculate the impact of VAT on the transactions described above.

Feedback

Taxable person	Cost £	Input tax £	Net sales price £	Output tax £	VAT payable to C&E £
Susan	0	0	200	35	35
Country Crafts	200	35	600	105	70
Country Clothes	600	105	1,000	175	70

Note that the VAT suffered by the final consumer is £175 which is exactly the amount payable to Customs and Excise (£35 + £70 + £70).

Hence the tax is charged by each registered person in the chain of production. Each person is charged input tax on taxable supplies received and charges output tax on taxable supplies by him. If there is an excess of input tax over output tax the excess can be reclaimed (VATA 1994 s25(3)). An excess of output tax over input tax must be paid to the Customs and Excise (VATA 1994 s25(2)). The person making the supply is liable for any tax which becomes due at the time of supply (VATA 1994 s1(2)).

In theory then, businesses are not affected by VAT except in so far as they have to administer the tax and suffer a loss of cash flow. However, as you will see, in practice VAT does affect the operation of business and they do incur compliance costs even if not directly paying VAT when registered.

The value of a taxable supply

If the supply is for a consideration in money the consideration is taken to be the VAT inclusive price meaning VAT should be added to whatever price the good or service would otherwise be charged at. We saw how this worked for standard-rated supplies above. If the supply is for a consideration which is not wholly in money the money value equivalent of the consideration is also taken to be the VAT inclusive price (VATA 1994 s19(3)).

If consideration in money is received for more than just a supply of goods or services a proportion of the consideration which is properly attributable to the taxable supply is attributed to it (VATA 1994 s19(4)).

The open market value of a supply of goods or services is deemed to be the amount which would be payable by a person in an arms' length transaction (VATA 1994 s19(5)).

Since the standard rate of VAT is 17.5% the VAT proportion of the total consideration is $17.5/(100 + 17.5) = 7/47$. This proportion is called the VAT fraction and can be used to find how much VAT will have been paid on any standard rated supply.

Accounting for VAT

Before you can study the special schemes for VAT we discuss later in this chapter you need to understand the principles of accounting for VAT and you need to know the basic legislation and practices which deal with the accounting for VAT.

VAT returns

Registered traders must submit a VAT return, together with any VAT payable, within one month of the end of a tax period.

A tax period is a period covered by a VAT return. It is normally three months long and ends on the last day of the month. The Customs and Excise have classified trades and businesses and allocated tax periods by reference to the type of trade that is being carried on when a business registers for VAT. This enables HM Customs and Excise to spread their work evenly throughout the year. However, variations on this general rule are allowed. For example, a trader who operates four-week periods can apply to use this basis for VAT periods rather than using month ends. Some businesses also prefer to have one of the tax periods ending on the same date as the accounting year end and this is likely to be acceptable to the Customs and Excise. It is even possible to shorten the length of the tax periods to one month. This would be attractive to traders who regularly receive a repayment of VAT (i.e. their input tax exceeds their output tax), and so could improve their cash flow, but carries the penalty of having to complete 12 VAT returns a year. At the other extreme, small businesses can elect to complete only one tax return a year although they must still pay VAT throughout the year.

A transaction must be accounted for in the tax period in which the tax point occurs. The transaction is subject to the rate of VAT which prevails on the date of the tax point.

A VAT return, called VAT 100, is completed at the end of each tax period and sent to Customs and Excise (in paper form or also now via electronic submission). The VAT return includes the following information:

- output tax collected in the period
- input tax paid in the period
- net amount payable or repayable
- value of supplies to other EU countries
- value of acquisitions from other EU countries
- input VAT due on acquisitions from other EU countries.

If an excess of input over output tax exists for the period this is repayable to the business. If the output tax exceeds the input tax (as would be normal) this difference will be paid over to Customs and Excise.

The details of different payment arrangements are discussed in the special schemes section of this chapter as the actual payment arrangements for VAT can differ from business to business for a variety of reasons.

Tax invoices

Once a trader is registered for VAT the trader must supply a tax invoice to other registered traders (VATA 1994 Sch 11 s2(1)). He or she must also retain a copy of the tax invoice.

A tax invoice must include:

- supplier's name, address and registration number
- tax point
- invoice number
- name and address of the customer
- description of the goods or services including, for each type of goods or services supplied:
  - quantity purchased
  - rate of tax
  - tax exclusive amount
  - type of supply, for example sale or hire
  - rate of any cash discount available and separate totals of the cash discounts which applies to zero rated and exempt supplies.

Retailers may issue less detailed invoices when the VAT inclusive total is less than £100. They need only disclose:

- supplier's name, address and registration number
- date of the supply
- a description of the goods or services supplied
- rate of tax
- the total amount chargeable including VAT.

If a less detailed invoice is used it must not include supplies which are taxable at different rates.

Cash operated machines, for example in car parks, do not need to provide a tax invoice provided that the total value of the invoice is less than £25. Purchasers can still reclaim the input tax even though they do not have a tax invoice.

Sometimes goods and services are sold as a unit but are, in fact, made up of a mixture of standard rated, zero rated and exempt supplies. For example if a book and cassette tape are sold together, perhaps as a foreign language course, the book is zero rated and the tape is standard rated. In this case the supplier must apportion the value of the supply between the different components using an equitable basis. VAT is then levied on each part at the appropriate rate. The legislation does not offer one method to be used to apportion the value, but acceptable methods are likely to include apportionment by reference to the cost to the supplier of the components and apportionment by reference to the open market value of each component. Sometimes it is not possible to apportion the value in this way. It is then necessary to consider the sale as a composite supply and one rate will be applied to the whole of the supply.

New invoicing rules are currently being introduced in the UK as part of a European wide development of new accounting practices for VAT. These are being implemented in the UK in stages up to the end of 2003. These new rules will make the general items of information mandatory plus four additional items if necessary. They will allow invoicing small businesses and small valued items to be simplified and allow for electronic transfers of VAT invoices in some circumstances. They will also introduce new rules for outsourcing the burden associated with accounting for VAT– even allowing customers to self bill under some circumstances.

Cash discounts

With the exception of imports from non-EU-member states, if a cash discount is offered for early settlement of the invoice the VAT is levied on the value of the supply net of the cash discount (Sixth VAT Directive 77/388 art11 s11(A)). For imports from outside the EU the discount offered is ignored for the purposes of VAT unless it is actually taken up.

Input tax

So far we have simply suggested that registered traders can reclaim input tax against output tax they charge provided that they have a VAT invoice. In principle this is correct, but there are a number of special situations that you need to know about.

We will start by considering capital expenditure and then list the occasions on which input tax cannot be reclaimed.

Capital expenditure

Capital expenditure is not differentiated from revenue expenditure for VAT purposes. Hence all input tax is fully recoverable and when the asset is disposed of VAT is charged as for any other taxable supply.

The exception is the treatment of cars. Generally, input tax on cars cannot be reclaimed. Equally, registered traders need not account for output tax when the car is subsequently sold, unless it is sold at a profit, when output tax must be levied on the profit element. However, there are a number of exceptions to the rule. VAT can be reclaimed on cars:

- acquired new and intended to be sold (i.e. if you are a car dealer)
- intended to be leased to or used in a taxi business, a self-drive hire business or a driving school
- bought after 1st August 1995 wholly for business purposes, primarily leasing. If there is any use of the car for private motoring only 50% of the input VAT can be recovered.

Where input VAT on a car is recoverable, output VAT must be accounted for when the car is eventually disposed of.

Accessories bought at the same time as the car suffer the same treatment but if they are acquired and fitted after the car was acquired, the input VAT can be reclaimed provided that the expenditure is for business use.

Bad debts

Where a person has supplied goods or services for a consideration in money and has accounted for and paid tax on the supply, and the whole or any part of the consideration for the supply has been written off in his or her accounts as a bad debt, and a period of six months from the date on which payment was due has elapsed, the person is be entitled to a refund of the amount of tax chargeable on the outstanding amount (VATA 1994 s36(1) & (2)).

A refund can be claimed only if the value of the supply is less than or equal to its open market value and, in the case of goods, title to the goods has passed from the trader to either the purchaser or a person deriving title from, through or under that person (VATA 1994 s36(4)). If payments on account are made they are treated as meeting the earliest liabilities first for the purposes of this legislation. If the debtor subsequently repays all or part of the debt a corresponding proportion of the VAT repaid must be reimbursed to Customs and Excise.

The Chancellor introduced a new measure in the budget in November 1996 which was intended to enable Customs and Excise to claw back bad debt relief. Registered traders must now repay any VAT which they reclaimed on supplies for which they have not paid and on which bad debt relief was claimed by the supplier.

Registered traders who use the annual accounting scheme and hence only complete one VAT return a year will be able to account for output tax and claim bad debt relief on the same return.

Input tax specifically disallowed

In addition to unrecoverable input tax on the acquisition of cars discussed above even a registered trader cannot reclaim input tax on expenditure on:

- Business entertaining unless the expense is allowable for either income tax or corporation tax purposes (see Chapter 5).
- Living accommodation for directors.
- Non-business items which have been recorded in the business accounts. If the taxable supply is acquired partly for a business use and partly for private use, the registered trader may either reclaim all of the input tax and then account for output tax on the value of the supply taken for private use or reclaim only the business element of the input tax. If the taxable supply is a service only the second method can be used.

Note that non-deductible input tax is deductible for income tax, corporation tax and capital gains tax purposes if the related expenditure is deductible for Schedule D Cases I and II or capital gains tax purposes.

Mixed output

Input tax is only recoverable by a registered trader if it has been paid on supplies which are attributable to taxable supplies made by the trader.

If a trader's outputs consist of both taxable and exempt supplies (see list later for examples of these supplies) the basic rule is that only input tax which relates to taxable outputs is recoverable. This type of trader is referred to as 'partially exempt'.

This matching is achieved by firstly determining how much input tax can be related directly to taxable outputs and exempt outputs. The input tax which relates to taxable outputs is fully reclaimable and that which relates to exempt supplies is not deductible. The remaining input tax is apportioned between taxable supplies and exempt supplies by using the percentage (taxable turnover excluding VAT/total turnover excluding VAT) × 100% rounded up to the next whole percentage point. The following items are omitted from the calculation:

- Tax on goods acquired and sold without any work being carried out on them.
- Tax on self-supplies. A self-supply occurs when a trader produces a marketable output and then uses it during the course of the business. For example, a business may own a printing operation which produces stationery which is used by the business.
- Tax on capital goods acquired for use within the business.

The Customs and Excise may be willing to allow an alternative basis to be used to allocate input tax between taxable and exempt supplies.

If the amount of input tax which is deemed to relate to exempt supplies is less than an average of £600 a month the above apportionment is ignored and all of the input tax is reclaimable.

Cars and travelling costs

As you have already seen the VAT on the acquisition of a new car is generally not recoverable, although the VAT on accessories bought at a later date is recoverable provided that the accessories are acquired for a business purpose. In this section we will concentrate on the VAT on petrol and maintenance costs.

By concession, provided that the car is used for business purposes, the VAT on the full cost of any repair and maintenance costs is reclaimable even if the car is also used for private purposes.

VAT on fuel used for business purposes is deductible even if the fuel is bought by an employee who is then reimbursed, either through a mileage allowance or by repayment of the cost of the fuel.

If a business provides its employees with petrol for private use and the employee does not fully reimburse the company for the cost of the fuel the business is considered to have made a taxable supply. Consequently the business can reclaim the input tax on the petrol but must also account for output tax using a scale charge. However, if the business chooses not to reclaim the input tax on the fuel they do not have to account for output tax. The scale charge is approximately equal to a quarter of the fuel scale charge rounded up to the nearest pound. If the employee does fully reimburse the company for the cost of the fuel used privately VAT must be accounted for on the amount reimbursed as if it were VAT inclusive. The VAT car fuel scale charge tables can be accessed from the Customs and Excise website.

VAT on fuel for private use is also deductible unless the employee fully reimburses the cost of the fuel. However, the business must also account for output tax using the scale charges per quarter, or per month.

If an employee reimburses an employer for the cost of either the use of the car or any private fuel used the payment is treated as if it were VAT inclusive provided that the payment is equal to or exceeds the cost of the private fuel.

Self-supply

If a person makes a supply to themselves, input tax on the supply is only allowable up to the level of output tax charged on the supply. (i.e. input tax cannot exceed output tax on the supply so specific input tax paid to others will not be reclaimable). (Statutory Instrument Value Added Tax (General) Regulations 1985 s32A).

If a registered trader made a self-supply of a motor car the input tax cannot be reclaimed (SI VAT (Cars) Order 1992 s5). This legislation also applies if the trader originally acquired a car and used it for a purpose which enabled the input tax to be reclaimed, specifically as a taxi, a self-drive hire car or a driving school car and subsequently the car was used for other purposes (SI VAT (Cars) Order 1992 s6).

Where a person produces printed matter in the course of their business and the printed matter is not supplied to another person or incorporated in other goods produced in the course or furtherance of that business, but is used by that person for the purpose of a business carried on by them, then the printed matter shall be treated as a self-supply provided the value of the self-supply exceeds the VAT threshold a year (Statutory Instrument Value Added Tax (Special Provisions) Order 1992 s7(1)). From 1 June 2002 businesses which are partially exempt, who fall into this category no longer have to account for VAT under the self-supply rules.

Registration and deregistration

A registered trader is a sole trader, partnership or company who is registered for VAT. It is important that a trader who is liable to register does notify the Customs and Excise because failure to register carries severe penalties as well as a liability to pay the VAT which should have been accounted for.

Initial registration

A person who makes taxable supplies, but is not registered for VAT, becomes liable to be registered:

- at the end of any month, if the value of taxable supplies in the period of one year then ending has exceeded £55,000 (FY2001 : £54,000), or
- at any time, if there are reasonable grounds for believing that the value of taxable supplies in the period of 30 days then beginning will exceed £55,000 (VATA 1994 Sch 1 s1(1)).

In determining the value of a person's supplies for this purpose supplies of goods or services that are capital assets of the business are ignored (VATA 1994 Sch 1 s1(7)).

The trader will then be registered for VAT from the end of the month following the 12-month period in which they exceeded the limit. If the Customs and Excise and the trader agree to an earlier date this will be used instead.

Registration must also take place if there are reasonable grounds for believing that the taxable supplies will exceed the annual limit in the next 30 days.

However, if the Commissioners are satisfied that the value of a trader's taxable supplies in the period of one year from the date on which he would be required to register under section 1(1) will not exceed £55,000 the trader is not liable to register (VATA 1994 Sch 1 s1(3)).

There is legislation to prevent the avoidance of registration by dividing the business between a number of persons each of whom would not be liable to register under the turnover rule contained in Schedule 1 section 1(1).

The Commissioners can make a direction under which all the persons named in the direction are treated as a single taxable person carrying on the activities of the business described in the direction. The traders named in the direction are liable to be registered for VAT from the date of the direction, unless a later date is specified in the direction (VATA 1994 Sch 1 s2(1)). The Commissioners shall not make such a direction unless they are satisfied that:

- The trader is making, or has made taxable supplies, and
- The trader's activities in making those taxable supplies form only part of the total activities which can be considered to be the business that is described in the direction. The other activities are carried on by one or more other persons, and
- If all the taxable supplies of that business were taken into account, a person carrying on that business would at the time of the direction be liable to be registered under Schedule 1 section 1(1), and
- The main reason or one of the main reasons for the person concerned carrying on the activities described in the direction in the way he or she does is the avoidance of a liability to be registered, whether that liability would be his, another person's or that of two or more persons jointly (VATA 1994 Sch 1 s2(2)).

Connected businesses which avoid registration by artificially separating are liable to be treated as one business regardless of the reason for the separation. This enables Customs and Excise to treat independent businesses which are conducted at arm's length as one business under some circumstances.

As soon as it becomes known that a trader is required to register they should keep VAT records and begin to charge VAT on any taxable outputs (although they cannot issue VAT invoices until a VAT registration number is received). During this period the trader should notify customers that the price charged is VAT inclusive and a full tax invoice should be sent within 30 days of receiving the registration number.

Traders who fail to register will be liable for VAT on taxable supplies from the date on which they should have registered. If it is not possible to collect the VAT due from customers they will still be liable for the tax due.

Traders making only zero-rated supplies can request exemption from registration. Traders with this exemption are responsible for notifying Customs and Excise if there is any change in the nature of their supplies.

Voluntary registration

Where a person who is not liable to be registered under the Act and is not already so registered satisfies the Commissioners that he or she either makes taxable supplies or is carrying on a business and intends to make such supplies in the course of that business, they shall, if he or she so requests, register them with effect from the day on which the request is made or from an earlier date as agreed between them (VATA 1994 Sch 1 s9).

There are a number of benefits and disadvantages of voluntary registration.

The following are advantages of voluntary registration:

- the input tax can be reclaimed
- customers who are VAT registered can reclaim the output tax charged to them
- the trader may appear to be a larger business than he or she actually is which may increase his or her status with customers.

The following are disadvantages of voluntary registration:

- customers who are not VAT registered cannot reclaim the output tax and so the trader may lose his competitive edge with non-registered customers
- the administrative burden of registration should not be overlooked.

It appears then that the tax status of a trader's customers is an important factor when deciding whether voluntary registration is likely to be beneficial. Let's consider this in a little more detail.

Activity

Elaine makes patchwork quilts. She can make a maximum of 40 quilts in a year which she can sell to members of the general public for £500 each. She does not think that her customers would be willing to pay any more. Alternatively she could sell her total production for the year to an exclusive retail outlet, again for £500 a quilt excluding VAT. The materials to make a quilt cost £100 before VAT. Under what circumstances should Elaine apply for voluntary registration?

Feedback

Sales to public	Registered £	Not registered £
Value of supply		
40 × £500	20,000	20,000
Less output VAT	(2,979)	
Net sales	17,021	20,000
Less costs 40 × £100 excluding VAT	(4,000)	(4,000)
Non-reclaimable VAT		(700)
Profit	13,021	15,300

If Elaine chooses to sell her quilts directly to the public she should not register for VAT.

	Registered £	Not registered £
Value of supply		
Value of supply		
40 × £500		20,000
20,000 × 117.5%	23,500	
Less output VAT	(3,500)	
Net sales	20,000	20,000
Less costs as above: net costs	(4,000)	(4,700)
Profit	16,000	15,300

If Elaine chooses to sell her quilts to the retailer she should register for VAT. Of the four options the most profitable is to register for VAT and sell her quilts to the retailer.

Deregistration

Deregistration may be voluntary or compulsory.

A person who has become liable to be registered for VAT purposes shall cease to be so liable, and become compulsorily deregistered, if the Commissioners are satisfied that he or she has ceased to make taxable supplies and is not included in a directive under Schedule 1 section 1A(1) (VATA 1994 Sch 1 s3).

A person who has become liable to be registered for VAT purposes shall cease to be so liable if the Commissioners are satisfied that the value of his or her taxable supplies in the next 12 months will not exceed £53,000 (FY 2001– £52,000) (VATA 1994 Sch 1 s4(1)).

A person cannot be registered under two or more different provisions under the Act. A registered trader who ceases to make or have the intention of making taxable supplies shall notify the Commissioners within 30 days unless, when he or she so ceases, he or she would still be liable or entitled to be registered under the VATA 1994 (VATA 1994 Sch 1 s11).

A trader may claim to be voluntarily deregistered if Customs and Excise are satisfied that the traders taxable supplies, net of VAT, in the following 12 months will not exceed £53,000. Note that traders will not be able to claim to be voluntarily deregistered if they intend to cease to trade or if there will be a suspension of taxable supplies for a continuous period of 30 days or more in the next 12 months.

The date of a voluntary deregistration is the later of the date on which the request is made or an agreed date.

If a trader who is voluntarily registered ceases to make or have the intention of making taxable supplies he or she shall notify the Commissioners within 30 days unless, when he or she so ceases, they would still be liable or entitled to be registered under the VATA 1994 (VATA 1994 Sch 1 s12).

When a registered trader takes goods or services from the business for non-business purposes, for example a retailer taking goods for self-consumption, VAT is chargeable on their cost rather than the selling price.

Taxable supplies and exempt supplies

Now that you are able to discuss the need for and consequence of registration for VAT purposes we can turn our attention to identifying taxable and exempt supplies. Unless a supply is specifically exempt or zero rated it is taxable at the standard rate of 17.5% (or the lower rate of 5%). At the beginning of this chapter there was a list of taxable supplies however any supply which is not-exempt or zero-rated will be taxable at the standard rate.

Exempt supplies

The exemptions to VAT are contained in Schedule 9 of the VATA 1994. The Schedule contains a number of groups, which are listed here, together with some important examples of exempt goods and services.

Group 1 – land.
    Including:
- granting of any interest in or right over land
- holiday accommodation
- mooring fees including anchoring and berthing.

Group 2 – insurance.
Group 3 – postal services provided by the post office.
Group 4 – betting, gaming and lotteries.
Group 5 – financial services.
    Including:
- provision of credit
- issue, transfer or receipt of, or any dealing with, any security or secondary security.

Group 6 – education.
Including:
- provision of education or research by a school, eligible institution or university or independent private tutor
- supply of any goods or services incidental to the provision of any education, training or re-training.

Group 7 – health and welfare.
Including:
- supply of services by registered medical practitioners, ophthalmic opticians and dentists
- provision of spiritual welfare by a religious institution as part of a course of instruction or a retreat.

Group 8 – burial and cremation.
Group 9 – supplies to trade unions and professional bodies if in consideration for membership.
Group 10 – entry fees for sports competitions (if non profit making).
Group 11 – works of art when disposed of to public bodies.
Group 12 – fund-raising events by charities and other qualifying bodies (this was extended in the 2000 Budget to include participative events and events on the internet).

Group 13 – Provision of cultural services (e.g. admission charges for museums, zoos, galleries, exhibitions, etc).

Group 14 – Supplies of goods with unrecoverable input tax.

Group 15 – Gold purchased as an investment.

The implications of making an exempt supply are that VAT can not be charged on the supply and if you only make exempt supplies you cannot register for VAT and therefore cannot reclaim input tax.

Zero-rated supplies

The goods and services which are zero rated are contained in Schedule 8 of the VATA 1983. The Schedule contains a number of groups, which are listed here, together with some important examples of zero-rated goods and services.

Group 1 – food.
  Including:
  - food of a kind used for human consumption
  - animal feeding stuffs.
  Exceptions include (these are standard rated instead):
  - supply in the course of catering, including all food which is consumed on the premises and all hot food
  - ice cream, confectionery and chocolate biscuits
  - spirits, beer and wine
  - pet food.

Group 2 – sewerage services and water for non-industrial use.

Group 3 – books.
  Including:
  - books, booklets, brochures, pamphlets and leaflets
  - newspapers, journals and periodicals.

Group 4 – talking books for the blind and handicapped and wireless sets for the blind when supplied to a charity.

Group 5 – construction or conversion of buildings, for residential or charitable purposes.

Group 6 – sale by builders of restored 'protected buildings' (i.e. listed buildings) if used for residential or charitable purposes.

Group 7 – international services.

Group 8 – transport (apart from those with less than 10 seats which are standard rated – reduced from 12 or more in 2001 Budget announcements).

Group 9 – caravans and houseboats.

Group 10 – gold supplied between capital banks (through a new scheme of invest ment gold was introduced at the start of 2000).

Group 11 – bank notes.

Group 12 – drugs, medicines, as prescribed by a medical practitioner and aids for the handicapped.

Group 13 – certain exports, etc.

Group 14 – tax-free shops.

Group 15 – sales by charities of donated goods and some supplies to charities e.g. some advertising (not for paid staff), etc.

Group 16 – children's clothing and footwear and some protective clothing e.g. crash helmets and bike helmets (children's and adults – latter added in 2001 Budget).

The VAT system is complex and full of anomalies, for example, individual knitting patterns are taxable supplies but booklets containing more than one pattern are zero rated.

The implications of supply being zero rated is that VAT is calculated at 0% – but it still is in effect charged – it is not the same as being exempt. This means businesses making zero-rated supplies can still reclaim input tax as a taxable person.

Lower-rated supplies

A handful of items that would normally fall into the standard rated category are, by special exception, taxed at a rate of 5%. These are termed lower rate supplies. This category includes:

- domestic fuel or power (or for charity use)
- installation of energy-saving materials in the home or a charity property (e.g. loft insulation)
- Government grant-funded installation, maintenance and repair of central heating systems in homes
- qualifying security goods installed in the homes of qualifying pensioners (when installed as part of a Government grant funded scheme).
- women's sanitary products (new from 1 January 2000)
- children's car seats (new in 2001 as announced in Budget BN 56/01, and amended paragraph of Schedule A1 of VAT Act 1994).

The VAT fraction on lower-rated items is 1/21 (i.e. 5/(100 + 5)).

Special schemes

You need to be aware of some of the special VAT schemes which are available to registered traders. The payments on account scheme is compulsory for large organisations but other schemes are offered to taxpayers on a voluntary basis. None of the schemes alters the amount of VAT which must be paid; they merely affect either the date of payments to Custom and Excise or the administration of VAT. In practice the take-up of these voluntary schemes is very low despite the apparent attractiveness of some of them. This may be partly due to the stringent conditions for joining the schemes some of which have been relaxed in the 2002 Budget to encourage wider take-up as we will see.

The payments on account scheme

Companies which have to pay £2 million a year or more to the Customs and Excise complete their VAT returns in the normal way but are required to make two payments on account in each quarter, in addition to the end of quarter payment. The first payment is made a month before the end of the quarter, the second payment is made at the end of the tax period and the final payment, which is sufficient to cover the remaining VAT liability for the tax period, is made at the usual time, one month after the end of the tax period.

This means that the trader will make a payment to the Customs and Excise at the end of each month of the year.

Registered traders with a VAT liability of £2 million or more for the last accounting period are required to operate the payments on account scheme. The Customs and Excise will use current information in order to determine the monthly payments of the members of the scheme usually on the basis of 1/24th of the trader's total VAT liability for the previous year. (Statutory Instrument 1993/2001 as amended by Statutory Instrument 1995/291). Traders can opt to pay their actual VAT liability instead however if they so wish.

The cash accounting scheme

The cash accounting scheme uses the following tax points:

- for output tax, the day on which payment or other consideration is received, or the date of any cheque, if later
- for input tax, the date on which payment is made or other consideration is given, or the date of any cheque, if later (Statutory Instrument VAT (Cash Accounting) Regulations 1987 s3).

This means they can ignore the usual tax points and only pay VAT on actual cash transactions. This can provide a considerable cash flow help to many businesses.

Taxable persons are eligible for admission to the scheme if:

- they have reasonable grounds for believing that the value of taxable supplies made by them in the period of one year beginning at the date of their application for authorisation will not exceed £600,000
- they have made all the returns which they are required to make and all VAT payments are up to date
- they have not, in the twelve months preceding the date of application for authorisation, been convicted of any offence in connection with VAT (SI VAT (Cash Accounting) Regulations 1987 s4(1)).

The scheme does not apply to hire purchase agreements, conditional sale agreements or credit sale agreements (SI VAT (Cash Accounting) Regulations 1987 s4(3)).

Authorised persons may remain in the scheme unless:

- at the end of any quarter or prescribed accounting period the value of taxable supplies made in the year then ended has exceeded £750,000 and in the year then beginning is expected to exceed the figure of £750,000, in which case they shall within 30 days notify the Commissioners and cease to operate the scheme at the anniversary of joining, or

Authorised persons may withdraw from the scheme if:
- they derive no benefit from remaining in the scheme
- they are unable, by reason of accounting systems, to comply with the requirements of the scheme

and following written notification of that fact by them to the Commissioners they shall terminate authorisation at the end of the prescribed accounting period in which such notification is received by them (SI VAT (Cash Accounting)

Regulations 1987 s6(3)).

The Commissioners may terminate an authorisation if:

- a false statement has been made by or on behalf of an authorised person in relation to the application for authorisation
- an authorised person has, while admitted to the scheme, been convicted of an offence in connection with VAT
- an authorised person has failed to leave the scheme despite having a turnover which exceeds £750,000 a year
- an authorised person has claimed input tax as though he or she had not been admitted to the scheme (SI VAT (Cash Accounting) Regulations 1987 s10(1)).

A person whose authorisation has been terminated shall account for and pay on a return made in respect of his or her current prescribed accounting period all tax which has not been accounted for and paid in accordance with the scheme, subject to any adjustment for credit for input tax (SI VAT (Cash Accounting Regulations 1987 s10(2)).

The annual accounting scheme

The Commissioners may authorise taxable persons to account for tax in accordance with a scheme by which they:

- pay, by direct debit on their bank account normally in nine equal monthly installments commencing on the last day of the fourth month of their current accounting year, 90% of tax liability as estimated by the Commissioners for that current accounting year (an option to pay in three larger installments was introduced in the 2002 Budget with effect from 25 April 2002)
- furnishes by the last day of the second month following the end of that current accounting year a return for that year, together with any outstanding payment due to the Commissioners in respect of their liability for tax declared on that return (SI VAT (Annual Accounting) Regulations 1988 s3).

Taxable persons shall be eligible to apply for authorisation under the scheme if:

- they have been registered for at least one year at the date of application for authorisation (unless they have taxable turnover of less than £100,000 and can join immediately they register after 25 April 2002)
- they have reasonable grounds for believing that the value of taxable supplies in the period of one year beginning at the date of application for authorisation will not exceed £600,000
- they have made all the returns which they are required to make
- total credits for input tax did not exceed total output tax in the year prior to application for authorisation
- registration is not in the name of a group or a division
- they have not, in the three years preceding the date of application for authorisation, had authorisation terminated (SI VAT (Annual Accounting) Regulations 1988 s4(1)).

An authorised person may start to use the scheme at the beginning of the accounting year stated in the notification of the authorisation (ST VAT (Annual Accounting) Regulations 1988 s5(1)).

Authorised persons may remain in the scheme unless:

- at the end of any current accounting year the value of the taxable supplies made by them in that year has exceeded £750,000, in which case their authorisation shall be terminated immediately
- at any time there is reason to believe that the value of taxable supplies made in the current accounting year will exceed £750,000 in which case they shall within 30 days notify the Commissioners who may terminate authorisation
- they are expelled from the scheme (SI VAT (Annual Accounting) Regulations 1988 s5(2)).

Authorised persons who cease to operate the scheme either of their own volition or because the value of taxable supplies made by them exceeds £750,000 a year shall account for and pay tax as provided for, by or under the Act (SI VAT (Annual Accounting) Regulations 1988 s6).

The Commissioners may terminate an authorisation in any case where:

- a false statement has been made by or on behalf of an authorised person in relation to the application for authorisation
- an authorised person fails to furnish by the due date a return in respect of the current accounting year
- an authorised person fails to make any payment due under the scheme
- an authorised person has failed to leave the scheme although his or her taxable supplies exceed £750,000 (SI VAT (Annual Accounting) Regulations 1988 s8(1)).

Activity

Why may a business choose the annual accounting scheme?

Feedback

The annual accounting schemes is useful in managing business cash flows as payments are predictable throughout the year and only one VAT return must be completed, helping to reduce compliance costs. However, it does require monitoring of limits to ensure the turnover maximum is not exceeded and some planning for payments must be performed to ensure monies are available for payments when they fall due irrespective of the cash flow position of the underlying business. Larger payments may also be collected than would otherwise be the case if you are down scaling your business activity as payments are based on the previous year's figures.

Retail schemes

There are 12 schemes which are used by about 270,000 retailers and which are legislated for by the VAT (Supplies by Retailers) Regulations 1972. The normal VAT legislation requires registered traders to maintain detailed records of every transaction. Retailers who make a mixture of standard rated, zero rated and exempt supplies face particular problems. Retailers are able to keep less detailed records by using one of the schemes and calculate output tax in a way which suits their circumstances. Some of the schemes require totals for different sorts of supply rather than details of individual transactions while others allow the VAT liability to be estimated using purchases and mark-up percentages. The retail schemes are only available to retailers who cannot reasonably be expected to account for VAT in the normal way.

From 1st March 1997 the tax point on self-financed credit sales is based on the time of supply rather than on the date of payment as in the past. Individually agreed schemes for businesses with taxable retail turnover in excess of £10 million per annum have recently been introduced.

The secondhand goods scheme

The secondhand goods scheme is available to traders who buy secondhand goods from individuals who are not registered traders. The Commissioners can make an order allowing a reduction on the supply of such secondhand goods (VATA 1994 s32(1)).

The maximum reduction available is equal to the amount of tax which would have been due had the acquisition of the goods been a taxable supply (VATA 1994 s32(2)).

This means that VAT is due only on the trader's margin rather than on the sales price of the goods. Hence the trader has to account for 7/47 of the difference between his purchase price and his selling price (VATA 1994 s50A).

A registered trader who buys goods from a trader who is using the secondhand goods scheme will not be able to reclaim the input tax because he will not have received a tax invoice.

Orders under this scheme can apply to all secondhand goods, works of art, antiques and collectors' items. The scheme cannot be applied to precious metals and gemstones.

A system of global accounting for VAT on secondhand goods was introduced in 1994. Under the global accounting system registered traders only need to account for VAT on the difference between the total purchases and the total sales of eligible goods in a tax period, rather than on an item by item basis.

Flat Rate scheme

The 2002 Budget introduced a new scheme for VAT payment aimed at offering smaller businesses a significant compliance cost saving in handling VAT issues. The new scheme, available since 25 April 2002, is for businesses with:
- VAT - exclusive taxable turnover of up to £100,000 per annum and
- VAT - exclusive total turnover (i.e. including exempt or other non-taxable (income) up to £125,000 per annum.

The scheme allows businesses to account for VAT based on a flat rate percentage applied to their tax-inclusive turnover (including exempt or zero-rated income). The rate that applies depends on the nature of the business as different flat rates will apply to different types of business.

Businesses using this scheme will continue to issue VAT invoices to their customers but will no longer have to track input or output VAT specifically to calculate their VAT charge. This could save businesses significant compliance effort by saving much of the separate accounting that otherwise needs to occur for handling the input and output VAT appropriately.

The Government has said this scheme will be excluded to extended turnovers up to £150,000 from 2003/04.

Imports and exports

With the creation of a Europe without trade barriers on 1st January 1993 it has become necessary to differentiate between transactions with traders resident in other countries in the European Union and those resident in countries outside the European Union.

Imports

Imports may come from other EU member states or from countries which are not members of the EU. The tax treatment of imports depends on the source of the goods.

We will discuss the detail of the arrangements which are currently in force within the EU member states later in this section. First, we will consider imports from countries from outside the EU.

Tax on the importation of goods from places outside the member states will be charged and payable as if it were a duty of customs (VATA 1994 s16(1)). The rate of the duty is the same as the rate which would apply if the same goods were supplied in the home market by a registered trader. The person who is to be treated as importing any goods from outside the member states is the person who would be liable to discharge any such EU customs debt (VATA 1994 s15(2)). The registered trader is then able to reclaim the duty on the goods which are used for the purposes of a business carried on by him or her as input tax in the normal way (VATA 1994 s24(6)).

A registered trader may apply for approval under the Customs Duties (Deferred Payment) Regulations 1976 in order to make deferred payments. The Commissioners will grant an approved person deferment of customs duty until payment day (Statutory Instrument Customs Duties (Deferred Payment) Regulations 1976 s5). Payment day is the 15th day of the month next following that in which the amount of duty deferred is entered into the Commissioners' accounts, or in the case of import entries scheduled periodically, the 15th day of the period following that in which deferment is granted. A period commences on the 16th day of any month and ends on the 15th day of the month next following (SI Customs Duties (Deferred Payment) Regulations 1976 s2(1)). On each payment day an approved person shall pay to the Commissioners the total amount of customs duty of which he has been granted deferment (SI Customs Duties (Deferred Payment) Regulations 1976 s6).

If relevant services are supplied to a registered trader who is UK resident by a person resident overseas, either within the EU or a place outside the EU, the reverse charge system will be used. Relevant services include:
- transfers and assignments of copyright, patents, licenses, trademarks and similar rights
- advertising services
- services of consultants, engineers, consultancy bureaux, lawyers, accountants and other similar services; data processing and provision of information
- banking, financial and insurance services including re-insurance
- any other service supplied to a registered trader provided that it is not exempt under VATA 1994 Sch 9 (VATA 1994 Sch 5).

VAT will be accounted for as if the registered trader had supplied the services in the UK in the course of business and that supply were a taxable supply (VATA 1994 s8 (1)).

If the recipient is not VAT registered and the supply is only a relevant supply because it is not exempt under VATA 1994 Sch 9 the supplier, if registered, will be required to account for VAT in the normal way.

Under new EU rules, non-EU based suppliers of services to UK based non-registered recipients will also be required to charge VAT from July 2003. This will require non-EU based suppliers to become registered traders in at least one EU member country and to comply with their VAT regulations in making suppliers of services in the rest of the EU.

Multinational groups which are registered as a group for VAT purposes will be prevented from obtaining services from overseas without accounting for VAT. The reverse charge system only allows a business to recover tax due as input tax to the extent that it relates to the business's taxable supplies. Hence, where the reverse charge relates to exempt supplies the tax due cannot be recovered.

Telecommunication services supplied to UK businesses from outside the EU are liable to VAT.

Imports of works of art, antiques and collectors' pieces from outside the EU are subject to VAT at a reduced rate of 2.5%.

Exports

A supply of goods is zero-rated if the Commissioners 'are satisfied' that the person supplying the goods has:

- exported them to a place outside the EU member states (evidence must be produced)
- shipped them for use as stores on a voyage or flight to an eventual destination outside the UK, or as merchandise for sale by retail to persons carried on such a voyage or flight in a ship or aircraft (VATA 1994 s30(6)).

VAT in the EU

The European Union, brought into effect as a single market in 1993, requires that no borders exist when goods and services are sold or purchased between suppliers and customers in more than one member state. This means that VAT should be applied as if both parties were infact in the same state.

In reality this situation has not yet come about. The current position is as follows.

If a registered person in one member state supplies goods or services to a registered person in another member state they should make the supply at a zero-rate in the country of origin (no output tax is accounted for, but input tax associated with the supply can be reclaimed). The customer will then account for output VAT on the purchase at whatever VAT rate is applicable in their country. The VAT suffered can also then be treated as their input tax in their country and accounted for as normal. This implies a net effect of zero of course and the trader is in the same position as if they have acquired the goods from a UK trader. For this system to be applied evidence of the transfer or supply of the goods or services must be available to prove it did infact occur.

If the supply from a registered trader is to a non-registered customer (or one who has not proved their registered status by providing their registration number) then the supply should be made including VAT at the origin country's rate, as if it had been supplied within their own country.

Tax planning points

We have already seen that it is possible for a trader to register voluntarily for VAT, but there are some more options when registering which we should consider.

Groups of companies under common control can elect to register as a group. One company must be appointed as the representative member who deals with all VAT matters for the group. For the purposes of VAT a VAT group is deemed to be a single taxable person, that is, although each company within the group has a separate legal identity for VAT purposes they are not considered to have a discrete identity. Intra-group transfers are ignored for VAT purposes and all taxable supplies to and from any member of the group are treated as a taxable supply by or to the representative member.

If a group registration is made it is not necessary for all members of the group to participate. This may be useful if one member of the group is making exempt supplies.

In order to be eligible for group registration all companies in the group must be resident in the UK or have an established place of business in the UK. In addition either one company must control each of the others, or one person, an individual or a company, must control all of the companies, or two or more persons who are partners in business must control them all.

Any special status attributed to the representative member of the group cannot be used to obtain relief from VAT by other members of the group who are not otherwise entitled to the relief. Examples of special status companies include:

- companies providing insurance and reinsurance who are permitted to carry on insurance business in accordance with section 2 of the Insurance Companies Act 1982 (VATA 1994, Sch 9 Group 2)
- eligible bodies providing education, research or vocational training. An eligible body is a school, including state schools, independent schools and grant-maintained schools, Colleges of Further and Higher Education, UK universities and youth clubs (VATA 1994, Sch 9 Group 6)
- charities supplying goods and services in connection with a fund-raising event organised for charitable purposes (VATA 1994, Sch 9 Group 12).

Customs and Excise retain the right to refuse any application for group registration if they deem that it is necessary in order to protect the revenue.

In contrast to group registration it is possible for a company to apply for divisional registration. Provided that the Commissioners see fit registration is in the names of the divisions (VATA 1994 s46(1)). This would be advantageous if the organisation of the company is divisional and it is simpler administratively to operate as divisions for VAT purposes. However, the company is still liable for any VAT liability. In order to obtain divisional registration it is necessary to fulfill the following conditions:

- all divisions must register regardless of the size of their turnover
- each division must be distinct from the other divisions in terms of their accounting function and business activities
- the input tax which relates to exempt supplies must be, on average, less than

£600 a month for the whole company
- each division must use the same tax periods
- supplies from one division to another are not supplies for VAT purposes and so tax invoices should not be issued.

Summary

In this chapter you have read about the operation of VAT, one of our most important taxes.

VAT has to be paid whenever a taxable person makes a taxable supply of goods or services in the course of business. Unless a supply of goods or services is specifically exempt in the legislation it is a taxable supply. With the exception of domestic fuel, which is taxable at 5%, taxable supplies are either standard rated or zero rated. The standard rate of VAT for the UK is 17.5% in this tax year.

A trader must register if turnover exceeds certain limits, for this tax year the limit is £55,000 a year. A trader whose turnover is lower than the registration limit may elect to register voluntarily.

A registered trader is able to reclaim allowable input tax but must account for output tax on taxable supplies.

VAT is paid quarterly to Customs and Excise on the invoices received and issued in the quarter. However, there are a considerable number of special schemes, some of which are compulsory for some businesses, which require VAT to be accounted for on a different basis.

There is debate about the acceptability of further increases in the amount of revenue which is raised using indirect taxation. This debate was considered in the first three chapters.

We have suggested that, with the exception of non-deductible input tax, VAT is merely a cash flow and administrative issue for registered traders. However, in Chapter 3 we discussed the nature of VAT and concluded that the burden of VAT fell on traders as well as final consumers. In the budget of 1991 the standard rate of VAT was increased from 15% to 17.5% to fund a reduction in the community charge. At the time the economy of the UK was in recession and a large number of retailers, including Marks and Spencer, announced that they would absorb the increase in VAT themselves rather than pass it on to their customers. The retailers recognised that increases in prices would lead to a decrease in demand which would reduce their profits.

Project areas

The harmonisation of VAT within the EU provides considerable scope for dissertation titles.

There are also opportunities for comparative studies, for example the special schemes on offer to small businesses in EU member states.

Since 1979 there has been a significant shift in taxation in the UK from direct taxation to indirect taxation. A number of titles suggest themselves, for example, is it possible for there to be further shifts from direct taxes to indirect taxes? Alternatively would a shift back towards direct taxation be possible or desirable?

Case Study materials

Having completed this chapter you should now review and extend your knowledge by undertaking the KPMG Tax Business School® VAT Case Study you will find on the website for the book (http://www.taxstudent.com).

Computational questions

Question 1. (based on CIMA May 1988).

(a) A trader started in business, selling mainly foodstuffs which are zero rated for VAT purposes, on 1st January 2002 and the following information was extracted from his records for the year ended 31st December 2002.

The purchases (but not the sales) are inclusive of VAT.

	£
Fixed assets purchased (all standard rated)	8,000
Other standard rated purchases and expenses	4,000
Sales of zero rated foodstuffs	48,000
Sales of standard rated items	9,000

He approaches you shortly after the end of the year and informs you that he does not intend to register for VAT since 'the sales liable to VAT were well below the threshold'.

Required Advise him on the position regarding registration for VAT, and show the final value added tax position which would have applied for the above year if the trader had registered voluntarily at the start of the year.

Question 2. (based on CIMA November 1992).

You are the chief accountant of Z Ltd, a UK-resident company, whose activities to date have been confined wholly to the UK.

The company is about to acquire three UK-resident subsidiaries, and the members of the newly formed group will engage, for the first time, in import and export activities.

Required Draft a brief report to the board on the VAT implications of the above changes.

Question 3. (based on ACCA Paper 3.3. December 1993).

Part c. Alison Able, the senior partner in Able, Keane and Ready, is planning to set up a new business venture in the near future that she will run herself, rather than as part of the partnership. None of the partnership assets or staff will be involved in the new business. The income from the new business is expected to be £60,000 p.a., net of VAT. All the income is in respect of standard-rated supplies, 80% of which will be made to VAT-registered persons. Because of the highly competitive nature of the business, it will not be possible to pass on the additional cost of VAT to the 20% of customers who are not VAT registered.

The business is to be run from Alison's home, so the only expenses of the new business will be:

	£
Leased office equipment	2,820 p.a.
Telephone (40% private)	1,175 p.a.
Entertaining clients	705 p.a.
Insurance	470 p.a.

Alison also plans to spend £5,875 on a pre-launch advertising campaign. All the above figures include VAT where applicable.

Required

(i) Will Alison automatically have to account for VAT on the income of her new business as a result of the partnership being registered for VAT?

(ii) Assuming that the answer to (i) is that Alison does not automatically have to account for VAT on her income, would it be beneficial for her to register voluntarily for VAT in any case?

(iii) Would it be beneficial for Alison to defer the pre-launch advertising expenditure until after she has commenced trading? Your answer should consider both the VAT and the income tax implications.

(Note: answer available via lecturer's website)

Question 4. (based on ACCA Paper 11 June 1994).
Part b. Skunk Ltd owns 70% of the ordinary share capital of both Zebra Ltd and Emu Ltd. All three companies are involved in the construction industry. Skunk Ltd's sales are all standard rated, whilst Zebra Ltd's and Emu Ltd's are zero-rated and exempt respectively. The companies' sales and purchases for the year ended 31st March 2003 are as follows:

	Sales £	Purchases £
Skunk Ltd	1,170,000	480,000
Zebra Ltd	540,000	270,000
Emu Ltd	390,000	150,000

The purchases for all three companies are standard rated. In addition Skunk Ltd incurred standard rated overhead expenditure of £300,000 which cannot be directly attributed to any of the three companies' sales. Skunk Ltd charges both its subsidiary companies a management charge of £40,000 p.a. each in respect of the services of its accountancy department. All the above figures are exclusive of VAT where applicable. Skunk Ltd and its two subsidiaries are not registered as a group for VAT purposes.

Required

(i) Calculate the VAT position of Skunk Ltd, Zebra Ltd and Emu Ltd for the year ended 31st March 2003.

(ii) Advise Skunk Ltd of the conditions that must be met for itself and its two subsidiaries to register as a group for VAT purposes, and the consequences of being so registered.

(iii) Advise Skunk Ltd of whether or not it would have been beneficial for itself and both its subsidiaries to have been registered as a group for VAT purposes throughout the year ended 31st March 2003. Your answer should be supported by appropriate calculations.

(Note: answer available via lecturer's website)

Appendix A: Tables of tax rates and allowances

Rates and allowances for income tax, corporation tax, capital gains tax, inheritance tax and the pension schemes earnings cap are set out below. All allowances, thresholds and limits for 2000–01 have risen in line with statutory indexation and rounding rules.

	2002/03	2001–02(£)	Increase (£)
Income tax allowances			
Personal allowance	4,615	4,535	80
Personal allowance – age 65–74	6,100	5,990	110
Personal allowance – age 75 and over	6,370	6,260	110
Married couple's allowance – age 65 before 6 April 2000	5,465	5,365	100
Married couple's allowance – age 75 or more	5,535	5,435	100
Married couple's allowance – minimum amount	2,110	2,070	30
Income limit for age-related allowances	17,900	17,600	300
Blind person's allowance	1,480	1,450	30
Children's Tax Credit (10% relief, income related)	5,290	5,200	90
In year of birth (baby rate)	10,490	5,200	
Capital gains tax annual exempt amount			
Individuals, etc.	7,700	7,500	200
Other trustees	3,850	3,700	100
Inheritance tax threshold	250,000	242,000	8,000

Taxable bands 2002/3 (2001/2 in brackets)	Non-savings	Savings/Capital Gains Tax	Dividends
0 – £1,920 (1,880)	10% (10%)	10% (10%)	10% (10%)
£1,921 – 29,900 (1,881 - 29,400)	22 % (22%)	20% (20%)	10% (10%)
over £29,900 (over 29,400)	40% (40%)	40% (40%)	32.5% (32.5%)

Corporation tax profits	2002/3 (2001/2)	(£)
Starting rate	0% (10%)	£0–10,000*
Marginal rate	23.75% (22.5%)	£10,001–50,000*
Small companies' rate	19% (20%)	£50,001–300,000*
Marginal rate	32.75% (32.5%)	£300,001–1,500,000*
Main rate	30% (30%)	£1,500,001 or more*
Marginal relief fraction	1/40	1/40
Profit threshold for quarterly instalment payments	£1,500,000*	£1,500,000*

*reduced where associated companies exist

National Insurance Contributions

Item	2002/03	2001/02
Class 1:		
Lower Earnings Limit (per week)	£75	£72
Upper Earnings Limit (per week – employees only)	£585	£575
Primary (employees) Threshold (per week)	£89	£87
Secondary (employers) Threshold (per week)	£89	£87
Employee's contributions	10%	10%
Employee's Contracted-out Rebate	1.6%	1.6%
Employer's Contribution Rates	11.8%	11.9%
Employer's Contracted-out Rebate		
Salary Related	3.5%	3%
Money Purchase	1.0%	0.6%
Married women's reduced rate	3.85%	–
Class 2: Self employed Contribution (per week)	£2.00	£2.00
Small Earnings Exception (per annum)	£4,025	£3,955
Class 3: (voluntary) Contribution (per week)	£6.85	£6.75
Class 4: Contributions – Upper Profits Limit	£30,420	£29,900
Contributions – Lower Profits Limit	£4,615	£4,535
Contribution Rate	7.0%	7.0%

Working Families Tax Credit

	2002/03 from June (£)	2001/02 from June (£)
Basic Tax Credit (one per household)	62.50	59.00
Additional credit where one earner works 30 or more hours/week	11.65	11.45
Additional child tax credits		
Under 16	26.45	26.00
16–18	27.20	26.75

Personal Pensions and Retirement Annuity Premiums

Age at start of tax year	Retirement annuity (%)	Personal and Stakeholder pensions (%)
< 35	17.5	17.5
36–45	17.5	20.0
46–50	17.5	25.0
51–55	20.0	30.0
56–60	22.5	35.0
61–75	27.5	40.0

Pension maximum cap for tax relief £97,200 (£95,400 for 2001/02). Maximum contribution to Personal Pension is the higher of £3,600 or the relevant age and earnings percentage.

Fuel Benefit for Company Cars

Car engine capacity	2002/03		2000/01	
	Petrol	Diesel	Petrol	Diesel
0–1400cc	2,240	2,850	1,930	2,460
1,401–2000cc	2,850	2,850	2,460	2,460
> 2000cc	4,200	4,200	3,620	3,620

Authorised private car mileage rates

Business Miles	Allowance rate per mile
0-10,000	40p
10,000+	25p

Excess payments over these rates are taxable. Shortfalls can be claimed as tax relief by the employee.

Taper Relief (for disposals after 5 April 2002)

Number of complete tax years in holding period	% of gain taxable Business assets	Non-business assets
< 1	100	100
1	50	100
2	25	100
3	25	95
4	25	90
5	25	85
6	25	80
7	25	75
8	25	70
9	25	65
10 or more	25	60

VAT

	after 1 April 2002	after 1 April 2001
Standard Rate	17.5%	17.5%
Annual Registration Limit	£55,000	£54,000
De-registration Limit	£53,000	£52,000
VAT Fraction	7/47	7/47
Cash Accounting Scheme		
– max turnover	£600,000	£600,000
Annual Accounting Scheme		
– max turnover	£600,000	£600,000
Optional Flat Rate Scheme (from 25 April 2002)		
– max turnover	£100,000	

Retail prices index (January 1987 = 100.0)

	1982	1983	1984	1985	1986	1987	1988	1989	1990	1991
Jan		82.6	86.8	91.2	96.2	100.0	103.3	111.0	119.5	130.2
Feb		83.0	87.2	91.9	96.6	100.4	103.7	111.8	120.2	130.9
Mar	79.4	83.1	87.5	92.8	96.7	100.6	104.1	112.3	121.4	131.4
Apr	81.0	84.3	88.6	94.8	97.7	101.8	105.8	114.3	125.1	133.1
May	81.6	84.6	89.0	95.2	97.8	101.9	106.2	115.0	126.2	133.5
Jun	81.9	84.8	89.2	95.4	97.8	101.9	106.0	115.4	126.7	134.1
Jul	81.9	85.3	89.1	95.2	97.5	101.8	106.7	115.5	126.8	133.8
Aug	81.9	85.7	89.9	95.5	97.8	102.1	107.9	115.8	128.1	134.1
Sept	81.9	86.1	90.1	95.4	98.3	102.4	108.4	116.6	129.3	134.6
Oct	82.3	86.4	90.7	95.6	98.5	102.9	109.5	117.5	130.3	135.1
Nov	82.7	86.7	91.0	95.9	99.3	103.4	110.0	118.5	130.0	135.6
Dec	82.5	86.9	90.0	96.0	99.6	103.3	110.3	118.8	129.9	135.7

	1992	1993	1994	1995	1996	1997	1998	1999	2000	2001
Jan	135.6	137.9	141.3	146.0	150.2	154.4	159.5	163.4	166.6	171.1
Feb	136.3	138.8	142.1	146.9	150.9	155.0	160.3	163.7	167.5	172.0
Mar	136.7	139.3	142.5	147.5	151.5	154.4	160.8	164.1	168.4	172.2
Apr	138.8	140.6	144.2	149.0	152.6	156.3	**162.6**	165.2	170.1	173.1
May	139.3	141.1	144.7	149.6	152.9	156.9	163.5	165.6	170.7	174.2
Jun	139.3	141.0	144.7	149.8	143.0	157.5	163.4	165.6	171.1	174.4
Jul	138.8	140.7	144.0	149.1	152.4	157.5	163.0	165.1	170.5	173.3
Aug	138.9	141.3	144.7	149.9	153.1	158.5	163.7	166.5	170.5	174.0
Sept	139.4	141.9	145.0	150.6	153.8	159.3	164.4	166.2	171.7	174.6
Oct	139.9	141.8	145.2	149.8	153.8	159.6	164.5	166.5	171.6	174.3
Nov	139.7	141.6	145.3	149.8	153.9	159.6	164.4	166.7	172.1	173.6
Dec	139.2	141.9	146.0	150.7	154.4	160.0	164.4	167.3	172.2	173.4

	2002
Jan	173.3
Feb	173.8
Mar	174.5

Note: Only companies can continue to receive the indexation allowance for capital disposals after April 1998. For individuals, indexation allowance stops at April 1998 and taper relief is then applied.

Capital gains tax indexation allowance for individuals for disposals after April 1998

	Jan	Feb	Mar	Apr	May	Jun	Jul	Aug	Sep	Oct	Nov	Dec
1982	–	–	1.047	1.006	0.992	0.987	0.986	0.985	0.987	0.977	0.967	0.971
1983	0.968	0.960	0.956	0.929	0.921	0.917	0.906	0.898	0.889	0.883	0.876	0.871
1984	0.872	0.865	0.859	0.834	0.828	0.823	0.825	0.808	0.804	0.793	0.788	0.789
1985	0.783	0.769	0.752	0.716	0.708	0.704	0.707	0.703	0.704	0.701	0.695	0.693
1986	0.689	0.683	0.681	0.665	0.662	0.663	0.667	0.662	0.654	0.652	0.638	0.632
1987	0.626	0.620	0.616	0.597	0.596	0.596	0.597	0.593	0.588	0.580	0.573	0.574
1988	0.574	0.568	0.562	0.537	0.531	0.525	0.524	0.507	0.500	0.485	0.478	0.474
1989	0.465	0.454	0.448	0.423	0.414	0.409	0.408	0.404	0.395	0.384	0.372	0.369
1990	0.361	0.353	0.339	0.300	0.288	0.283	0.282	0.269	0.258	0.248	0.251	0.252
1991	0.249	0.242	0.237	0.222	0.218	0.213	0.215	0.213	0.208	0.204	0.199	0.198
1992	0.199	0.193	0.189	0.171	0.167	0.167	0.171	0.171	0.166	0.162	0.164	0.168
1993	0.179	0.171	0.167	0.156	0.152	0.153	0.156	0.151	0.146	0.147	0.148	0.146
1994	0.151	0.144	0.141	0.128	0.124	0.124	0.129	0.124	0.121	0.120	0.119	0.114
1995	0.114	0.107	0.102	0.091	0.087	0.085	0.091	0.085	0.080	0.085	0.085	0.079
1996	0.083	0.078	0.073	0.066	0.063	0.063	0.067	0.062	0.057	0.057	0.057	0.053
1997	0.053	0.049	0.046	0.040	0.036	0.032	0.032	0.026	0.021	0.019	0.019	0.016
1998	0.019	0.014	0.011	–	–	–	–	–	–	–	–	–

Some Other Useful Rates

	2002/03 £	2001/02 £
Basic Retirement Pension (per week)		
– Single Person	75.50	72.50
– Married Couple	120.70	115.90
Child Benefit (per week)		
– First Eligible Child	15.75	15.50
– Each Extra Child	10.55	10.35
Statutory Sick Pay		
£75 or more (2001/02 £72)	63.75	62.20
Statutory Maternity Pay		
Average Weekly Earnings		
£75 or over (2001/02 £72)		
Higher Weekly Rate (first six weeks)	90% of weekly earnings	
Lower Weekly Rate (next twelve weeks)	75.00	62.20
Job Seekers Allowance		
– Single Person	53.95	53.05
– Married Couple	84.65	83.25
National Minimum Wage	From October 2001 £4.10 per hour	
	From October 2002 £4.20 per hour	
Disabled Person's Tax Credit	62.10	61.05

Appendix B: UK Budget Summaries

This appendix reviews recent UK Budgets, and their associated Finance Bills/Acts to provide a summary of recent changes to the UK tax system.

The April 2002 Budget and Finance Bill 2002

The 2002 Budget was given on 17th April 2002 – very late compared to previous years. It was put back one month due to the personal circumstances of the Chancellor, Gordon Brown. As the Budget statement was then actually made after the start of the tax year it necessitated release of some information that is normally announced in the Budget as separate, earlier, Press Releases from the Treasury. This section combines these various releases however into one analysis as the timing of the releases is not important after the event (other than for political analysis of course).

A key theme of the 2002 Budget was support for the UK's National Health Service with an increase in National Insurance contributions (from April 2003) announced to provide extra money to the NHS.

Despite relatively few changes to the tax system last year, ahead of the General Election which re-elected the Labour Government in June 2001, the 2002 Budget tweaked many issues in small, but often significant ways. This included the introduction of a flat rate VAT system for smaller businesses which may enable them to save costs on managing their compliance with the complicated UK VAT system. The rate of Corporation Tax was also changed for small businesses to 0% for the starting rate (from 10%) and lowering the small companies rate by 1% to 19%. For larger businesses details were provided of the Research and Development Tax Credit that can now also be claimed by them (previously having been restricted to small and medium sized businesses).

Income Taxation

The rates of income tax (10%, 20%, 22%, 32.5% and 40%) are not changed this year. The bands of income to which they apply;y have increased - starting rate band is now the first £1,920 of taxable income (2001/2: £1,880), the basic rate band now becomes the next £27,980 of taxable income (2001/2: £27,520) with the higher rate being applied with taxable incomes of more than £29,900 (2001/2: £29,400).

Personal Allowances increased to £4,615 (2001/2: £4,535), £6,100 if you are between 65 and 75 (2001/2 – £5,990) and £6,370 if you are more that 75 (2001/2: £6,260) The Blind Persons allowance rose by £30 to £1,480. (2001/2: £1,450).

Children's Tax Credit was raised to £5,290 (2001/2: £5,200) but remained at 10% (ie actual deduction that can be claimed is £529 for the 2002/3 year).

Married Couples Allowance (now only available to those over 65 at 6 April 2000) also rose to £5,465 (2001/2: £5,365) or £5,535 if you were more than 75 at 6 April 2000 (2001/2: £5,435). This also is restricted still to 10%.

National Insurance Contributions

The rates for NIC for 2002/3 were originally announced in the Pre-Budget Report in November 2001 and confirmed before the start of the 2002/3 tax year. Class 1 employee contributions will be due on earnings between £89 (2001/2: £87) and £585 (2001/2: £575) per week and from £89 (2001/2: £87) per week upwards for employers. The rates of NIC remains the same as before (normally 10%) for employees but drops slightly to 11.8% (2001/2: 11.9%) for employers.

Significant changes to NIC from April 2003 were announced in the Budget. Class 1 employee rates will rise to 11% normally and the extra 1% will also be applied to all earnings (i.e. not capped as for other employee NIC at £585 per week this year) An extra 1% will also be paid by employers on their contribution lifting their normal rate to 12.8% (this new rate will apply to Class 1A and 1B contributions also).

Class 2 contributions remain at £2 per week but the lower exemption limit was raised to £4,025 (2001/2 – £3,955). Class 3 contributions also were increased to £6.85 (2001/2: £6.75) and Class 4 contributions remained at 7% but with the bands to which it applies changing in line with the income tax bands as has been the case for the last few years - that is becoming £4,615 to £30,420 (2001/2 – £4,535 to £29,900). Class 4 contributions will also be increased by 1% to 8% from April 2003 to match the increase in Class 1 employee and employer contributions.

Business Taxation

The key change in the 2002 Budget related to business taxation was the alteration to the tax rates on small incorporated businesses. With effect from the start of the 2002/3 financial year the new starting rate of tax (on the first £10,000 of taxable profits) will be 0% (2001/2: 10%). The smaller companies rate was also reduced by 1% to 19%. This is a significant boost to small businesses and likely to encourage more to incorporate rather than remain as sole traders or partnerships.

The bands for marginal relief were not changed in the 2002 Budget.

Further changes were announced to the Enhanced Capital Allowance Scheme which will bring further capital assets into the 100% first year allowance scheme. This includes expenditure on new low emission cars - which also are removed from the expensive car allowance limitation of £3,000 writing down allowance each year, where the low emission car cost more than £12,000.

Cars and Fuel Benefit

From April 2002 a new company car benefit in kind computation has been introduced that is no longer based not on the previous business mileage formula but instead on the levels of the emissions of the car.

While the current fuel benefit scheme remains in place for the 2002/3 tax year. This too will be replaced by an emissions based scheme from April 2003.

The fixed profit car scheme (FPCS), used to determine the maximum expense allowance that can be paid to an employee for use of their own vehicle on their employer's business, has also been simplified. Instead of car capacity based formula for determining the allowed maximum expense, a simple formula of 40p a mile on the first 4,000 business miles and 25p per mile on subsequent mileage in the year will be used. This may leave large capacity car drivers worse off than previously (2000+cc cars got up to 63p per mile on the first 4000 miles under the old scheme), and so an important concession was made that all employees will now be *entitled* to the 40p/25p per mile and where their employer pays them less than this the excess can be claimed as an expense relief against their schedule E income.

Corporation Tax

Larger businesses have been included in the Research and Development Tax Credit Scheme that previously was only available to small businesses. Whilst SMEs continue to get a 150% credit, large businesses will now be able to claim 125% on their direct research and development expenditure.

VAT

No changes are being made to the various rates of VAT, but the compulsory registration and deregulation limits will increase to £55,000 and £53,000 respectively (2201/2: £54,000 and £52,000).

A more significant change, for small businesses at least, will be the introduction of another VAT payment scheme - this time aimed at reducing the compliance cost of VAT for many businesses by allowing VAT to be paid on the basis of a flat rate payment. This flat rate will not be the same for all businesses but will vary based on the nature of the business. It may, however, allow for significant cost savings as businesses will not need to account for VAT separately, as currently, on each invoice received and supplied. As with other VAT schemes, the flat rate scheme will be optional.

Previous budgets – key changes to the UK's tax system

2001 Budget and Finance Act

The 2001 Budget was given by the Chancellor, Gordon Brown, on 7th March 2001. It was his fifth Budget speech. This Budget was shortly before a General Election in the UK (held in June 2001) as is often the case with such Budgets it made few changes to the tax system. Income tax bands and personal allowances were increased by inflation. The Children's Tax Credit was introduced as replacement for the Married Couple's Allowance.

For businesses a key change was the extension of 100% first year allowances for designated, energy-saving, plant and machinery. There were also significant increases in the turnover bands for various of the VAT schemes (eg cash scheme was doubled to £600,000 turnover) to widen the availability of schemes that could reduce compliance costs for smaller businesses.

2000 Budget and Finance Act

The 2000 Budget was given on 21st March 2000. Generally the Chancellor, Gordon Brown, painted a picture of the UK as growing and looking healthy. This did not, however, encourage him to give away very much and many of the changes to the direct tax burden on individuals and companies that are affecting them in the 2000/01 tax year were actually announced in the 1999 Budget, or the pre-Budget speech in November, as to start in April 2000. This included the further 1% cut in the basic rate of income tax. Instead, the Government chose to use the extra revenues they were raising from the growing economy to fund increased expenditure in areas like health and education.

Overall the UK continued to have fiscal surplus (tax income being greater than public expenditure), generally considered a healthy position to be in. Individuals were affected by the final removal of interest relief on their homes (MIRAS) and other tax reducers such as the Married Couples Allowance and Additional Persons Allowance. There was also an increase in house Stamp Duty – the tax paid on the purchase price of a house for some properties.

The biggest change for personal income tax calculations in the 2000/01 tax year was the scrapping of a number of tax reducers. This includes the Married Couples Allowance for everyone except people born before 6th April 1935 who will be able to continue to collect the MCA as in 1999/2000 (i.e. £1,970 at a 10% rate). It also included the related tax-reducers of the widows bereavement allowance and additional personal allowances.

Mortgage Interest Relief was also abolished from 6th April 2000 as was relief for maintenance payments (again unless one of the parties was born before 6th April 1935 when the relief will now be restricted to a maximum of £200 i.e. £2,000 at 10%).

Income tax rates on savings were changed. From 6th April 2000 the starting rate of tax (10%) applied to savings income (1999/2000: 20% for starting and basic rate bands) as well as non-savings income. The rate withheld at source remained at 20% however, with any excess withheld being reclaimable or extra being payable if a higher rate taxpayer at the difference between 20% and 40% of the income.

A theme of the 2000 Budget was support of technology. This included giving extra share ownership plan concessions to reduce the amounts of tax that were paid by key employees in small businesses (of which many new ones are directly related to technology industries such as Internet companies). This year also saw the start of 100% first year allowances for small businesses for any money invested in computers, software and Internet-enabled mobile phones over the three years from 1st April 2000.

A new starting rate for corporation tax of 10% was introduced for taxable profits up to £10,000. For profits between £10,000 and £50,000 marginal relief was to be given with the small companies' rate only then applying between £50,000 and £300,000. These new rules significantly lowered the amount of tax paid by many small businesses.

Some fairly significant amendments were also made in the area of capital allowances. These included the scrapping of the need for a separate pool for cars costing less than £12,000. Small and medium-sized enterprises were also given a new tax credit related to any money they spent on research and development.

From the start of the 2000/01 tax year any gains falling below the starting rate limit for income tax were taxed at 10%. Gains falling between the starting rate and basic rate limits were taxed at 20% and any gains above the basic rate limit at 40%. This brought capital gains into line with other savings income types (only dividends now continue to operate under a different rate scheme).

Another key change related to Capital Gains taxation brought in this year was the reduction in the holding period for maximum taper relief from capital gains tax from 10 years to 4 years. This reduction, however, only applied to business assets. This made owning business assets much cheaper, however, and was a very popular tax concession. These new rules applied for any disposals after 6th April 2000 and for holding periods from 6th April 1998.

The charity sector was particularly favoured by the 2000 Budget. This included abolishing the £250 minimum for gift aid donations and the £1,200 annual maximum for payroll giving, and introducing a 10% supplement on payroll giving donations for the subsequent three years.

Summary of main reforms, 1979–2000

Personal income taxes	Basic rate 33% down to 22% Top rate 98% (unearned income), 83% (earnings) down to 40% Lower rate 25% down to 10% Independent taxation introduced Married couple's allowance abolished, Children's Tax Credit introduced Mortgage interest tax relief abolished Life assurance premium relief abolished PEP, TESSA and ISA introduced Capital gains tax at income tax rates
National Insurance	Rate for employee increased from 6.5% to 10% Rate for employer reduced from 13.5% to 11.9% Ceiling abolished for employers Cuts for low earners Alignment of floor with income tax allowance Imposition of NI on benefits in kind
VAT	Standard rate increased from 8% to 17.5% Higher rate of 12.5% abolished Reduced rate introduced on domestic fuel and other selected items
Excises	Large real rise in duties on road fuels Smaller increase in tobacco duties Slight real decrease in duties on beer, larger decline for spirits Small increase in real duties on wine
Corporate income taxes	Rate cut from 52% to 30% General 100% first-year allowance replaced by 25% writing-down allowance Reintroduction of FYA for small businesses on selected other capital expenditure Advance corporation tax and refundable dividend tax credit abolished
Local tax	Domestic rates replaced by council tax (via poll tax) Locally varying non-domestic rates abolished, replaced by national non-domestic rates

(Source: based on 'A Survey of the UK Tax System', IFS Briefing Notes No 9 by L. Chennells, A. Dilnot and N. Roback)

Glossary

1982-holding   A pool of identical securities acquired between 6th April 1965 and 5th April 1982 used for capital gains tax matching purposes.

Ability to pay   A system of taxation under which tax is levied on a taxpayer according to his economic ability to pay tax. *See also* Benefit principle.

Accounting period   The interval for which corporation tax is assessed and charged on the profits arising during the interval.

Accruals basis   Under the accruals basis profits for an accounting period equal revenue earned in the period less expenses incurred in earning that revenue.

Accumulation and maintenance trust   A trust in which income is accumulated for minor children until they reach a specified age.

Additional personal allowance (APA)   An allowance that was given to any single person with a child living with them (not available from 6 April 2000).

Additional voluntary contributions   Payments made by an employee to increase retirement benefits due from the approved pension scheme run by his employer.

Advance corporation tax   A payment which was made to the Inland Revenue whenever a UK company paid a dividend (no longer paid).

AESP   All employee share-ownership plans that enable share ownership in their own companies to employees with tax advantages.

Age allowance   An allowance available to individuals over 65 years of age instead of the ordinary personal allowance.

Agricultural buildings allowance   An allowance, for income tax and corporation tax purposes, available for capital expenditure on farmhouses, farm buildings cottages, fences, drainage and similar works.

Agricultural property relief   Relief from inheritance tax available on the agricultural value of agricultural property in the UK, the Channel Islands or the Isle of Man.

Annual accounting scheme   A method of accounting for VAT which only requires the registered trader to complete one VAT return each year.

Annual exemption   The amount of capital gains that an individual may make each year that is not subjected to capital gains tax. Also the amount which an individual may transfer each year which is not subjected to inheritance tax.

Annuity   An amount of money paid annually or at other regular intervals.

Arising basis   Income which is taxed as it arises regardless of if or when it is remitted to the UK.

Artificial scheme   A self-cancelling scheme used to avoid tax which is made up of a series of preordained steps which leaves taxpayers in the same position at the end as they were at the beginning.

Associated companies   Companies who are either under common control or where one company controls the other.

Associated disposal   One of a series of linked disposals of related assets to connected persons.

Associated operations   Two or more operations which are related are deemed to take place at the time of the last of the operations for inheritance tax purposes.

Average rate of tax   Equal to the total tax paid in the tax period, usually one year, divided by the total income received in the period.

Avoidance   The legal manipulation of a taxpayer's affairs in order to reduce the taxpayer's tax liability.

Bad debt relief   Relief for VAT paid on a taxable supply made by a registered trader who has subsequently written off all or part of the debt in his accounts.

Badges of trade   The six elements which the Royal Commission identified as helping to determine whether or not trading is taking place.

Balancing allowances and charges   Relief for capital expenditure, or the claw back of relief already given, given in the year in which an asset is disposed of or the business ceases to trade.

Basic rate of tax   The main rate at which income and capital gains taxes are levied (see Rates and Allowances for current rate).

Basis period   The time period whose profits are taxed in the fiscal year.

Beneficial loan   A loan given to an employee who derived the benefit of the loan because of their employment.

Beneficiary   Individual who may derive benefit from a trust.

Benefit principle   In contrast to the ability to pay principle, under the benefit principle tax is raised by reference to the amount of benefit a taxpayer is deemed to receive from the public sector. *See also* Ability to pay.

Benefits in kind   A benefit received by an employee or members of his or her family or household due to their employment.

Bills delivered basis   Income expenditure recognition basis which allows for inclusion in tax computation only on issuing/receipt of bills.

Blind person's allowance   An allowance given to taxpayers that are registered blind.

Board of Inland Revenue   Civil servants appointed by the Treasury who administer income tax, corporation tax and capital gains tax.

Bonus issue   An issue of additional shares in proportion to existing holdings to shareholders.

Budget   An annual statement by the Chancellor of the Exchequer setting out proposals for taxation and government expenditure in the following fiscal year.

Burden of tax   The amount by which a taxpayer's income or wealth is reduced because of taxation.

Business property relief   Relief from inheritance tax on transfers of relevant business property.

Capital allowances   Relief from income tax and corporation tax on capital expenditure on eligible assets.

Capital Allowances Act 1990 (CAA 1990)   The Act that governs capital allowances for income tax and corporation tax purposes.

Capital distribution   A repayment of capital by a company to its shareholders.

Capital gains   The net increase in the value of an asset after the indexation allowance on its disposal by an individual.

Capital gains tax   The tax levied on capital gains. The liability to tax only arises when the asset is disposed of.

Capitalisation of future tax benefits   Future tax benefits are capitalised when the current value of an asset includes an allowance for the increased expected yield from the asset due to future tax benefits.

Cash accounting scheme   A method of accounting for VAT which depends on payments and receipts rather than invoices for identifying tax points.

Cash basis Income and expenditure recognition basis which allows for inclusion in tax computation when each flow occurs.

Cash voucher A voucher, stamp or similar document capable of being exchanged for a sum of money.

Cash-flow tax base Under a cash-flow tax based system cash flows rather than profits are taxed.

Certificate of tax deposit A payment to the Inland Revenue which can be used to meet a tax liability.

Charge on income A recurring, legally enforceable, liability which income tax law allows as a deduction from the payer's total income.

Chargeable asset All assets are chargeable assets unless they are specifically exempted from capital gains tax.

Chargeable business asset The whole or part of a business or assets used in a business until it ceased to trade or shares or securities of a company.

Chargeable lifetime transfer A transfer of value made by an individual during their lifetime that is not an exempt or potentially exempt transfer. In practice, only transfers into a discretionary trust are chargeable lifetime transfers.

Chargeable transfer A transfer of value made by an individual who intended to confer a gratuitous benefit that is not an exempt transfer.

Chattel Tangible movable property.

Children's Tax Credit New tax reducer introduced 2001/02 in replacement for old tax reducers removed from April 2000.

Class 1 national insurance contributions Payments made by employees, primary contributions, and employers, secondary contributions.

Class 1A national insurance contributions Payments made by employers when employees are provided with most benefits in kind.

Class 2 national insurance contributions Flat rate payments made by the self-employed.

Class 3 national insurance contributions Voluntary payments made to individuals in order to maintain rights to some state benefits.

Class 4 national insurance contributions Payments made by the self-employed based on a percentage of taxable profits.

Close company A UK resident company which is under the control of five or fewer participators or of participators who are directors.

Close investment-holding company A close company which is a non-trading company.

Collector of taxes Civil servants appointed by the Board of Inland Revenue to collect the tax which is assessed to be payable.

Commissioners of Customs and Excise Civil servants appointed by the Crown who are responsible for collecting and accounting for, and otherwise managing, the revenues of Customs and Excise.

Commissioners of Inland Revenue Individuals appointed by the Lord Chancellor to hear taxpayers' appeals against the assessment of the inspectors.

Compliance costs Costs which are incurred by taxpayers in order to enable them to comply with a specific tax or more generally with the tax system.

Composite supply A taxable supply for VAT purposes made up of a mix of standard rated, zero rated or exempt supplies where it is not possible to apportion the value of the supply to each of the rates. One rate is applied to the whole of the supply.

Comprehensive income tax A tax which is levied on an individual's comprehensive income. An individual's comprehensive income is the amount which an individual could consume without diminishing the value of their wealth. *See also* Economic income.

Connected persons Persons who are defined as having a special relationship for tax purposes and transactions between them are sometimes accorded special treatment (see Chapter 7: Gross proceeds on disposal for complete list of connected persons).

Consortium A group of companies in which one company is at least 75% owned by UK resident companies who are called members of the consortium.

Consortium relief Allows trading losses to be surrendered from a member of a consortium to a consortium held company and vice versa.

Consumption taxes Also called expenditure taxes, a consumption tax taxes the resources which an individual has consumed during a set period of time.

Corporate PEP A single company personal equity plan which invests in the securities of only one company.

Corporation tax The tax that is levied on the profits of companies and unincorporated associations such as clubs and political associations but not partnerships.

Corrective taxes A tax which is intended to affect the behaviour of taxpayers. Tax relief on pension contributions is intended to encourage individuals to provide for a private pension.

Corresponding accounting period An accounting period of a company claiming group relief which falls wholly or partly within an accounting period of the surrendering company.

Crowding out This is the effect which may occur when public expenditure increases and causes a reduction in size of the private sector, thus reducing the tax base.

Cum div A quoted security which carries the right to an imminent dividend.

Cum int A quoted security which carries the right to an imminent interest payment.

De minimis limit Various taxes use a minimum value rule below which different rules to usual often apply. For example, expenditure on long life assets for single companies below £100,000 will not be subject to a writing down allowance of only 6%. They continue to receive allowances at 25%.

De-pooling An election made by taxpayers for nominated items of plant and machinery with a short life to be maintained outside the pool so that balancing allowances may be claimed on their disposal.

Deed of covenant A promise to pay over a number of years relating to the old system of relief for charitable payments.

Depreciating asset An asset which is, or within the next ten years will become, a wasting asset. Wasting assets have a useful life of 50 years or less thus a depreciating asset has a useful life of less than 60 years.

Deregistration The process by which a registered trader voluntarily or otherwise ceases to be registered for VAT.

Diminution in value The loss in value of an item, for example, of the donor's estate when a transfer of value for inheritance tax purposes occurs.

Direct taxes A tax which is levied on the taxpayer who is intended to bear the final burden of paying tax. Examples include income tax and employee national insurance contributions.

Disabled person's tax credit Benefit paid to person with illness or disability.

Discovery assessment An assessment made by the Inland Revenue based on evidence they discover after a self-assessment return became final.

Discretionary trust A trust in which no beneficiary has an absolute right to the income.

Disincentive effect of taxation Where a transaction, such as employment, is subject to tax there is a gap between the selling price and the purchase price which is equal to the tax levied. This gap may act as a disincentive to the transaction. For example an employee may be unwilling to undertake overtime at the rate offered if he is subject to a high marginal rate of tax.

District inspector Each Inland Revenue district is headed by a district inspector who has other inspectors working for them.

Divisional registration Registration by a company so that each division is registered separately for VAT purposes.

Domicile A domicile is the place that an individual thinks of as home. He or she may not live in the place of domicile but he or she is likely to retain some links with it.

Duality test When expenditure has both a business and a private purpose the expenditure is likely to fail the 'wholly and exclusively' test and be disallowable for tax purposes because of a duality of purpose.

Due date The date on which tax is due to be paid.

Earnings basis Income and expenditure recognition basis which allows for inclusion in tax computation on normal accounting accrual and realisation concepts.

Earnings cap The upper limit on the earnings on which an approved pension scheme can be based.

Economic efficiency A tax is economically efficient if it does not distort the economic decisions which are made by individuals or companies *See also* Fiscal Neutrality.

Economic income The maximum value which an individual can consume during a period and still expect to be as well off at the end of the period as at the beginning. *See also* Comprehensive income tax.

Economic rent The amount that a factor of production, such as land, earns over and above what could be earned if it was put to its next best use.

Effective incidence of tax The effective incidence of tax falls on those individuals whose wealth is reduced by the tax. This may not be the same as the formal incidence of tax.

Eligible interest Interest paid on loans to purchase annuities or other qualifying loan interest payments.

Emoluments Income (not necessarily just money) from an office or employment.

Employee An individual with a contract of services.

Employee share ownership plan (ESOP) A trust into which a UK resident company transfers funds for the benefit of some or all of its employees.

Enhanced Capital Allowance Scheme Government Scheme under which extra capital allowances are given to the normal arrangements

Enhancement expenditure Capital expenditure incurred to enhancing an asset.

Enterprise zone An area designated as benefiting from tax and other incentives in order to encourage investment.

Error or mistake relief Relief for tax overstated due to some error or mistake on the part of the taxpayer.

Estate at death The value of all the assets owned on the date of death together with any interest held as a joint tenant and capital held by a trust in which the deceased had an interest in possession.

Evasion The illegal manipulation of a taxpayer's affairs so as to reduce the taxpayer's tax liability.

Ex div   A quoted security which does not carry a right to the imminent dividend.

Ex int   A quoted security which does not carry a right to the imminent interest payment.

Excepted estate   An estate in respect of which it is not necessary to deliver an account of the property for inheritance tax purposes.

Excess burden of tax   Where a tax is not economically efficient the loss to the economy caused by the distortion is termed the excess burden of tax.

Excluded property   Property which is specifically excluded from an estate at death for the purposes of inheritance tax.

Exempt income   Income which is specifically exempt from income tax.

Exempt supply   A supply of goods or services which is specifically exempt from VAT.

Exit charge   Charge made at the end of the life of an asset such as an inheritance charge levied when funds leave a discretionary trust.

Expenditure taxes   A tax on the amount consumed by an individual in a given period of time.

Extra-statutory concession   A series of statements made by the Inland Revenue or Customs and Excise which give concessions to taxpayers over and above those allowed by legislation.

FA 1985 pool   A pool of shares of the same class in the same company acquired on or after 6th April 1982 and held on 6th April 1985 and those acquired on or after 6th April 1985, maintained for capital gains tax purposes.

Factor of production   Resources used as inputs into a production activity to produce outputs such as goods and services. Typically include land, labour and capital. Some argue entrepreneurship should also be included in this list.

Fall in value relief   An inheritance tax relief available if assets are disposed of within a given period after death for less than their value at the date of death.

Finance Act   Usually an annual Act of Parliament which contains the fiscal legislation needed to implement the budget.

Financial year   Runs from 1st April to the following 31st March. The rate of corporation tax is set for financial years.

First year allowance   A capital allowance which may be available in the year in which an asset is acquired.

Fiscal neutrality   A fiscally neutral tax system does not discriminate between economic choices.

Fiscal year   A tax year for individuals which runs from 6th April until the following 5th April. A particular fiscal year is described using the two calendar years crossed by the fiscal year, e.g. fiscal year 2000/01 is the tax year starting 6th April 2000 and ending 5th April 2001.

Fixed profit car scheme   Maximum allowance available to an employee for use of their own car on their employer's business. Expense payments in excess of this amount is a taxable benefit in kind. Scheme ceased to exist April 2002 when new approved rate scheme commenced.

Follow-up account   A TESSA which was set up using some of the proceeds of an earlier TESSA on its maturation.

Foreign emoluments   The emoluments of a person, not domiciled in the UK, from an office or employment with an employer not resident in the UK.

Franked investment income (FII)   Dividends together with the related tax credit received by a UK company from another UK company which are not treated as group income.

Franked payment (FP)   Dividends together with the related tax credit paid by a UK company to another UK company which are not treated as group income.

Free estate   The value of all the assets owned outright by an individual at his death.

Free-standing additional voluntary contributions   Payments made by an employee who is a member of an occupational pension scheme in order to increase retirement benefits.

Full rent   A rent paid under a lease which is sufficient, taking one year with another, to defray the cost to the lessor of any expenses which are borne by him.

Functional test   A test to identify assets which are actively used in the business and thus are eligible for capital allowances as opposed to those which form part of the setting in which the business was carried on.

Furnished holiday lettings   Holiday lettings taxed under Schedule A using the regulations for Schedule D Case I. The income is treated as earned income for tax purposes.

Furnished letting   A letting of furnished property which is taxed under Schedule D Case VI.

General Commissioners   Part time and unpaid individuals who hear taxpayers' appeals against the assessments of the inspectors.

Gift relief   A relief from capital gains tax when a qualifying asset is disposed of and both the transferor and transferee elect for the transferor's gain to be reduced to nil.

Gift with reservation   A gift which the donor is not able to benefit from to the exclusion of the donor during the period.

Gratuitous disposition   A disposal of an asset which was intended to confer some benefit to the recipient.

Gross amount of tax   The aggregate of the input tax and output tax included in the VAT return for a period.

Grossing up   The conversion of net receipts to gross receipts such as in tax computations.

Group charge   A charge paid under an election by one member of a 51% group to another without deduction of income tax.

Group   Companies which are either associated, 51% subsidiaries, 75% subsidiaries or consortia.

Group income   Dividends paid under an election by one member of a 51% group to another member of the same group.

Group interest   Interest paid under an election by one member of a 51% group to another without deduction of income tax.

Group registration   Registration for VAT purposes by a group of companies under common control.

Group relief   Trading losses incurred by one member of a 75% group can be surrendered to another member of the same group.

Higher rate tax   Taxable income of an individual in excess of £29,400 is taxed at the higher rate of 40%.

HM Customs and Excise   A government department which is responsible to the Treasury and administers VAT.

Holdover relief   Relief from capital gains tax which can be claimed when a business asset is replaced by a depreciable asset.

Horizontal equity   A tax system displaying horizontal equity treats similar individuals, companies or situations in similar ways.

Hypothecated taxes   Taxes raised to provide designated benefits.

Imputation system   A system under which shareholders are given a tax credit for the corporation tax paid by a company on the payment of a dividend.

Incidence of taxation   The formal incidence of tax falls on those who must actually pay the tax while the effective incidence of tax falls on those whose wealth is reduced by the tax. *See also* Indirect taxes; Regressive taxes.

Incidental costs of acquisition   Costs incurred when an asset was acquired which are allowed when calculating a chargeable gain for capital gains tax purposes.

Incidental costs of disposal   Costs incurred when an asset was disposed of which are allowed when calculating a chargeable gain for capital gains tax purposes.

Incidental expenses   Small payments to employees to cover expenses.

Income and Corporation Taxes Act 1988 (ICTA 1988)   Act of Parliament which contains the majority of the legislation dealing with the taxation of individuals and companies.

Income tax   A tax levied on all income, earned and unearned, attributed to an individual in a given period.

Income taxed at source   Income paid net of tax at the rate of 20% or 22%.

Income taxed by assessment   Income paid gross on which income tax is levied.

Income   Valuable consideration received in exchange for the provision of goods or services.

Incorporation   Creation of a company from a business run by a sole trader or partnership.

Independent taxation   The taxation of spouses as individuals rather than as a family unit.

Indexation allowance   An allowance intended to compensate for the effect of inflation on the value of capital assets when determining a capital gains tax liability.

Indirect taxes   A tax which is ultimately borne by someone other than the taxpayer on whom it is levied. However, it is not always possible to identify the effective incidence of an indirect tax. VAT is an example of an indirect tax which is intended to be suffered by the final consumer. However, market forces might lead to manufacturers absorbing some of the VAT themselves, rather than passing it on to the final consumer. *See also* Incidence of taxation.

Individual Savings Account (ISA)   Savings product providing tax free income. Used to replace TESSAs and PEPs.

Industrial buildings allowances (IBA)   Capital allowance available on expenditure on industrial buildings and hotels.

Inheritance tax   Tax levied on certain lifetime transfers and estates on the death of individuals.

Inheritance Tax Act 1984 (IHTA 1984)   Act of Parliament containing the majority legislation dealing with inheritance tax.

Inland Revenue   The government department responsible for income tax, corporation tax, capital gains tax and inheritance tax.

Input VAT   VAT levied on the purchases of goods and services by a registered trader.

Inspector of taxes   Civil Servants who assess individuals, companies and other organisations liability to tax.

Instalment option   Facility which allows some capital, gains tax and inheritance tax to be paid in instalments.

Intending trader registration   Registration for VAT by an individual or organisation which has not yet begun to trade.

Interest in possession trust   A trust in which the beneficiaries, the life tenants, have a right to receive the income from the trust for a period of time.

Interim payments   Payments of income tax on account on 31st January in the fiscal year and 31st July following the end of the fiscal year.

Intra-group transfer   A transfer of assets between two members of a group which would in other circumstances give rise to a capital gains tax charge.

Irrecoverable VAT   VAT levied on the purchases of goods or services that cannot be recovered as input tax.

ISA   *See* Individual Savings Account

Job-related accommodation   Accommodation provided to an employee which is eligible for some tax relief.

Landlord repairing lease   A lease of property at a full rent. That is the rent paid under the lease is sufficient taking one year with another, to defray the cost to the lessor of any expenses subject to the lease which fall to be borne by him.

Large business   For tax purposes a large business would be one that exceeds two or more of the conditions necessary to be a medium sized business.

Lease   The granting of a right to the use of an asset for a specified period.

Less detailed VAT invoice   May be issued by retailers when the VAT inclusive total is less than £100.

Letting exemption   Relief from capital gains tax available when part or all of a property, which was at some time the taxpayer's principal private residence, is let.

Life interest trust   A trust in which beneficiaries have an interest in possession throughout their life.

Life tenant   An individual who has a right to receive the income from a trust for a period of time.

Linked transactions   A series of transactions to connected persons where the disposal proceeds of each disposal are taken to be a proportion of the value of the aggregate of the assets transferred for capital gains tax purposes.

Long-life assets   For capital allowance purposes assets with useful lives of more than 25 years receive writing down allowances of 6% per annum.

Loss relief   Tax relief for trading or capital losses given by setting losses against taxable income or chargeable gains.

Lower rate of tax   The rate of tax, currently 20%, levied on savings income and capital gains that falls into the basic rate band.

Lump sum taxes   A fixed amount of tax paid by an individual regardless of his or her income.

Maintenance payments   Payments to a spouse, former spouse or children.

Management expenses   Expenses incurred in managing an investment company.

Marginal rate of tax   This is the rate at which a taxpayer would be taxed if his income increased by a small amount.

Marginal relief   Relief given to companies with taxable profits lying within given limits.

Marriage exemption   Relief from inheritance tax on gifts made in consideration of marriage.

Married couple's allowance   An allowance available to a married man whose wife lives with him (not available from 6th April 2000 unless aged over 65 as at that date).

Matching rules   The rules used to match acquisitions and disposals of quoted securities for capital gains tax purposes.

Medium-sized business   To be classed as medium-sized for tax purposes the business must be larger than a small business and satisfy at least two of the following conditions: turnover not more than £11.2 million, assets not more than £5.6 million and not more than 250 employees.

Minor   An unmarried child under the age of 18.

MIRAS   The mechanism used to give individuals tax relief on the interest paid on their mortgages called Mortgage Interest Relief At Source (not available from 6th April 2000).

Mixed supply   A supply of goods and services by a registered trader which is made up of a separable mix of elements. The appropriate VAT rate to be applied to each part.

National insurance contributions   A tax paid by individuals and employers to secure certain benefits such as a state pension.

National Savings Bank   A government owned bank in which individuals can invest in order to obtain interest.

National Savings Certificate   Certificates issued by the Government which offer tax-free returns.

Negligible value claim   A capital gains tax relief that can be claimed by a taxpayer when an asset becomes effectively worthless.

Net Relevant Earnings   Schedule D Case I and II, Schedule E and income from furnished holiday lettings taxed under Schedule D Case VI net of loss relief and excess of trade charges over other income.

Nil rate band   The band of transfers for which the rate of inheritance tax is nil.

No gain/no loss transfer   Disposal of an asset without a gain or loss for capital gains tax purposes regardless of the actual costs and the value of any proceeds.

Nominal rent lease   A lease which is not expected to generate a profit over a number of years.

Non-cash voucher   A voucher which can only be exchanged for goods or services.

Non-savings income   Income other than interest and dividends.

Normal expenditure out of income exemption   Exemption from inheritance tax where the gift or gifts are not so large that the donor's residual income is inadequate to maintain his or her usual standard of living.

Occupational pension scheme   Pension schemes available for employees set up by their employers.

OECD   Organisation for Economic Co-operation and Development. A grouping of the major economic world powers part of whose remit is to provide an international forum for tax issues (see http//www.oecd.org).

Ordinary residence   A taxpayer is ordinarily resident if the UK is a regular choice of abode which forms part of the regular order of an individual's life.

Output VAT   The VAT on supplies made by a registered trader or on the acquisition by a registered trader of goods from another member state.

Overlap losses   Losses incurred by a trader in a period which forms all or part of the basis period of more than one fiscal year.

Overlap profits   Profits earned by a trader in a period which forms all or part of the basis period of more than one fiscal year.

Part disposal   The disposal of part of an asset for capital gains tax purposes.

Partial exemption   Where a trader makes some taxable supplies and some exempt supplies he may be unable to recover all of his input tax.

Participator   A person who has a share or interest in the capital or income of a close company.

Partnership   Two or more individuals carrying on a business.

Pay and file   The system used to collect corporation tax.

Pay As You Earn (PAYE)   The system used to collect income tax and national insurance contributions from employees.

Payment basis   Charges are recognised for tax purposes when they are paid.

Payroll deduction scheme   Payments to charity from an employee's gross income under the PAYE scheme.

Period of account   The period for which a business prepares accounts.

Personal allowance   An amount of income that can be received tax free by an individual.

Personal company   A company is an individual's personal company if he exercises at least 5% of the voting rights in the company.

Personal equity plan (PEP)   A plan which enables individuals to invest in equities either directly or using unit trusts free of income tax or capital gains tax.

Personal pension scheme   A pension scheme which employees can invest in provided that they are not a member of their employer's occupational pension scheme.

Plant and machinery   Apparatus used by a business person for carrying on business not their own stock-in-trade which they buy or make for resale. Capital expenditure on plant and machinery may qualify for capital allowances.

Political accountability   Tax raising bodies should be accountable to those they raise taxes from. This usually takes the form of requirement to obtain a mandate from the electorate in regular elections.

Potentially exempt transfer (PET)   A lifetime transfer of value, other than one to a discretionary trust, made by an individual which is not an exempt transfer for inheritance tax purposes. A potentially exempt transfer becomes a chargeable transfer if the donor dies within seven years of making the transfer.

Premium   A payment in return for the granting of a lease on land or property.

Principal charge   A charge of 15% of the inheritance scale rate on the value of a discretionary trust every ten years.

Principal private residence   The main residence of an individual or a married couple. An individual who owns more than one residence may nominate one as his or her main residence.

Profit sharing scheme   A scheme for employees which enables shares in their employer company to be distributed to them.

Profits chargeable to corporation tax (PCTCT)   Tax adjusted profits of a company excluding franked investment income after deducting charges and loss relief.

Profits for small companies rate purposes   Profits chargeable to corporation tax plus franked investment income.

Progressive taxes   A tax is progressive if individuals with a larger taxable capacity pay proportionately more of their income in tax than individuals with a lower taxable capacity.

Proportional taxes   A tax is proportional if tax paid is a fixed proportion of taxable capacity.

Qualifying corporate bond   A sterling bond which is a normal commercial loan which is exempt from capital gains tax for individuals (but not for companies).

Quarter days 25th March, 24th June, 29th September and 25th December. Often rents are due on the quarter days.

Quarter up rule A valuation rule for quoted securities for capital gains tax purposes. The valuation is equal to the lower of the two prices quoted in the Daily Official List plus a quarter of the difference between the two prices.

Quarterly accounting The system used by large companies to account for corporation tax under self-assessment.

Quick succession relief Relief from inheritance tax when a chargeable transfer increased the value of a person's estate within the previous five years.

Ramsay principle A principle that if an artificial scheme is used to avoid or delay a tax liability the courts can set aside the scheme and instead compare the position of the taxpayer in real terms at the start and finish of the scheme.

Rate applicable to trusts The 34% rate for income tax and capital gains tax applied to discretionary trusts.

Rebasing The procedure under which capital gains are calculated by assuming that assets owned on 31st March 1982 were bought on that date at their market value on that date.

Receipts basis A way of allocating income to fiscal years on the basis of when it is received.

Receivable basis A way of allocating income to fiscal years on the basis of when it was due to be received.

Regressive taxes A tax is regressive if the proportion of tax paid increases as income falls. *See also* Incidence of tax.

Reinvestment relief Relief from capital gains tax available to individuals or trustees, but not companies, when some or all of the proceeds from the disposal of an asset or a material disposal of shares in a qualifying company are reinvested in a qualifying investment.

Related property Property held in the estates of spouses.

Relief A reduction in tax allowed to a taxpayer.

Relevant supplies Supplies to a non-taxable person in the UK from another EU member state. The supplier may be liable to register for VAT in the UK.

Remittance basis A way of determining taxable income on the basis of amounts remitted to the UK.

Remoteness test A test for determining whether an expense is deductible. An expense which is considered to be too remote from the trade will not be deductible.

Renewals basis An allowable deduction from income from furnished letting for the replacement of furniture.

Rent a room scheme A scheme under which if an individual lets one or more furnished rooms in their main residence rents received up to £4,250 a year are exempt from tax under Schedule A.

Residence An individual is deemed to be resident in the UK for a fiscal year if he or she spends more than 183 days in the UK during the tax year.

Retail prices index (RPI) An index used to calculate the indexation allowance for capital gains tax purposes.

Retail schemes Schemes for accounting for VAT which are available to some retailers.

Retirement relief Relief from capital gains tax is given in any case where a material disposal of business assets is made by an individual who, at the time of the disposal, has attained the age of 50 or has retired on the grounds of ill-health below the age of 50.

Reverse charge   A system of accounting for VAT on supplies made to a UK resident registered trader by a person resident overseas.

Reversionary interest   An interest in a trust which will depend on the termination of another interest in the trust.

Rollover relief   Relief from capital gains tax available if the proceeds from the disposal of certain classes of assets are reinvested in other qualifying assets.

Royalty   Payments made in consideration for the use of, or right to use, intellectual property (e.g. patents, copyrights, design plans, trademarks, business processes etc).

Savings income   Income source, primarily interest and dividends.

Schedular system of taxation   Income is taxed under the schedular system in the UK. The income to be taxed, the deductible expenses and the date of the payment of tax is laid down in the schedular system.

Secondhand goods scheme   A VAT scheme available to traders who buy secondhand goods from individuals who are not registered traders.

Self assessment   A system of administration of taxation in which taxpayers are responsible for assessing their own liability to tax.

Self-employed person   An individual who has a contract for services. An employee has a contract of service.

Self-supply   A supply of goods or services by a registered person which is used by themselves in the course of their business.

Settled property   Assets held within a trust.

Settlement   A trust.

Seven year cumulation   An inheritance tax computation depends on the transfers of value which have occurred in the seven years prior to the most recent transfer.

Share option scheme   A scheme open to employees and directors which grants them share options.

Short-life asset   Plant or machinery which is kept separate from the general pool for the purposes of calculating capital allowances.

Single company PEP   A personal equity plan which only holds shares in one company.

Small Business   To be classed as a small company requires at least two of the following conditions to be true: turnover not more than £2.8 million, assets not more than £1.4 million, not more than 50 employees.

Small companies rate   The rate at which profits chargeable to corporation tax are taxed provided the profits for small companies rate purposes lie below a given limit.

Small gifts exemption   An inheritance tax exemption for gifts to the same person provided that they have a total value of less than £250 in the fiscal year.

Special Commissioners   Full-time paid individuals who have been legally qualified for at least ten years who hear complex appeals of taxpayers against the assessment of the inspectors.

Stakeholder Pension   Pension scheme available from 6 April 2001 to widen provision for own retirement income. Not tied to earnings and low cost.

Stamp duty   A tax on documents usually involving transfers of property (e.g. houses or shares).

Standard rated supply   A supply of goods or services by a registered trader which is not VAT exempt or zero rated.

Starting rate   Introductory rate of income and corporation taxation.

Statement of practice   A statement issued by the Inland Revenue in order to clarify the application of some aspect of the legislation.

Statutory total income   An individual's total income before deduction of allowances.

Substitution effect of tax   A substitution distortion occurs when individuals consume one item rather than another because of the effect of taxation.

Surplus ACT   Used to arise when ACT was paid by a company that could not be set against its corporation tax liability for the period in which the ACT was paid.

Tapering relief   Relief given to companies with taxable profits lying within given limits. Also called marginal relief. Also used to refer to relief given for capital gains from ownership of assets after April 1998 by individuals.

Tax avoidance   The use of legal means to reduce tax liabilities.

Tax base   The liability of a collection of items collectively form the tax base. Tax may be levied on income, wealth or expenditure, making these the primary tax bases.

Tax borne   The tax on an individual's taxable income less tax relief on tax reducers other than those paid net.

Tax credit   A credit received with dividends from UK companies which is equal to the amount of tax deemed to have been suffered by the taxpayer.

Tax evasion   The use of illegal means to reduce tax liabilities.

Tax exempt special savings account (TESSA)   Savings accounts which give tax free returns provided that they are held for five years.

Tax liability   Tax borne plus income tax retained on charges paid net.

Tax life   The deemed life of an industrial or agricultural building. The life is currently 25 years.

Tax payable   Tax liability less tax already suffered and tax credits.

Tax point   The date on which a supply of goods or services is treated as taking place for VAT purposes.

Tax reducer   An allowance or relief which has the effect of reducing the tax due on taxable income.

Tax relief   The deduction allowed to reduce the amount that must be paid of a specific tax.

Tax system   The collection of specific taxes and tax rules that together describe how revenue is raised for a Government.

Tax wedges   In the case of an indirect tax the tax wedge is the difference between the marginal cost of producing a good or service and the marginal benefit of consumption.

Tax year   Also called a fiscal year or a year of assessment. A tax year runs from 6th April to the following 5th April.

Taxable capacity   This is the capacity of an individual to pay tax and may be measured by reference to the individual's income, expenditure, wealth or even ability to generate income.

Taxable income   Statutory total income less allowances.

Taxable person   A person who is, or should be, registered for VAT.

Taxable supply   A supply of goods or services by a registered trader which is not an exempt supply.

Taxable turnover   The turnover of a business which is subject to VAT at any rate.

Taxation of Chargeable Gains Act 1992 (TCGA 1992)   The Act which provides the majority of the legislation for capital gains tax.

Taxed income   Income received net of basic rate or lower rate tax.

Taxpayer's Charter   A statement setting out what a taxpayer is entitled to expect from the Inland Revenue.

Tenant's repairing lease   A lease where the tenant is obliged to maintain or repair the whole or substantially the whole, of the premises which are the subject of the lease.

Terminal loss relief   An income tax relief available to individuals for losses incurred in the final 12 months of trading.

TESSA   *See* Tax exempt special savings account.

Transfer of value   A disposition by an individual which reduces the value of their estate.

Treasury   A government department responsible to the Chancellor of the Exchequer which is responsible for the Inland Revenue and HM Customs and Excise.

Trust   A trust is created when a settler transfers assets to trustees who hold the assets for the benefit of one or more persons.

Trustees   Hold assets within a trust for the benefit of one or more persons.

Unfranked investment income (UFII)   Taxed income received by a UK resident company.

Value Added Tax Act 1994 (VATA 1994)   The Act containing the principal legislation for VAT.

Value added tax (VAT)   An indirect or expenditure tax borne by the final consumer which is charged whenever a taxable person makes a taxable supply of goods or services in the course of his or her business.

VAT invoice   An invoice which must be supplied by registered traders to other registered traders.

VAT period   The period of time, usually three months, which is covered by a VAT return.

VAT return   Form VAT 199 which must be submitted to HM Customs and Excise together with any VAT payable within one month of the end of the VAT period.

Vertical equity   A tax system has vertical equity if those in differing economic circumstances are taxed differently, e.g. those on higher incomes pay more tax than those on lower incomes.

Void period   A period in which there is no tenant leasing property and the property is not occupied by the owner.

Wasting asset   Assets with an estimated remaining useful life of 50 years or less.

Wealth taxes   A wealth tax is levied on a taxpayer's assets at a particular date. The primary difficulty with a wealth tax comes from valuing assets, especially intangibles like pension funds.

Wear and tear allowance   A deduction from the income from furnished lettings to give relief for the wear and tear of furniture and equipment provided.

Widow's bereavement allowance   An allowance given to a widow in the fiscal year in which her husband dies and the following fiscal year provided that she has not remarried by the beginning of that year.

Withholding taxes   Some income, such as debenture interest, has tax deducted at source regardless of the personal circumstances of the recipient. The tax so deducted is termed a withholding tax.

Work effort and taxes   There is a potentially complicated relationship between work effort and taxes. If marginal rates of tax are too high they may act as a disincentive to work.

Working Families' Tax Credit   Benefit available to families in which the parent (or parents) are currently working.

Writing down allowance   A capital allowance which is given as a deduction from profits to determine the Schedule D Case I or II assessment.

Year of assessment   A fiscal or tax year which runs from 6th April to the following 5th April.

Zero rated supply   A supply of goods or services made by a registered trader which is subjected to a nil rate of VAT.

Suggested solutions to questions

Chapter 4

Question 1

(a) The general strategy to be adopted in order to maximise the benefits of the system of independent taxation should aim to:

- Ensure that each spouse has sufficient income to fully utilise their personal allowances.
- Ensure that, if possible, each spouse fully utilises their lower and basic rate bands. The situation where one spouse pays tax at 40% while the other is a lower or basic rate taxpayer should be avoided if possible.
- Chargeable disposals should be made by the spouse with the lowest marginal rate of tax. Wherever possible each spouse should fully utilise their exemption limit.
- Chargeable disposals should be made in such a way as to fully utilise any allowable losses.

(b) This strategy can be achieved by:

- Transferring income generating investments to the spouse with the lowest marginal rate of tax.
- Taking the spouse of a self-employed taxpayer into partnership or providing employment in the business in order to generate income for the spouse with the lower marginal rate of tax.
- Using charges and other tax deductible payments to reduce the taxable income of the spouse with the highest marginal rate of tax. Remember that the spouse who wishes to claim such reliefs must actually make the relevant payment.
- Transferring chargeable assets between spouses on a no gain/no loss basis in order to ensure that:
  - Annual exemption limits are fully used
  - Chargeable gains are realised by the spouse with the lowest marginal rate of tax
  - Allowable losses are not wasted by being relieved against chargeable gains which would otherwise have been relieved by the annual exemption limit.

Question 2

Personal tax computation for Janet for 2002/03

	£ (Savings)	£ (Non-savings)	£ (Total)
Income			
Schedule E: Salary		26,000	26,000
Bonus		3,000	3,000
Building society interest			
£2,500 × 100/80	3,125		3,125
Schedule A			
6/12 × £8,000		4,000	4,000
less expenses		(1,000)	(1,000)
Statutory total income	3,125	32,000	35,125
(no charges)			
less personal allowance		(4,615)	(4,615)
Taxable income	3,125	27,385	30,510
Tax due			
Non-savings income	1,920 @ 10%		192.00
	25,465 @ 22%		5,602.30
Savings income	2,515 @ 20%		503.00
	616 @ 40%		244.00
	30,510		
Tax liability			6,541.30
(no charges)			
less tax deducted at source:			
Building society interest			(625.00)
PAYE			(5,000.00)
Tax payable			916.30

Notes: Janet

The first £70 in interest received from a National Savings Bank ordinary account and any premium bond winnings are tax free and therefore do not need to form part of her tax computation.

Personal tax computation for Dave for 2002/03

	£ (Dividends)	£ (Savings)	£ (Non-savings)	£ (Total)
Income				
Schedule E: Salary			27,500	27,500
Bank deposit account				
£3,000 × 100/80		3,750		3,750
Schedule F (dividends)				
£5,760 × 100/90	6,400			6,400
Total income	6,400	3,750	27,500	37,650
less charges on income				
£312 × 100/78			(400)	(400)
Statutory total income	6,400	3,750	27,100	37,250
less personal allowances			(4,615)	(4,615)
Taxable income	6,400	3,750	22,485	32,635

Tax due			
	Non-savings	1,920 @ 10%	192.00
		20,565 @ 22%	4,524.30
	Savings	3,750 @ 20%	750.00
	Dividends	3,665 @ 10%	366.50
		2,735 @ 32.5%	888.87
		32, 635	

Tax borne		6,721.67
Add: Tax withheld on charge and credits		
£400 × 22%		88.00
Tax liability		6,809.67
less: tax deducted at source and tax credits		
Bank £3,750 @ 20%		(750.00)
Dividends £6,400 @ 10%		(640.00)
PAYE		(5,200.00)
Tax payable		219.67

Chapter 6

Question 1

The treatment of each of the items, for tax purposes, is as follows:

(a) *Reconstruction of the roof*
  The expenditure was incurred to renovate an asset soon after it was acquired

and the asset, a building, was not in a usable condition immediately after acquisition. Following the decision in Law Shipping the expenditure will be deemed to be capital and hence will be disallowable for tax purposes. If the use of the warehouse qualifies the building for an industrial buildings allowance the expenditure will qualify for capital allowances.

The expenditure on the roof should be added back to the net profit in order to determine the Schedule D Case I profit.

(b) *Embezzlement by the Director*

Defalcations by staff are not allowable deductions for Schedule D Case I purposes. Hence the expense should be added back to the net profit in order to determine the Schedule D Case I profit. Embezzlement of a staff member (not a partner or director) is an allowable tax expense. All payments in connection with criminal offences (e.g. fines or bribes) are explicitly excluded as deductions.

(c) *Redundancy payment to a works manager*

Redundancy payments made wholly and exclusively for the purpose of trade are allowed without limit, provided that the business continues to trade. If Jones ceases to trade there is a limit on the amount of any redundancy payment of the statutory amount plus up to three times the statutory amount. In the case of the works manager the maximum deductible is £48,000 (£12,000 × 3 + £12,000). Since the actual payment is lower than this it will be an allowable expense even if Jones ceases to trade.

Hence no adjustment needs to be made in order to determine the Schedule D Case I profit.

(d) *Salary of senior manager seconded to a charity*

Such a payment is specifically allowable for tax purposes and hence no adjustment needs to be made in order to determine the Schedule D Case I profit.

Salary of manager working entirely for the subsidiary

Salaries are only deductible for tax purposes if they are incurred for the purposes of trade. Hence the manager's salary will only be deductible if Jones' trade benefits from his work.

Provided that Jones does benefit from the manager's work, by for example, charging the associate for his work, no adjustment needs to be made in order to determine the Schedule D Case I profit. Otherwise the expense should be added back to the net profit in order to determine the Schedule D Case I profit.

(e) *Costs of the crèche*

The construction costs are capital expenditure and as such are not allowable for tax purposes, although if Jones trade is a qualifying trade it may be eligible for industrial buildings allowance.

The running costs of the crèche are incurred in order to provide a benefit in kind for employees and as such are allowable deductions for tax purposes.

Hence the construction costs should be added back to the net profit in order to determine the Schedule D Case I profit while no adjustment is required for the running costs.

(f) *Receipt from insurance company*

The cost of repairing the asset is an allowable expense. The receipt from the insurance company will reduce the allowable expenditure by £18,000 because the company has been reimbursed for its costs.

The receipt of £6,000 in compensation for loss of profits is taxable.

Since the company has reduced the balance on the repairs account by £18,000 and increased the balance on the profits and loss account by £6,000 no adjustments in respect of these items are necessary.

(g) *Gain on the sale of investments*

Capital gains are not taxed under Schedule D Case I. Hence the gain of £30,000 should be deducted in order to calculate the Schedule D Case I profits.

(h) *Sales to X Ltd*

Drawings in the form of goods or services made by sole traders or partners have to be dealt with at market prices. The sales figure should therefore be increased by £30,000.

Question 2

(i) Bill and Ben make a joint election for industrial buildings legislation to apply.

Period	Computation £	Allowances claimed £
Bill		
y/e 31.3.01		
Cost	30,000	
Less WDA	(1,200)	1,200
WDV c/f	28,800	
y/e 31.3.02		
Less WDA	(1,200)	1,200
WDV c/f	27,600	
y/e 31.3.03		
Proceeds	(20,000)	
Balance allowance	7,600	7,600
Ben		
y/e 30.6.03		
Residue before sale	27,600	
Balancing allowance	(7,600)	
Residue after sale	20,000	

The total tax life of the poultry house is 25 years. Bill owned the house for two years so the remaining tax life is 23 years.

The writing down allowance which Ben can claim for each of the next 23 years is £870 (£20,000/23).

(ii) No election is made.

Period	Computation £		Allowances claimed £
Bill			
<y/e 31.3.01			
Cost	30,000		
Less WDA	(1,200)		1,200
WDV c/f	28,800		
y/e 31.3.02			
Less WDA	(1,200)		1,200
WDV c/f	27,600		
y/e 31.3.03			
Less WDA	(900)	(Note 1)	900
	26,700		
Ben			
y/e 30.6.03			
Allowable cost	26,700		
Less WDA	(600)	(Note 2)	600
WDV c/f	26,100		

For the accounting periods from y/e 30th June 2004 to y/e 30th June 2024 the writing down allowance of £1,200 can be claimed and in the accounting period ended 30th June 2025 Ben will be able to claim an allowance of £900, which is simply the difference between the original cost of the building and the total allowances given to date. Thus by the 30th June 2025 the total allowances given will equal the original cost of the building.

Note 1
Without an election Bill is entitled to the writing down allowance in the year of disposal restricted by reference to the proportion of the period of account during which he owned the asset. Bill owned the asset for nine months and hence the writing down allowance is £1,200 × 9/12.

Note 2
Similarly Ben's writing down allowance will be restricted by reference to the proportion of the period of account during which he owned the asset. Ben owned the asset for six months and hence the writing down allowance is £1,200 × 6/12.

Accounting period	Pool £	Car (1) £	Car (2) £	Allowance £
15 months to 31.12.2000				
Additions:				
Expensive car (1)		12,200		
WDA (max allowable)		(3,750) × 80%		3,000
£3000 × 15/12 (Note 1)				
Others (trailer and plant)	10,000			
FYA (10,000 × 40%)	(4,000)	6,000		4,000
WDV of total allowances	4,000	8,450		7,000
y/e 31.12.2001				
Disposals:		2,000	7,000	
		2,000	1,450	
Additions:			13,000	
WDA	(750)		(3,000) × 80%	3,150
Balancing allowance		(1,450) × 80%		1,160
WDV c/f total allowances	1,250	—	10,000	4,310
y/e 31.12.2002				
WDA	(562)		(2,500) × 80%	2,562
WDV c/f total allowances	688		7,500	2,562

The Industrial Buildings Allowance for the y/e 31.12.2002 is £800 (£20,000 × 4%).

Accounting	Profits £	Capital allowances £	Net profits £
15 months to 31.12.2000	35,000	7,000	28,000
y/e 31.12.2001	24,000	4,310	19,690
y/e 31.12.2002	42,000	2,562	39,438

Fiscal year	Basis period	Taxable profits £
1999/2000	1.10.1999–5.4.2000 (Note 2)	11,457
2000/01	1.1.2000–31.12.2000 (Note 3)	22,363
2001/02	1.1.2001–31.12.2001	19,690
2002/03	1.1.2002–31.12.2002	39,438

The overlap period is 1st January 2000 to 5th April 2000 a period of 95 days. Hence the overlap profits carried forward are £5,820 (£28,000 × 95/457).

Note 1
The first period of account is 15 months long and so the maximum writing down

allowance is increased by 15/12. (Note FYAs are not scaled to the period length).

Note 2
The basis period is 187 days long and the accounting period is 457 days long. Hence the taxable profits are £28,000 × 187/457.

Note 3
The basis period is 365 days long and the accounting period is 457 days long. Hence the taxable profits are £28,000 × 365/457.

Chapter 7

Question 1

Schedule E assessment for Martin for 2002/03

	£
Salary £30,000 × 9/12	22,500
Commission (none paid in fiscal year)	–
Car (£30,000 × 33%) – (50 × 9) × 9/12	7,162
Fuel (Note 1)	–
Clothing allowance £600 × 10/12	500
Flat (£1,200 – 9/12) + £(120,000 – 75,000) × 9/12 × 10%	4,275
Furniture £10,000 × 9/12 × 20%	1,500
Schedule E assessment	35,937

Note 1
The cost of private fuel is chargeable as a benefit if any of it is provided by the employer. A calculation is necessary to find out if Martin's employer actually paid for any of his private fuel. The actual cost of his private fuel is £160.00 (1,000/5 × 80p). This is less than the amount reimbursed by Martin of £180 (£20 × 9) and hence no benefit exists.

Question 2

Tax computation for Mr Thistlethwaite for 2002/03

	Dividends £	Savings £	Non-savings £	Total £
Earned income:				
Schedule E				
Salary			24,407	
Less pension contributions			(1,220)	23,187
Benefits in kind:				
Car £14,500 × 23% × 5/12			1,389	1,389
Fuel 2,850 × 5/12			1,187	1,187
Less professional subs			(100)	(100)
Schedule D			3,000	3,000
Less pension contributions				
(30% × 3,000)			(900)	(900)
Savings income:				
Bank interest £300 × 100/80		375		375
Building Society £2,000 × 100/80		2,500		2,500
Dividends £1,750 × 100/90	1,944			1,944
Less charges on income				
£250 × 100/78			(320)	(320)
Statutory total income	1,944	2,875	27,443	32,262
Less personal allowance			(4,615)	(4,615)
Taxable income	1,944	2,875	22,828	27,647

		£
Income tax due		
Non-savings	£1,920 × 10%	192.00
	£20,908 × 22%	4,599.76
Savings	2,875 × 20%	575.00
Dividends	1,944 × 10%	194.40
	27,647	
Tax borne		5,561.16
Add		
Tax retained on charge 320 × 22%		70.40
Less		
Tax credit on dividend 1,944 × 10%		(194.40)
Tax liability		5,437.16

Tax computation for Mrs Thistlethwaite for 2002/03

	Dividends £	Savings £	Non-savings £	Total £
Earned income:				
Schedule E				
Salary			17,000	17,000
Less pension contributions			(1,020)	(1,020)
Less AVC Contribution				
900 × 100/78			(1,153)	(1,153)
Less professional subs			(60)	(60)
Savings income:				
Bank interest £300 × 100/80		375		375
Building Society £2,000 × 100/80		2,500		2,500
Dividends £1,750 × 100/90	1,944			1,944
Statutory total income	1,944	2,875	14,767	19,586
Less personal allowance			(4,615)	(4,615)
Taxable income	1,944	2,875	10,152	14,971

Income tax due:		£
Non-savings	£1,920 × 10%	192.00
	8,232 × 22%	1,811.04
Savings	2,875 × 20%	575.00
Dividends	1,944 × 10%	194.00
	10,152	
Tax borne		2,772.04
Add		
Tax retained on AVC		
£1,153 × 22%		253.66
Less		
Tax credit on dividend		
£1,944 × 10%		(194.40)
Tax liability		2,831.30

Note: it is unlikely that the academic gown purchased by Marjorie will be tax deductble under the wholly, exclusively and necessary rule, despite her employer requesting it.

Chapter 8

Question 1

(a) Adrienne

The FA 1985 pool

	Number of shares	Cost (£)	Indexed pool (£)
Acquisition May 88	1,500	5,000	5,000
Indexed rise to April 1998			
$\dfrac{162.6 - 106.2}{106.2} \times £5,000$			2,655
			7,655
Disposal	(1,500)	(5,000)	(7,655)

Disposal from FA 1985 pool

Proceeds £18,000 × 1,500/2,000	13,500
Less cost	(5,000)
Unindexed untapered gain	8,500
Less indexation allowance	
£(7,655 – 5,000)	(2,655)
Indexed untapered gain	5,845
Tapered gain £5,845 × 85%	4,968

Disposal from 1982 holding

	Cost (£)	31 March 1982 value (£)
Proceeds £18,000 × 500/2,000	4,500	4,500
Less – cost 500/1,500 × £4,000	(1,333)	
– 31.3.1982 value £4 × 500		(2,000)
Unindexed untapered gain	3,167	2,500
Less indexation allowance		
1.047 × £2,000	(2,094)	(2,094)
Indexed untapered gain	1,073	406
Taper relief 1,073 or 406 × 85%	912	345

The chargeable gain is the lower gain of £345

Adrienne's chargeable gain (before annual exemption) is £5,313 (£4,968 + £345).

(b)   James

Dates	Commentary	Exempt months	Chargeable months
Jul 86–Dec 86	(i)	6	–
Jan 87–Jun 89	(ii)	30	
Jul 89–Jun 90	(iii)		12
Jul 90–Jun 99	(iv)		108
Jul 99–Jun 2002	(v)	36	–
Total		72	120

Commentary

(i)   The property was occupied as a principal private residence.
(ii) James was working overseas. It was not necessary for James to return to the property on his return to the UK because he was required by his employers to live elsewhere in the UK.
(iii) James did not return to the property after working elsewhere in the UK although not required to live elsewhere by his employers. Hence the period is chargeable.
(iv) James did not occupy the property as his principal private residence.
(v)   The final 36 months of ownership are exempt.

Capital gains tax computation	£
Proceeds	200,000
Less cost	50,000
Unindexed untapered gain	150,000
Less indexation allowance	
0.667 × £50,000	(33,350)
Indexed untapered gain	116,650
Less exempt proportion [72/(72 + 120)]	(43,744)
Untapered gain	72,906
Taper relief £72,906 × 85%	61,970

Question 2

(a) Arthur

Capital gains tax computation

	£
Proceeds	40,000
Less allowable cost	
$£120,000 \times \dfrac{40,000}{40,000 + 187,500}$	21,099
Unindexed untapered gain	18,901
Less indexation allowance	
$0.568 \times £21,099$	(11,984)
Indexed untapered gain	6,917
Tapered gain £6,917 × 25%	1,729

(Assuming land was a business asset for taper relief purposes)

(b) Margaret

	£	£
Proceeds		65,000
Less allowable costs:		
– 31.3.82 market value (Note 1)	25,000	
– enhancement expenditure	4,000	(29,000)
Unindexed untapered gain		36,000
Indexation allowance		
$1.047 \times £25,000$	26,175	
$0.708 \times £4,000$	2,832	(29,007)
Indexed untapered gain		6,993
Tapered gain £6,993 × 25%		1,748

Note 1

It is not necessary to calculate the indexed gain using the original cost because it will clearly give rise to a larger gain.

(c) Anne

The following reliefs may be claimed by Anne and Jocelyn:

- retirement relief
- gift relief.

The effect of claiming the reliefs is as follows:

- Where both gift relief and retirement relief are available retirement relief must be claimed first. Then gift relief is calculated without reference to retirement relief. Gift relief cannot exceed the gain after retirement relief.

- The maximum retirement relief available to Anne on the disposal of this business is £50,000, plus 50% of the next £150,000 gain, (i.e. another £75,000). Retirement relief is only available on the disposal of chargeable business assets. Chargeable business assets are all chargeable assets which are used for the purposes of trade. Assets which are held for investment purposes only are not chargeable business assets.
- Gift relief can be claimed when business assets are transferred provided that both the transferrer and the transferee make an election. Once the election has been made the transferrer's gain is reduced to nil and the base cost to the transferee will be taken to be the market value on the date of transfer less the amount of the gift relief.

Chapter 9

Question 1

Ultimate Upholsterers Ltd
Corporation Tax Computation for the 12 months to 30th September 2002

	£
Schedule D Case I (Note 1)	313,136
Chargeable gain (Note 2)	25,160
Profits chargeable to corporation tax	338,296
Franked investment income	
(£18,000 × 100/90)	20,000
'Profits'	358,296
Corporation tax: £338,296 × 30%	101,488.80
Less taper relief	
1/40 × £(1,500,000 − 358,296)	
$\times \dfrac{338,296}{358,296}$	26,949.36
	74,539.44

Note 1: calculation of Schedule D Case I assessment

In order to calculate the Schedule D Case I assessment we need to calculate the capital allowances. The writing down allowance is given in the question. Ultimate Upholsterers cannot claim capital allowances on Factory 1 because the right to capital allowances on a lease of less than 50 years rests with the lessor. However, tax relief will be available on the lease premium paid. The landlord will be assessed on £24,000 (£50,000 × (25 − 1) × 2%). Ultimate Upholsterers will be able to claim relief of £1,040 (£26,000/25).

Factory 2 is eligible for an industrial buildings allowance. The remaining tax life of Factory 2 is 17 years (25 years − 8 years) because it was 8 years old when Ultimate Upholsterers Ltd acquired it. The writing down allowance on Factory 2 is calculated as follows:

	£	£
Original cost (lower than purchase price)	150,000	
Annual writing down allowance (£150,000/17)		8,824
Extension cost	125,000	
Writing down allowance (4%)	(5,000)	5,000
Written down value carried forward	120,000	
Total allowances available		13,824

	£	£
Trading profit		375,000
Loan interest accrued	120,000	
Less Debenture Interest accrued	(10,000)	2,000
Less Capital Allowances:		
plant and machinery	49,000	
industrial building	13,824	(62,824)
Less relief on lease premium paid		(1,040)
Schedule D Case I		313,136

Note 2: calculation of chargeable gain on land

	£
Proceeds	47,000
Less 31st March 1982 value	(10,000)
Unindexed gain	37,000
Less indexation allowance	
$\dfrac{173.4 - 79.4}{79.4} = 1.184$	
$1.184 \times £10,000$	(11,840)
Indexed gain	25,160

There is no need to undertake a computation based on the original cost because it will clearly give a higher gain than using the March 1982 valuation.

Question 2

ABC Ltd has a corporate tax liability of more than £1.5 million so is required to make instalment payments of their tax liability.

a) Instalment dates will be

1st instalment	31st October 2001 + 6 months + 13 days	14th May 2002
2nd instalment	14th May + 3 months	14th August 2002
3rd instalment	14th August + 3 months	14th November 2002
Final instalment	14th November + 3 months	14th February 2003

Amounts due on each date above is:

$$\frac{[3 \times £1,800,000 \times 60\%]}{12} = £270,000$$

The balancing payment of £720,000 (40% × £1,800,000) will be due on the normal due date of 1st August 2003.

b)   Instalment dates

Final instalment	31st June + 3 months + 14 days	14th September 2002
First instalment	31st October + 6 months + 14 days	14th May 2002
Second instalment	14th May + 3 months	14th August 2002
Third instalment	(not due as falls beyond final instalment date)	

Amounts due each instalment

$$\frac{[3 \times £1,800,000 \ 60\%]}{8} = £405,000$$

The balancing payment of £585,000 will be due on the normal due date of 1st April 2003.

Chapter 10

Question 1

A person who makes taxable supplies becomes liable to be registered for VAT:

- at the end of any month, if the value of his or her taxable supplies in the period of one year then ending has exceeded £55,000, or
- at any time, if there are reasonable grounds for believing that the value of his or her taxable supplies in the period of thirty days then beginning will exceed £55,000.

Taxable supplies are made up of both standard rated and zero rated supplies. Since the trader's taxable supplies total £57,000 (£48,000 + £9,000) does exceed the annual limit of £55,000 the trader is liable to register for VAT. The trader must notify the Customs and Excise within 30 days of the end of the 12 months in which the limits were exceeded. The trader will then be registered from the first day of the following month.

Had the trader voluntarily registered from the beginning of the accounting period his VAT position would have been:

	£
Output tax:	
– standard rated supplies £8,000 × 17.5%	1,400
Less input tax:	
– (7,000 + 3,000) × 7/47	1,489
VAT recoverable	89

Question 2

To: The Board of Directors
From: D Hancock
Date: 12 June 2002
Subject: VAT implications of forming a group and trading overseas

Group Position
Groups of UK registered companies under common control can elect to register for VAT as a group. Either one company must control each of the others, or one person, an individual, two or more persons in partnership, or a company, must control all the companies. It is not necessary for all members of the group to participate in the scheme. One company must be appointed as the representative member who deals with all VAT matters for the group. All members of the group are jointly and severally liable for any tax due from the representative member.

Intra-group transfers are ignored for VAT purposes and all taxable supplies to and from any member of the group are treated as a taxable supply by or to the representative member.

Imports
Tax on goods imported from outside the EU is charged and payable as if it were a duty of customs and the rate which would apply if the same goods were supplied in the home market by a registered trader. The registered trader is then able to reclaim the duty on the goods which are used for the purposes of a business carried on by him as input tax in the normal way.

Goods supplied by a registered trader resident in another EU country are zero rated. The importing trader will be required to account for VAT as both a taxable supply and input tax at the rate in force in his own country.

Exports
A supply of goods is zero rated if the Commissioners are satisfied that the person supplying the goods will be exporting to a place outside the EU.

Goods supplied to registered traders in other member states are zero rated.

Index

Index of cases

Chapter numbers are given in bold, page numbers within chapters are given in non-bold type.

Subject index

Note:
- G = Defined in Glossary,
- Chapter numbers are given in bold, page numbers within chapters are given in non-bold type.